INVITATION TO THE Septuagint

Karen H. Jobes (Ph.D., Westminster Theological Seminary) is Gerald F. Hawthorne Professor of New Testament Greek and Exegesis at Wheaton College. Karen is the author of *The Alpha-Text of Esther: Its Character and Relationship to the Masoretic Text*, *The NIV Application Commentary: Esther,* and *1 Peter* (BECNT).

Moisés Silva (Ph.D., University of Manchester) has taught biblical studies at Westmont College, Westminster Theological Seminary, and Gordon-Conwell Theological Seminary. Moisés is the author of various books on biblical interpretation, including *Biblical Words and Their Meaning: An Introduction to Lexical Semantics*, *Philippians*, and *Explorations in Exegetical Method.*

INVITATION TO THE

Septuagint

Karen H. Jobes

and

Moisés Silva

BakerAcademic
Grand Rapids, Michigan

Published by Baker Academic
a division of Baker Publishing Group
P.O. Box 6287, Grand Rapids, Michigan 49516-6287
www.bakeracademic.com

ISBN 978-0-8010-3115-1

Printed in the United States of America

The Library of Congress Cataloging-in-Publication Data has cataloged the hardcover edition as follows:

Jobes, Karen H.
Invitation to the Septuagint / Karen H. Jobes and Moisés Silva.
p. cm.
Includes bibliographical references and index.
ISBN 0-8010-2235-5
1. Bible. O.T. Greek—Versions—Septuagint. I. Silva, Moisés. II. Title
BS744.J63 2000
221.4′8′09—dc21 00-063082

Contents

Appendixes

Indexes

Illustrations

Preface

The inspiration for a book like this was born during my doctoral studies at Westminster Theological Seminary in a course entitled "The Greek Old Testament," taught by Moisés Silva. I had previously heard Professor Silva comment that this course was the hardest one offered at the seminary. Being a woman who enjoys a reasonable challenge and having become enamored with Biblical Greek, I registered for the course with enthusiasm.

Very quickly I began to appreciate both the technical and conceptual complexities of Septuagint studies. So many of my naive assumptions about texts, manuscripts, and the Scriptures I hold dear were quickly shattered. I began to see a more profound, mysterious, and wonderful picture that captured my scholarly imagination. I've been hooked on Septuagint studies ever since.

Professor Silva was right, it was a difficult course. But one of the difficulties for me as a student completely new to the subject was that everything I read about the Septuagint seemed to presume a great deal of prior knowledge. I could find nothing that provided an introduction to the scholarly discussions that had been going on for decades. I needed a concise primer that would define the jargon, delineate the most fundamental and elementary concepts, and trace out the overarching issues of what Septuagint studies was all about. As I worked through the course under Professor Silva's able guidance, I began to make notes of things I wish someone had written in clear, easy language. Although I was unaware of it at the time, the outline for this book had begun to take shape.

This book is intended to be a relatively brief and inviting introduction for the student who has no prior knowledge of the Septuagint. It aims to introduce both the history and current state of the scholarly discussion by presenting the terminology, foundational concepts, and major issues in Septuagint studies. Nevertheless, those interested in pursuing the technical use of the Septuagint in textual criticism and biblical studies will also find resources here to further their understanding. If successful, this book will serve as a bridge to the more sophisticated literature produced by scholars working in the field. We trust that our book not only honors the work done by previous generations of Septuagint scholars and accurately presents the work now being done by our colleagues in the field, but will also inspire future generations to take up this fascinating field of research.

Karen H. Jobes
Santa Barbara, California

In my student days at Westminster Theological Seminary, unlike Professor Jobes, I did not even have the option of taking a class in Septuagint studies. I was, however, able to sign up for an independent reading course on the subject as part of my Th.M. program; and later the text of the Septuagint became a major focus of attention in my doctoral research at the University of Manchester. In my experience, learning the basic facts related to the Septuagint proved painless, but I soon realized how superficial, and therefore dangerous, that knowledge was. Moving to the next level—that is, being able to handle the Greek text responsibly and to understand specialized articles—required considerable effort, especially without the benefit of structured guidance.

When I began to offer a course on the Greek Old Testament, my aim was to help students profit from my mistakes. While there is no such thing as "Septuagint without tears" (indeed, without the affliction of trial-and-error, one seldom learns anything), pedagogical direction can prevent much wasted time and unnecessary frustration. This book seeks to perform that service. We have made a special effort to write part 1 in a simple and user-friendly fashion, but without minimizing the problems and ambiguities inherent in the subject. The qualifications and nuances in those first chapters are essential if one is to avoid building a shaky foundation.

It is in part 2, however, that we seek to guide the reader through the thicket of the Septuagintal forest. The chapters in this section are intended for students who already have some knowledge of the biblical languages and who wish to attain an intermediate level of proficiency in the use of the Greek Bible. With the additional help of part 3, which reviews the state of scholarship on selected topics, a few readers may even decide that advanced study of the Septuagint is worth pursuing.

The great challenge in teaching a course (or writing a book) on a complex subject is that explaining any one detail seems to assume some understanding of many other items not yet covered. This problem is particularly acute in the field of Septuagint studies. Some repetition is therefore unavoidable, but in dealing with individual topics we have also relied heavily on the use of cross-references to both prior and subsequent discussions within the book. In the end, however, a second reading of the volume may be necessary to tie loose ends.

I must add that this book would never have been written without the productive and persevering efforts of Professor Jobes, on whom fell the lion's share of the work in its initial stages. Throughout the project, however, we have been in frequent consultation, reading and critiquing each other's work, and discussing every aspect of the book before it took its final form. As a result, this book represents a collaborative effort in the fullest sense of the term. It is our wish that others will find as much delight in reading these pages as we have found in writing them.

Moisés Silva
Ipswich, Massachusetts

Acknowledgments

It is a pleasure to acknowledge the significant help we have received throughout the course of this project. We are especially grateful to David Aiken for proposing the idea of such a book in the first place, for promoting the work in many ways, and for agreeing to copyedit the typescript. His personal and scholarly interest in Septuagint studies has much to do with the successful completion of the book.

Several specialists have generously given of their time to assist us. Leonard J. Greenspoon, Emanuel Tov, Robert A. Kraft, and Martin G. Abegg read portions of the typescript at an early stage and provided valuable criticisms. Other colleagues, including Natalio Fernández Marcos, Peter W. Flint, Peter J. Gentry, Robert H. Gundry, Galen Marquis, Bruce M. Metzger, Takamitsu Muraoka, Bradley Nassif, Gerard Norton, Albert Pietersma, Eugene C. Ulrich, and John W. Wevers, were kind enough to respond to inquiries or otherwise support our research.

To the staff of the Septuaginta-Unternehmen in Göttingen we extend our sincere thanks. During a visit to its facilities, the authors were able to discuss some important questions and to gather information unavailable anywhere else. We are particularly indebted to its director, Anneli Aejmelaeus, for the time that she unselfishly spent with us, and to Udo Quast, whose unique knowledge of Septuagint manuscripts and of the work of the institute proved invaluable.

We also profited greatly from a brief visit to the Centre for Septuagint Studies and Textual Criticism (Katholieke Universiteit, Leuven, Belgium). Our thanks to Erik Eynikel and Katrin Hauspie for their assistance during that time and to its director, Johan Lust.

The authors also thank the staff of the Ancient Biblical Manuscript Center at Claremont, California, for their assistance in selecting and acquiring the photographs of manuscripts that appear in this volume.

David L. Palmer, Byington scholar at Gordon-Conwell Theological Seminary, read a near-final draft of the typescript with great care, identifying some remaining problems and offering numerous suggestions for improvement.

Bradford Zinnecker, also a Byington scholar at Gordon-Conwell Theological Seminary, prepared an initial draft of appendix D that greatly facilitated our work.

Finally, the authors express their thanks to Westmont College and Gordon-Conwell Theological Seminary for the support they have received in the production of this book.

Abbreviations

General and Bibliographical

AT	Alpha-Text of Greek Esther
BAGD	Walter Bauer, *A Greek-English Lexicon of the New Testament and Other Early Christian Literature*; trans. William F. Arndt and F. Wilbur Gingrich; 2d ed. rev. by F. Wilbur Gingrich and Frederick W. Danker (Chicago: University of Chicago Press, 1979)
BDF	*A Greek Grammar of the New Testament and Other Early Christian Literature* by Friedrich Blass and Albert Debrunner, trans. and rev. Robert W. Funk (Chicago: University of Chicago Press, 1961)
BIOSCS	*Bulletin of the International Organization for Septuagint and Cognate Studies*
CATSS	Computer Assisted Tools for Septuagint Studies
IOSCS	International Organization for Septuagint and Cognate Studies
LSJ	Henry G. Liddell and Robert Scott, *A Greek-English Lexicon*, 9th ed. rev. by Henry S. Jones et al. (Oxford: Clarendon, 1968)
LXX	Septuagint
MT	Masoretic Text
NETS	*A New English Translation of the Septuagint*
NIV	New International Version
NRSV	New Revised Standard Version
NT	New Testament
OG	Old Greek
OL	Old Latin
OT	Old Testament
SBLSCS	Society of Biblical Literature Septuagint and Cognate Studies

Bible Books

Gen.	Genesis	Eccles.	Ecclesiastes
Exod.	Exodus	Song	Song of Songs
Lev.	Leviticus	Isa.	Isaiah
Num.	Numbers	Jer.	Jeremiah
Deut.	Deuteronomy	Lam.	Lamentations
Josh.	Joshua	Ezek.	Ezekiel
Judg.	Judges	Dan.	Daniel
Ruth	Ruth	Hos.	Hosea
1 Sam.	1 Samuel	Joel	Joel
2 Sam.	2 Samuel	Amos	Amos
1 Kings	1 Kings	Obad.	Obadiah
2 Kings	2 Kings	Jon.	Jonah
1 Chron.	1 Chronicles	Mic.	Micah
2 Chron.	2 Chronicles	Nah.	Nahum
Ezra	Ezra	Hab.	Habakkuk
Neh.	Nehemiah	Zeph.	Zephaniah
Esth.	Esther	Hag.	Haggai
Job	Job	Zech.	Zechariah
Ps.	Psalms	Mal.	Malachi
Prov.	Proverbs		

The Hellenistic World
MACEDONIA
ITALY
Rome
GREECE
Athens
Byzantium
(Constantinople)
Ephesus
ASIA MINOR
Antioch
SYRIA
Caesarea
JUDEA
Jerusalem
Alexandria
EGYPT
Dan Malda

The Hellenistic and Roman Periods

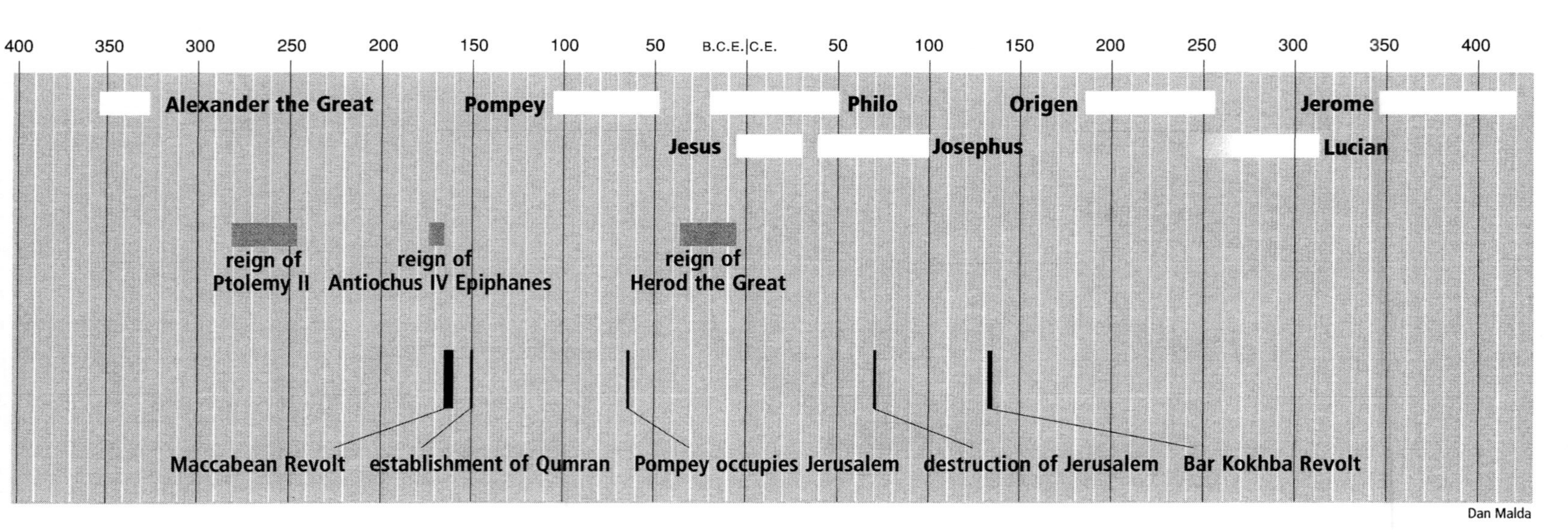

Introduction: Why Study the Septuagint?

The Septuagint—commonly abbreviated LXX—is a fascinating treasure from the ancient past.[1] Whether you are Christian or Jewish or neither,[2] whether you are only generally interested in religious studies or are an aspiring biblical scholar, it is worth your while to become acquainted with it. Because the Septuagint was the first translation made of the Hebrew Bible (or of any literary work of comparable size) into another language, it marks a milestone in human culture. Any knowledge of the ancient world would be incomplete without understanding the significance of the Septuagint and the history that brought it into existence. In this book, we invite you to learn about the place of this translation in history, to appreciate its value for modern scholarship, and to come away with some of our enthusiasm for it. The present chapter is intended as an overview of the field, with a brief description of issues that will be treated later in greater detail.

The Septuagint and the Hebrew Bible

The Bible contains ancient writings that have been continuously read from the time of its authors until our own. The first and oldest part of the Bible was written originally in Hebrew (with some small

1. The "proper" way to pronounce *Septuagint* is the subject of lighthearted debate among specialists. English dictionaries typically suggest the pronunciation *SEP-too-a-jint* or *sep-TOO-a-jint* or the like, but many scholars in the discipline treat it as a three-syllable word, *SEP-twa-jint*. In Europe, one often hears the last syllable pronounced with hard *g*, after the pattern of Latin *Septuaginta*.

2. The authors are Christian, but recognize and value the Jewish heritage of the Bible and its translations. Accordingly, the term *Hebrew Bible* will be used mainly when the text is discussed in the context of Judaism, and *Old Testament* when in the context of the church.

portions in Aramaic: Ezra 4:8–6:18; 7:12–26; Dan. 2:4–7:28; Jer. 10:11; and two words in Gen. 31:47). The abiding importance of these sacred writings—first to the Jews and later to the Christians—demanded that throughout history they be translated into the languages of the peoples who received them as Scripture.

After the Near East was conquered by Alexander the Great (ca. 333 B.C.E.), the Jewish people came under the influence of Hellenistic culture. Their religious values and ancient ways collided with Greek practices, philosophies, and language. Just as today most Jews live outside of Israel, so it was during the Hellenistic period. Because as a rule the Jews of the Diaspora (Dispersion) scattered throughout the Mediterranean no longer spoke Hebrew, they needed to translate their sacred writings into Greek, which had become the *lingua franca* of the Hellenistic world. Thus the Greek version of the Hebrew Bible, now known as the Septuagint, became Scripture to the Greek-speaking Jewish communities in the Diaspora. Together with the Greek New Testament, it would become the Bible of most Christians during the first centuries of the church. The Greek version remains even today the canonical text for the Orthodox Christian tradition, which traces its heritage to the earliest Greek-speaking Christians.

Because of its widespread importance, numerous copies of the Greek Bible were produced by scribes in many places throughout the centuries. More manuscripts of the Greek Old Testament survive than of any other ancient Greek text except the New Testament. Counting both complete and fragmentary manuscripts, nearly 2,000 handwritten copies of the Septuagint have survived.[3] In comparison, we have only about 650 extant manuscripts of Homer's *Iliad*, the most popular work of antiquity, and fewer than 350 of the works by the famous Greek tragedian, Euripides.[4] For scholars interested in the complexities of textual criticism and the tendencies of scribes, the manuscripts of the Septuagint provide an enormous amount of material for study.

The Septuagint is written in Koine, that is, the common Greek of the Hellenistic age, a form of the language that had developed from the Classical Greek of fifth-century Athens. For students of the Greek language during the Hellenistic period, the Septuagint is a major source of information. Moreover, because it is a translation of a Hebrew text into Greek, it provides a unique opportunity for those interested in comparing translation Greek to composition Greek.

The Greek version also has great value for the study of the Hebrew text. The issues surrounding this use of the version are quite complex,

3. This estimate comes from the Septuaginta-Unternehmen in Göttingen (personal communication). See below, chap. 2, pp. 57–63, for further detail.

4. Bruce M. Metzger, *The Text of the New Testament: Its Transmission, Corruption, and Restoration*, 3d ed. (New York: Oxford University Press, 1992), 34.

but the fact remains that the Septuagint was translated from some Hebrew text that was not identical to the Hebrew text we use today. That original Greek translation, which was produced much earlier than any surviving copy of the Hebrew Bible, is an indirect witness to its *Vorlage*, that is, the Hebrew parent text from which it was translated. In theory, the Septuagint should allow scholars to reconstruct that earlier Hebrew text, though in practice this activity is fraught with difficulties.

Already in the first chapter of the Bible we come across some interesting examples where the Greek differs from the Hebrew. Compare Genesis 1:6–7 in the two forms (translated literally into English):

	Hebrew	**Greek**
6	And God said, "Let there be a firmament in the midst of the waters, and let it be separating between waters to waters."	And God said, "Let there be a firmament in the midst of the water, and let it be separating between water and water." And it was so.
7	And God made the firmament and separated between the waters that [were] under the firmament and between the waters that [were] above the firmament. And it was so.	And God made the firmament and God separated between the water that was under the firmament and between the water above the firmament.

A few minor differences may be observed, such as the repetition of "God" in the Greek version of verse 7. Note especially, however, that the Greek has transposed the words "and it was so" from verse 7 to verse 6. Does that mean, as some scholars argue, that the Hebrew manuscript used by the Greek translator also had the phrase in verse 6? Or is there some other way to account for the difference?

One of the reasons scholars cannot be certain that the Greek exactly represents its Hebrew *Vorlage* is that translation between any two languages always involves a degree of interpretation. The translators who produced the Greek version of the Hebrew Bible were also interpreters who came to the text with the theological and political prejudices of their time and thus had to deal with hermeneutical issues similar to those we face today. Their translations were no doubt influenced, whether deliberately or subconsciously, by what they believed the Hebrew meant in light of their contemporary situation, which may not have been what the author of the Hebrew intended. Clearly, this is bad news to the textual critic, who wants to use the Greek version to reconstruct its Hebrew parent text. It is possible that the Greek translator deleted the phrase "and it was so" from Genesis 1:7, perhaps because it sounded out of place, and inserted it in 1:6, where it seemed more appropriate immediately following God's command (similarly, the Greek text includes this phrase after the command in Gen. 1:20, where it is absent in extant Hebrew texts).

On the other hand, precisely because the Septuagint reflects the theological, social, and political interests of the translator, it provides valuable information about how the Hebrew Bible was understood and interpreted at the time the translators were working. In the Greek we find passages that are given a particular political or religious spin. This feature is especially clear in the Book of Isaiah. For example, the Hebrew text of Isaiah 65:11 reproaches those who, forsaking the Lord, "set tables for Gad [a god of fortune] and fill cups of mixed wine for Meni [a god of fate]." The names of these Semitic gods were probably not familiar to Alexandrian Jews, and so the translator replaced these names with the Greek words for "demon" and "fate," both of which could be understood as names for deities.[5] With this technique, the translator managed not only to clarify the meaning of the text, but also to contemporize it.

One must also remember that the Septuagint was produced in the wake of Alexander's conquest and death, when Palestine was coveted by the Ptolemies to the south in Egypt and the Seleucids to the north in Syria. Because Palestine was caught in the middle, political allegiances among the Jews were often divided. Moreover, great internal turmoil resulted as Jews in favor of Hellenization clashed with those who opposed it. Just as people today use the Bible to support their agendas, so also were the sacred writings appealed to for authority at that time. And just as a given verse today can be interpreted to support the claims of opposing parties, so also were specific sacred texts understood differently by different communities. This conflict may be seen, for instance, in the Essenes' understanding of Scripture when compared with that of the Pharisees. To what extent such interpretations can be identified in the Greek translation of the Bible is a subject of debate, but it would be strange indeed if the political loyalties and religious convictions of translators were not reflected in their work.[6]

5. See Isaac L. Seeligmann, *The Septuagint Version of Isaiah: A Discussion of Its Problems* (Leiden: Brill, 1948), 99, who argues that the Greek words should be taken as a reference to Agathos Daimon and Tyche, deities in the Hellenistic cult.

6. See Isa. 15:7b, which in the Hebrew reads, "They [i.e., the Moabites] will carry away their possessions over the brook of willows." The Greek translator, however, misunderstood the text (the Hebrew word for "willows" has the same consonants as the word for "Arabs") and rendered it, "For I will bring Arabians upon the valley, and they will take it." Seeligmann (*Septuagint Version of Isaiah*, 89) suggests that this rendering alludes to the conquest of Transjordan by the Nabateans, an Arab state, in the second century B.C.E.

In any case, the Septuagint provides invaluable material showing how the Hebrew Bible was used in this crucial period of Jewish history.

The Septuagint in the Christian Church

The Septuagint, not the Hebrew Bible, was the primary theological and literary context within which the writers of the New Testament and most early Christians worked. This does not mean that the New Testament writers were ignorant of the Hebrew Bible or that they did not use it. But since the New Testament authors were writing in Greek, they would naturally quote, allude to, and otherwise use the Greek version of the Hebrew Bible. This process is no different from that of a modern author writing, for instance, in Spanish, and quoting a widely used Spanish translation of the Bible.

Consequently, familiarity with the Greek Old Testament cannot help but enlighten the student of the Greek New Testament. Biblical scholar Adolf Deissmann once wrote, "A single hour lovingly devoted to the text of the Septuagint will further our exegetical knowledge of the Pauline Epistles more than a whole day spent over a commentary."[7] The connection can be illustrated at several levels.

In the first place, the Septuagint provided some of the vocabulary that the New Testament writers drew upon. To be sure, it is often difficult to determine whether a New Testament writer used a given Greek word, such as *sabbaton* ("Sabbath"), because of its use in the Septuagint or simply because it was already a part of the vocabulary among Greek-speaking Jews of first-century Palestine. There is no doubt, however, that the New Testament writers often use Septuagint terms or phrases that were not in common usage in the first century (e.g., *pasa sarx*, "all flesh," in Luke 3:6). In such cases, they may be borrowing the terms from the Septuagint to affect a "biblical" style. Most of us have heard someone pray using the archaic English pronouns *thee* and *thou*. Although these pronouns are not current in modern English, people still use them on certain occasions if they want to imitate or suggest the style of biblical language as found in the enormously influential King James Version. The Septuagint certainly left its mark in Greek, just as the King James Version has in English.

Second, the New Testament writers sometimes used expressions found in the Septuagint to draw the reader's mind to specific passages of Old Testament Scripture. Paul, for instance, uses the phrase *every knee shall bow* in Philippians 2:10 to describe the ultimate exaltation

7. Adolf Deissmann, *The Philology of the Greek Bible* (London: Hodder & Stoughton, 1908), 12.

of Jesus. This Greek phrase occurs in Septuagint Isaiah 45:22–23, which may be translated as follows:

> Turn to me and you will be saved,
> you from the ends of the earth.
> I am God and there is no other.
> By myself I swear
> —surely righteousness will come out of my mouth,
> my words will not be thwarted—
> that every knee will bow to me
> and every tongue will confess to God.

Clearly Paul is using vocabulary from the Greek version of Isaiah 45:23, not just to sound "biblical" but to bring that passage to mind in order to identify Jesus with God.

Third, the New Testament writers frequently quote the Greek Old Testament directly—perhaps as many as three hundred times. This accounts for some of the differences readers note when comparing these quotations with the corresponding Old Testament passages. For example, in Hebrews 11:21 dying Jacob is said to have worshiped leaning on the top of his *staff*, a reference to the Greek text of Genesis 47:31. In almost all English Bibles, however, Genesis says that Jacob worshiped at the top of his *bed*, which is indeed what the Hebrew manuscripts say. The reason for the discrepancy is that the Hebrew text used by the Greek translator of Genesis consisted only of consonants; the appropriate vowels were to be inferred by the reader from the context. The Hebrew noun *mṭh* in Genesis could be read as either *maṭṭeh* ("staff") or *miṭṭah* ("bed"), and the Greek translator inferred that the word *staff* was meant. Some centuries later, when vowel points were added to the Hebrew biblical texts, the noun in Genesis 47:31 was taken to mean "bed."[8]

One must appreciate that the continuity and development of thought between the Old and New Testaments is of particular concern for biblical theology. The Septuagint provides essential, but often overlooked, theological links that would have been familiar to Christians of the first century, but are not so obvious in the Hebrew version. No New Testament scholar can afford to ignore the Septuagint.

After New Testament times, the Septuagint, not the Hebrew text, was the Bible used by the early church fathers and councils. As Chris-

8. The NIV translates Gen. 47:31 so as to agree with Hebrews 11:21, presumably on the grounds that the traditional vowel-pointing of the Hebrew text is incorrect and that the Greek version preserves the correct sense. For a discussion of this quotation, see Moisés Silva, "The New Testament Use of the Old Testament: Text Form and Authority," in *Scripture and Truth*, ed. D. A. Carson and J. W. Woodbridge (Grand Rapids: Zondervan, 1983; repr. Grand Rapids: Baker, 1992), 147–65.

tian doctrine on the nature of Jesus and the Trinity developed, discussion centered on the exegesis of key Old Testament texts. Because most of the church fathers could not read Hebrew, exegetical debates were settled using the Greek Old Testament. Some of the Greek words used to translate the Old Testament had connotations associated with Greek culture and philosophy that were probably alien to the thought of the original Hebrew author. The simple fact that the Hebrew Scriptures existed in the Greek language and were read by people living in Greek culture led to exegesis by both Jewish and Christian interpreters (e.g., Philo and Arius, respectively) that was heavily influenced by Greek philosophy.

Of course, one must also consider that the Greek translator himself originally rendered the Hebrew in ways that were to some extent influenced by Greek culture and thought, making the text even more congenial to a later exegesis that would be similarly influenced. A good example is the Septuagint text of Proverbs 8:22–31, which held a prominent place in the early discussions about the nature of Jesus and his place in the Trinity. In this passage, wisdom is personified as the first of the Lord's works prior to the creation of the universe. Primarily because of the opening verses of John's Gospel, Jesus became associated with this divine wisdom (*sophia*) or rationality (*logos*). In Greek philosophy, however, the Greek concept of an impersonal divine wisdom permeating the universe was very prominent, and so the nature of Jesus and his relationship to God the Father had to be carefully delineated. Many early theologians, such as Origen and Tertullian, used this passage in their discussions of the relationship between the Son and the Father. Subsequently Arius, a Christian presbyter of Alexandria (died 336), argued on the basis of Septuagint Proverbs 8 that the Son was a created being, not coeternal with the Father. Subtle differences between the Greek and Hebrew worked in favor of Arius's argument, which led to years of intense debate.[9]

This example is only one of many that show how the doctrines of orthodox Christianity were hammered out with exegetical appeals to an Old Testament that was written in Greek, not Hebrew. While no point of orthodox Christian doctrine rests on the Greek text in contradiction to the Hebrew, it is also true that the Septuagint text was the Word of God for the church in its first three centuries. Moreover, the Eastern Orthodox churches—Greek, Russian, and Syrian—inherited the Greek text as their Bible. Traditionally, the Orthodox churches have considered the Greek version to be divinely inspired (and even in

9. The exegesis of this passage was settled by the Council of Nicea in 325, when the Arian controversy was pronounced a heresy. For further details, see Jaroslav Pelikan, *The Christian Tradition: A History of the Development of Doctrine*, 5 vols. (Chicago: University of Chicago Press, 1971–89), 1.191–210.

some sense to have superseded the Hebrew text), although this is a matter of debate among Orthodox scholars today.[10]

Because of the Protestant Reformation of the sixteenth century, most Christians in the Western church today are completely unfamiliar with the Septuagint. Part of the reason for this development is that the Reformation shifted attention away from the early translations of the Hebrew Bible, whether they be Greek or Latin, back to the original Hebrew text. Today's English translations of the Old Testament are quite rightly based, not on the Greek or Latin versions, but on the best available Hebrew text, known as the Masoretic Text. While the Hebrew is the best textual base for modern translations, we cannot forget that the ancient Greek version of the Old Testament was nevertheless the Bible of the earliest Christian writers.[11]

As we have seen, the Septuagint contains textual links not found in the Hebrew text that provide historical and literary continuity for the important task of biblical theology and for accurately understanding the exegetical debates of the early church fathers. The student of Bible at the college or seminary level must learn to appreciate the Septuagint and to understand its use in modern biblical scholarship and exegesis. Although few students will pursue Septuagint studies as a specialty at the graduate level, all students of the Bible, regardless of their religious identity, should understand the historical importance of the Septuagint and its significant contribution to the development of the Bible that we hold in our hands today. As the eminent biblical scholar Ferdinand Hitzig is said to have remarked to his students, "Gentlemen, have you a Septuagint? If not, sell all you have, and buy a Septuagint."[12]

10. See the discussion below in chap. 3, pp. 84–85.

11. Mogens Müller, *The First Bible of the Church: A Plea for the Septuagint* (Journal for the Study of the Old Testament Supplement 206; Copenhagen International Seminary 1; Sheffield: Sheffield Academic Press, 1996), goes so far as to argue that the Christian church in the West was quite wrong to follow Jerome's preference for the Hebrew text over that of the Septuagint (see, e.g., p. 143). While Müller's arguments are not persuasive, they are helpful in showing the great importance of the Greek text for early Christianity.

12. Quoted without documentation by Frederick W. Danker, *Multipurpose Tools for Bible Study*, 3d ed. (St. Louis: Concordia, 1970), 63. Apparently, Professor Hitzig had no female students. Today, women are among the outstanding scholars contributing to Septuagint studies.

PART 1

The History of the Septuagint

In this first part of the book, the reader is introduced to the basic facts and concepts related to Septuagint studies. We begin in chapter 1 by defining our terms and describing the historical origins of the Septuagint. We then discuss in chapter 2 the complications that developed in the following centuries as the Greek text underwent various revisions. Chapter 3 provides a summary of the manuscripts that have survived and of the printed editions available today, followed by a description of the contents of the Septuagint in the light of historical developments regarding the biblical canon. Finally, chapter 4 is devoted to the nature of the Septuagint as a translation document.

These chapters are written with the general reader and the beginning student in mind. Although most readers will probably have a basic familiarity with biblical studies, no knowledge of Greek or Hebrew is assumed in this part of the book, and a special effort has been made to explain new terms as they appear (these terms are also included in the glossary).

1

The Origin of the Septuagint and Other Greek Versions

Defining Our Terms. The term *Septuagint*, which has been used in a confusing variety of ways, gives the inaccurate impression that this document is a homogeneous unit. Important distinctions sometimes need to be made, such as the contrast between the initial translation of the Pentateuch (the Septuagint proper) and the earliest translation of other books (the Old Greek).

The First Greek Translation. The *Letter of Aristeas*, in spite of its legendary character, seems to preserve some valuable information. The Pentateuch was originally translated in Alexandria around the year 250 B.C.E., and the rest of the Hebrew Bible was translated within the following two centuries. The precise reason for the translation of the Pentateuch at that time is debated by scholars. Later traditions, which provide little help in sorting out the origins of the Septuagint, are in part responsible for the present terminological confusion.

The Later Greek Translations. For several reasons, such as dissatisfaction with the Septuagint, other attempts were made to render the Hebrew Bible into Greek. ***Aquila*** was a Jewish proselyte who tried to represent almost every detail of the Hebrew text consistently. ***Symmachus*** produced a careful translation that can be characterized as moderately "literal," while showing sensitivity to Greek idiom. The translation associated with ***Theodotion*** has some points of contact with that of Aquila, but its origin is the subject of much scholarly debate. We know little about the ***Other Versions*** from antiquity.

Defining Our Terms

Strictly speaking, there is really no such thing as *the* Septuagint. This may seem like an odd statement in a book entitled *Invitation to the Septuagint*, but unless the reader appreciates the fluidity and ambiguity of the term, he or she will quickly become confused by the literature.[1]

One might think that the Septuagint is the Greek version of the Bible in the same way that the Vulgate, for example, is the Latin version. The difference between them, however, is much greater than simply the language used. The Vulgate was largely the work of one man (Jerome) at one time (the end of the fourth century) in one place (Bethlehem).[2] As a result, the Latin Vulgate is characterized by unity throughout. Not so with the Septuagint, which was produced by many people unknown to us, over two or three centuries, and almost certainly in more than one location. Consequently, the Greek Old Testament does not have the unity that the term *the Septuagint* might imply.

Because the Greek translation of the Hebrew Bible has such a long and complicated history, the name *Septuagint* is used to refer to several quite different things. In its most general sense, the term refers to any or all ancient Greek translations of the Hebrew Bible, just as one might now refer in general to the "English Bible," with no particular translation in mind. This is the sense in which the term is used in the title of our book—a book about the ancient Greek version(s) of the Hebrew Bible. Often, the term is also used to refer to a particular printed edition of the Greek text, whether that edition reproduces the text of a particular manuscript or prints a reconstructed text.[3]

Given these typical uses of the term *Septuagint*, one might understandably, though mistakenly, infer that the Greek translation found in a given ancient manuscript or modern edition is a homogeneous text produced in its entirety at one point in time. In fact, no such homogeneity exists in any collection of the Greek books of the Old Testament. Each edition—whether an ancient, hand-copied manuscript such as

1. See Leonard J. Greenspoon, "The Use and Abuse of the Term 'LXX' and Related Terminology in Recent Scholarship," *BIOSCS* 20 (1987): 21–29.

2. Jerome's work began as a revision of earlier Latin versions (the Old Latin), which had themselves been translated from the Septuagint. His own translation of the Hebrew text was produced in the years 390–405 and much later came to be known as the Vulgate, from Latin *vulgatus* ("commonly known, in general circulation").

3. For example, *The Old Testament in Greek according to the Septuagint*, 3 vols., ed. Henry Barclay Swete (Cambridge: Cambridge University Press, 1887–94), is a diplomatic edition that, aside from minor corrections, simply prints the text of Codex Vaticanus. On the other hand, *Septuaginta*, 2 vols., ed. Alfred Rahlfs (Stuttgart: Württembergische Bibelanstalt, 1935), prints an eclectic text based on several manuscripts. Both of these editions include at the bottom of the page a brief apparatus that indicates some of the more important differences ("textual variants") among the manuscripts.

Vaticanus or a modern, printed book such as the Rahlfs edition—is an amalgam, with each section of the Bible having a long and separate textual history.

The books of the Hebrew Bible were originally translated independently into Greek by different translators over several centuries. What we call books were at that time written on individual scrolls. Typically no longer than thirty-five feet, a single scroll could not contain the Greek version of the Hebrew Bible in its entirety, and so each book was usually written on a separate scroll. A different format, the codex,[4] came into use in the second century of the Christian era. This format made it possible to bind originally separate texts (which would fill many scrolls) into one volume, giving a false impression of homogeneity. Just because the texts were bound together, one should not infer that they shared a common origin. In fact, there was no one uniform Greek version of the entire Hebrew Bible—just individual scrolls that had been copied from other scrolls through the ages. For instance, a medieval Greek codex might contain the text of Genesis copied from a manuscript produced in the first century of our era and containing the translation originally made in the third century B.C.E. in Alexandria, while the text of Esther bound in the same codex may have been copied from a manuscript produced in the fourth century of our era and containing a translation made in the first century B.C.E. in Jerusalem.

The particular collection of Greek texts of the biblical books that comprise the earliest one-volume Bibles, such as Codex Sinaiticus and Codex Vaticanus, usually came to be by the historical happenstance of whatever texts were at hand, irrespective of their origin and character. Therefore, whatever one may say about the history and characteristics of the Greek text of one biblical book may not be true of the others, even though they are bound together in one codex. And because modern critical editions of the Septuagint are based on the ancient manuscripts, the same misleading appearance of homogeneity exists today.

When one enters the highly specialized world of textual criticism, the name *Septuagint* takes on a more precise and technical sense. It may be used specifically to distinguish the oldest Greek translation from subsequent translations and revisions of the Greek. If the term is used in this narrower sense, it refers only to the original Greek version of the Pentateuch, for that was the first part of the Hebrew Bible translated in the third century B.C.E. The remaining books of the Hebrew canon were translated by different people in different places during

4. The term *codex* refers to ancient books, the leaves of which were handwritten and stitched together by hand, thus resembling the modern book format. The earliest complete copies of the Greek Bible survive in this form.

the next two centuries. It has become customary, however, to extend the term *Septuagint* to refer to the complete Greek canon of the Hebrew Bible.

It is probably better to refer to the original translation of books other than the Pentateuch as the Old Greek (OG) so as to distinguish them from the original translation of the Pentateuch and from the later revisions and new translations. (When referring to these initial Greek translations of the Hebrew Bible as a whole, some scholars prefer the combined abbreviation "LXX/OG" as a continual reminder of the diversity that characterizes the corpus.) However, when the Greek version of a biblical book survives in more than one form, it is not always possible to know with certainty which is the older. Nor is it possible to know for sure if the oldest surviving form was in fact the first Greek translation made of that book. Therefore, even the term *Old Greek* is not totally satisfactory. Unless the context requires a distinction, we will in this book continue to use the term *Septuagint* in its general sense (but enclosed in quotation marks if some ambiguity is present).

The scope of modern Septuagint studies extends beyond the canon of the Hebrew Bible. It includes texts from the Hellenistic period that are not translations from the Hebrew at all, but rather Jewish writings composed in Greek, such as 3 Maccabees, 4 Maccabees, and the Wisdom of Solomon. Some other books, such as Judith, survive as complete copies only in Greek, even though they were probably translated from a Semitic source that is no longer extant. These texts may also be in mind when the term *Septuagint* is used.

The reader is cautioned, therefore, that there is really no such thing as *the* Septuagint. One must pay particular care to the context in which the term is used, even by the same writer—and even in the present book! Unfortunately, some writers use the term carelessly and equivocally, and the inevitable confusion that results from such ambiguity has led Septuagint scholars to call for standard terminology. This may be easier said than done, however, for the ambiguities of the term go back to antiquity.

We have no evidence that any Greek version of the Hebrew Bible, or even of the Pentateuch, was called the "Septuagint" prior to the second century of this era. The word came into English from Latin *Septuaginta* ("seventy"), a shortened form of the title *Interpretatio septuaginta virorum*: "The Translation of the Seventy Men." This title arose from the Greek word for "the seventy" (*hoi hebdomēkonta*), which had been used by second-century Christian writers to refer to the entire Greek Old Testament, even though only the first five books were traditionally said to have been produced by seventy (either a round figure or an abbreviation for seventy-two) translators in Alexandria, Egypt, in the third century B.C.E.[5] These circumstances also explain why the Septuagint is commonly abbreviated today with the Roman numeral for seventy, LXX.

The First Greek Translation

The earliest extant account of the original Greek translation of the Hebrew Bible is found in the *Letter of Aristeas* (or *Pseudo-Aristeas*).[6] This document purports to be a lengthy, personal letter from a man named Aristeas to his "brother" (or friend) Philocrates. It describes, among other things, how the Jewish Torah was first translated from Hebrew into Greek for the great library of the Egyptian king Ptolemy Philadelphus (285–247 B.C.E.) in Alexandria. Copies of this so-called letter survive in about two dozen medieval manuscripts, the earliest of which dates to the eleventh century. The length and character of the *Letter of Aristeas* and its apparently wide copying and circulation suggest that the document was not personal correspondence from one person to another, but was intended as an "open letter" to a wider audience.

According to the author of the letter, the king's librarian requested the high priest of the temple in Jerusalem to send translators with the Hebrew Torah scrolls to Alexandria. The high priest complied, sending six men from each of the twelve tribes of Israel, that is, seventy-two translators, with a large escort carrying gifts for the king. The twelve tribes of Israel had long before been dispersed, so if there is any truth to this unlikely story, the number of people sent would have been merely a symbolic gesture. Aristeas was among the envoys.

The entourage from Jerusalem was welcomed to Alexandria with a royal banquet lasting several days, during which time the king and the envoys from the high priest discussed questions of theology and ethics. Finally, the translators were escorted to an island called Pharos, connected by a causeway to Alexandria. Working there for seventy-two days, they produced the first Greek translation of the Pentateuch. When the translation was complete, it was read to an assembly of the

5. Because the Greek letter *omicron* is used to represent the numeral 70, the Septuagint (or Old Greek) is often referred to with the abbreviation οι ο′ or simply ο′.

6. For an English translation of Aristeas, see R. J. H. Shutt, "Letter of Aristeas," in *The Old Testament Pseudepigrapha*, ed. James H. Charlesworth, 2 vols. (New York: Doubleday, 1985), 2.7–34. The Greek text of the document is printed in Henry Barclay Swete, *An Introduction to the Old Testament in Greek*, 2d ed. (Cambridge: Cambridge University Press, 1914; repr. Peabody, Mass.: Hendrickson, 1989), 533–606. See also Moses Hadas, *Aristeas to Philocrates (Letter of Aristeas)* (Dropsie College Edition: Jewish Apocryphal Literature; New York: Harper, 1951), which includes a full introduction, the Greek text and English translation on facing pages, and notes.

Jews of Alexandria, who enthusiastically received it and gave the translators a great ovation. The Jews asked the king's librarian to make a copy of the new translation for use in their community. To ensure that the original words of the translators would be preserved in perpetuity, the priests and elders pronounced a curse on anyone who should later change the text in any way.

Scholars today believe that this letter was written, not at a time contemporaneous with the events it describes, but in the second century B.C.E., to defend Judaism in general and the Greek version in particular.[7] During the conflict in Judaism over Hellenization, some Jews embraced the Greek language and culture while others resisted such acculturation on religious principle. It is also very likely that the Greek translation of the Pentateuch did not enjoy universal favor among the Jews. A hundred years or more after the translation was produced, the *Letter of Aristeas* was probably written to address this situation. Claiming that the translation was made from the Jerusalem scrolls under circumstances that paralleled the giving of the law on Sinai, the author seeks to give the Greek version of the Scriptures used in Alexandria authority and veneration, such as the Hebrew texts in Jerusalem enjoyed.

Even though the authenticity of the letter should be rejected, some of its information is probably reliable. The first Greek translation of the Hebrew Torah would have been needed by Jews living in the Diaspora during the Hellenistic period (i.e., after Alexander's conquest in 333 B.C.E.). Even earlier, during the Persian period, significant communities of Aramaic-speaking Jews already lived in Egypt: papyri from Elephantine show an established Jewish community there as early as 495 B.C.E. After Alexander's conquest of the Persian Empire, Alexandria became home to a large Greek-speaking Jewish population. It is therefore likely that the Pentateuch was first translated into Greek by or for the Alexandrian Jews during the reign of Ptolemy Philadelphus in the middle of the third century B.C.E. (The historical and prophetic books of the Hebrew Bible were probably translated into Greek during the following century, but we do not know where or by whom.)[8]

7. The debate about the origin, date, and purpose of the *Letter of Aristeas* is itself a well-defined topic of research within Septuagint studies.

8. Around the middle of the second century, Jewish historian Eupolemos seems to have used a Greek version of Chronicles (Swete, *Introduction to the Old Testament in Greek*, 24–25). The Greek text of the Wisdom of Joshua ben Sira (also known as Sirach or Ecclesiasticus), dated about 132 B.C.E., contains a prologue that makes reference to a translation of "the law, the prophets, and the rest of the books." (The original Hebrew of this book was written by Joshua ben Sira ca. 180, then later translated into Greek by his grandson, who added the prologue.) In spite of this statement, scholars believe that most of the Writings, such as the wisdom books, were not translated until the first century B.C.E.

But what about the other details of the story? The language of the translation bears the marks of the Greek spoken in Egypt, and it seems improbable that it would have been produced by a large group of Palestinian scholars. It is much more reasonable to believe that a handful of Greek-speaking Alexandrian Jews were responsible for it. As for the claim that the translation was based on Hebrew scrolls brought from Jerusalem, we have no clear evidence to refute it, but few scholars accept its validity.

More difficult to assess is the role supposedly played by the king's librarian. Many scholars, thinking it unlikely that the Greeks themselves would have taken the initiative to produce a translation of the Hebrew Scriptures, reject this element of the story as pure embellishment. On the other hand, some specialists are hesitant to dismiss altogether the possibility that court officials may have had an active interest in gaining access to the formative documents of the large and significant Jewish population. The *Letter of Aristeas* may reflect some reliable information concerning the Ptolemaic court's support, if not sponsorship, of the translation.

But the questions do not end here. Even if the Greeks had some involvement in this project, the interests of the Jewish population itself must have been prominent. Was the translation then undertaken because of the needs of the Greek-speaking worshipers who no longer understood Hebrew? Or was it done rather for the academic purposes of Hebrew students and scholars who would be more likely to make sense of the translation's many difficult, literal renderings? It may well be that all of these concerns, and perhaps others as well, were motivating factors in the production of the Septuagint.

The very intensity with which the *Letter of Aristeas* defends the legitimacy of the translation raises an additional question. A great Hebraist of a previous generation, Paul Kahle, argued forcefully that the author of this document was in fact defending the Alexandrian version against competing Greek translations.[9] Septuagint scholars, following the lead of Paul de Lagarde in the nineteenth century, have generally believed that there was only one initial Greek translation of the Hebrew Bible and that the recovery of that "Proto-Septuagint" (Ur-Septu-

9. Kahle articulated some of his views on the Septuagint very early in his career. For a mature statement, see *The Cairo Geniza*, 2d ed. (Oxford: Clarendon, 1959), chap. 3. Part of the argument was based on the meaning of the Greek verb *sēmainō* in the *Letter of Aristeas* §30, which says that the Jewish laws found in the Hebrew language had been "written" carelessly. Kahle claimed that the verb means "translated" and that this statement refers to the existence of previous and unsatisfactory Greek translations rather than to imperfect Hebrew manuscripts. This interpretation has been refuted by several scholars. See especially the articles by David W. Gooding and Günther Zuntz reprinted in *Studies in the Septuagint: Origins, Recensions, and Interpretations*, ed. Sidney Jellicoe (New York: Ktav, 1974), 158–80, 208–25.

aginta) is the great task at hand.[10] Kahle insisted, however, that originally simultaneous Greek translations were produced over time, in a manner not unlike that of the Aramaic Targumim, and that the *Letter of Aristeas* sought to impose the authority of one such translation over the other ones. Although Kahle's theories created heated controversy during his lifetime, relatively few scholars were persuaded by them. Lagarde's position, with some modifications, has been confirmed by later investigation and functions as the working assumption for most specialists.[11]

Writers subsequent to the *Letter of Aristeas* add little information of substance.[12] Philo, a Jewish Alexandrian philosopher who lived in the first century of our era, embellished the story of the origin of the Greek version of the Bible. Probably relying on an earlier tradition, he writes that the translators worked independently of each other, yet produced the same translation word-for-word through divine dictation. Philo believed that the Greek translation had been divinely inspired just as the original Hebrew had been.

By the second century, we have evidence of an alternate Jewish tradition, found in rabbinic material, that gives the number of translators who went to Alexandria as seventy, not seventy-two.[13] This detail is probably intended to justify the claim that the Greek version, like the Hebrew, was divinely inspired. Seventy elders of Israel accompanied Moses to Mount Sinai and saw God (Exod. 24:1–2, 9–11); moreover, seventy elders received a share of the Spirit that was in Moses (Num. 11:10–25). By numbering the translators of the Torah as seventy, the tradition portrays them as assistants to Moses working centuries later to administer the law. The name *Septuagint* reflects this tradition. It first appears in Greek (*hoi hebdomēkonta*, "the seventy") in the mid-second century and thereafter only in Christian writers, such as Justin, Irenaeus, Eusebius, and Chrysostom. The term was most often used by these writers to refer in general to the entire Greek Old Testament, without distinguishing its various revisions and forms.

10. For further information on Lagarde, see below, chap. 11, pp. 242–45.

11. See especially John W. Wevers, "Proto-Septuagint Studies," in *The Seed of Wisdom: Essays in Honour of T. J. Meek*, ed. W. S. McCullough (Toronto: University of Toronto Press, 1964), 58–77; idem, "Barthélemy and Proto-Septuagint Studies," *BIOSCS* 21 (1988): 23–34, esp. 24–26.

12. For a description of embellishments to the story as it was transmitted through history, see Sidney Jellicoe, *The Septuagint and Modern Study* (Oxford: Clarendon, 1968), 38–47.

13. See *Sefer Tora* 1.8 (a minor tractate in the Babylonian Talmud). Still another tradition gives the number of translators as five. The minor tractate *Soferim* 1.7–8 combines two of these traditions by stating that an initial unsatisfactory translation was made for Ptolemy by five elders, but that subsequently seventy-two elders who had divine assistance produced a successful work.

In the third century, the use of the term became even more confused. As we shall see in the next chapter, Origen revised the Greek translation commonly used in the third century, "correcting" it on the basis of the Hebrew text available to him. After his work, the name *Septuagint* began to be used to refer both to the Greek text he had used as his base *and* to the text that resulted from his revisions!

The term *the Seventy* is found in colophons in biblical manuscripts as early as the fourth century.[14] It is not known if such a notation was used to distinguish the text of these manuscripts from other Greek versions known to the scribes at that time or was intended simply to identify the proper textual pedigree of the manuscript. In any case, the confusion resulting from the imprecise and ambiguous use of the name *Septuagint* today reflects the long and complicated history of the term and the texts to which it refers.

The Later Greek Translations

As we have seen, early Christian writers made frequent use of the Greek Old Testament and referred to it with the Greek or Latin term meaning "the Seventy." From time to time, however, they would also refer to alternate renderings found in other translations. These references are often vague, but many passages specifically identify translations attributed to three scholars: Aquila, Symmachus, and Theodotion. Sometimes they are referred to as a group, "the Three (Translators)."[15] Today they are often called "the Later Versions" or (for reasons to be discussed in the next chapter) "the Hexaplaric Versions." None of these works has survived, except for a few fragments,[16]

14. A colophon is a scribal notation at the end of a manuscript (or of a section in the manuscript), giving indications regarding its production. For example, a note following the Book of Genesis in Codex Vaticanus (fourth century) says that the Greek text is *kata tous hebdomēkonta* ("according to the seventy"; see Rahlfs's *Septuaginta*, 1.86). In Codex Ephraemi (fifth century), the Greek text of Proverbs is followed by the comment *para hebdomēkonta* ("from the seventy"; see Swete's *Old Testament in Greek*, 2.479). Since both of these codices also contain the books of the New Testament, the manuscripts were apparently produced within the Christian tradition.

15. These translations are often referred to by the initial Greek letter of each name: α΄, σ΄, θ΄. As a group, they may be called οἱ τρεῖς ("the three"), abbreviated οι γ΄, or οἱ λοιποί ("the others"), abbreviated οι λ΄.

16. In 1897, for example, as a result of excavations in the genizah (a storage area for worn-out documents) of a synagogue in Cairo, a sixth-century palimpsest was discovered. (A palimpsest is a manuscript that was erased and rewritten with a second text. By applying chemicals and ultraviolet light, the erased text can be read with some difficulty.) When the manuscript was brought to Cambridge, England, its underwriting was found to preserve two small portions of an uncial manuscript of Aquila's translation of 1–2 Kings. See Swete, *Introduction to the Old Testament in Greek*, 34.

but we have valuable evidence in numerous patristic quotations, as well as in marginal notations in manuscripts. With regard to their origin, these later translations are to be clearly distinguished from the "Septuagint," but as we shall see, the textual transmission of all these documents eventually became closely intertwined.

The rise of Christianity from Judaism in the first century of our era is usually given as the reason new Greek versions of the Hebrew Bible were needed. The Christian church first flourished in Jerusalem among Jews who recognized Jesus of Nazareth as the Messiah and who interpreted the death and resurrection of Jesus in light of the sacred Scriptures of the Judaism of their day. When Christianity spread outside the borders of Palestine, it was apparently the Greek version of the Jewish Scriptures from which the apostles, especially Paul, preached Christ. It is usually said that the resulting tension between Christians and Jews, both of whom used the Greek Bible but understood it differently, was the primary reason that the synagogue abandoned the "Septuagint" to the church and produced a new translation of the Hebrew texts.

While the early relationship between Christians and Jews no doubt played a major role in the history of the Greek versions, there was another factor that should not be overlooked. The recently discovered Dead Sea Scrolls provide indisputable evidence that at the turn of the era, before the birth of Christianity, the text of at least some books of the Hebrew Bible circulated in more than one form. One of these textual forms, however, emerged as *the* standard text by the beginning of the second century C.E., apparently supplanting all previous Hebrew texts. This situation alone could provide the need for a new Greek translation faithful to the newly standardized Hebrew text.

In addition, it is now clear that, even apart from Jewish-Christian polemics, there were different ideas among the Jews themselves about what a translation should look like. The discoveries in the Judean Desert have shed light on this issue as well. One of the more significant manuscripts found there is actually a Greek translation of the Minor Prophets.[17] Dated no later than the first century of our era, it appears to be a revision of the "Septuagint" for those books of the Bible. This find provides clear evidence that prior to the second-century debates among Jews and Christians, more than one Greek version of the Bible was in circulation.

Aquila

According to ancient testimony, Aquila was a Gentile who had been commissioned by his relative, the Roman emperor Hadrian, to superin-

17. This discovery will be discussed in greater detail in chap. 8, pp. 171–73.

tend the rebuilding of Jerusalem (renamed Aelia Capitolina) around the year 128 C.E.[18] While there, he became a Christian, but later converted to Judaism and studied under prominent rabbis. Aquila eventually undertook a new Greek translation of the Hebrew Bible that (a) was based on the recently standardized Hebrew text; (b) sought to correct perceived deficiencies in the Septuagint, including those that affected Jewish-Christian disputes;[19] and (c) adopted a very literalistic approach that possibly reflected certain rabbinic methods of interpretation. Aquila's work, perhaps completed around the year 140, was received enthusiastically by the Greek-speaking Jewish communities and remained the form trusted by the synagogue well into the sixth century and beyond.

The literal character of Aquila's translation has not always been adequately understood. Some scholars give the impression that Aquila was either incompetent or eccentric, but the facts suggest otherwise. To begin with, we should note that Aquila allowed himself some flexibility in the area of syntax. Instead of representing Hebrew grammatical forms in one-to-one fashion, he would sometimes use the resources of the Greek language to provide stylistic variation.[20]

In the area of vocabulary, undoubtedly, Aquila's policy was to represent every detail in the most consistent fashion, even at the cost of acceptable Greek. For example, Psalm 22:12b says, "Strong [bulls] of Bashan *surrounded* me." The Hebrew verb here, *kittēr*, happens to be related to the noun *keter* ("crown, turban"). Because this Hebrew noun is elsewhere rendered with the Greek *diadēma* ("band, diadem"), Aquila boldly makes up a new Greek verb, *diadēmatizō*, so that his translation would carry over into English as "strong ones of Bashan diademized me."[21] We must not think that Aquila misunderstood the

18. For the evidence, see Swete, *Introduction to the Old Testament in Greek*, 31–34. Unfortunately, ancient statements can seldom be taken at face value.

19. The classic example is Isa. 7:14, where the Hebrew word *ʿalmâ* had been rendered *parthenos* ("virgin") by the Septuagint; Aquila used a different Greek word, *neanias* ("young woman"). Similarly, to represent the Hebrew word *māšiaḥ* ("anointed, messiah") in Ps. 2:2, Aquila chose the Greek word *ēleimmenos* rather than *christos*, both of which mean "anointed."

20. Note, for example, his use of the optative and of the genitive absolute, for which Hebrew has no equivalents. See Kyösti Hyvärinen, *Die Übersetzung von Aquila* (Coniectanea biblica, Old Testament 10; Lund: Gleerup, 1977), 86. We strongly recommend that those who read Greek study carefully the specimens of Aquila's translation reproduced in Swete, *Introduction to the Old Testament in Greek*, 35–38, as well as the sample from Mal. 2:13 on p. 51 (the latter also includes the "Septuagint," Theodotion, and Symmachus).

21. See the evidence in Frederick Field, *Origenis Hexaplorum quae supersunt sive veterum interpretum graecorum in totum Vetus Testamentum fragmenta*, 2 vols. (Oxford: Oxford University Press, 1875), 2.118. LSJ 393 has an entry for this verb (the only reference is this passage from Aquila) but gives the misleading meaning, "wear the [diadem]." The Hebrew verb is properly translated by the Septuagint (Ps. 21:13b) with *periechō* ("to surround").

meaning of the Hebrew verb or that he was simply being reckless. He was clearly guided by the principle of providing one-for-one lexical correspondences, and he did so even in the case of particles and certain word endings.

Almost surely, Aquila's method was intended as an aid to biblical exegesis, perhaps for people who had a minimal knowledge of Hebrew.[22] We also have reason to believe that he may have been following a specific rabbinic approach to interpretation, although this point is disputed.[23] In any case, we should remember that some distinguished writers, even today, argue that translations ought to preserve both the content and the form of the original.[24] And for modern biblical scholars interested in reconstructing the Hebrew *Vorlage* or parent text of a Greek translation, Aquila's consistent method makes that task simpler.

Symmachus

Little is known about the origins of the Greek version attributed to Symmachus. He is said by some sources to have been an Ebionite Christian who produced his translation around the year 170 of our era.[25] A major recent study identifies Symmachus as a Jew (not an Ebionite) who undertook this task around the year 200 for the Jewish community in Caesarea of Palestine.[26]

Scholars who have studied what remains of this translation agree that the work was carefully done. After examining the exegetical features of Symmachus's version of the Pentateuch, as well as its syntax and vocabulary, Alison Salvesen concludes that Symmachus produced a Greek translation of the Hebrew text of the Pentateuch that "combined the best Biblical Greek style, remarkable clarity, a high degree of accuracy regarding the Hebrew, and the rabbinic exegesis of his day: it might be described as a Greek Targum, or Tannaitic Septuagint."[27]

22. Compare the way that "literal" English translations of the Bible are sometimes advertised as the next best thing to knowing Greek and Hebrew.

23. See below, chap. 13, p. 286.

24. See the discussion in Moisés Silva, *Has the Church Misread the Bible? The History of Interpretation in the Light of Current Issues* (1987); repr. in *Foundations of Contemporary Interpretation*, ed. Moisés Silva (Grand Rapids: Zondervan, 1996), 45–47.

25. The Ebionites were a second-century sect of Palestinian Christians who held fast to the practices of Judaism, especially circumcision and observance of the Sabbath. Some scholars identify Symmachus as a disciple of Rabbi Meir mentioned in the Talmud, a Samaritan who converted to Judaism.

26. Alison Salvesen, *Symmachus in the Pentateuch* (Journal of Semitic Studies Monograph 15; Manchester: University of Manchester, 1991), 296–97, building on the work of Arie van der Kooij.

27. Ibid., 297. The term *Tannaitic* refers to the rabbinic tradition during the first two centuries of our era.

On the basis of syntactic and lexical characteristics found also in the other Greek versions, Salvesen concludes that Symmachus "certainly knew Aquila," "probably knew Theodotion," and "likely" knew of the Septuagint as he produced his translation for the Jewish community of Caesarea in Palestine around the year 200. In short, Symmachus

> aimed to produce a translation in clear Greek which accurately reflected the sense of the Hebrew original. His respect for the LXX is evident: he revised it in the spirit of the original translators of the Pentateuch, ironing out their lexical inconsistencies and inaccuracies, yet preserving smooth diction where he found it and extending it where it was absent.[28]

Another specialist similarly states that Symmachus's work on the Major Prophets is characterized by clarity (representing Hebrew idioms with natural Greek expressions), variety (one Hebrew term may be represented with several Greek terms), and coherence. Although the translator allowed himself the use of exegetical expansions, his approach was sober. In general, the translation stands midway between Aquila and the Septuagint.[29]

Theodotion

The Greek translation attributed to Theodotion is especially problematic. According to the traditional view, Theodotion was a convert to Judaism who lived in Ephesus in the late second century. Taking the existing Greek version as his base, he revised it toward the standard Hebrew text. His work—which may fairly be characterized as literal, but not excessively so—includes features reminiscent of Aquila. One peculiarity is his penchant for transliterating (i.e., using Greek letters to represent the sound of the Hebrew) rather than translating certain words, such as the names for animals and plants. His translation of the Book of Daniel supplanted that of the "Septuagint" (better, the Old Greek), which was widely regarded as defective.[30]

28. Ibid., 262. Leonard J. Greenspoon believes that Symmachus's work is primarily a revision of Theodotion; see "Symmachus, Symmachus's Version," in *The Anchor Bible Dictionary*, ed. David N. Freedman et al., 6 vols. (New York: Doubleday, 1992), 6.251.

29. José González Luis, *La versión de Símaco a los profetas mayores* (diss., Universidad Complutense de Madrid, 1981), 367–68. The last comment, like all comparisons with the "Septuagint" as a whole, could be misleading. In books where the Septuagint is very literal, Symmachus does not stand midway between it and Aquila. For example, the literal Septuagint rendering *huios thanatou* ("a son of death") in 2 Sam. 12:5 becomes *axios thanatou* ("worthy of death") in Symmachus.

30. Specifically, all but two surviving manuscripts have Theodotion's translation, not the Old Greek, for Daniel. The exceptions are manuscripts 88 (11th century) and 967 (a second-century papyrus that is part of the Chester Beatty collection, discovered in 1931). The Old Greek is also reflected in a Syriac version known as the Syro-Hexaplar.

One of the problems with this description is that certain renderings once thought distinctive to Theodotion are now known to have existed a century or two before he lived. Note, for example, the reference to Daniel 6:23 in Hebrews 11:33. Although the author of Hebrews is otherwise heavily dependent on the "Septuagint" or the Old Greek, this passage reflects Theodotion's rendering: "[God] shut the mouths of the lions" (*enephraxe ta stomata tōn leontōn*), rather than the Old Greek, which says, "God saved me from the lions" (*sesōke me ho theos apo tōn leontōn*). This phenomenon led to speculation about the existence of a "Proto-Theodotion," and recent discoveries have confirmed the view that, for at least parts of the Hebrew Bible, a translation very similar to Theodotion's was already in use in the first century B.C.E. For reasons to be discussed elsewhere in this book,[31] most scholars now prefer to speak of *Kaige*-Theodotion, meaning by that term a well-defined, pre-Christian revision of the Old Greek; it is also thought that this revision became the basis for the work of both Aquila and Symmachus. The work of the historical Theodotion may then be viewed as a later updating of the revision.

Also debated is the question of Daniel-Theodotion in particular. Some argue that the characteristics of this translation do not fit those found in materials otherwise attributed to Theodotion.[32] Moreover, doubts have been raised about the usual view that Daniel-Theodotion is a revision of the Old Greek.[33] These and other questions will continue to occupy scholars for years to come.

Other Versions

In addition to the Three, other attempts were made to translate parts of the Hebrew Bible into Greek. Some church fathers, for example, make reference to *ho hebraios*,[34] an ambiguous term that in some contexts appears to mean "the Hebrew translator." One also finds quite a few references to "the Syrian" (*ho syros*) and nearly fifty to "the Samariticon" (*to samar[e]itikon*).

31. See chap. 8, pp. 171–73, and chap. 13, pp. 284–86.

32. See A. Schmitt, *Stammt der sogennante θ'-Text bei Daniel wirklich von Theodotion?* (Mitteilungen des Septuaginta-Unternehmens 9; Göttingen: Vandenhoeck & Ruprecht, 1966); and his update in a later article, "Die griechische Danieltexte («θ'» und o') und das Theodotionproblem," *Biblische Zeitschrift* 36 (1992): 1–29.

33. See Tim McLay, *The OG and Th Versions of Daniel* (SBLSCS 43; Atlanta: Scholars Press, 1996).

34. Greek ὁ Ἑβραῖος (also τὸ ἑβραϊκόν), abbreviated ο εβρ'. For a fine summary of the research on this and other versions, see Natalio Fernández Marcos, *Introducción a las versiones griegas de la Biblia*, 2d ed. (Textos y Estudios "Cardenal Cisneros" 23; Madrid: Consejo Superior de Investigaciones Científicas, 1998) = *The Septuagint in Context: Introduction to the Greek Version of the Bible*, trans. Wilfred G. E. Watson (Leiden: Brill, 2000), chaps. 10–11.

Little can be said with confidence about these versions. Moreover, as we shall see in the next chapter, Origen was familiar with three anonymous translations that have come to be known as Quinta, Sexta, and Septima. Of these, the Quinta is best attested, but not sufficiently to give us a complete picture.

The existence of such a variety of translations in addition to the original "Septuagint" needs to be taken seriously. Although the primary focus of the present book is indeed on that earlier form, subsequent developments shed considerable light on the subject as a whole. Moreover, the other translations and revisions had a deep effect on the transmission of the earlier work.

To Continue Your Study

Because we learn best when material is presented from more than one perspective, students are encouraged to supplement the present chapter, as well as the rest of part 1, with brief treatments found elsewhere. Dictionary and encyclopedia articles are well suited for this purpose. Note, for example, Melvin K. H. Peters, "Septuagint," in *The Anchor Bible Dictionary*, ed. David N. Freedman et al., 6 vols. (New York: Doubleday, 1992), 5.1093–1104. Older, but still very useful, is John W. Wevers, "Septuagint," in *The Interpreter's Dictionary of the Bible*, ed. George A. Buttrick et al. (Nashville: Abingdon, 1962), 4.273–78, which was updated by Emanuel Tov and Robert A. Kraft in *The Interpreter's Dictionary of the Bible: Supplementary Volume*, ed. Keith Crim et al. (Nashville: Abingdon, 1976), 807–15. Compare also Ernst Würthwein, *The Text of the Old Testament: An Introduction to the Biblia Hebraica*, trans. Erroll F. Rhodes, 2d ed. (Grand Rapids: Eerdmans, 1995), 49–63, and comparable textbooks.

The classic source for information on Septuagint studies is Henry Barclay Swete, *An Introduction to the Old Testament in Greek*, 2d ed. (Cambridge: Cambridge University Press, 1914; repr. Peabody, Mass.: Hendrickson, 1989). See pages 1–58 for a more detailed treatment of the material covered in the present chapter. In spite of its age, Swete's book provides data not found anywhere else, though readers should keep in mind that he assumes knowledge of biblical scholarship and proficiency in Greek and Latin. Sidney Jellicoe provided an indispensable updating of that volume in *The Septuagint and Modern Study* (Oxford: Clarendon, 1968), which assumes that the reader is familiar with Swete's work; pages 29–99 provide extensive supplementary information on the origins of the Septuagint and the early revisions.

Introductory works in other modern languages include Natalio Fernández Marcos, *Introducción a las versiones griegas de la Biblia*, 2d ed. (Textos y Estudios "Cardenal Cisneros" 23; Madrid: Consejo Superior de Investigaciones Científicas, 1998),[35] chapters 3–11, the most thorough and up-to-date summary and evaluation of current scholarly work; it includes extensive bibliographies. Also important though addressed to a more general audience is *La Bible Grecque des Septante: Du judaïsme hellénistique au christianisme ancien*, 2d ed. (Initiations au christianisme ancien; [Paris]: Cerf/Centre National de la Recherche Scientifique, 1994), coauthored by Marguerite Harl, Gilles Dorival, and Olivier Munnich; see chapter 2 for a discussion of the origins of the Septuagint, and pages 142–61 for a treatment of Aquila, Symmachus, and Theodotion. Finally, note the important essay by B. Botte and P.-M. Bogaert, "Septante et versions grecques," in *Dictionnaire de la Bible, Supplément* 12.536–692.

35. Now available in English translation: *The Septuagint in Context: Introduction to the Greek Version of the Bible*, trans. Wilfred G. E. Watson (Leiden: Brill, 2000).

2

The Transmission of the Septuagint

Recensions of the Septuagint. Among systematic revisions of the Septuagint, the most important was the ***Hexaplaric Recension***, a work produced by Origen in connection with his larger project, the Hexapla, which contained the biblical text in six columns (the Hebrew text, a transcription of the Hebrew text in Greek letters, and four Greek translations). Also significant was the ***Lucianic Recension***, a stylistic revision made in Antioch around the year 300, but apparently based on a much earlier textual recension.

Witnesses to the Septuagint Text. The primary evidence consists of a very large number of ***Greek Manuscripts***, usually divided into three categories: papyri (ancient manuscripts written on leaves made from the papyrus plant), uncials (early parchment manuscripts that use a script based on capital letters), and minuscules (medieval manuscripts written in a cursive style). Scholars also depend on the evidence provided by the ***Secondary Versions***, that is, translations of the Septuagint into other languages, and by ***Ancient Citations***, that is, many thousands of passages from the Greek Bible quoted by early Jewish and Christian writers.

As we saw in the previous chapter, the Pentateuch of the Hebrew Bible was translated into Greek in Alexandria, Egypt, probably all within a short period, in the third century B.C.E. When and where the other books were translated, and by whom, has not been determined, but we have good reason to believe that by the middle of the first century B.C.E., the rest of the Hebrew Bible, with the possible exception of one or two books, had been translated into Greek.

In the case of Judges, Daniel, and Esther (as well as Tobit, Susanna, and Judith—books not included in the Hebrew canon), two quite different Greek forms are found among surviving manuscripts. The current consensus among Septuagint scholars, with few exceptions, is that only one "original" Greek translation was made of each book prior to the Christian era, and that whatever differences are found between surviving texts of the same book reflect a revision of the Greek. In any case, by the turn of the era, at least one Greek translation of virtually every book of the Hebrew Bible was in circulation among Greek-speaking Jews.

Recensions of the Septuagint

In the past, scholars made a fairly sharp distinction between two types of work produced subsequent to the "original" Septuagint: (a) new Greek translations of the Hebrew Bible (i.e., primarily the three versions made by Aquila, Symmachus, and Theodotion) and (b) major recensions[1] of the Septuagint itself (illustration 1). Following this traditional understanding, we dealt with the Three at the end of the previous chapter and treated them as independent works to be distinguished from the Septuagint. In this chapter, however, we focus again on the Septuagint as the original Greek version and ask questions about its transmission and revisions.

1. Traditional understanding of the relationship between the Septuagint and the later Greek versions

Were the later Greek versions original translations?

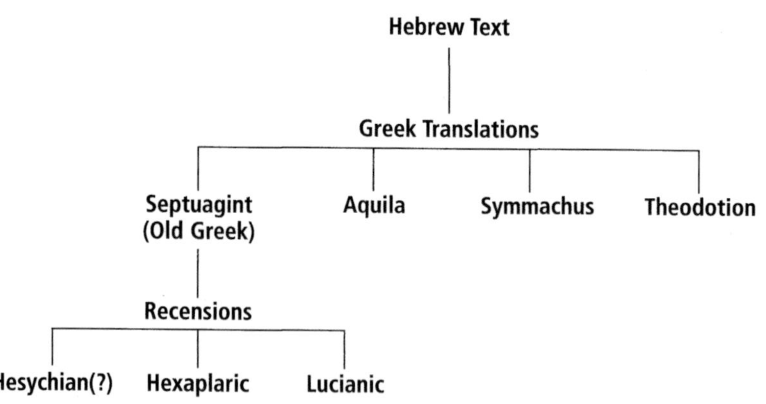

Unfortunately, the distinction between a revision and a new translation is difficult to define clearly.[2] After all, scholars today speak of

1. In this book, we use the term *recension* to indicate a self-conscious, systematic, and clearly identifiable revision of an existing text. The resulting work is viewed not as a new entity, but as the updating (or restoration or improvement) of an earlier work.

2. Compare in English the New Revised Standard Version. If it had a different name and if we did not know that historically this work descends directly from the King James Version, might we not regard it as a new, independent translation (such as the NIV, for example)?

Kaige-Theodotion as a revision, and even the work of Aquila is sometimes described this way. An approach that does not differentiate between revisions and new versions may be represented with the diagram in illustration 2.[3] It remains true, however, that the Three were historically perceived and probably intended as new works more or less in competition with the Septuagint, whereas the "recensions" (Origen's in particular) were meant to provide reliable editions of the Septuagint itself.

2. Alternative understanding of the relationship between the Septuagint and the later Greek versions

Were the later Greek versions revisions of the Septuagint?

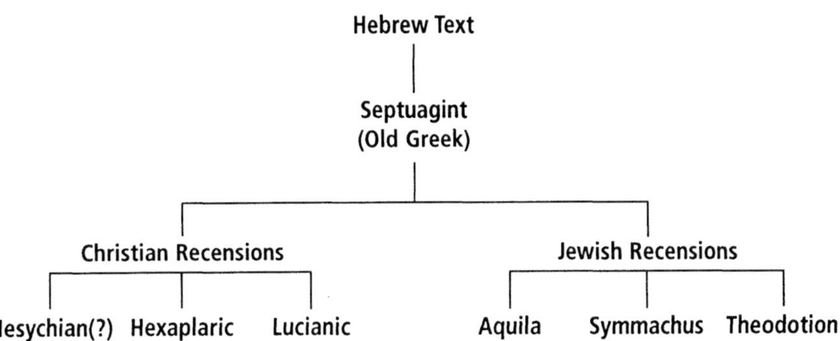

The usual starting point for a discussion of recensions is a well-known comment by Jerome (ca. 340–420), the most knowledgeable biblical scholar of his day. In his preface to Chronicles, Jerome complained that the Christian world was in conflict over three forms (*trifaria varietas*) of the Septuagint text: (a) one in Egypt, attributed to Hesychius; (b) a second dominant from Constantinople to Antioch and attributed to Lucian; and between them (c) Origen's (Hexaplaric) recension, used in Palestine. We know nothing about Hesychius, and scholars have been unsuccessful in identifying a Hesychian recension among the manuscripts (although most biblical books have an Egyptian form of the text, which may be the basis for Jerome's comment).[4]

3. The distinction in illustration 2 between Jewish and Christian recensions is followed, for example, by Natalio Fernández Marcos, *Introducción a las versiones griegas de la Biblia*, 2d ed. (Textos y Estudios "Cardenal Cisneros" 23; Madrid: Consejo Superior de Investigaciones Científicas, 1998) = *The Septuagint in Context: Introduction to the Greek Version of the Bible*, trans. Wilfred G. E. Watson (Leiden: Brill, 2000), parts 3–4. Emanuel Tov prefers a threefold, chronological distinction: (a) pre-Hexaplaric revisions, (b) the Hexapla, and (c) post-Hexaplaric revisions; see his *Textual Criticism of the Hebrew Bible* (Minneapolis: Fortress, 1992), 144.

4. For the text of Jerome's statement, see Sidney Jellicoe, *The Septuagint and Modern Study* (Oxford: Clarendon, 1968), 134. With regard to Hesychius and his alleged recen-

For all practical purposes, therefore, a description of the Christian recensions must be limited to those attributed to Origen and to Lucian of Antioch.

The Hexaplaric Recension

Origen's Hexapla

The most important work on the text of the Greek Old Testament was done by Origen, the Christian theologian of Alexandria (ca. 185 to ca. 254). After heading up the Christian catechetical school in Alexandria, Origen eventually settled in Palestine, in the city of Caesarea. During this period he undertook the massive project of comparing the Greek versions known to him with the Hebrew text of his day, which apparently was close to the form that has come to us as the Masoretic Text. Most of what is known about this work comes from two brief descriptions by Origen himself and from the writings of later church fathers who saw the work.[5] Aware of the differences between the Septuagint and the Hebrew text, he set out to produce an edition that would take those variations into account. To accomplish his task, he wrote the available texts in parallel columns. For most of the Old Testament he needed to use six columns, the feature from which the name of this work, the Hexapla, is taken. These columns contained the following texts:

1. Hebrew text
2. transliteration of the Hebrew text into Greek letters
3. Aquila's translation
4. Symmachus's translation
5. translation of the Seventy
6. Theodotion's translation

The purpose of the second column, containing a transliteration of the Hebrew into Greek letters, is somewhat puzzling. Some suggest that it would have allowed a Greek speaker who did not know Hebrew

sion, see pp. 146–56; and especially Fernández Marcos, *Introducción a las versiones griegas*, chap. 15. A Christian bishop of that name lived in Alexandria and died during the persecutions of Diocletian. The name Hesychius, however, was common, and we have no evidence to link this martyr with a Greek version of Scripture.

5. For the relevant Greek and Latin texts, see Henry Barclay Swete, *An Introduction to the Old Testament in Greek*, 2d ed. (Cambridge: Cambridge University Press, 1914; repr. Peabody, Mass.: Hendrickson, 1989), 60 (Origen's *Letter to Africanus* 5 and his *Commentary on Matthew* 15:14) and 64 (esp. Eusebius's *Ecclesiastical History* 6.16 and Jerome's *Commentary on Titus* 3:9). Because some of the ancient testimony is contradictory, very few points can be established with certainty. The description given here should be viewed only as a possible way of explaining the data.

to "read" (i.e., pronounce) the Hebrew Bible aloud, perhaps in the synagogue service. To give an example with English letters, try reading the following aloud: *be-ray-sheeth ba-ra e-lo-heem*. You have just "read" the Hebrew words that open the Book of Genesis: בְּרֵאשִׁית בָּרָא אֱלֹהִים ("in the beginning God created").

J. A. Emerton argues that the transliteration of the Hebrew into the Greek alphabet was used "to enable those who knew both the Hebrew language and alphabet to vocalize a consonantal text in Hebrew characters."[6] Before the early Middle Ages, the Hebrew text consisted of consonants only; the vowel sounds were to be inferred by the reader. Origen's second column may represent an earlier attempt to preserve the correct pronunciation of the Hebrew vowels for people whose native language was Greek and whose knowledge of Hebrew was not extensive. Although Origen possibly created the transliteration himself, it seems consistent with his purposes that he was using a text already available in the Jewish synagogue, a text that allowed Greek-speaking Jews to hear the ancient scriptures "read" in the original Hebrew.[7]

The translations in columns 3 (Aquila), 4 (Symmachus), and 6 (Theodotion) of the Hexapla were described in the previous chapter. Column 5 contained the "Septuagint," apparently the standard Greek translation used by the Christian church at the time. It is usually thought that this column included the corrections that Origen made in light of the Hebrew text. For example, as he compared the texts of Isaiah, he found that several lines of Hebrew in chapter 40 (vv. 7b–8a) were missing from the Septuagint, so he inserted that material into the text of the fifth column. According to some scholars, however, the fifth column contained an uncorrected text, so that the revised translation was really a separate, subsequent project for which the Hexapla was the preparatory work.[8]

6. J. A. Emerton, "The Purpose of the Second Column of the Hexapla," *Journal of Theological Studies* 7 (1956): 79–87, quotation from 79; repr. in *Studies in the Septuagint: Origins, Recensions, and Interpretations*, ed. Sidney Jellicoe (New York: Ktav, 1974), 347. The article includes a summary of other theories.

7. Because Origen was interested in reconciling the Septuagint text to the Hebrew, it was appropriate for him to include in the Hexapla the aural version that Greek-speaking Jews would have heard in the synagogue. Unfortunately, no manuscript containing such a transliteration of the Hebrew Bible has survived. Its existence and use is hypothetical and debated. If it was a provincial text used only in the synagogues of Alexandria, it may have existed in a limited number of copies, none of which has survived.

8. See the clear summary of the issues by Joachim Schaper, "The Origin and Purpose of the Fifth Column of the Hexapla," in *Origen's Hexapla and Fragments: Papers Presented at the Rich Seminar on the Hexapla, Oxford Centre for Hebrew and Jewish Studies, 25th [July]–3rd August 1994*, ed. Alison Salvesen (Texte und Studien zum antiken Judentum 58; Tübingen: Mohr Siebeck, 1998), 3–15. This volume contains several important essays that have a bearing on the subject of the present chapter.

We do not know Origen's rationale for the order of the columns. One interesting theory was proposed by Harry M. Orlinsky, who argued that Origen wanted "to provide his [Christian] contemporaries with the much needed facilities to learn Hebrew, and thus to be able to make use of all six columns of his Hexapla." After supplying the Hebrew text and a second column to help the reader pronounce it, Origen next included Aquila's version because its word-for-word representation of the Hebrew provided a "crib" for the reader. Since Aquila is often unintelligible, however, Symmachus was needed to clarify it. "And equipped with the knowledge gained from the first four columns, the reader was ready to tackle the most important column of them all, the Septuagint."[9]

For the Book of Psalms and possibly for a few other books, Origen was able to use three more Greek versions (but not more than two at a time), so for these books he expanded his work to eight columns—thus the term *Octapla*. Virtually nothing is known about the origin of these anonymous versions, referred to as Quinta, Sexta, and Septima.[10] Since Origen included their text for only a few books, apparently none of these three versions contained the complete Old Testament in the manuscripts available to him. Quinta—the best attested of these three versions—is believed to have included 2 Kings, Job, Psalms, Song of Songs, and the Minor Prophets.

Given the way modern scholars refer freely to the Hexaplaric texts, including the translations of Aquila, Theodotion, and Symmachus, readers may be left with the impression that fairly complete and reliable copies of these Greek texts exist. In fact, actual specimens are preserved only in (a) quotations by other ancient writers, (b) marginal notes in a handful of manuscripts,[11] and (c) a very few fragments of copies of the Hexapla. The largest and most significant Hexapla fragment is the Mercati palimpsest in the Ambrosian Library of Milan. In 1896 Giovanni Mercati discovered that the underwriting of this tenth-

9. Theodotion had to be included somewhere, so the only place left was the sixth column. See Harry M. Orlinsky, "The Columnar Order of the Hexapla," *Jewish Quarterly Review* 27 (1936–37): 137–49, quotation from 146–47; repr. in *Studies in the Septuagint: Origins, Recensions, and Interpretations*, ed. Sidney Jellicoe (New York: Ktav, 1974), 378–79.

10. That is, the fifth (abbreviated ε′), sixth (ς′), and seventh (ζ′) versions used by him. See the discussion in Jellicoe, *Septuagint and Modern Study*, 118–24, to be supplemented by Fernández Marcos, *Introducción a las versiones griegas*, 163–69 (= *Septuagint in Context*, 155–61). The Sexta apparently included at least Job, Psalms, Song of Songs, and Habakkuk. According to the somewhat conflicting explanations of Eusebius and Epiphanius, Origen himself unearthed these Greek manuscripts. One or two he found in earthenware jars at Jericho in the year 217 and one in Nicopolis while visiting Greece in 231. In other words, whatever the origin and history of these three additional versions, they apparently were not in wide circulation at the time of Origen.

11. For example, codices G and Q; see below, pp. 59–64.

century cursive manuscript contained five columns of the Hexapla for about 150 verses of the Psalms. It apparently never contained the first column, the Hebrew text.[12]

What a precious treasure Origen's Hexapla would be for biblical scholars had it survived! It is estimated that the Hexapla would have required about six thousand pages bound in fifteen volumes. Such a massive work would probably never have been copied in its entirety. The only copy we know of was deposited in the library in Caesarea, Palestine, under the care of Pamphilus, the Christian martyr (ca. 250–310). It was presumably destroyed with the library by Muslim Saracens in the seventh century, if not earlier.

A comprehensive collection of Hexaplaric remains was published by Frederick Field over a century ago.[13] Since then, new fragments have been discovered and studied. In 1994, a new project was begun at the University of Oxford under the leadership of Leonard J. Greenspoon, Alison Salvesen, and Gerard Norton to produce a new, electronic database containing all the surviving evidence.[14]

The Fifth Column

For students of the Septuagint, the most important issue surrounding Origen's work is the character of his revised Greek text, which according to many scholars was to be found in the fifth column. (As mentioned earlier, other scholars argue that this column contained an *un*revised text and that Origen's own recension was published separately.) Origen had set out to produce a restored Greek version of the Bible for the church, and his corrected text quickly became the standard Old Testament for the Eastern churches from Antioch to Alexandria. It was copied and promoted by church leaders for centuries. It, too, was called the "Septuagint," although it was no longer the same "Septuagint" text with which Origen had started out.

Origen himself states the purpose of this work in the *Letter to Africanus*, while the method he used is explained in his *Commentary on Matthew*.[15] Apparently his purpose was to settle the dispute between Christians and Jews about the biblical texts. The Hexapla would show at a glance the Hebrew and all known Greek versions of it. Where the Greek Bible disagreed with the Hebrew Bible, Origen felt it important to "correct" the Greek version used at that time by the church to agree

12. See Ernst Würthwein, *The Text of the Old Testament: An Introduction to Biblia Hebraica*, trans. Erroll F. Rhodes, 2d ed. (Grand Rapids: Eerdmans, 1995), pl. 34, for a photo of this interesting manuscript; see also Swete, *Introduction to the Old Testament in Greek*, 62–63, for a transcribed specimen of Ps. 45:1–3.

13. *Origenis Hexaplorum quae supersunt sive veterum interpretum graecorum in totum Vetus Testamentum fragmenta*, 2 vols. (Oxford: Oxford University Press, 1875).

14. See below, appendix A.

15. See above, n. 5.

with the Hebrew version used at that time by the synagogue. In other words, Origen's purpose in constructing the Hexapla was quite different from the task of modern textual critics.

Origen may have been unaware that the Hebrew text available to him did not fully correspond with the Hebrew parent text from which the Greek translation had been produced. He could have easily been misled by the fact that in his day one standard Hebrew text—the one that has survived today as the Masoretic Text—already reigned supreme. We now know, however, that this text had undergone at least some development in the centuries before becoming standardized and that, for at least some books, the Hebrew Bible existed in more than one textual form. This means that the parent text from which any Greek translation had been made may not have had the same general form as the Hebrew text used by Origen. From the perspective of textual criticism, therefore, the basic assumption upon which he based his method was wrong. On the other hand, what looks like the work of a wrongheaded textual critic in the production of the Hexapla was actually the careful and valuable work of a well-intentioned Christian apologist.

As for his method, Origen compared the Greek Septuagint text, bit by bit, to the Hebrew text. The Greek sometimes had text that was not found in the Hebrew. These pluses may have been in the Hebrew *Vorlage* from which the Greek was originally produced,[16] or maybe they were introduced later as the Greek version developed independently of the Hebrew. In either case, out of respect for the sanctity of the Septuagint, Origen did not wish simply to delete Greek material not found in the Hebrew text. So he marked material found in the Septuagint but not in the Hebrew with an obelus (– or ∸ or ÷); if the reading included more than one word, he marked the end of the reading with a metobelus (⁄. or ⁒ or ⸔). The signs used by Origen to mark his text are sometimes referred to as the Aristarchian symbols, because they had previously been used by an Alexandrian scholar named Aristarchus to do similar text-critical work on the various Greek texts of Homer.

Origen also found, however, that some Hebrew material was not in the Septuagint text. Perhaps the Hebrew *Vorlage* of the original translation did not contain this material, either because that Hebrew text was quite different from the one Origen had before him or because the material was added to the Hebrew text after the Greek translation had been made. Or perhaps these minuses had originally been in the Greek translation, but were omitted, either intentionally or accidentally, at

16. Septuagint scholars often refer to a word or passage found in the Greek but not in the Hebrew as a *plus* because the term *addition* prejudices the discussion (i.e., it implies that the Hebrew text used by the translator did not have this passage). Similarly, a passage found in the Hebrew but not in the Greek is usually called a *minus* rather than an *omission*.

some later time. In any case, Origen felt compelled to insert Greek text to correspond to his Hebrew text. He did this by referring to the other existing Greek versions. If one of them contained a reading that in his opinion corresponded well to the Hebrew reading, he inserted that reading into the Greek text of the fifth column, placing it between an asterisk (※) and a metobelus (⸔).

Through this process, Origen introduced isolated readings pulled from Aquila, Symmachus, and Theodotion (and possibly from Quinta, Sexta, and Septima) into the "Septuagint" text. Although he marked the original material, those markings were not always preserved. After Origen completed his work, the fifth column—that is, his recension of the Septuagint—was copied separately and became the authorized Greek version of the Bible for the Christian church in Palestine. Because Origen's symbols were reproduced imperfectly or not at all, it became impossible to identify the origin of the various readings. Subsequently this text was widely copied and circulated, which means that surviving manuscripts of the "Septuagint," with few exceptions, have a mixed text.

Origen may have accomplished his goal successfully, but he greatly complicated the work of modern textual critics, who are often tempted to view the Hexapla as "a monument to misguided industry."[17] In effect, the great task of Septuagint textual criticism is to reconstruct the pre-Hexaplaric text, which means *undoing* Origen's labors so as to rediscover the form of the "Septuagint" in the second century. Without Greek manuscripts predating Origen,[18] however, that goal is not easily reached. The challenges of Septuagint textual criticism are explored below (chap. 6).

The Lucianic Recension

Lucian of Antioch, born in Syria about the middle of the third century, died as a martyr in the year 312. He was a controversial theologian and an influential biblical scholar. While the specific extent and nature of his textual work remain uncertain, he apparently updated an existing Greek text of both the Old and New Testaments. His revisions seem to have been primarily stylistic in nature.[19]

17. John W. Wevers, "Proto-Septuagint Studies," in *The Seed of Wisdom: Essays in Honour of T. J. Meek*, ed. W. S. McCullough (Toronto: University of Toronto Press, 1964), 58.

18. A few fragmentary exceptions are Papyrus 967, the Greek biblical manuscripts from the Judean Desert (see below, pp. 58–59), and quotations of the Septuagint by early writers.

19. For a survey of Lucian's life and work, see especially Bruce M. Metzger, "The Lucianic Recension of the Greek Bible," in *Chapters in the History of the New Testament* (New Testament Tools and Studies 4; Leiden: Brill, 1963), 1–41. Most of this article (the sections dealing with the Old Testament) is reprinted in *Studies in the Septuagint: Origins, Recensions, and Interpretations*, ed. Sidney Jellicoe (New York: Ktav, 1974), 270–91. It is important to note that many scholars are skeptical about the traditions concerning Lucian's role as reviser. A few writers go so far as to deny that Lucian himself had any-

The resulting Lucianic recension is also referred to as the Antiochene or Antiochian text, partly because Lucian may have used as his base the Greek text then current in Antioch of Syria, partly because his revision was best known in that city. Lucian's recension (perhaps based on Origen's fifth column) is believed to be quoted in the writings of later Antiochene scholars such as Chrysostom and Theodoret. Moreover, isolated readings in the margins of several Greek and Syriac manuscripts are marked respectively by the Greek letter *lambda* (λ) and the Syriac letter *lomadh* (ܠ), and many of these readings should no doubt be recognized as Lucianic.[20] With these clues, scholars are able to identify, for most books, a large number of Septuagint manuscripts containing the Lucianic recension.

The revision attributed to Lucian is especially evident in the Book of Psalms and in the New Testament.[21] Indeed, most of the surviving manuscripts that include either of those two portions of the Greek Bible contain a revised text that is somewhat fuller—and stylistically more homogeneous—than other text forms. Whether or not Lucian was responsible for this work, it is generally agreed that the revision can be traced back to Antioch around the year 300. In addition to the Psalter, the Lucianic or Antiochene recension of the Septuagint is clearly attested in the Prophets and in some of the historical books (especially Samuel–Kings–Chronicles). Scholars have been unable to identify a Lucianic text in the Pentateuch.

The most difficult and important problem related to this recension has to do with the presence of so-called Lucianic readings attested long before Lucian lived.[22] The Old Latin version (a translation from the Greek Old Testament produced in the second century of our era),

---

thing to do with a Greek revision of the Old Testament, though they recognize such a thing as an Antiochene (Syrian) recension for both the Old and the New Testament.

20. Because Greek *lambda* also serves as an abbreviation for *hoi loipoi* (οἱ λοιποί ["the others"], that is, the versions of Aquila, Symmachus, and Theodotion), much care needs to be exercised in the interpretation of this marginal notation. The ambiguity is intensified by the fact that the Lucianic readings often coincide with those of the Three.

21. When Fenton J. A. Hort, building on the work of earlier textual critics, identified and described the Syrian text of the New Testament, he hesitantly suggested that Lucian may have had some responsibility for it: "Of known names his has a better claim than any other to be associated with the early Syrian revision," but "no critical results are affected by the presence or absence of his name"; see Brooke Foss Westcott and Fenton J. A. Hort, *The New Testament in the Original Greek: Introduction* [*and*] *Appendix* (Cambridge/London: Macmillan, 1881), 138–39. This suggestion has not been picked up by many scholars, and some flatly reject it. Most New Testament textual critics, however, acknowledge that the text found in the majority of surviving manuscripts (the Byzantine text) reflects a revision marked by smoothness and comprehensiveness, and developed primarily in Antioch of Syria in the late third or early fourth century.

22. See especially Metzger, "Lucianic Recension of the Greek Bible," 31–35 (repr. 284–88).

as well as biblical quotations from Latin fathers such as Tertullian (who died early in the third century) and Cyprian (died 258), occasionally reflect a text that has some distinctives normally associated with the Antiochene text. Even earlier, Greek writers such as Justin Martyr (died ca. 165) and especially Josephus (died ca. 100) appear to have used a biblical text resembling that of the Antiochene recension. Most puzzling of all, one of the Hebrew fragments of Samuel discovered at Qumran (4QSam^{a}) also shows important points of contact with the Lucianic text.[23]

Although some of the evidence is disputed, many scholars speak of a Proto-Lucianic text, meaning by that term an early revision of the Septuagint (better, Old Greek) that brings it closer to the Hebrew text. If so, the historical Lucian may have used such a revised text as the basis for his own revisions. This two-layer view helps to explain why the Lucianic or Antiochene text is characterized by two opposing tendencies: on the one hand, the Lucianic manuscripts contain many readings that are closer to the Hebrew text than are those found in the other Septuagint manuscripts; on the other hand, many of the stylistic changes in the Lucianic recension tend to move the Greek text away from the Hebrew. This problem is solved if "Lucian" made his stylistic alterations on a text that had earlier been adjusted toward the Hebrew.

Recensions: A Summary

The recensions produced by Origen and Lucian (and perhaps Hesychius) were the texts of the Greek Bible most commonly in use in the Christian church after the late third century. The Greek-speaking Jewish synagogues continued to use either the "Septuagint" or Aquila's version well into the latter half of the first millennium and possibly beyond. Since the exact pedigree of any surviving manuscript cannot be established beyond doubt, it is difficult to untangle the history of the various Greek texts and how they have influenced each other. Much work by Septuagint scholars today is directed toward identifying and isolating those texts in order to get behind them and approximate as much as possible the original form of the Greek Old Testament.

To summarize, the textual history of the Greek version of the Hebrew Bible can be divided generally into at least five stages:

23. For example, the Masoretic Text of 2 Sam. 13:3 identifies Amnon's friend as Jonadab. Most manuscripts of the Septuagint have the same name, but the Lucianic/Antiochene recension has Jonathan, as does 4QSam^{a}. Josephus writes the name as Jonathes. See Emanuel Tov, "Lucian and Proto-Lucian: Toward a New Solution of the Problem," *Revue biblique* 79 (1972): 101–13; repr. in *Qumran and the History of the Biblical Text*, ed. Frank M. Cross and Shemaryahu Talmon (Cambridge: Harvard University Press, 1975), 293–303. Tov wants to allow for the possibility that the Proto-Lucianic text may have been not a revision of the Old Greek but a different Greek translation altogether (p. 103).

1. the original translation of each biblical book from Hebrew into Greek (the Old Greek)
2. early revisions evolving from the originals (e.g., *Kaige*-Theodotion, possibly Proto-Lucian and others)
3. the versions/revisions of Aquila, Symmachus, and Theodotion
4. Origen's recension (probably the fifth column in the Hexapla)
5. Lucian's recension (possibly also Hesychius's recension) known to Jerome.

Illustration 3 attempts to visualize some of the more important connections. A solid line indicates direct descent; a dotted line suggests only a measure of influence from one document to another. As with all such charts, the reader should keep in mind its tentative and simplified nature.

3. Textual history of the Greek versions

Only the complexity of the textual history of the Greek versions is certain. This diagram illustrates one possible reconstruction.

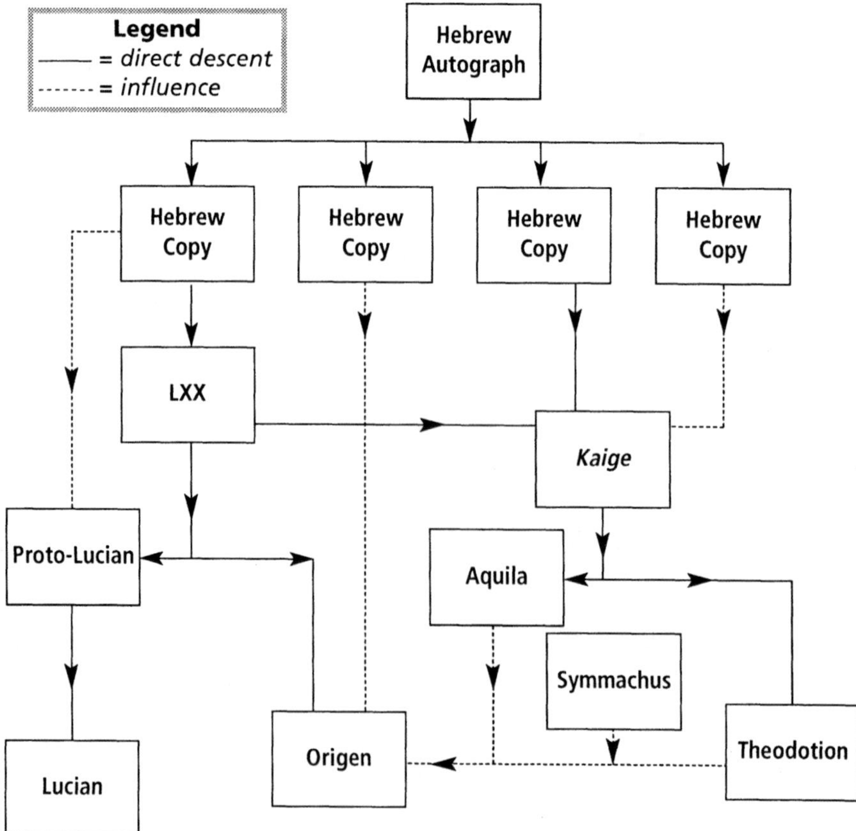

Witnesses to the Septuagint Text

If you wanted to examine the Greek text of the Septuagint, you would most likely take a look at the text prepared by Alfred Rahlfs or some other modern edition. Editors like Rahlfs, however, can do their work only by making use of textual witnesses, that is, Greek manuscripts produced throughout the centuries, ancient translations of the Septuagint into other languages, and citations by the church fathers and other ancient writers. These collectively comprise the pieces to the great puzzle of the history of the Greek Old Testament. Although an extensive list of such witnesses would be out of place in the present textbook, students need at least a general knowledge of the materials that have preserved the text of the Greek Bible.

Greek Manuscripts

Paleographers—scholars who study the physical characteristics of ancient writings—make a basic distinction between two kinds of Greek manuscripts: older ones written in the uncial script (a style developed from the majuscules or capital letters used in inscriptions) and later ones written in minuscule script (a style developed from cursive handwriting in the ninth century). A further distinction is based on the material used: papyrus,[24] parchment (an expensive alternative made from the skin of animals), and paper (beginning in the late Middle Ages). It is important to keep in mind that, because of the special importance attached to the papyri, these are placed in a separate category and thus distinguished from the uncials. This terminology can prove confusing, since the uncial script was used to write on the papyri as well.

Manuscripts are given a name or number or both based on the cataloguing system of the library or museum that holds them. In addition, scholars in a particular discipline give manuscripts a different designation as part of a comprehensive system of cataloguing manuscripts that have similar content. Thus, for example, a thirteenth-century minuscule manuscript of the Gospels in the British Library has the designation Burney 20; New Testament scholars, however, refer to it as manuscript 482.

Septuagint scholars have their own system. Most uncial manuscripts are designated by capital letters; the famous Codex Sinaiticus,

24. Papyrus was a relatively inexpensive material made from the papyrus plant, which grew abundantly along the banks of the Nile. For many centuries Egypt was the major producer and exporter of rolls of papyrus used throughout the ancient Mediterranean world. Documents written on papyrus wear out quickly under normal use, but many such texts have survived thousands of years buried in the dry sands of desert areas. For a useful treatment of biblical paleography, including numerous photographic plates, see Bruce M. Metzger, *Manuscripts of the Greek Bible: An Introduction to Palaeography* (New York/Oxford: Oxford University Press, 1981).

for example, is referred to as S.[25] Minuscules, according to one system, are designated by lowercase letters, but the preferred approach (developed by Rahlfs for the Septuagint project in Göttingen) uses numbers. The first thousand numbers are used for manuscripts of books other than Psalms, with numbers 800–1000 reserved for the papyri and for uncial fragments; numbers 1001–2000 are used for the copious manuscripts of the Psalms (2001 and following are reserved for especially ancient witnesses to the Psalms).[26]

Papyri

While most of the surviving biblical texts have come to us through continuous transmission over the centuries, many other manuscripts have come to light only in modern times as a result of archeological work. Indeed, ancient biblical texts dating as far back as the pre-Christian era have been found in archives of papyri excavated by archeologists. Manuscripts discovered in this way are extremely valuable, because they preserve the text as it existed when they were buried. These documents, which have not been subjected to the vicissitudes of copying throughout subsequent centuries, provide a snapshot of the text at an earlier time. One of the most significant finds, fourth-century Chester Beatty Papyrus IV (Rahlfs 961), contains Genesis 9:1–44:22. Most papyri, however, are fragmentary and contain small portions of biblical text—sometimes only a few letters or words. Therefore, while the papyri provide ancient and important testimony of the text at the time they were buried, the sparsity of the material makes it difficult to generalize about which form of the Greek Bible the papyrus represents.

Collections of papyri may be designated by the name of the place they were discovered (e.g., POxy. is a collection of papyri excavated in Oxyrhynchus, Egypt), the name of the library where they are now housed (PRyl. is the collection at the John Rylands Library in Manchester, England), or the name of the person who discovered, purchased, or published them (PBod. is named for Martin Bodmer, 1899–1971). As mentioned above, these papyri also receive a Rahlfs number.

Among important biblical texts in Greek, the two earliest documents deserve special notice. Papyrus Fouad 266, dated to ca. 100 B.C.E., contains small portions of Deuteronomy that have great significance for the reconstruction of the text.[27] Even earlier by perhaps half

25. New Testament scholars refer to this important manuscript with the Hebrew letter א (*ʾālep̱*) or the number 01. Papyri are designated in New Testament scholarship with the letter P (often in its gothic form, 𝔓) and a superscript number, e.g., P[56] or 𝔓[56].

26. See Alfred Rahlfs, *Verzeichnis der griechischen Handschriften des Alten Testaments* (Mitteilungen des Septuaginta-Unternehmens 2; Berlin: Weidmann, 1914).

27. This papyrus, which at one point may have covered the whole Pentateuch, includes two small fragments of Genesis. (The Genesis fragments have been assigned Rahlfs number 942, while the portions from Deuteronomy have two Rahlfs numbers:

a century is Papyrus Rylands 458 (Rahlfs 957), which contains about twenty scattered verses from Deuteronomy 23–28. A few additional documents from the following two centuries have survived, and many other papyrus fragments of the Greek Bible date from the third century of our era and later.

One of the most dramatic papyrological finds began in 1947 when the first of the Judean Desert materials (popularly known as the Dead Sea Scrolls) came to light. Over the following decade, texts were found in eleven caves at Qumran, on the northwestern shore of the Dead Sea, and its environs. Most of these texts are in Hebrew and Aramaic, but caves 4 and 7 preserved a small number of biblical texts in Greek containing fragments of the Pentateuch, specifically Leviticus, Numbers, and Deuteronomy.[28] A wider area of the Judean wilderness produced other significant finds, especially an entire scroll of the Minor Prophets in Greek (not to be confused with the Minor Prophets scroll in Hebrew discovered at Murabbaʿat). All of these documents are dated to the first century of our era or earlier.

Uncials

The three best-known biblical uncials contain the books of both the Old Testament and the New. Pride of place must be given to Codex Vaticanus (B), a fourth-century manuscript of exceptionally high quality (illustration 4). For most books of the Old Testament, this codex preserves a text relatively free from Hexaplaric influence.[29] Codex Sinaiticus (S or ℵ), produced about the same time, was discovered in the nineteenth century by Count Friedrich von Tischendorf at the Monastery of St. Catherine on Mount Sinai (illustration 5). Unfortunately, very little of the Pentateuch or of the historical sections is preserved; for most of the other books, however, its text is similar to that of B. Finally, Codex Alexandrinus (A), copied in the fifth century, contains all the books with only a few minor gaps (illustration 6). Its text, which often shows signs of Hexaplaric influence, is mixed but valuable; in the Book of Isaiah, for example, it is our best witness.

Several other important uncials are worth special attention. Codex Colberto-Sarravianus (G), dated about the year 400, preserves portions

847 and 848.) For photos of Fouad 266 and other papyri, see Würthwein, *Text of the Old Testament*, pls. 28–29; and Metzger, *Manuscripts of the Greek Bible*, pls. 1–3, 5, 10–11.

28. These Greek texts have been published in the series Discoveries in the Judaean Desert, vols. 3, 9, 12 (Oxford: Clarendon, 1962, 1992, 1994). See below, chap. 8, pp. 168–73, for a list of the relevant fragments and for a discussion of the Greek Minor Prophets Scroll. As will become clear in that chapter, the greatest impact the Judean Desert documents have had on Septuagint studies comes not from these Greek manuscripts, but from the Hebrew biblical texts found there.

29. Vaticanus is missing the first 46 chapters of Genesis. In a few books, especially Isaiah, its text is less trustworthy.

4. Codex Vaticanus (B), containing Isaiah 52:10–54:2; fourth century C.E.

This carefully produced uncial is the best extant witness for most books of the Septuagint, but in Isaiah it contains many secondary readings.

source: Vatican Library; Vat. Graecus 1209 part II, folio 1052

5. Codex Sinaiticus (S or א), containing the first page of Psalms; fourth century C.E.

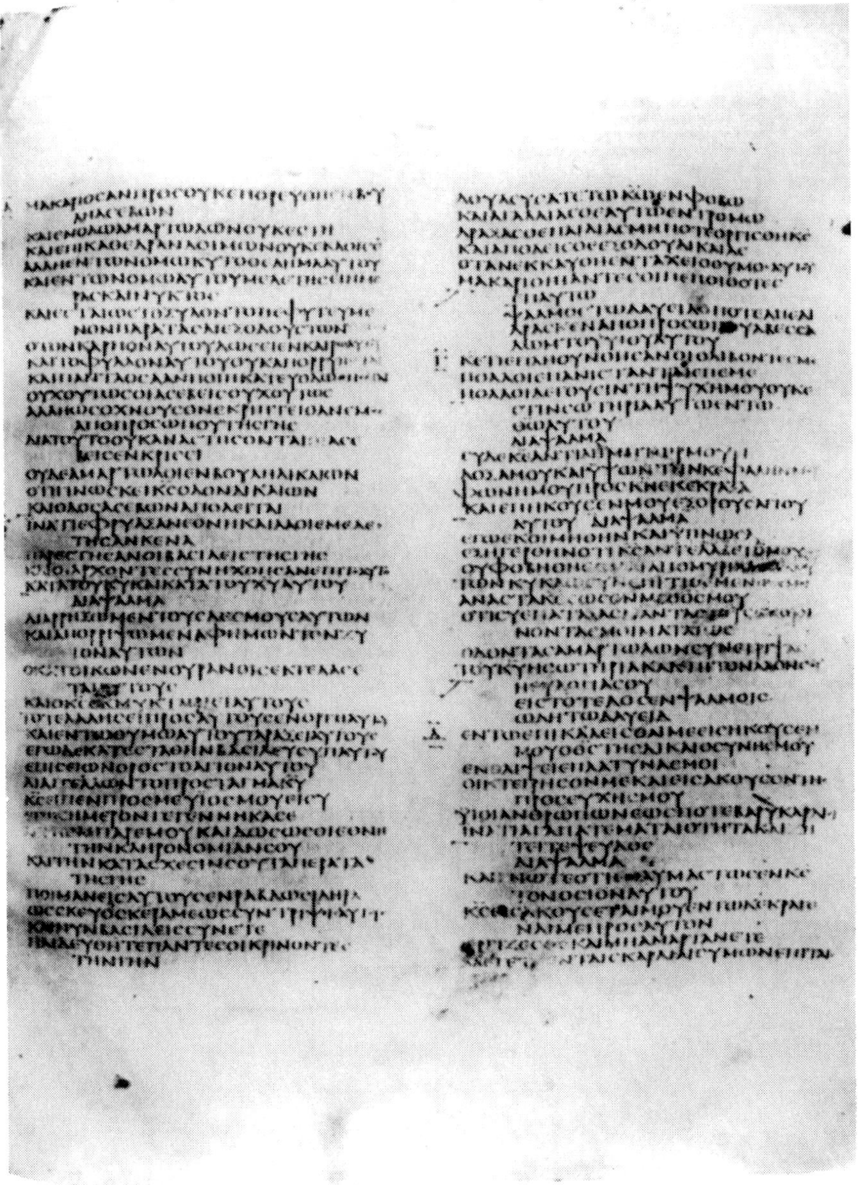

Although the Psalms are written in two columns, most of the codex is presented in four columns.

source: British Library; folio 134 (front)

6. Codex Alexandrinus (A), containing the end of Malachi and the first chapter of Isaiah; fifth century C.E.

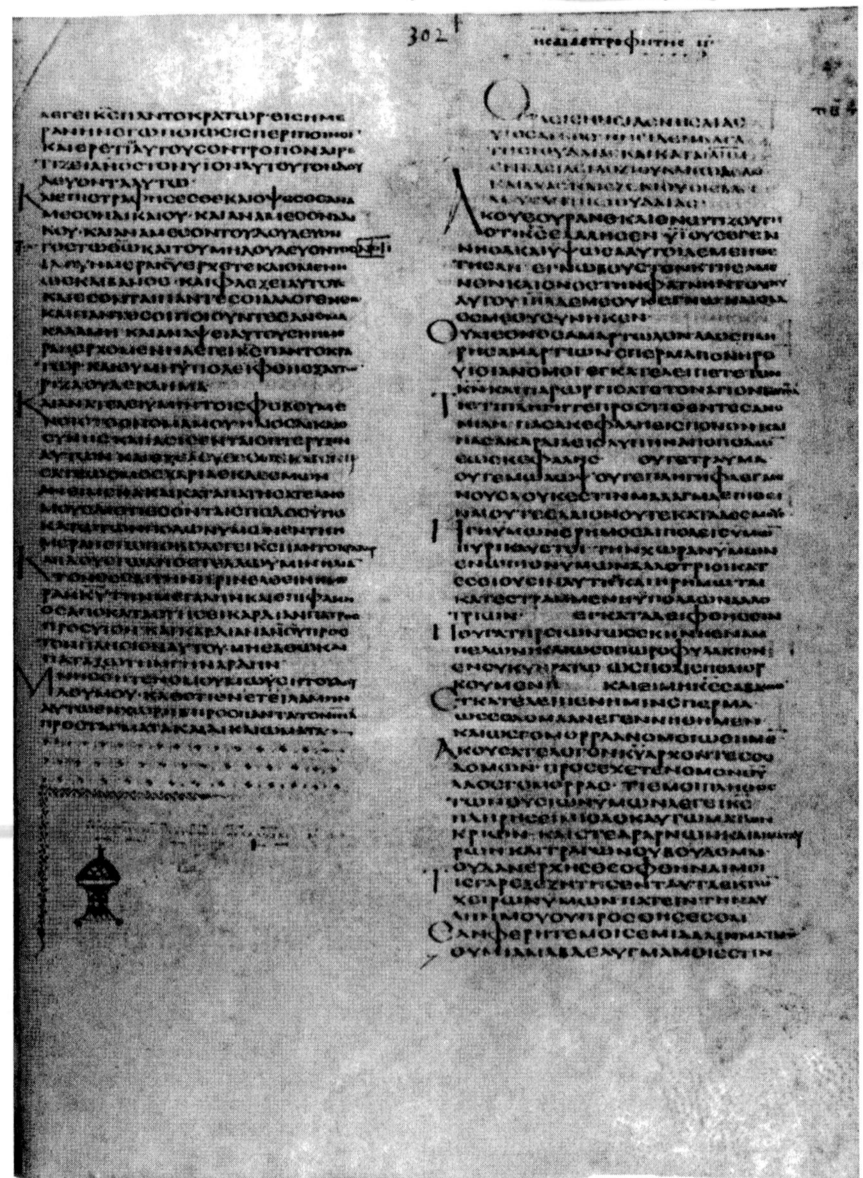

In the Septuagint, the Minor Prophets are placed before the Major Prophets.

source: British Library; folio 302 (front)

of Genesis to Judges; its significance lies in the fact that it retains the Hexaplaric signs (although these are not always trustworthy). Codex Coislinianus (M), copied in the seventh century, includes Genesis to 2 Samuel and the first chapters of 1 Kings (3 Reigns or 3 Kingdoms). Codex Basiliano-Vaticanus is an eighth- or ninth-century uncial with the double designation N-V; one portion (N) is in the Vatican Library and contains half of the Pentateuch (beginning with Lev. 13:59) and the historical books; the other portion (V, also known as Codex Venetus) is in Venice and contains most of the poetic books, the Prophets, Tobit, Judith, and 1–4 Maccabees. Finally, Codex Marchalianus (Q) is a beautiful and well-preserved manuscript of the Prophets, dating from the sixth century; it contains an excellent text and includes the Hexaplaric signs (illustration 7).[30]

Minuscules

Well over 1,500 cursive manuscripts containing at least parts of the Septuagint have been preserved. Because they are later than the papyri and the uncials, they are relatively less important, but it would be a great mistake to ignore them. In the first place, a minuscule produced, say, in the thirteenth century may be a copy of an uncial dated many centuries earlier; if so, the text preserved in the minuscule is much more ancient than the manuscript itself. Moreover, the minuscules broaden our knowledge base significantly and thus help us to assess the value of the uncials in a more accurate way (a specific reading in a valuable uncial may be suspect if it is not broadly attested).

Among interesting cursives, we may note especially the famous Chigi manuscript (88), which has two distinctions: it is one of the few manuscripts that include the Hexaplaric signs, and it is the only Greek manuscript that preserves the Old Greek (rather than the Theodotionic) version of Daniel in its entirety (illustrations 8 and 9). An important group of cursives that deserves attention is most frequently referred to by the lowercase letter designations boc_2e_2; these minuscules constitute our primary witnesses to the Lucianic or Antiochene text of Samuel–Kings.[31]

Secondary Versions

As the Christian church expanded, the translation of the Bible into other languages became necessary. Such translations, when made

30. For photos of several uncials, see Würthwein, *Text of the Old Testament*, pls. 33–36. See also Metzger, *Manuscripts of the Greek Bible*, pls. 13–21; students should pay special attention to plate 21 (Codex Q) and attempt to read the Hexaplaric readings in the margin with the help of Metzger's notations.

31. See below, chap. 7, pp. 159–161, for a discussion of the text in these manuscripts.

7. Codex Marchalianus (Q), containing Ezekiel 1:28–2:6; sixth century C.E.

Note the Hexaplaric signs in the left margin.

source: Vatican Library; Vat. Graecus 2125, folio 283

8. Manuscript Chigi (19), containing the beginning of Daniel; tenth century C.E.

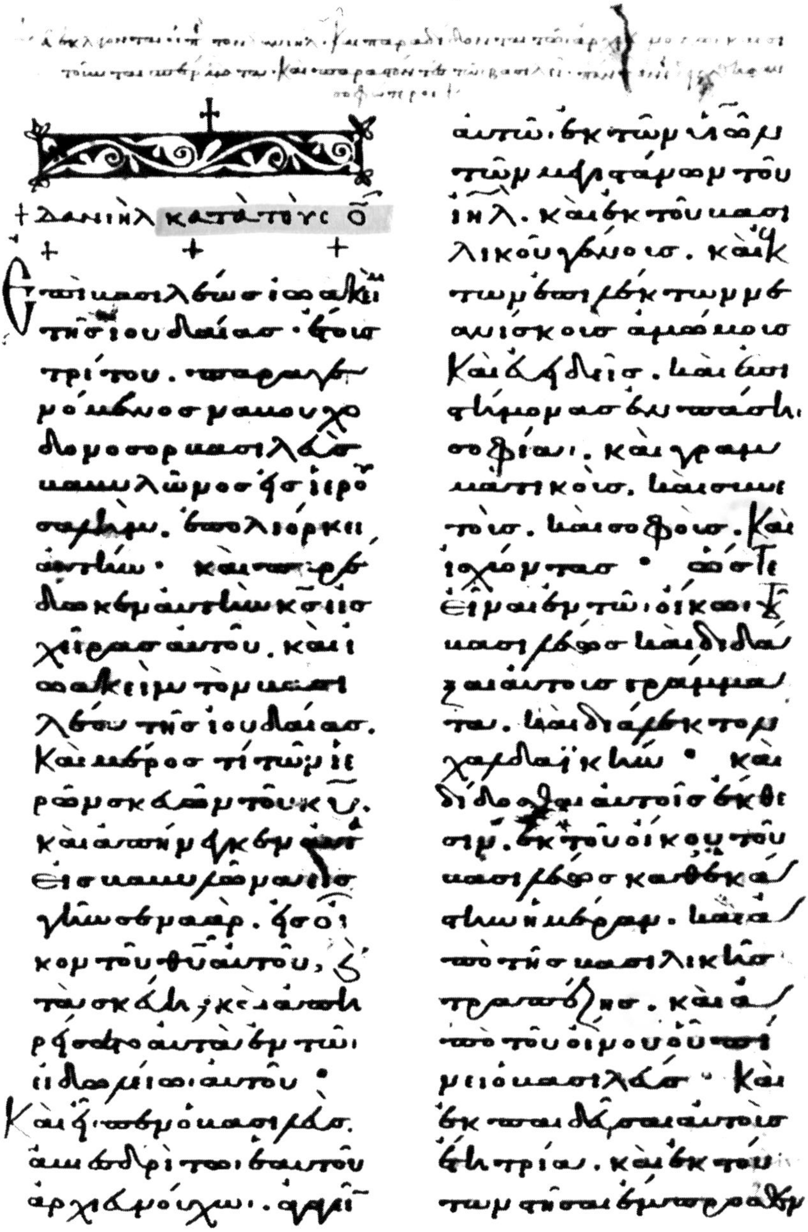

This is the only extant manuscript that preserves the Old Greek version of Daniel in its entirety. Notice κατα τους ō ("according to the seventy").

source: Vatican Library; R.VII.45, folio 135

9. Manuscript Chigi (19), containing Ezekiel 47:8–14; tenth century C.E.

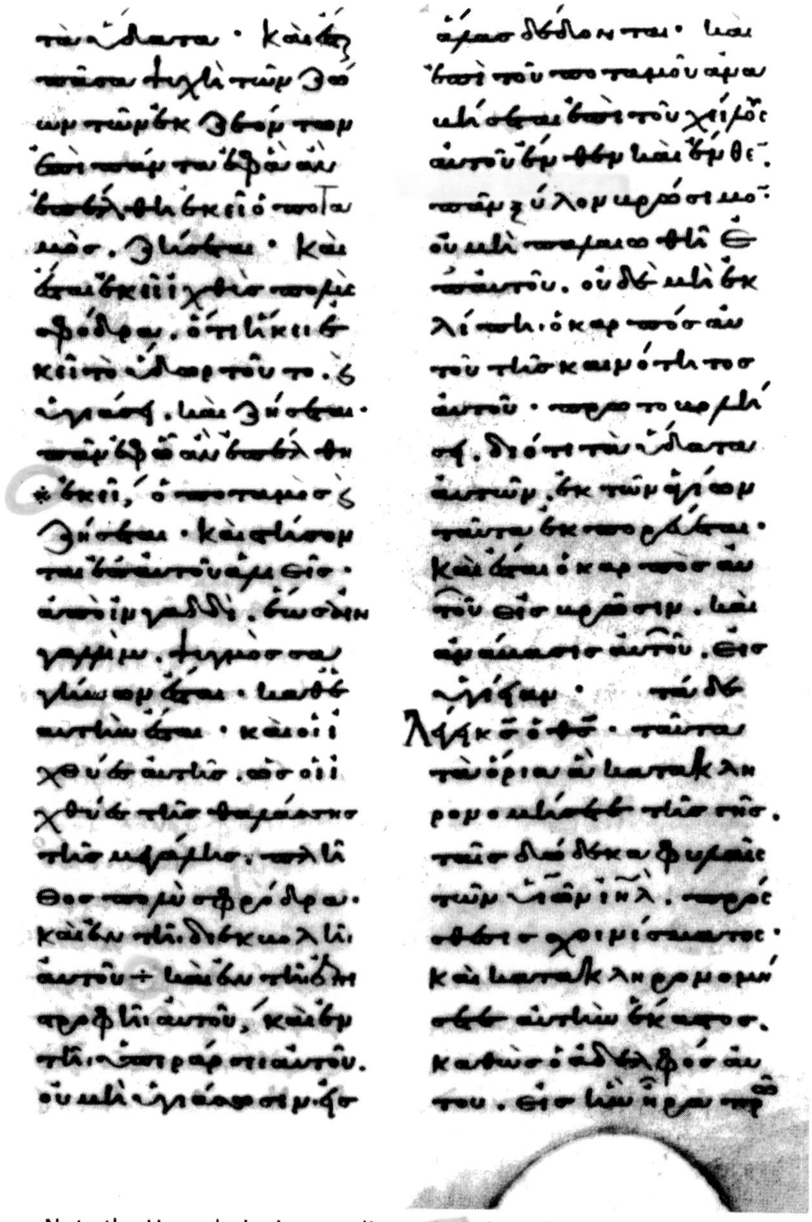

Note the Hexaplaric signs on lines 12 and 24 of the left column.

source: Vatican Library; R.VII.45, folio 312

from the Greek (rather than from the Hebrew), have great value to scholars who try to identify and date distinctive features of the different Greek versions. If a translation of the Greek into another language was made before Origen produced the Hexapla, that translation offers, at least in theory, a witness to what the Greek text(s) looked like in the earliest centuries of the church. However, since the secondary translation too has suffered the vicissitudes of time and transmission, then *its* original text must be established before we can use it to reconstruct its Greek *Vorlage*. It should also be kept in mind that these "daughter" translations cannot always represent the Greek parent text precisely, and therefore their witness must be used with caution. For example, the Coptic verb system has only an active form, and therefore the presence of an active verb in a Coptic translation does not necessarily tell us that the Greek it renders was an active rather than a middle or passive verb.

In the first few centuries of this era, Latin was the language not only of Italy but of other areas as well, including parts of northern Africa. When the first translation of the Bible was made into Latin, it was made from a Greek text. This Latin version, referred to as the *Vetus Latina* or Old Latin, was eventually replaced in the Latin-speaking church by Jerome's translation made in the early fifth century. Jerome's work, known as the Vulgate, was a direct translation of the Old Testament in Hebrew. In contrast, surviving manuscripts of the Old Latin translation attest to a Greek *Vorlage*.

Syriac (a member of the Aramaic family) was the language of a large and important section of the Christian church for many centuries. The Syro-Hexaplar (sometimes spelled Syro-Hexapla), an important secondary translation of Origen's Hexaplaric recension, was produced between 613 and 617. This work, translated from the Greek, is to be distinguished from the standard Syriac Bible, known as the Peshitta, which had been translated from the Hebrew about the second century.[32]

Translations of the Septuagint into Coptic (a late form of the Egyptian language) have been preserved in both the Sahidic and Bohairic dialects; they are important witnesses to an early Greek text used in Egypt. Other languages into which the Septuagint was translated include Arabic, Ethiopic, Armenian, Slavonic, Gothic, and Georgian. Not many Septuagint scholars have mastered one or more of these languages, and relatively few manuscripts of these translations have survived.[33]

32. See Würthwein, *Text of the Old Testament*, pls. 37 and 39, for photos of the Syro-Hexaplar and the Peshitta.

33. For photos of manuscripts of the secondary versions, see Würthwein, *Text of the Old Testament*, pls. 37, 40–46. See also below, chap. 13, pp. 278–80.

Ancient Citations

Another secondary or indirect source for the Greek texts consists of quotations from the Bible surviving in ancient writings, especially the large corpus of the Christian fathers. In many ways, the value of these quotations for establishing the Greek text in use at that time is even more tenuous than consulting the secondary translations. The writings of the fathers were themselves copied by scribes who may have edited the quotations to agree with the text known and used in their time and locale. Therefore, the textual critic must first establish how patristic writers originally quoted the passage. Moreover, one cannot be sure that they quoted a biblical verse word-for-word. They may have paraphrased it or omitted short phrases that were irrelevant to their point.

These complications notwithstanding, the quotations of certain fathers appear to agree more closely with the readings of some surviving manuscripts than with others. For instance, Chrysostom and Theodoret, both of Antioch, are considered to be primary witnesses to the Antiochene text as revised possibly by Lucian. The study of biblical quotations by the church fathers who wrote in Greek is a major branch of Septuagint (and New Testament) studies.

To Continue Your Study

Henry Barclay Swete, *An Introduction to the Old Testament in Greek*, 2d ed. (Cambridge: Cambridge University Press, 1914; repr. Peabody, Mass.: Hendrickson, 1989), 59–170, covers the recensions, the secondary versions, and the manuscripts. Updated information on this material may be found in Sidney Jellicoe, *The Septuagint and Modern Study* (Oxford: Clarendon, 1968), chapters 5–8; Natalio Fernández Marcos, *Introducción a las versiones griegas de la Biblia*, 2d ed. (Textos y Estudios "Cardenal Cisneros" 23; Madrid: Consejo Superior de Investigaciones Científicas, 1998) = *The Septuagint in Context: Introduction to the Greek Version of the Bible*, trans. Wilfred G. E. Watson (Leiden: Brill, 2000), chapters 12–19; and Marguerite Harl, Gilles Dorival, and Olivier Munnich, *La Bible Grecque des Septante: Du judaïsme hellénistique au christianisme ancien*, 2d ed. (Initiations au christianisme ancien; [Paris]: Cerf/Centre National de la Recherche Scientifique, 1994), 130–42, 162–73. Much valuable relevant information on Septuagint manuscripts is to be found in B. Botte and P.-M. Bogaert, "Septante et versions grecques," in *Dictionnaire de la Bible, Supplément* 12.536–692, esp. 650–76.

3

The Septuagint in Modern Times

Printed Editions. The invention of the printing press made it possible to stabilize the text of ancient documents by producing numerous identical copies. ***Early Editions*** of the Septuagint were produced during the sixteenth century. The first one was the text included in the Complutensian Polyglot. Other important editions were the Aldine and especially the Sixtine. ***Critical Editions*** provide evidence of textual variations among the manuscripts with a view to reconstructing the original text. The Holmes-Parsons edition, completed in 1827, was the first large treasury of textual information. At the end of the nineteenth century, a small edition by Swete prepared the way for the Larger Cambridge project, only part of which was completed. Works that attempt to reconstruct the original text include the small and widely used edition by Rahlfs, as well as the more ambitious project of the Göttingen Septuagint, which is still in progress. ***Modern Language Translations*** of the Septuagint include early editions in English by Thomson and by Brenton and the projected *New English Translation of the Septuagint*. A French multivolume translation that includes commentary is La Bible d'Alexandrie, parts of which have already been published.

The Contents of the Septuagint. We are able to refer to portions of the Bible by providing ***Book, Chapter, and Verse***. Unfortunately, the Greek version does not always correspond to the Hebrew text or modern translations. Discrepancies in chapter and verse divisions, as well as in the order of the material, can prove confusing, especially in Exodus, Psalms, and Jeremiah. Major differences in content can be traced back to the history of the ***Biblical Canon***. Events such as the adoption of the Septuagint by the ancient Christian church, the division of the church between East and West in the Middle Ages, and the Protestant Reformation in the sixteenth century have left their mark on the Bibles used by various religious communities.

For our purposes, we may view the shift from medieval to modern times as having taken place in the fifteenth century, with the invention of the printing press. The Gutenberg Bible, an edition of the Vulgate published around 1450, was the first book known to be printed in the Western world with the new technology of movable type. Its production brought an end to an era.[1] Prior to this time, every book had to be copied by hand, and even the most careful scribe would produce imperfect copies. But now, for the first time in history, it became possible to produce numerous copies that were exact replicas of one another—and to do so in a single process. Mass duplication virtually eliminated the tedious work of scribes and prevented the inevitable errors and changes they introduced into the texts. The effect of this new technology was to stabilize the biblical text, which in turn made possible the systematic and consistent work of textual criticism, that is, the attempt to restore the text to its original form.[2]

Printed Editions

Early Editions

When the first printed editions of the Septuagint were produced, the choice of a biblical text by the printers was sometimes based simply on which manuscripts were conveniently at hand rather than on deliberate selection, much less scholarly scrutiny. By the fifteenth century there were thousands of handwritten codices in existence, and no two contained completely identical texts. Furthermore, in a given codex the text of one biblical book may have been from Theodotion, for example, while another book in the same codex may have contained the Hexaplaric recension of the Septuagint. If a given codex was damaged (e.g., lacking all or part of a biblical book), any missing text would be supplied from another codex near at hand, without thought to the pedigree of the texts contained therein. While the advent of modern printing technology stabilized the printed editions of the Bible, giving the appearance of homogeneity, the particular version it preserved and propagated was in fact an arbitrary amalgam of texts with various pedigrees and characteristics.

The first printed edition of the entire Greek Old Testament was produced by Christian scholars in Spain between 1514 and 1517, then published a few years later, as part of the Complutensian Polyglot

1. In likening the revolutionary effects of computer technology to that of Gutenberg's press, Bill Gates comments that before Gutenberg there were about thirty thousand books in Europe, mostly Bibles or biblical commentaries. By 1500, there were more than nine million books on many topics. See *The Road Ahead* (New York: Viking, 1995), 8.

2. In limited fashion, textual criticism took place earlier whenever a reader compared two manuscripts and drew conclusions or made changes based on the differences between them. The result of that work, however, could be used only by people who had access to the one revised manuscript. Furthermore, any copies based on it would contain new changes (deliberate or inadvertent), thus contributing to textual instability.

Bible.[3] The Old Testament was presented in three columns: the Latin Vulgate with pride of place in the middle, the Hebrew text on its right, and the Greek text (with a Latin interlinear translation) on its left. In addition, the Aramaic Targumim, accompanied by a Latin translation, were placed at the bottom of the page. This work was initiated and directed by Cardinal Francisco Jiménez de Cisneros, who claimed to have carefully selected his manuscripts, including some supplied by Pope Leo X from the Vatican library.

At about the same time, the so-called Aldine edition of the Greek Bible, based on a few, relatively late manuscripts, was published in Venice. Of greater importance is the Sixtine edition, published in 1587 under the auspices of Pope Sixtus V. This project was undertaken with care and thoroughness. After searching for manuscripts in various libraries, the editors, led by Cardinal Antonio Carafa, became convinced that what is now known as Codex Vaticanus or B (Vatican Library Gk. 1209) was the best manuscript upon which to base the new edition. Other manuscripts were used to fill the large gaps and correct errors in B, as well as to provide alternate readings from time to time. The Sixtine edition became the standard Septuagint text and was used by many subsequent editors.[4]

Critical Editions

In the seventeenth and eighteenth centuries, scholars began to collect and publish variant readings, that is, differences among the manuscripts for any given verse. This process gave birth to modern textual criticism. Collation is the tedious process of comparing the readings of various manuscripts against a selected standard text and noting where and how each one differs from the standard. A section of notes indicating variant readings, usually found at the bottom of the page in a critical edition,[5] is called the critical apparatus.

3. A polyglot edition is one that prints the text on each page in more than one language. The name *Complutensian* designates the place of publication, Complutum, the Latin name for the city otherwise known as Alcalá de Henares. See Ernst Würthwein, *The Text of the Old Testament: An Introduction to Biblia Hebraica*, trans. Erroll F. Rhodes, 2d ed. (Grand Rapids: Eerdmans, 1995), pl. 47, for a photo of a page from this interesting edition. Other polyglots were later published at Antwerp (1569–72), Heidelberg (1586–1616), Hamburg (1596), and Paris (1645).

4. An edition based on Codex Alexandrinus was produced by John Ernest Grabe early in the eighteenth century. Because of various idiosyncrasies, this edition was not widely used, but at the time it provided a great service to Septuagint scholarship. See the description in Henry Barclay Swete, *An Introduction to the Old Testament in Greek*, 2d ed. (Cambridge: Cambridge University Press, 1914; repr. Peabody, Mass.: Hendrickson, 1989), 183–84.

5. Here we use the term *critical edition* for editions that document textual variations. Some scholars reserve the term for editions that contain a critical (reconstructed) text

British scholars Robert Holmes (until his death in 1805) and later James Parsons produced such a critical edition in five large volumes, published in Oxford between 1798 and 1827 under the title *Vetus Testamentum Graecum cum variis lectionibus* (illustration 10). Using the Sixtine text as their base, this monumental work provides readings from about 300 manuscripts collated by a large number of British and Continental scholars. From our later vantage point, the methods used in this work can be easily criticized; and since the quality of the collations was not uniform, the edition must be used with care. Even today, however, specialists know that certain kinds of information can be found only in Holmes-Parsons.

Other editions, including Tischendorf's,[6] were published during the 1800s, though none of them was truly satisfactory. Toward the end of that century, however, scholars in Cambridge, England, began to work on a diplomatic edition of Codex Vaticanus.[7] This important manuscript was collated against all the available uncials, many minuscules (thirty in Genesis, for example), the secondary versions, and quotations from Philo, Josephus, and the Christian fathers. A preliminary "portable" edition in three volumes, entitled *The Old Testament in Greek according to the Septuagint*, was produced by Henry Barclay Swete in 1887–94 (third edition, 1901–7) and became the most widely used text during the first decades of this century. The more ambitious project, often referred to as the Larger Cambridge edition, was entrusted to Alan E. Brooke and Norman McLean and was published in fascicles under the title *The Old Testament in Greek according to the Text of Codex Vaticanus, supplemented from other uncial manuscripts, with a critical apparatus containing the variants of the chief ancient authorities for the text of the Septuagint*.[8] Although never completed, this work is a great treasure; for the books of Joshua through Chronicles, it remains our primary source of information.

---

as well. It should be pointed out that some of the earlier editions had already included selected variants; Brian Walton's Polyglot (1657), for example, recorded the variants of Codex Alexandrinus.

6. See below, chap. 11, p. 240.

7. A diplomatic edition reproduces as exactly as possible the text of one selected manuscript, although obvious scribal errors are corrected (e.g., the standard edition of the Hebrew Bible, *Biblia hebraica stuttgartensia*, is a diplomatic edition of Codex Leningradensis). In the case of Vaticanus, its *lacunae* (gaps) had to be filled with the text of Alexandrinus or Sinaiticus.

8. The nine fascicles of the Larger Cambridge Septuagint, published by Cambridge University Press, are as follows:

volume 1: The Octateuch (ed. Alan E. Brooke and Norman McLean)
- 1.1: Genesis (1906)
- 1.2: Exodus and Leviticus (1909)
- 1.3: Numbers and Deuteronomy (1911)
- 1.4: Joshua, Judges, Ruth (1917)

10. Holmes-Parsons Septuagint (Esther 5:1–5 including addition D)

Ε Σ Θ Η Ρ.

ΚΕΦ. V.

“ αὐτὸς ἐκάθητο ἐπὶ τȣ̃ θρόνου τῆς βασιλείας αὐτȣ̃, καὶ πᾶσαν ϛολὴν τῆς ἐπιφανείας αὐτȣ̃ ἐν-
“ δεδύκει, ὅλος διὰ χρυσȣ̃ καὶ λίθων πολυτελῶν, καὶ ἦν φοβερὸς σφόδρα. Καὶ ἄρας τὸ πρόσ-
“ ωπον αὐτȣ̃ πεπυρωμένον δόξῃ, ἐν ἀκμῇ θυμȣ̃ ἔβλεψεν· καὶ ἔπεσεν ἡ βασίλισσα, καὶ μετέβαλε
“ τὸ χρῶμα αὐτῆς ἐν ἐκλύσει· καὶ κατεπέκυψεν ἐπὶ τὴν κεφαλὴν τῆς ἄβρας τῆς προπορευομέ-
“ νης. Καὶ μετέβαλεν ὁ Θεὸς τὸ πνεῦμα τȣ̃ βασιλέως εἰς πραΰτητα, καὶ ἀγωνιάσας ἀνεπήδη-
“ σεν ἀπὸ τȣ̃ θρόνου αὐτȣ̃, καὶ ἀνέλαβεν αὐτὴν ἐπὶ τὰς ἀγκάλας αὐτȣ̃, μέχρις οὗ κατέϛη· καὶ
“ παρεκάλει αὐτὴν λόγοις εἰρηνικοῖς, καὶ εἶπεν αὐτῇ, Τί ἐϛιν Ἐσθήρ; ἐγὼ ὁ ἀδελφός σȣ, θάρ-
2. “ σει, Οὐ μὴ ἀποθάνῃς· ὅτι κοινὸν τὸ πρόςαγμα ἡμῶν ἐϛιν, Πρόςελθε. Καὶ ἄρας τὴν χρυσῆν
“ ῥάβδον, ἐπέθηκεν ἐπὶ τὸν τράχηλον αὐτῆς, καὶ ἠσπάσατο αὐτὴν, καὶ εἶπε, Λάλησόν μοι. Καὶ
“ εἶπεν αὐτῷ, Εἶδόν σε Κύριε ὡς ἄγγελον Θεȣ̃, καὶ ἐταράχθη ἡ καρδία μȣ ἀπὸ φόβȣ τῆς δόξης
“ σȣ, ὅτι θαυμαςὸς εἶ Κύριε, καὶ τὸ πρόσωπον σȣ χαρίτων μεϛόν. Ἐν δὲ τῷ διαλέγεσθαι αὐτὴν,
“ ἔπεσεν ἀπὸ ἐκλύσεως. Καὶ ὁ βασιλεὺς ἐταράσσετο, καὶ πᾶσα ἡ θεραπεία αὐτȣ̃ παρεκάλει
3. “ αὐτήν.” Καὶ εἶπεν ὁ βασιλεὺς, Τί θέλεις Ἐσθήρ; καὶ τί σου ἐϛὶ τὸ ἀξίωμα; ἕως τȣ̃ ἡμί-
4. σους τῆς βασιλείας μου, καὶ ἔϛαι σοι. Εἶπε δὲ Ἐσθὴρ, Ἡμέρα μȣ ἐπίσημος σήμερόν ἐϛιν· εἰ
5. οὖν δοκεῖ τῷ βασιλεῖ, ἐλθάτω καὶ αὐτὸς καὶ Ἀμὰν εἰς τὴν δοχὴν, ἣν ποιήσω σήμερον. Καὶ εἶ-

tem in sedili gloriæ suæ: et ipse erat vestitus purpurâ, et omni lapide pretioso, et aurea virga in manu ejus. Vet. Lat. ex MS. Corb. ἐνώπ. τȣ̃ βασιλ.] καὶ ἐνωπιον τȣ βασιλ. 93. b. καὶ αὐτὸς ἐκάθητο] και ὁ βασιλευς εκαθητο 93. a. ȣ̃ αυτος εκαθητο 93. b. ἐπὶ τȣ̃ θρόνου] ∧ τȣ 44, 93, 106, 236. τῆς βασιλείας αὐτȣ̃] ∧ της βασιλειας 19. καὶ πᾶσαν—ὅλος] ∧ cum intermed. 106. καὶ πᾶσαν ϛολὴν] και πασαν την ϛολην 93. b. καὶ τὴν ϛολὴν Alex. καὶ πᾶσαν τὴν ϛολὴν &c. ad fin. com.] habet sub ÷ 93. b. τῆς ἐπιφανείας αὐτȣ̃] επιφανειας tantum 93. a. ἐνδεδύκει] ενεδυκει II. ενεδιδυσκει XI. ενεδιδυσκει 55. ενεδεδυκει 93, a. 108. a. Compl. ενδεδυκη 93. b. εδεδυκει 108. b. ὅλος] ολως 52, 93. b. ὅλος διὰ χρυσȣ̃] ολως διαχρυσος 19. ολος διαχρυσος 93. a. διὰ χρυσȣ̃ καὶ λίθων] διαχρυσίου καὶ λίθων 249. λίθων πολυτελῶν] λιθοι πολυτελεις επ' αυτων 19. sic, nisi επ' αυτω, 93. a. καὶ ἦν φοβερὸς] ∧ ην 19, 93. a. φοβερὸς σφόδρα] φοβερως σφοδρα 52. Καὶ ἄρας] καὶ ἦρεν Alex. Καὶ ἄρας τὸ πρόσωπον αὐτȣ̃] *Et respiciens oculis suis* Vet. Lat. ex MS. Corb. πεπυρωμένον—ἐπέβλεψεν] *vidit eam sicut taurus in impetu iræ suæ, et iratus est ei:* Vet. Lat. ex MS. Corb. δόξῃ] εν δοξη 19, 93. a. habet δόξῃ in charact. minore Alex. ἐν ἀκμῇ θυμȣ̃] ∧ εν 44, 106. ἐν ἀκμῇ θυμȣ̃ ἔβλεψεν] ενεβλεψεν αυτη ως ταυρος εν ακμη θυμȣ αυτȣ 19, 93. a. ἔβλεψεν] + αυτην ως ταυρος 93. b. ∧ Alex. καὶ ἔπεσεν] και εφοβηθη 19, 93. a. καὶ ἔπεσεν ἡ βασίλ.] *et cogitabat perdere eam rex, et erat ambiguus clamans, et dixit: Quis ausus est introire in aulam non vocatus? Et timens regina cecidit* Vet. Lat. ex MS. Corb. καὶ μετέβ.—ἐκλύσει] *et convertit color ipsius in fletum* Vet. Lat. ex MS. Corb. τὸ χρῶμα αὐτῆς] το σωμα αυτης XI. το προσωπον αυτης 19, 93. a. ἐν ἐκλύσει] ἐνεκλύση (sic) 93. b. καὶ ἐπέκυψεν] επεκυψεν 19, 93, a. 108. b. Alex. καὶ ἐνέβλεψεν 44, 71, 74, 76, 106, 120. κατεκυψεν 52, 64, 108, a. 243. Compl. Ald. επεκαλυψεν 93. b. ἐπὶ τὴν κεφαλὴν] ∧ 55. ἐπὶ τῆς κεφαλῆς Alex. ἐπὶ τὴν κεφαλὴν τῆς ἄβρας] *supra caput abræ* Vet. Lat. ex MS. Corb. τῆς προπορευομένης] + αυτῃ 44, 74, 106, 120. + αυτης 71, 76, 93. b. Alex. τῆς πορευομένης Ald. Καὶ μετέβαλεν—πραΰτητα] *Deus autem iram convertit in miserationem et furorem ipsius in tranquillitatem;* Vet. Lat. ex MS. Corb. εἰς πραΰτητα] και μετεθηκεν τον θυμον αυτȣ εις πραοτητα 19, 93. εἰς πραότητα Compl. καὶ ἀγωνιάσας] + ὁ βασιλευς 19, 93. a. ∧ αγωνιασας 108. a. *et conterritus* Vet. Lat. ex MS. Corb. ἀνεπήδησεν] καὶ επηδησεν 19, 93, a. 108. a. επηδησεν 93. b. ἀπὸ τȣ̃ θρόνου αὐτȣ̃] ∧ αυτȣ 248. Compl. habet αὐτȣ̃ in charact. minore Alex. *de sedili suo* Vet. Lat. ex MS. Corb. ἐπὶ τὰς ἀγκάλας αὐτȣ̃] *sub alis suis* Vet. Lat. ex MS. Corb. μέχρις ȣ̃ κατέϛη] ∧ 19, 93. a. *donec apud se rediret* Vet. Lat. ex MS. Corb. καὶ παρεκάλει] και παρεκαλεσεν 19, 93. a. παρεκ. αὐτὴν] παρεκ. αὐτῇ 93. b. *rogabat eam* Vet. Lat. ex MS. Corb. λόγοις εἰρηνικοῖς] ∧ 19, 93. a. *in verbis pacificis* Vet. Lat. ex MS. Corb. καὶ εἶπεν αὐτῇ] ∧ αυτῃ 19, 93. a. ∧ 106. *dicens:* Vet. Lat. ex MS. Corb. Τί ἐϛιν Ἐσθήρ] *Hester regina, soror mea Hester es, et consors regni.* Vet. Lat. ex MS. Corb. ἐγὼ ὁ] ∧ ὁ 76. ἐγὼ ὁ ἀδελφός σȣ] εγω ειμι ὁ αδελφος σου 93. a. θάρσει] θαρρει 74, 76. ὅτι κοινὸν—Πρόςελθε] *quoniam præceptum commune est nostrûm, non adversus te. Ecce sceptrum in manu mea est.* Vet. Lat. ex MS. Corb. τὸ πρόςαγμα] το πραγμα XI, 44, 106, 249. τὸ πρόςαγμα ἡμῶν ἐϛιν] εϛι το πραγμα ημων 19. sic, nisi προςαγμα, 93. a. Πρόςελθε] και ου προς σε ἡ απειλη· ιδȣ το σκηπτρον εν τη χειρι σου 19, 93. a. sic, præmisso προσελθε, 93. b.

II. Καὶ ἄρας] *Et sustulit* Vet. Lat. ex MS. Corb. τὴν χρυσῆν ῥάβδον] το σκηπτρον 19, 93. a. ῥάβδον] ῥαύδον Ald. ἐπέθ. ἐπὶ τὸν τράχηλον αὐτῆς] *et extendit in manu ipsius* Vet. Lat. ex MS. Corb. ἠσπάσ. αὐτὴν] ἠσπάσ. τὴν Ἐσθὴρ Alex. Καὶ εἶπεν &c. ad fin. com.] habet sub ÷ 93. b. Καὶ εἶπεν αὐτῷ] ∧ αυτῳ XI. *Et dixit illi Hester:* Vet. Lat. ex MS. Corb. Εἶδόν σε, Κύριε] ∧ Κυριε 93. a. καὶ ἐταράχθη] και εταχη 19, 93. a. ἀπὸ φόβου] απο τȣ φοβου 52, 64, 108, a. 243, 248, 249. Compl. Ald. habet φόβου in charact. minore Alex. ἀπὸ φόβου τῆς δόξης σου] απο της δοξης του θυμου σου Κυριε 19, 93. a. ὅτι θαυμαςὸς εἶ] *quam præclarus es domine* Vet. Lat. ex MS. Corb. ὅτι θαυμαςὸς εἶ—ἐταράσσετο] και επι το προσωπον αυτης μετρον ιδρωτος και εταρασσετο ὁ βασιλευς 19. εἶ Κύριε] εἶ Κυριε μου 249. χαρίτων] χαριτος 93. b. διαλεγ. αὐτὴν] διαλεγ. αὐτῇ 93. b. ἔπεσεν ἀπὸ ἐκλύσεως] + αυτης XI, 44, 52, 55, 71, 74, 76, 106, 120, 243, 248, 249. Compl. Ald. Alex. επεσεν απο εκδυσεως 93. b. *deficiente ejus spiritu* Vet. Lat. ex MS. Corb. Καὶ ὁ βασιλεὺς &c. ad fin. com.] *rex turbatur, et omnis curia ipsius.* Vet. Lat. ex MS. Corb. παρεκάλει αὐτήν] και παρεκαλουν αυτην 19, 93. a. παρακάλει αὐτήν Ald.

III. Καὶ εἶπεν] και ειπεν αυτῃ 44, 71, 93, b. 106. Alex. Καὶ εἶπεν ὁ βασιλ.] *Et ipse precabatur eam dicens:* Vet. Lat. ex MS. Corb. Τί θέλεις] τι εϛιν 19, 71, 93. a. Τί θέλεις Ἐσθήρ] *Succedanea et consors regni mei, quæ est postulatio tua* Vet. Lat. ex MS. Corb. Ἐσθήρ] + ἡ βασιλισσα sub ※ 93. b. καὶ τί σου &c. ad fin. com.] αναγγειλον μοι και ποιησω σοι εως ημισους της βασιλειας μȣ 19, 93. a. τί σου ἐϛὶ τὸ ἀξίωμα] τι εϛι το αξιωμα σου, cum σου sub ※, 93. b. *quod est desiderium tuum?* Vet. Lat. ex MS. Corb. τὸ ἀξίωμα] ∧ το 108. a. ἕως τȣ̃ ἡμίσους] ∧ του 64, 93, b. 248. Compl. Ald. εως ημισεως 249. καὶ ἔϛαι σοι] ∧ και 248. Compl. *et faciam.* Vet. Lat. ex MS. Corb.

IV. Εἶπε δὲ Ἐσθὴρ] και ειπεν Εσθηρ 19, 44, 71, 74, 76, 93, a. 106. *Et dixit regina* Vet. Lat. ex MS. Corb. Ἡμέρα μου—ἐϛιν] ημερα μοι επισημος εϛι σημερον sub ÷ 93. b. ἡμέρα μοι σήμερον ἐπίσημος ἐϛιν, cum ἐϛιν in charact. minore, Alex. Ἡμέρα μου ἐπίσημος] ∧ μου 19, 93, a. 120. ημερα μοι επισημος 249. Ἡμέρα μου ἐπίσημος &c. ad fin. com. seq.] *Postulatio mea rex, in convivio quod faciam: cras cœnabis apud me, tu et amicus tuus. Et dixit rex: fiat secundum desiderium reginæ.* Vet. Lat. ex MS. Corb. σήμερόν ἐϛιν] αυριον 19. αυριον μοι 93. a. μοι αυριον 108. b. εἰ ȣ̃ν δοκεῖ] εἰ δοκει ȣν 19, 93. a. ει ȣν ευδοκει 55. δοκεῖ τῷ βασιλεῖ] τῳ βασιλει δοκει 93. b. ἐλθάτω] ελθετω XI, 52, 55, 64, 93, b. 243, 248, 249. Compl. Ald. Alex. ελθετω ὁ βασιλευς 108. a. ἐλθάτω καὶ αὐτὸς καὶ Ἀμὰν] εισελθε συ και Αμ. ὁ φιλος σου 19, 93, a. 108. b. ελθετω ὁ κυριος μου και ὁ Αμαν 44. sic, sine ὁ secundo, 71, 74, 76, 106, 120, 236. καὶ αὐτὸς] και ὁ βασιλευς 52, 243. Compl. Ald. ὁ βασιλευς 64, 93. b. Alex. ∧ και 249. εἰς τὴν δοχὴν] εις τον ποτον 19, 93. a. ∧ την 71, 76. ἣν ποιήσω] ὃν ποιησω 19, 93. a. ἣν εγω

VOL. III. Z

source: Robert Holmes and James Parsons, *Vetus Testamentum Graecum cum variis lectionibus* (Oxford: Clarendon, 1798–1827).

Given that every manuscript contains scribal errors and that no one existing manuscript preserves in its entirety the Greek text as it originally came from the translator or reviser, a different approach can be taken, namely, the production of a critical text. Instead of printing the entire text of one manuscript, an editor or editorial committee examines the textual variants and decides which reading is most likely original. This approach produces a reconstructed text, often referred to as eclectic,[9] because the resulting printed text is not identical to any manuscript in its entirety. Although the text that appears on the printed page of such an edition is not found in any one surviving manuscript, it preserves the best readings selected from among all of them and is therefore closer to the text of the original documents. This is the approach used for most classical works, including the Greek New Testament in editions such as the United Bible Societies and Nestle-Aland.

The production of a critical text for the Septuagint has been the goal of many scholars. Above all, however, it was the vision of a brilliant and controversial scholar named Paul de Lagarde, whose work was taken up upon his death in 1891 by his student Alfred Rahlfs. As a means to that end, a scholarly center known as the Septuaginta-Unternehmen was established in Göttingen in 1908.[10] This organization soon became the world's primary center for Septuagint research. As its director, Rahlfs devoted his considerable talents and energies to searching for manuscripts, evaluating them, and designing a new system for their enumeration,[11] as well as producing some of the most penetrating textual studies in the history of Septuagintal scholarship.

---

volume 2: The Later Historical Books (ed. Alan E. Brooke, Norman McLean, and Henry St. John Thackeray):
- 2.1: 1–2 Samuel (1927)
- 2.2: 1–2 Kings (1930)
- 2.3: 1–2 Chronicles (1932)
- 2.4: 1 Esdras, Ezra–Nehemiah (1935)

volume 3 (ed. Alan E. Brooke, Norman McLean, and Henry St. John Thackeray)
- 3.1: Esther, Judith, Tobit (1940)

9. Because the word *eclectic* can have a mildly pejorative association (i.e., unsystematic or heterogeneous), some scholars reserve that term for the description of manuscripts that have a mixed text. It can be argued, incidentally, that the Sixtine and other early editions of the Septuagint were small-scale attempts at reconstructing a critical text.

10. The German word *Unternehmen* means "enterprise, undertaking." This institute, founded on the initiative of Rudolf Smend and Julius Wellhausen, is part of a larger umbrella organization, Die Akademie der Wissenschaften in Göttingen (originally, Königliche Gesellschaft der Wissenschaften).

11. See above, chap. 2, p. 58. Sidney Jellicoe, *The Septuagint and Modern Study* (Oxford: Clarendon, 1968), app. 2, provides a list of the manuscripts collated for the Cambridge and Göttingen editions, with their corresponding sigla.

Work on a full critical edition had to be postponed because of the First World War and its aftermath, but Rahlfs undertook the production of a provisional critical edition, which appeared just before his death in 1935. His text is based primarily on the three great uncials—Vaticanus, Sinaiticus, and Alexandrinus—but many other sources were used extensively. Rahlfs's edition, in spite of its provisional character, has since been regarded as the standard Septuagint text, even though for many books of the Bible it has now been superseded by individual volumes of the larger project, often referred to as "the Göttingen Septuagint."

For the fuller edition, Rahlfs himself published the volume on Psalms (and Odes) in 1931, though he emphasized the preliminary character of the work, since it was not based on fresh collations. Subsequently, Werner Kappler, Joseph Ziegler, Robert Hanhart, and John W. Wevers have produced over twenty full and authoritative volumes.[12] Entitled *Septuaginta: Vetus Testamentum Graecum*, this project combines a judiciously reconstructed critical text with a virtually exhaustive repository of information from all available sources.

Modern Language Translations

Two English translations of the Greek Old Testament are available, and others are in process. During the formative years of the United States of America, Charles Thomson (1729–1824) produced the first English translation of the Septuagint.[13] Having seen a copy of J. Field's 1665 edition of the Greek Old Testament, Thomson realized its value for better understanding the New Testament. Because no English translation existed, he endeavored to produce an English version of

12. Kappler was responsible for 1 Maccabees (1936) and 2 Maccabees (1959; completed by Hanhart). Ziegler edited Job (1982), Wisdom of Solomon (1962), Sirach (1965), the Twelve Prophets (1943), Isaiah (1939), Jeremiah, with Baruch, Lamentations, and the Epistle of Jeremiah (1957), Ezekiel (1952), and Daniel, with Susanna and Bel and the Dragon (1954). Hanhart completed 1 Esdras (1974), 2 Esdras (1993), Esther (1966), Judith (1979), Tobit (1983), and 3 Maccabees (1960). Wevers has been responsible for the Pentateuch: Genesis (1974), Exodus (1991), Leviticus (1986), Numbers (1982), and Deuteronomy (1977). Many of the earlier volumes have subsequently appeared in revised editions. The whole project is published by Vandenhoeck & Ruprecht in Göttingen, Germany.

13. Thomson served as Secretary of the Continental Congress from 1774 to 1789, making him probably the only Bible translator who directly participated in a political insurrection. One historian suggests that Thomson undertook his Bible translation work to dispel the political stresses of post-Revolutionary America; see John H. P. Reumann, *The Romance of Bible Scripts and Scholars* (Englewood Cliffs, N.J.: Prentice Hall, 1965), 122–44. In fact, Thomson did most of his Bible translation after retiring from politics in 1789 at the age of sixty. (In 1975 he became the only Septuagint translator to be honored by the United States Postal Service—albeit for his contribution to the Revolutionary cause—when he served as the subject of a 7¢ postcard.)

the Septuagint, followed by a translation of the New Testament that would allow the English reader to appreciate its heritage in the Greek Old Testament.[14] Although Thomson finished his translation of the Septuagint in 1792, it was not until 1808 that the complete Bible was published in four volumes.[15]

More familiar to English readers is the translation of the Septuagint by Sir Lancelot C. L. Brenton, published in England in 1851. Brenton was aware of Thomson's translation, but had never seen it and so could not make direct use of it in his work.[16] Brenton's translation is the one most frequently used today, especially in a reprint that gives the Greek and English texts in parallel columns;[17] it is also the version included in some Bible software programs.

A New English Translation of the Septuagint (NETS) is currently in process under the auspices of the International Organization for Septuagint and Cognate Studies and edited by Albert Pietersma and Benjamin G. Wright. When the Greek text represents a Hebrew *Vorlage* similar to that which underlies the New Revised Standard Version (NRSV), NETS reproduces the NRSV. Where, however, the Greek does not follow the Hebrew as it is represented by the NRSV, NETS reflects that difference. Therefore NETS provides the English reader with the distinctive traits of the Greek text in a version already familiar to English Bible readers. Unlike the two previous English translations, NETS is based on the best Greek texts, using the Göttingen critical edition for those books where it is available and Rahlfs's edition where it is not. NETS includes the deuterocanonicals, and for books with two distinct Greek versions extant, both will be translated.

14. Thomson's rules for Bible translation were preserved in his notebook: "To translate well is 1, to give a just representation of the purpose of the author; 2, to convey into the translation the author's spirit and manner; 3, to give it the quality of an original, by making it appear natural, a natural copy without applying words improperly, or in a meaning not warranted by use, or combining them in a way which renders the sense obscure, and the construction ungrammatical or harsh." Quoted in Reumann, *Romance of Bible Scripts*, 133–34.

15. The apocryphal (deuterocanonical) books were not included in Thomson's translation. Thomson's English Septuagint was reprinted by S. F. Pells in 1904. Pells had received a letter from a friend encouraging him in his publication of papers in biblical studies. The letter happened to arrive in the seventy-second month after Pells's wife had died, which struck him as coincidentally the same number of the original translators of the Septuagint. He had recently become aware of Thomson's work and took this as a divine sign that he should make it available in England (Reumann, *Romance of Bible Scripts*, 138–40). A revised and expanded edition by C. A. Muse was published as *The Septuagint Bible: The Oldest Version of the Old Testament in the Translation of Charles Thomson* (Indian Hills, Colo.: Falcon's Wing, 1954).

16. Reumann, *Romance of Bible Scripts*, 138.

17. Lancelot C. L. Brenton, *The Septuagint with Apocrypha* (Grand Rapids: Zondervan, n.d.).

A Septuagint translation is being produced as part of the *Orthodox Study Bible: Septuagint and New Testament*. Directed by Jack N. Sparks, this work is intended to meet the needs of Orthodox Christians in North America. Using the New King James Version as a base, the translators change it where it differs from the standard printed text of the Septuagint used in the Greek Orthodox Church (apparently, the Hebrew text is not taken into account). The study notes are exegetical and theological rather than textual.[18]

Translations of the Septuagint into other modern languages are rare. Special mention should be made, however, of *La Bible d'Alexandrie* (The Bible of Alexandria), a French translation of the Septuagint with a philological and exegetical commentary that pays special attention to the patristic use of the Greek Old Testament. Under the direction of Marguerite Harl, professor of postclassical Greek at the University of Paris-Sorbonne, the first volume (on Genesis) appeared in 1986, published in Paris by Cerf. The rest of the Pentateuch, as well as volumes on Joshua, Judges, 1 Kings, and several Minor Prophets, have also been published.[19]

An Italian project, *La Bibbia dei Settanta*, has been undertaken by a team of scholars mainly from the University of Bologna and coordinated by Luciana Mortari. Their purpose is to produce a very literal translation, even if the results are stylistically harsh. The translation will be accompanied by introductions and footnotes, the latter focusing on discrepancies between the Greek and Hebrew texts.[20] Efforts are also underway to produce translations of the Septuagint in German (main editors Martin Karrer and Wolfgang Kraus) and in Spanish.

The Contents of the Septuagint

Book, Chapter, and Verse

The modern biblical student who wishes to make use of the Septuagint and opens a printed edition of the Greek text (or an English translation) will come across some unexpected and confusing features. The titles and order of the books do not always correspond to those in our English Bibles; within some books, chapter and verse divisions look wrong; and at times whole sections appear to be out of place.

Take, for example, Rahlfs's *Septuaginta*, which uses the Latin name of the books in the table of contents. The Octateuch (i.e., the first eight

18. For further information, including some samples, see the project's Web page (http://www.lxx.org).

19. For further information on both this French project and NETS, see appendix A below, and *BIOSCS* 31 (1998): 26–35.

20. See the summary in *BIOSCS* 31 (1998): 36–38.

books, from Genesis to Ruth) corresponds to what we find in English Bibles. The books of 1–2 Samuel and 1–2 Kings, however, are listed as 1–4 Regnorum, that is, Reigns or Kingdoms (Greek *Basileiōn*), while the books of Chronicles bear the name Paralipomenon (Greek *Paraleipomenōn*, "things left out"; that is, books that include material not found in Samuel–Kings). Then follows 1 Esdras, which is not part of the Hebrew canon;[21] 2 Esdras, which consists of *both* Ezra and Nehemiah; and Esther, which has some significant additions. The rest of the "historical" books in the Septuagint are all missing from the Hebrew canon: Judith, Tobit, and 1–4 Maccabees (4 Maccabees is largely philosophical rather than historical in character).

The poetic books include Psalms, Odes,[22] Proverbs, Ecclesiastes, Song of Songs, and Job, followed by three works not included in the Hebrew canon: Wisdom of Solomon, Ecclesiasticus (Wisdom of Jesus ben Sirach), and Psalms of Solomon. Next appear the twelve Minor Prophets, in an order slightly different from that of our English versions. Finally, we have the other prophetic books: Isaiah, Jeremiah, Baruch (not in the Hebrew canon), Lamentations, the Epistle of Jeremiah (not in the Hebrew canon), Ezekiel, and Daniel (with the additional stories of Susanna and Bel and the Dragon).[23]

It is important to note that Greek manuscripts do not present the books in uniform order. For example, in Sinaiticus and Alexandrinus the poetic books rather than the prophets come at the end, while in Vaticanus (which does not include any of the books of Maccabees) the group Esther–Judith–Tobit comes between the poetic and the prophetic books.[24]

Chapter and verse divisions developed over the centuries in a less than systematic fashion, resulting in inconsistencies among the various traditions. Within individual books, the chapter-and-verse numbering of the Septuagint sometimes differs from what we find in English Bibles. In the case of the Book of Psalms, it is mainly a matter of remembering two details. (a) The Septuagint, followed by the Vulgate

21. In the Vulgate (where 1 and 2 Esdras correspond respectively to Ezra and Nehemiah), this book has the title 3 Esdras. Moreover, the Vulgate includes 4 Esdras, an apocalyptic book that is often and confusingly referred to as 2 Esdras.

22. The Odes, which are appended to the Psalms in a few manuscripts, form part of the liturgical services in the Eastern Orthodox Church. This book consists of a series of prayers taken from both the Old and New Testaments; it is therefore somewhat misleading to include it within the corpus of the Septuagint.

23. The Prayer of Azariah and the Song of the Three Young Men, found in Roman Catholic Bibles after Dan. 3:23, are included in Rahlfs as Odes 7 and 8.

24. For a detailed description of the order of the books in various uncials as well as in patristic and ecclesiastical lists, see Swete, *Introduction to the Old Testament in Greek*, 201–14; also B. Botte and P.-M. Bogaert, "Septante et versions grecques," in *Dictionnaire de la Bible, Supplément* 12.536–692, esp. 541–43.

and Roman Catholic Bibles, treats Psalms 9 and 10 as a single psalm, while Psalm 147 is divided into two psalms: 146 and 147. This means that the chapter numbering is off by one from Psalm 10 to 147, with Psalms 1–8 and 148–50 being the same in both traditions.[25] (b) As in the Hebrew, the titles of the Psalms are given a verse number, which means that verse numbers are usually off by one in comparison with English Bibles. Thus, for example, Psalm 12:1 in an English Bible corresponds to 12:2 in the Hebrew Bible and to 11:2 in the Septuagint.

In other books the discrepancies are less predictable. Exodus 35–40, for example, displays a disconcerting series of variations in sequence. Especially important is Jeremiah: among other problems, chapters 25–45 in our English Bibles roughly correspond to chapters 32–51 in the Septuagint. Additional scattered discrepancies are found in Genesis (a few verses in chaps. 31 and 35), Exodus (chaps. 20 and 35), Numbers (chaps. 1, 6, and 26), Joshua (chaps. 8 and 19), 1 Kings (chaps. 4–11, with chaps. 20 and 21 reversed), Proverbs (chaps. 16 and 20), and Ezekiel (chap. 7).

The Biblical Canon

The discrepancies in content between the Septuagint and our English Bibles cannot be understood without reference to differences among the canons accepted by various groups. We must therefore revisit history.

The first books of the Bible were written in Hebrew, and so the Hebrew Bible has an unequaled place as the divinely inspired text of Judaism and Christianity. The Greek version, as far as we know, was the first written translation of the Bible. From that day until this, it has been received by many people as the Word of God, just as modern translations are so regarded by many Jews and Christians whose language is not Greek. The indirect influence of the Septuagint also explains differences in some modern English translations that have been made from the Hebrew.

If one compares the modern English Bibles of Judaism to the Old Testaments of Roman Catholicism, Protestantism, and the Eastern Orthodox Church, differences will quickly be found (the New Testament books and their sequence are identical in all Christian traditions). All of the Scriptures of these great religious communities by and large contain the same books, but in a different order (illustration 11). The Roman Catholic and Orthodox Bibles, however, contain additional books not found in the Jewish or Protestant scriptures. If a more care-

25. The matter is a bit more complicated, since Ps. 116–17 are off by two. For a comparative chart of all the discrepancies in the Old Testament books, see appendix D below.

11. Order of Books in the Hebrew Bible, the Greek Septuagint, and the English (Protestant) Bible

Hebrew Bible	Septuagint	English (Protestant)
Torah (Law)	***Pentateuch***	***Pentateuch***
Genesis	Genesis	Genesis
Exodus	Exodus	Exodus
Leviticus	Leviticus	Leviticus
Numbers	Numbers	Numbers
Deuteronomy	Deuteronomy	Deuteronomy
Neviʾim (Prophets)	***Historical Books***	***Historical Books***
Former Prophets	Joshua	Joshua
Joshua	Judges	Judges
Judges	Ruth	Ruth
1 Samuel	1 Reigns	1 Samuel
2 Samuel	2 Reigns	2 Samuel
1 Kings	3 Reigns	1 Kings
2 Kings	4 Reigns	2 Kings
Latter Prophets	1 Paralipomenon	1 Chronicles
Isaiah	2 Paralipomenon	2 Chronicles
Jeremiah	1 Esdras	Ezra
Ezekiel	2 Esdras	Nehemiah
The Twelve	Esther	Esther
Hosea	Judith	***Poetic Books***
Joel	Tobit	Job
Amos	1 Maccabees	Psalms
Obadiah	2 Maccabees	Proverbs
Jonah	3 Maccabees	Ecclesiastes
Micah	4 Maccabees	Song of Songs
Nahum	***Poetic Books***	***Prophets***
Habakkuk	Psalms (+ Odes)	Isaiah
Zephaniah	Proverbs	Jeremiah
Haggai	Ecclesiastes	Lamentations
Zechariah	Song of Songs	Ezekiel
Malachi	Job	Daniel
Ketuvim (Writings)	Wisdom of Solomon	The Twelve
Psalms	Sirach	Hosea
Job	Psalms of Solomon	Joel
Proverbs	***Prophets***	Amos
Ruth	The Twelve	Obadiah
Canticles	Hosea	Jonah
Ecclesiastes	Amos	Micah
Lamentations	Micah	Nahum
Esther	Joel	Habakkuk
Daniel	Obadiah	Zephaniah
Ezra	Jonah	Haggai
Nehemiah	Nahum	Zechariah
1 Chronicles	Habakkuk	Malachi
2 Chronicles	Zephaniah	
	Haggai	
	Zechariah	
	Malachi	
	Isaiah	
	Jeremiah	
	Baruch	
	Lamentations	
	Epistle of Jeremiah	
	Ezekiel	
	Susanna	
	Daniel	
	Bel and the Dragon	

ful comparison is made, the versification and the content of certain books is found to be somewhat different. These discrepancies in modern English Bibles can be traced to the ancient differences between the Hebrew and Greek Bibles.

Jewish communities usually refer to the Bible as the *Tanak* (or *Tanakh*), an acronym formed from the first consonant of the Hebrew names for the three major parts that comprise the Hebrew Bible: **T**orah (Law), **N**eviʾim (Prophets), and **K**etuvim (Writings). If you open an English translation of the *Tanakh*, such as the 1985 New Jewish Publication Society Version, the table of contents lists the same books of the Old Testament—though in a different order—as those found in Protestant Bibles. The reason for this agreement is that books were included in both Jewish and Protestant Bibles on the basis of the Hebrew manuscript tradition.

English Old Testaments bearing the imprimatur of the Roman Catholic Church—for instance, the Jerusalem Bible and the New American Bible—contain all of the books found in the Jewish Bible and the Protestant Old Testament, and in almost the same sequence as the Protestant Bible. However, the Catholic Old Testament includes additional books found in the Septuagint but not in the Hebrew Bible or the Protestant canon: Tobit, Judith, 1–2 Maccabees, Wisdom (of Solomon), Ecclesiasticus (i.e., Wisdom of Joshua ben Sirach, not to be confused with the Book of Ecclesiastes), and Baruch (with the Epistle of Jeremiah). These additional writings are called deuterocanonical books by the Roman Catholic Church.[26] In printed editions, these books are interspersed within the sequence of the other books of the Old Testament. Moreover, the books of Esther and Daniel contain additional material not found in the Jewish or Protestant Bibles. Six additional chapters are found within Esther; and additional material is found in Daniel 3, with chapters 13 and 14 being discrete stories entitled "Susanna" and "Bel and the Dragon."[27]

Books were included in the Roman Catholic Bible not on the basis of the Hebrew canon, but according to the contents and sequence of the Latin Vulgate. The Vulgate included books translated from the He-

26. The term *deuterocanonical* reflects the fact that the Roman Catholic Church officially declared such books as canonical on a "second" occasion, that is, in the sixteenth century after a period of debate. Traditionally, non-Roman Catholics have referred to these books as *apocryphal* (see below, p. 85).

27. Although Hebrew or Aramaic fragments of some of these books (e.g., Tobit and Ecclesiasticus) are extant, modern English translations generally are based on the Greek version. *The New Oxford Annotated Bible with the Apocryphal/Deuterocanonical Books: New Revised Standard Version*, ed. Bruce M. Metzger and Roland E. Murphy (New York: Oxford University Press, 1994), includes an English translation of all of the deuterocanonical books and informative introductory articles.

brew and books and material found only in the Greek. Today's Catholic Old Testaments in English still include all of the books found in the Vulgate. The books originally written in Hebrew, however, are now translated from the Hebrew text rather than from the Latin, though often distinctive readings and additional material found only in the Greek or the Vulgate are also included.

To understand how this situation came to be, one must remember the use of the Septuagint in the ancient Jewish synagogue and later in the early Christian church.[28] In the two centuries before Jesus, most Jews in the world spoke Greek, not Hebrew or Aramaic, just as most Jews today do not speak modern Hebrew, at least not as their native language. For them, the Greek translation of the Hebrew Scriptures was the only Bible with which they could have been personally familiar. As we saw in chapter 1, one of the motives of the *Letter of Aristeas* was apparently to defend the belief that the Greek Scriptures had as divine an origin in translation as the original Hebrew texts had in their composition. Philo's later elaborations confirm that in the Hellenistic period the Septuagint was revered by many Jews as the divinely inspired text, perhaps on a par with the Hebrew Scriptures.

The earliest Christian apostles were Jews who, wishing to show that Jesus was the long-awaited Messiah, appealed to the ancient Scriptures of Judaism. When they wrote their gospels and epistles, they wrote in the Greek language. Therefore, it was quite natural for them to quote from the existing Greek Bible, regardless of whether they themselves knew and used the Hebrew (or Aramaic) and whether they held the Greek as divinely inspired.

Within the first decades of the church, a situation similar to that of Judaism quickly developed. Although the church had begun with Jewish converts in Jerusalem and Galilee, soon the majority of Christians were Greek-speaking residents of other Mediterranean regions. Consequently, the Septuagint became the church's Old Testament while it continued to function as the Bible used by the majority of Jews. By the end of the first century, debates between Christians and Jews led to a close comparison of the Septuagint with the Hebrew. For instance, Hebrew Psalm 96:10 contains the phrase "the LORD reigns," while a Greek text used in the church read "the Lord reigns from a tree." As a result, Justin Martyr (ca. 100–165 C.E.) accused the

28. For what follows, see also Martin Hengel and Roland Deines, "Die Septuaginta als 'christliche Schriftensammlung', ihre Vorgeschichte und das Problem ihres Kanons," in *Die Septuaginta zwischen Judentum und Christentum*, ed. Martin Hengel and Anna Maria Schwemer (Wissenschaftliche Untersuchungen zum Neuen Testament 72; Tübingen: Mohr Siebeck, 1994), 182–284.

Jews of deleting from their text an obvious reference to the crucifixion of Jesus.[29]

The scrutiny of the texts that occurred when the Septuagint was adopted as Scripture by the Christians highlighted the differences of the Greek texts in circulation from the Hebrew text that had become the standard in Judaism. In the second century, most Jews became distrustful of the Septuagint. As discussed in chapter 1, Aquila made a new Greek translation faithful to the standardized Hebrew text, and this version continued to be used in Greek-speaking synagogues until at least the sixth century. The Jewish scholars who produced the Talmud and other rabbinic writings, however, worked on the basis of the Hebrew text, with only passing references to the existence of Greek versions.

The Greek versions have virtually no place in modern Jewish worship, although they had occupied a very prominent place in the lives of Jews of the Hellenistic period. In effect, by the end of the second century the Septuagint had passed into the care and keeping of the Christian church. It is no surprise that virtually all surviving Greek manuscripts of the Bible have been produced by Christian, not Jewish, scribes.

Christians, however, inherited not only those scrolls that had been translated from the books of the Hebrew Bible, but also a corpus of highly esteemed Greek texts written by Jews in the two centuries before Jesus. These include the additions to Esther and Daniel and the books found today in the Roman Catholic (but not in the Protestant) Old Testament. So at the end of the first century, the church's Bible consisted of all the books of the Hebrew Bible in Greek translation, some additional books, and the collection of writings that became the New Testament.

Christians appear to have preferred the codex over the scroll from a very early date, perhaps because the codex made it possible to bind many biblical books together in a single volume. But of course there was no standard sequence for them as yet. Furthermore, some of the Greek books that had no counterpart in the Hebrew Bibles were sometimes bound with the biblical texts into one codex. That is why the order and contents of the books differ among the manuscripts.

About the time of the Roman emperor Constantine (died 337), the empire split into two parts: the Western Empire, ruled from Rome, and the Eastern Empire, ruled from Constantinople (ancient Byzantium, now Istanbul, Turkey). Latin was the predominant language of the Western Empire, while Greek remained the language of the East. Eventually, the Christian church too was split into East and West.

29. Jaroslav Pelikan, *The Christian Tradition: A History of the Development of Doctrine*, 5 vols. (Chicago: University of Chicago Press, 1971–89), 1.20. Modern textual criticism has vindicated the Jews on this point, showing that the phrase *from a tree* was in fact a Christian addition to the Greek text of Ps. 96:10.

The ancient Greek Bible continued to be copied and used in the Christian churches of the Eastern (Byzantine) Empire. Today's Eastern Orthodox churches, such as the Greek, Russian, and Syrian, inherited the Greek text as their Bible. Traditionally, the Orthodox churches have treated the Greek version as divinely inspired, although this issue is a matter of some debate among Orthodox scholars today. Those who hold to the inspiration of the Greek translation understand it to have superseded the Hebrew. An attendant theological corollary is that God has continued his revelation beyond the original authors of the Old Testament books. In his general introduction to Eastern Orthodoxy, Timothy Ware explains this viewpoint:

> The Orthodox Church has the same New Testament as the rest of Christendom. As its authoritative text for the Old Testament, it uses the ancient Greek translation known as the Septuagint. When this differs from the original Hebrew (which happens quite often), Orthodox [Christians] believe that the changes in the Septuagint were made under the inspiration of the Holy Spirit, and are to be accepted as part of God's continuing revelation.[30]

While the ancient Eastern church continued to use the Greek scriptures, the Western, Latin-speaking church needed the Bible in its language. Jerome produced the standard Latin translation (the Vulgate) toward the end of the fourth century. His intention was to replace the many imperfect Latin versions then in use, which had been translated from the Greek, with a new, accurate translation made directly from the Hebrew. Although Jerome personally believed that the Christian Old Testament canon should correspond to that of the Hebrew Bible, his Latin version included those books and additions found only in the Greek. Because the Roman Catholic Church descends from the ancient Western church, the Roman Catholic Bible stands in the Latin tradition shaped by Jerome's Vulgate.

At the time of the Reformation, the unique authority of the Latin Vulgate was challenged by Protestants. The books of the Protestant Old Testament were translated afresh from the Hebrew canon, which does not include the additional Greek books, although the latter were also written by Jews. Therefore, even today the differences among some English versions of the Bible have their distant origin in the split

30. Timothy (Kallistos) Ware, *The Orthodox Church,* new ed. (New York: Penguin, 1993), 200. For a more nuanced view, see Harold P. Scanlin, "The Old Testament Canon in the Orthodox Churches," in *New Perspectives on Historical Theology: Essays in Memory of John Meyendorff*, ed. Bradley Nassif (Grand Rapids: Eerdmans, 1996), 300–312, esp. 311: "The Greek form of the books of the proto-canon has generally been regarded to have an exegetical primacy over the Hebrew by the contemporary Eastern Churches."

of the textual tradition of the Jews into Hebrew and Greek before the coming of Jesus.

The additional Greek Jewish writings were apparently widely known among ancient Jews and no doubt highly esteemed by many, but none of them was included in the canon of the Hebrew Bible. Among these books, 1 Maccabees and 2 Maccabees deserve special mention, since they record from two different perspectives the history of how the Jews reclaimed Jerusalem from the Seleucids in 164 B.C.E. and rededicated the temple. Although 1–2 Maccabees are not in the Hebrew Bible, they are important to Judaism because they document, among other things, the historical basis for the Feast of Hanukkah (or Dedication; mentioned in the New Testament in John 10:22).

Recognizing the esteem given these books by ancient Jews and Christians, the Roman Catholic and Eastern Orthodox churches consider them to be (deutero)canonical. The Protestant churches, however, refer to them as apocryphal;[31] while they may be helpful and interesting reading, they play no authoritative role in the spiritual life of the church. Because the apocryphal books are not normally bound in the Protestant Bible, most Protestant Christians have, unfortunately, never heard of them, much less read them.

To Continue Your Study

For a history of the printed texts of the Septuagint through the nineteenth century, see Henry Barclay Swete, *An Introduction to the Old Testament in Greek*, 2d ed. (Cambridge: Cambridge University Press, 1914; repr. Peabody, Mass.: Hendrickson, 1989), 171–94. For a description of subsequent editions, see Sidney Jellicoe, *The Septuagint and Modern Study* (Oxford: Clarendon, 1968), chapter 1. Swete also devotes considerable attention (pages 197–288) to the contents and order of the books. Questions about canon are discussed in Marguerite Harl, Gilles Dorival, and Olivier Munnich, *La Bible Grecque des Septante: Du judaïsme hellénistique au christianisme ancien*, 2d ed. (Initiations au christianisme ancien; [Paris]: Cerf/Centre National de la Recherche Scientifique, 1994), 112–19, 321–44. Among introductions to the deuterocanonical books, see most recently Daniel J. Harrington, *Invitation to the Apocrypha* (Grand Rapids: Eerdmans, 1999).

31. The term *apocryphal* means "hidden," that is, unrecognized. Roman Catholics reserve this adjective for a large number of additional Jewish books otherwise known as *pseudepigraphic*.

4

The Septuagint as a Translation

From One Language to Another. If we wish to understand the Septuagint, we must appreciate the difficulties involved in the work of translation. Rendering a statement into a different language presents some ***Linguistic Challenges***. The translator must first understand the original text, then find proper equivalents in the target language; decisions must be made as to whether figurative expressions should be translated literally. Moreover, ***Conceptual Factors*** must be taken into account. The translator is involved in re-expressing the subject matter in a different language. When the Greek text differs from the Hebrew, the variations sometimes provide access to theological and hermeneutical concepts present in the translator's Jewish Hellenistic culture.

Interpretation in the Septuagint. Interpretative features in the Greek version may be especially evident when the translators omit or add words or phrases. At times we can detect ***Theological Interpretation:*** debated topics include anthropomorphic expressions, eschatology, and messianic expectations. At other times the translator may be reflecting ***Influence from Exegetical Tradition*** that sought to clarify the text in the light of oral teaching and liturgy. Finally, there may have been ***Sociopolitical Considerations*** motivating the translator's work. All attempts to draw interpretative inferences from the Greek texts, however, must be made with great caution, in light of the complexities and subtleties involved.

Before concluding part 1 of this book, we need to give focused attention to a somewhat more technical question, namely, the character of the Septuagint as a translation document. It is commonly said that every translation is an interpretation. Rendering a statement from one language into another unavoidably involves the translator's understanding and, therefore, interpretation of the statement. The nature of this process and the linguistic results it produces are appreciated, at least at a basic level, by everyone who has attempted translation between any two languages, ancient or modern.

From One Language to Another

Linguistic Challenges

Several levels of interpretation are involved in translation. The first level—inherent in the very process of reading—is simply the basic comprehension of the meaning of the text. A translator must make many decisions, most of which are not subject to conscious thought, let alone long deliberation, but which flow more or less naturally from his or her own competency in the language, familiarity with the topic, wealth of vocabulary, and personal bias. Even understanding the most basic unit of meaning, the word, is subject to interpretation. A given word in any language has a semantic range of meaning, sometimes narrow, sometimes quite broad. The specific meaning of the word in a sentence is determined only by the context. For instance, the English word *play* can be a verb, as in *children play* or *I play the piano*, two examples illustrating that even as a verb *play* has a fairly broad range of meaning. As a noun, moreover, the word can refer to several events: a stage performance, as in *I saw a play*, or a sporting event, as in *he made the play that won the game*.

Every word in any language also shares a semantic field or domain with other words to which it is related in meaning. For instance, as a noun, *play* shares a semantic domain with words that also refer to visual objects of recreation, such as *movie*, *performance*, and *stage show*. A given word may not only have two or more quite different senses, but each of these senses may also belong to a different semantic domain. Therefore, a translator must be able to identify the context of a statement well enough to understand the sense of a given word correctly and not to confuse it with a different sense belonging to another semantic domain.[1]

A second level of interpretation is the task of finding adequate equivalents in the "target" language. To complicate matters, the semantic range of a given word is usually not identical to the range of its corresponding word in another language. This affords the opportunity for interpretation, and thus for error. When someone translates a word from one language into another, he or she must decide what sense the

1. For a more detailed discussion of how vocabulary works, see Moisés Silva, *Biblical Words and Their Meaning: An Introduction to Lexical Semantics*, rev. ed. (Grand Rapids: Zondervan, 1994). The linguistic character of the Greek texts produced by translation is treated further below in chap. 5.

original word carries and identify an equivalent word in the target language. Thus, even if the sense of the original thought has been correctly understood, a word in the target language may be chosen that has a more specific or more general meaning than the original word. Moreover, the translator may tend to choose in the target language one word instead of another for various reasons, such as to make the translation sound pleasant or to avoid suggesting a social, political, or religious taboo in the target culture.

The Hebrew word *tôrâ* is an example of a word with a fairly broad sense but translated by a Greek word with a narrower sense, *nomos* (both terms have usually been translated into English as "law"). The Hebrew word *tôrâ*, however, is used to refer to the whole body of biblical instruction, which certainly includes the commandments and statutes of the Pentateuch, but also much more. The Greek word *nomos*, in the period the Greek translation was made, had a sense fairly close to that of the English word *law*. According to Charles H. Dodd, it referred to the legal statutes and codes by which good Greek citizens lived.[2] By choosing to translate the Hebrew word *tôrâ* with the Greek word *nomos*, the translators introduced an understanding of biblical instruction in the Hellenistic period that focused on the normative regulations of religious life. Dodd summarizes the relationship between these words as follows: "[*Tôrâ*] in its widest sense means divine teaching or revelation; [*nomos*] in its widest sense means a principle of life or action. When divine teaching is of the nature of commandments regulating conduct, and when the principle of life is conceived as dictated by a legislative authority, then [*nomos*] and [*tôrâ*] have approximately identical meaning."[3] Therefore, the choice of equivalent words in translation introduces some element of interpretation.

The translator must also decide whether literal translation of idioms, metaphors, and other figurative language makes sense in the target language and, if not, what to say instead. For instance, as discussed further below, the Greek translators seem to have consistently avoided translating the metaphor of God as a rock, substituting non-

2. Charles H. Dodd, *The Bible and the Greeks* (London: Hodder & Stoughton, 1935), 26.

3. Ibid., 40. Dodd's extensive discussion of this topic, though influential, has been subjected to criticism. One of his main concerns was to show that, as a result of the Greek translators' choice, the Hebrew concept became distorted: using the Greek word to render the Hebrew word in its broader sense gives "a misleading legalistic tone to much of the Old Testament" (p. 41). This claim possibly has a measure of truth, but subsequent work has questioned its validity. Indeed, some authors argue that *nomos* had a broad meaning and was a fine choice as a rendering of *tôrâ*. See, for example, Laurent Monsengwo Pasinya, *La notion de nomos dans le Pentateuque grec* (Analecta biblica 52; Rome: Pontifical Biblical Institute Press, 1973), 201–5; Alan F. Segal, *The Other Judaisms of Late Antiquity* (Brown Judaic Studies 127; Atlanta: Scholars Press, 1987), 144.

figurative language instead. Moreover, many syntactic constructions could be rendered word-by-word, but at the expense of sounding unnatural or even unintelligible.

Depending on how translators see their role and the purpose of the translation, the resulting document can fall anywhere between the extremes of a strictly literal rendering and a completely reworded paraphrase. Some of these choices are quite deliberate, but many are made unconsciously. The people who translated the Hebrew Bible into Greek faced all of these linguistic decisions.

Conceptual Factors

The distinction between language and concept is a blurry one, but also valid and necessary.[4] Translators, in addition to making strictly linguistic choices, must deal with a "higher" level of interpretation, namely, deciding how the subject matter should be construed and reexpressed in the target language.[5] This level of interpretation is involved to some extent in every translation, regardless of the subject matter, but especially so in the process of translating the Bible.

Because the biblical texts were both ancient and sacred, the translators were concerned with relating the translation to the religious understanding, traditions, and sensibilities of their contemporary target audience. They worked not only within the linguistic context of Hellenistic Greek, but also within a social, political, and religious context that shaped their translation, probably both deliberately and unconsciously. The audience of the translation is different from the audience the author of the original work was writing for, and the concerns of the translator may well have been different from those of the original author. Not surprisingly, the Septuagint is regarded as one of the earliest witnesses to the history of biblical interpretation. It has the potential of enlightening our understanding of how the Hebrew Bible was used at the time it was translated into Greek. The Septuagint can provide access to the theological trends and hermeneutical principles of Judaism in the Hellenistic period. It also provides clues about the social and political concerns of its day.

But there are complications. As we emphasized in chapter 1, there really is no such thing as *the* Septuagint. If the entire corpus of the Hebrew Bible had been translated at one point in history by one group of translators in one location and for one purpose, then it would be much

4. See Silva, *Biblical Words and Their Meaning*, 26–30.

5. For this twofold distinction in interpretation, see James Barr, *The Typology of Literalism in Ancient Biblical Translations* (Mitteilungen des Septuaginta-Unternehmens 15; Göttingen: Vandenhoeck & Ruprecht, 1979), 291 (offprint p. 17). This monograph is an offprint from the 1979 Nachrichten der Akademie der Wissenschaften in Göttingen, Philologisch-Historische Klasse 11.279–325.

easier to use the Septuagint as a snapshot of the history of interpretation and theological thought. However, apart from the translation of the Pentateuch (for which we have very limited information), the when, where, who, and why of the Greek translation of other books is basically unknown. We have reason to believe that the Greek version of Isaiah is later than that of Psalms, Ezekiel, and the Minor Prophets, but earlier than that of Samuel–Kings and Daniel.[6] Even if such a relative sequencing of the books could be established, however, the precise period of origin remains unknown. Therefore, it is difficult to show correspondence between the tendencies of a given Greek text and the circumstances of its historical period. Furthermore, most manuscripts of the Septuagint available to us contain mixed texts that do not always represent the original translation. Given these complications, we must be careful about making broad generalizations or drawing narrowly specific inferences, but it is still possible to glean from the Greek texts valuable and interesting information about ancient interpretation and the circumstances that shaped it.

The astute reader will realize that the value of a Greek translation for understanding the theology and interpretation of the Hebrew Bible actually runs counter to its text-critical value in establishing the Hebrew *Vorlage* or parent text from which it was translated. Generally speaking, if a given reading has arisen from translation technique, whether linguistically or theologically motivated, it has not arisen from a variant Hebrew text. There are no doubt instances where a textual corruption in the Hebrew, if it made some sense, led the translator to misconstrue the meaning of the verse. But it is helpful to keep these two concepts—translation method versus variant parent text—quite distinct. Unfortunately, it is often impossible to determine with certainty which explanation is correct.

Although each reading must be judged individually, the modern scholar will typically approach the differences between the Greek and Hebrew versions with a general preference toward one explanation or the other. Certain scholars tend to argue that a given Greek reading is certainly due to the translator's technique. Other scholars argue with equal enthusiasm that the same reading is due to a variant Hebrew text. The tension between these two opposing solutions constitutes what is perhaps the weightiest problem in Septuagint scholarship.

The question of how differences between the Greek and Hebrew should be explained is important for biblical studies in general. If differences between the Greek and the Hebrew are understood primarily as resulting from a variant *Vorlage*, for example, then clearly there must have been (at least) one Hebrew form in circulation that differed

6. Isaac L. Seeligmann, *The Septuagint Version of Isaiah: A Discussion of Its Problems* (Leiden: Brill, 1948), 75.

widely from the surviving Masoretic Text we have today.[7] Questions of social, political, and theological bias must then be directed to the differing Hebrew texts. What accounts for the two different Hebrew readings? And which, if either, was original? The implications of how one explains the differences between the Greek and the Hebrew are far-reaching and can significantly affect a scholar's approach to the documents.

One of the reasons it is so difficult to determine whether a Greek reading is due to translation technique is that no uniform method characterizes the Septuagint overall. Some books seem to be translated quite literally, others quite freely. The lack of a consistent translation technique frustrates our attempts to use the Septuagint confidently to establish the Hebrew text from which it was produced. But when we consider what the translators were up against, this lack of uniformity is hardly surprising.

In our modern world, translation between languages is so common that many helps—such as bilingual dictionaries and translators' guides—are available to aid the process. Because countless texts in numerous languages have already been translated, we have more or less standard ways of proceeding. The translation of the Pentateuch, however, was in many ways a pioneering work.[8] The translators were attempting a project of unprecedented scope and had few standards to guide them. Complicating their work was the difficulty that they were not translating between two related languages (e.g., Hebrew to Aramaic), but between two distinct linguistic families, Northwest Semitic to Indo-European. Moreover, they were taking thoughts that had arisen in the ancient oriental culture and trying to render them into the intellectual milieu of Greek culture.

Given the lack of precedent for translation on this scale, and therefore the absence of proven tools and guidelines, the translators were pretty much on their own. We must also keep in mind that their concept of what it meant to translate from one language to another may have been somewhat different from our modern standards. Chaim Rabin observes that "Greek society did not go in for translation, but for independent rewriting of information."[9] Therefore, what may ap-

7. The discoveries at Qumran have proven that at least for some books of the Bible there was indeed more than one Hebrew form in circulation during the Second Temple period. The existence of variant Hebrew texts does not, however, preclude the possibility that any given difference between the Hebrew and the Greek was caused by the translator's method of work.

8. See the discussion in Sebastian P. Brock, "The Phenomenon of Biblical Translation in Antiquity" (1969), repr. in *Studies in the Septuagint: Origins, Recensions, and Interpretations*, ed. Sidney Jellicoe (New York: Ktav, 1974), 541–71.

9. Chaim Rabin, "The Translation Process and the Character of the Septuagint," *Textus* 6 (1968): 1–26, quotation from 19. This incisive article is highly recommended for further study.

pear as a translator's taking liberties with his text may have been quite appropriate to the expectations of the culture in which he worked.

In making linguistic decisions, translators had no choice but to rely upon the exegetical traditions of their day, the context of a given thought, and the etymology of words. They apparently often used assumptions that have been shown to be linguistically unsound. For instance, they sometimes assumed that the meaning of a given Hebrew word had not changed over time or that the meaning of contemporary Aramaic words could be used to shed light on the meaning of an obscure Hebrew expression.

Under such conditions, naturally, each translator's attempt produced an almost idiosyncratic translation. Once the Pentateuch was translated, it is possible that later translators would use it as a reference, checking to see how "the Seventy" handled a particular word or idiom.[10] For example, the translation of certain words in the Septuagint of the Pentateuch appears to have encouraged stereotyping, that is, the tendency to use a Greek word consistently to represent a given Hebrew word in a variety of contexts. A common example is the routine use of Greek *diathēkē* ("testament") to translate the Hebrew term *bĕrît* ("covenant"). Ancient translators sometimes seemed unaware or unconcerned that a given Hebrew word could have more than one sense and rendered it using the same Greek word even where the context suggests a different choice.

When we compare the Greek version with the Masoretic Text, we should keep in mind that the differences may have arisen from any of several factors:

1. The Hebrew *Vorlage* from which it was translated was different from the Hebrew text extant today.
2. The translation process was unprecedented and therefore does not reveal a pattern.
3. The translator made a mistake.
4. The translator had an interpretative bias.
5. Some complicated combination of these circumstances affected the resulting translation.

The theology and hermeneutics of the translator can be determined only to the extent that readings arising from his method of translation

10. See Emanuel Tov, "The Impact of the LXX Translation of the Pentateuch on the Translation of the Other Books," in *Mélanges Dominique Barthélemy: Études bibliques offertes à l'occasion de son 60e anniversaire*, ed. P. Casetti et al. (Orbus biblicus et orientalis 38; Fribourg: Éditions Universitaires/Göttingen: Vandenhoeck & Ruprecht, 1981), 577–92.

(# 4 above) can be distinguished from the other possible factors. Clearly this is no easy task.

Interpretation in the Septuagint

Careful study shows that the Greek translators made choices that introduced interpretative elements into their text. One example of an apparently deliberate lexical choice is the distinction made in the Greek Pentateuch when translating the Hebrew word *mizbēaḥ* ("altar"). If the reference is to a Jewish altar, the Greek word *thysiastērion* is consistently used; where the text refers to a pagan altar, however, the translators chose a different Greek word, *bōmos*.[11]

Interpretative features are especially evident when the translators omit and add words or phrases. An element in the Hebrew may be omitted by the translators simply because it sounds redundant in Greek, but the omission may reflect a hermeneutical concern. Conversely, an element may be added to clarify or specify the thought, to harmonize the text with another biblical passage, or to make a historical or theological point. Translators may choose to highlight a certain thought by omitting phrases that distract from it or by adding phrases that heighten it. For instance, Hebrew Isaiah 5:13 says God's people will go into exile "for want of knowledge." In the Greek this expression is expanded to "because they do not know the Lord," clarifying the thought as the translator apparently understood it.[12]

The choices made by a translator can be examined for their interpretative bias (usually referred to as *Tendenz*, a German word meaning "tendency"). The translators who produced the Greek version were motivated to introduce such elements for three general reasons. First, their rendering of the Hebrew text was sometimes influenced by the theology of their time. Second, interpretative elements were introduced into the Greek text because of the translators' respect for the oral tradition and liturgy that had developed alongside Scripture. Third, just as the original biblical authors wrote with a target audience in mind, the translators produced their work for a people living within certain social and political situations, and thus they were motivated to actualize the Scripture, making it both comprehensible and relevant for their contemporary situation.

Assuming that we can identify interpretative elements in the Greek text, inferences can then be made about the development of theology, extrabiblical traditions, and the sociopolitical situation of the transla-

11. Emanuel Tov, "Theologically Motivated Exegesis Embedded in the Septuagint," in *Translation of Scripture: Proceedings of a Conference at the Annenberg Research Institute, May 15–16, 1989* (Jewish Quarterly Review Supplement; Philadelphia: Annenberg Research Institute, 1990), 215–33, esp. 225.

12. Ibid., 226.

tors. Not all scholars are sure that we can draw many such inferences, but numerous studies attempt to do just that.[13] What follows is a sample of possible ways in which the Septuagint reflects the theology, traditions, and political concerns of Hellenistic Judaism.

Theological Interpretation

Theology, like all systems of thought, develops over time and is shaped by experience. For instance, Israel's theology at the time of King David was significantly different from the theological understanding of the Jews exiled in Babylon, which was different from that of the Jews living under Roman domination in the first century. Whatever theological elements the translator introduced into his text would presumably reflect the theological tendency of his day, which may not have been the same as or even consistent with the thought of the author of the original text. This issue is important not only for Septuagint studies, but also for tracing the development of thought in Judaism, the New Testament, and the patristic writings.

Of course, we should not assume that there was a homogeneous, codified theology to which the Greek translators subscribed. If such a thing existed in Hellenistic Judaism, it has not survived. The sources we do have are not sufficient to deduce a reconstruction of Jewish theology in the Hellenistic period. Therefore, it is impossible to know if the theological elements introduced by a translator were common to the thought of Judaism at that time, peculiar to the particular theological tradition of the translator, or idiosyncrasies of the translator alone.

And so, even if the theological elements introduced by the translator could be clearly distinguished from a variant Hebrew reading, generalizations implied by the expression "the theology of the Septuagint" are dangerous. Any inferences from the Greek version must be qualified by limiting them to the particular book from which they were drawn. For instance, the peculiar preference for the word *doxa* in Septuagint Isaiah has led scholars to conclude that "glory" is one of the central characteristics of God for the translator of that

13. One of the more highly regarded and influential works is Seeligmann's monograph, *Septuagint Version of Isaiah*, from which some of our examples are taken. See also *VI Congress of the International Organization for Septuagint and Cognate Studies: Jerusalem 1986*, ed. Claude E. Cox (SBLSCS 23; Atlanta: Scholars Press, 1987), which includes several technical papers that were part of a symposium on exegesis in the Septuagint; note especially the essay by Arie van der Kooij, "The Old Greek of Isaiah 19:16–25: Translation and Interpretation" (pp. 127–66). More generally, see the useful surveys by John W. Wevers, "The Interpretive Character and Significance of the Septuagint Version," in *Hebrew Bible/Old Testament: The History of Its Interpretation*, ed. Magne Sæbø, vol. 1.1 (Göttingen: Vandenhoeck & Ruprecht, 1996), 84–107; and Leonard J. Greenspoon, "The Septuagint," in *History of Biblical Interpretation*, ed. A. Hauser (Grand Rapids: Eerdmans, forthcoming), vol. 1.

book.[14] It would be precarious to generalize beyond this evidence and to attribute such a view to the Septuagint translators as a whole.

One debated theological topic is the question of how the Greek translators conceptualized God. The Hebrew Bible often speaks of the invisible God by means of anthropomorphic expressions, such as the hand or face or mouth of God. In the past, some scholars argued that the Greek translators avoided describing God in human terms so as not to confuse the God of the Bible with the anthropomorphic gods of the Greco-Roman pantheon.[15] For instance, in Joshua 9:14 the Hebrew statement "they did not ask at the mouth of the LORD" is rendered in Greek simply with "they did not ask the Lord." As scholars continue to explore this issue in the biblical corpus as a whole, most of them conclude that no consistent anti-anthropomorphic pattern is found throughout the Greek Bible.[16]

It is interesting that while the Greek translators did not avoid these metaphors in a systematic fashion, they were consistently reluctant to refer to God as a rock. Mostly in the Psalms, but also in Deuteronomy, Isaiah, and Habakkuk, the Hebrew text sometimes speaks of God as a rock or stone, a figure that likens God to a fortress, a secure place of refuge. For instance, consider Psalm 18:31, 46:

> For who is God except the LORD?
>   And who is a rock besides our God? . . .
> The LORD lives! Blessed be my rock,
>   and exalted be the God of my salvation! [NRSV]

The Greek translators of each of these books avoid rendering this metaphor literally. Instead, they substitute words such as *God*, *helper*, *guardian*, and *protector*, which preserve the sense but not the imagery of the metaphor.[17] Since these books were probably translated at dif-

14. See Tov, "Theologically Motivated Exegesis," 230.

15. Charles T. Fritsch, *The Anti-anthropomorphisms of the Greek Pentateuch* (Princeton: Princeton University Press, 1943), is usually mentioned as an example. Fritsch himself recognized that "the LXX reveals no consistent method of avoiding the anthropomorphisms of the Hebrew" (p. 62), but he argues that the tendency to avoid them "is strong enough to give the LXX a unique character and a somewhat different conception of God from that which is found in the Hebrew Old Testament" (p. 65). Harry M. Orlinsky, in his review of this book in the *Crozer Quarterly* 21 (1944): 156–60, argues that supposed instances of anti-anthropomorphism in the Septuagint do not reflect theological tendencies but merely stylistic concerns.

16. See, for instance, Arthur Soffer, "The Treatment of Anthropomorphisms and Anthropopathisms in the Septuagint of Psalms," *Hebrew Union College Annual* 28 (1957): 85–107.

17. See also Staffan Olofsson, *God Is My Rock: A Study of Translation Technique and Theological Exegesis in the Septuagint* (Coniectanea biblica, Old Testament 31; Stockholm: Almqvist & Wiksell, 1990), esp. table 1 on p. 155.

ferent times by different people, each of whom showed the same tendency, this pattern may well reflect a religious taboo of the Hellenistic period. It is difficult to say what motivated the translators to avoid referring to God as a rock, but Isaac L. Seeligmann suspects it was "an apologetic endeavor to escape even the semblance of approval of the worshipping of stone images."[18]

Another theological concept that apparently developed within Judaism in the Hellenistic period is an eschatology that involved personal resurrection at the final judgment. The Greek translation of the Psalms, produced within this period, may reflect such a tendency.[19] To cite one possible example, Hebrew Psalm 1:5 reads, "Therefore the wicked will not *stand* in the judgment," whereas the Greek has, "Therefore unbelievers will not *arise* in (the) judgment." The semantic range of the Hebrew word *qûm* includes both arising and standing. The Greek verb chosen by the translator, *anistēmi*, means specifically "to rise up," and the New Testament writers use it with reference to resurrection.

Clearly, the evidence for theological trends in the Septuagint can be very subtle. As in this last example, it often hangs on the issue of whether and to what extent the semantic range of a given Greek word encompasses the sense of the Hebrew. Equally competent scholars will give differing answers. Even if the sense of the chosen Greek word can be shown to be somewhat different from that of the Hebrew, it is still uncertain whether that means the translator was theologically motivated and, if so, whether the choice was deliberate or subconscious. Thus, no one rendering can be used by itself to argue for theological development. The evidential value of a particular reading depends on the overall character of the translation and on comparable patterns found in other biblical books. This is tedious work, and much remains to be done.

A further level of complication is illustrated by the debate whether the Septuagint, when compared to the Hebrew Scriptures, reflects a developing concept of the expected Messiah. Marguerite Harl observes that the concept of messianism declined among the Greek-speaking Jews of the Diaspora in the Hellenistic period but flourished during that same time in Palestine.[20] Accordingly, she lists several passages from the Greek version under the heading "A List of Verses that Reveal

18. Seeligmann, *Septuagint Version of Isaiah*, 100.

19. See Joachim Schaper, *Eschatology in the Greek Psalter* (Wissenschaftliche Untersuchungen zum Neuen Testament 2/76; Tübingen: Mohr Siebeck, 1995). See further below, chap. 14, pp. 301–2.

20. Marguerite Harl, Gilles Dorival, and Olivier Munnich, *La Bible Greque des Septante: Du judaïsme hellénistique au christianisme ancien* (Initiations au christianisme ancien; [Paris]: Cerf/Centre National de la Recherche Scientifique, 1988), 219–22.

a Process of 'Messianisation' in the Greek Version *or* that Facilitated a 'Messianic' Reading" (emphasis added). This heading makes an important distinction that is not limited to the concept of messianism, but applies to all theological topics later developed within the New Testament. It is very difficult to decide, for instance, if a rendering that could be read as evidence of a developing messianism actually reflected the state of messianic thinking when the translation was made or was simply the result of happenstance, a result that later during the Christian era was congenial to a messianic reading.

This distinction is well stated by Johan Lust, who refers to Septuagint readings congenial to Christian theology as "christological applications," reserving the term "messianic" readings for those passages that would have been so understood at the time they were produced.[21] This distinction should be kept in mind whether one is reading the Septuagint or the Hebrew Bible.

To further complicate matters, almost all manuscripts of the Septuagint are found in codices that date from the fourth century of our era or later and that also include the New Testament. They were evidently produced by Christian scribes, and so the question arises whether they edited Old Testament readings in light of Christian theology. The evidence that they did so is minimal, but the possibility cannot be excluded in principle. It should be clear to the reader at this point that the discussion of theological trends in the Septuagint is an intricate problem requiring expertise in semantics and textual criticism, as well as sensitivity to the historical vagaries to which the texts of the Greek version were subjected.

Influence from Exegetical Tradition

A second reason translators may have introduced interpretative elements into the Greek was to clarify the text or harmonize it to the way it had previously been understood, especially in consideration of the oral tradition and liturgies of Judaism. For instance, the Day of Atonement is sometimes referred to as "the great day" in the Greek version. Seeligmann suggests that this feature reflects the influence of a tradition that was later codified in the Mishnah and Talmud.[22] Of course, it is difficult to say in which direction the influence went. It would be surprising if the Greek version of Scripture did not also influence the wording of the liturgy and tradition among the Greek-speaking Jewish communities.

21. Johan Lust, "Messianism and the Greek Version of Jeremiah," in *VII Congress of the International Organization for Septuagint and Cognate Studies: Leuven 1989*, ed. Claude E. Cox (SBLSCS 31; Atlanta: Scholars Press, 1991), 87. This general topic will receive further discussion below in chap. 14, pp. 297–300.

22. Seeligmann, *Septuagint Version of Isaiah*, 102.

An interesting exegetical example concerns Genesis 2:2, where the Hebrew reads, "On the seventh day God ended his work." In contrast, the Greek version (and the Samaritan Pentateuch, the Peshitta, and the Genesis Midrash [Bereshith Rabbah]) reads, "On the sixth day God ended his work." The Hebrew expression could be construed to mean that God actually did some work on the seventh day before he rested. Because of the importance of this passage for Sabbath-keeping, this point apparently was argued and settled among Jewish exegetes, so texts subsequent to that exegetical discussion were reworded to avoid suggesting that God created anything on the seventh day. The cessation of work on the sixth day is meant to indicate that God may have worked right up to the last moment before the seventh day, but ceased his work as soon as the seventh day had begun.[23] This is an example where the Greek translator apparently chose not to follow the Hebrew text, but to make his translation consistent with the traditional exegesis of the law.

Study of 1 Kings shows that the Greek text may have been shaped by the midrashic discussion of the rise and fall of Solomon's power as indicated by the extent of his borders.[24] Four statements are found interspersed in Septuagint 1 Kings 4:6 that do not appear in the Hebrew. These four additions indicate a declining progression of Solomon's borders commensurate with his declining obedience to God. This same interest in the relationship between Solomon's life and the rise and fall of his power is found in the Midrash Rabbah of the Song of Songs and in the Babylonian Talmud, although the sequence differs. The written form of these texts was made much later than the Greek translation of Kings, but they probably preserve ideas that had been discussed for centuries among the Jews.

These examples illustrate how difficult it is to distinguish the work of the original translator from changes made later by an editor. The reader will recognize that although the substitution of a word in Genesis and the addition of four statements in Kings may be the work of the original translators, both could have been made to an already existing Greek text by a reviser anytime later. Whatever motivation can be ascribed to the original translator could also be ascribed to a subsequent editor. To complicate the situation further, the evidence that the Greek reading in Genesis 2:2 also appears in the Samaritan Pentateuch raises the question whether the Hebrew parent text from which the Greek was translated already contained the reading.

23. Sidney Jellicoe, *The Septuagint and Modern Study* (Oxford: Clarendon, 1968), 321–22.

24. David W. Gooding, *Relics of Ancient Exegesis: A Study of the Miscellanies in 3 Reigns 2* (Society for Old Testament Study Monograph Series 4; Cambridge: Cambridge University Press, 1976), 23–29.

In the Greek version(s) of some biblical books, such as Daniel and Esther, entire chapters have been added to the Greek that are not found in the Hebrew. In the case of Esther, a book notorious for its lack of any mention of God, the additional chapters in the Greek add the explicitly religious elements missing from the Hebrew. The syntax, vocabulary, and style of the Greek of these additions is so different from that of the rest of the book that they were certainly introduced by an editor some time after the original translation was produced. Some of the additions show a distinct interest in circumcision and the temple, central symbols of the Mosaic and Davidic covenants, respectively. These themes no doubt reflect the concerns of the person(s) who introduced them, but because they cannot be accurately dated, it is difficult to infer from them what historical moment motivated their inclusion.[25]

Sociopolitical Considerations

In Isaiah 11:11 we find a list of geographical places from which the Lord will gather the remnant of his people. The reference to "Hamath" in the Hebrew is replaced by "Arabia" in the Greek.[26] It is unclear whether Hamath and Arabia were the same territory, or whether the translator was using a contemporary location in place of one that was no longer known. In either case, the resultant rendering makes the list meaningful to the Diaspora Jews of the translator's own day.

This example illustrates how careful one must be in using the Septuagint for historical inferences. It would be erroneous to argue that simply because the Septuagint is a translation of a much older source it can be used to reconstruct the historical details of that source. In other words, it would be invalid to argue that because Septuagint Isaiah mentions Arabia, that name was current at the time of the historical prophet Isaiah. Although this point may seem obvious, it is easy to make similar fallacious use of the Septuagint on more subtle historical points by confusing the time of the translator with the time the Hebrew *Vorlage* was produced.

The Greek-speaking Jews who translated the Hebrew Bible were not only members of God's covenant people, they were also citizens of Greek cities living in politically volatile times. The translations they produced reflect sensitivity to those who ruled them and determined the quality of their lives. For instance, although the translator of Isaiah sometimes substituted the names of Hellenistic deities in place of pagan Semitic deities, the specific name of Agathos Daimon, the city-

25. See Karen H. Jobes, *The Alpha-Text of Esther: Its Character and Relationship to the Masoretic Text* (Society of Biblical Literature Dissertation Series 153; Atlanta: Scholars Press, 1996), 162–93.

26. Seeligmann, *Septuagint Version of Isaiah*, 79.

god of Alexandria, was not one of those chosen.[27] In the biblical texts, the pagan gods were usually being denounced, but the explicit denunciation of the city-god revered by the pagans with whom and under whose power they lived would have exposed the Jews of Alexandria to recrimination.

In the Greek versions of Esther, the theme of royal assassination is amplified.[28] Mordecai's role in saving the life of the king is elaborated in the additions, and moreover Haman is revealed as plotting a coup that would give the Persian Empire to the Macedonians. This addition in the Greek makes the point that having a Jew in high office is good not only for the Jewish people, but also for the personal well-being of the pagan king and for the tranquillity of the entire empire. Such a point, for instance, would have reassured the Ptolemies that the Jews of Alexandria were not a threat to the pagan king but were, on the contrary, a friend.

On the other hand, because the Septuagint was the Scripture used by dispersed Jews who lived in Greek cities far from Jerusalem, it also reflects veneration for the national symbols that defined and identified the Jews as a united people regardless of where they were living. This interest is found, as mentioned above, in the Greek additions to Esther, which include prayers by Esther and Mordecai extolling the covenant, circumcision, the Jerusalem temple, and that defining moment in Jewish history, the exodus. Esther and Mordecai are portrayed as models of Jews living in exile, but close in heart to Jerusalem.

The promises of the covenant that established the Jews as a people, gave them the land of Palestine, and promised them a king who would reign forever had to be rethought in the Hellenistic period when most of the Jews lived outside the land, did not speak one language, and were governed not by a theocratic descendant of David but by a pagan king. The cherished promises of a national leader of a united people were preserved in the Greek version, but a sensitivity to the political situation of the Jews is also evident.

Before being dispersed among the peoples of the earth, the Jews enjoyed a national identity within the land God gave to them, under the theocratic leadership of the Davidic dynasty. In 2 Samuel 7, God had established a covenant with David, promising him something no other human had ever had, an eternal dynasty. Nevertheless, the Jews of the Hellenistic period found themselves living in a foreign land under the domination of a pagan king. When the Hebrew Bible was translated into Greek within this new political situation, the Hebrew word for "king," *melek*, was sometimes translated not by the expected Greek

27. Ibid., 99. See also above, introduction, p. 22.
28. Jobes, *Alpha-Text of Esther*, 126–28.

word, *basileus*, but by words that indicated lesser political power, for example, *archōn* ("ruler").[29]

Such a lexical shift might be motivated by two different but related thoughts. First, there may have been a desire not to publicize the Jews' hope for a national identity under their own king if they were in a precarious political position; after all, the forces of a pagan empire could turn against them at any time. Second, the translation may represent an attempt among the Jews to reconcile God's promise to David with the contradictory reality in which they found themselves living. They could construe the Davidic covenant as fulfilled by Jewish leaders who occupied positions of power subservient to the pagan king (e.g., Mordecai in the Book of Esther). This lexical shift, from *king* in the Hebrew text to *ruler* in the Greek, no doubt gave opportunity for, or perhaps reflected, a difference of opinion among Jews as to what should be their ideal political structure: an independent national identity under a Davidic kingship or a submissive role within Hellenistic society.

Whatever their reasons, the lexical choice of the Greek translators to tone down the theme of the Davidic kingship in the Septuagint highlights the boldness of the Jews who wrote the New Testament Gospels, and who did not hesitate to proclaim Jesus as *basileus* ("king") of a new kingdom.[30]

Conclusion

This discussion shows the complex problems of separating what the Hebrew parent text read from the work done by both the original translator and subsequent revisers. The final, extant form of the Greek version of every biblical book is an amalgam of many changes made to the original text for many reasons by many hands over many centuries. It is impossible to reconstruct the textual history of the Greek text of a given book with complete certainty, and thus one must take into account this uncertainty when making inferences about how *the* Septuagint reflects the theology, exegetical practices, and historical setting of its time.

To Continue Your Study

For the character of the Septuagint, see Henry Barclay Swete, *An Introduction to the Old Testament in Greek*, 2d ed. (Cambridge: Cambridge University Press, 1914; repr. Peabody, Mass.: Hendrickson, 1989), 315–41; and Natalio Fernández Marcos, *Introducción a las ver-*

29. See R. A. Freund, "From Kings to Archons," *Scandinavian Journal of the Old Testament* 2 (1990): 58–72.

30. Ibid., 72.

siones griegas de la Biblia, 2d ed. (Textos y Estudios "Cardenal Cisneros" 23; Madrid: Consejo Superior de Investigaciones Científicas, 1998), 31–43 = *The Septuagint in Context: Introduction to the Greek Version of the Bible,* trans. Wilfred G. E. Watson (Leiden: Brill, 2000), 18–31. The subject is treated piecemeal in most discussions of the Greek versions. Among important articles, special mention should be made of Chaim Rabin, "The Translation Process and the Character of the Septuagint," *Textus* 6 (1968): 1–26; and an incisive essay by James Barr, published separately as *The Typology of Literalism in Ancient Biblical Translations* (Mitteilungen des Septuaginta-Unternehmens 15; Göttingen: Vandenhoeck & Ruprecht, 1979). The most significant attempt to use the Septuagint as evidence of Jewish theology is Isaac L. Seeligmann, *The Septuagint Version of Isaiah: A Discussion of Its Problems* (Leiden: Brill, 1948).

PART 2

The Septuagint in Biblical Studies

While it is not difficult to acquire a general knowledge of the LXX and other Greek versions, the transition to the next level can prove quite challenging. Traditionally, students have been pretty much on their own if they wished to achieve a higher degree of competence. The primary and distinctive purpose of this textbook is precisely to aid students in achieving that goal.

Part 2 assumes that the reader has a basic familiarity with biblical scholarship, as well as a knowledge of the biblical languages, especially Greek, at an intermediate level. While this part of the book is written so as to be accessible to a wide variety of readers, students who are at least in their second year of Greek are most likely to profit from the material.

Chapter 5 has a specific linguistic focus: it is intended to facilitate reading "Septuagintal Greek" by highlighting its distinctive features and clarifying its character. The next three chapters tackle the most demanding topic covered in this book, namely, textual criticism. Although a special effort has been made to write the exposition in as clear a fashion as possible, readers may find it necessary to go over this material with particular care. Chapter 9 discusses the specific problems that arise when the Greek OT is used in the study of the NT. Finally, chapter 10 provides commentary on three LXX passages as a means of illustrating how the previous material bears on the interpretation of the text.

5

The Language of the Septuagint

Semitic Influence in the Vocabulary of the Septuagint. The Hebrew language has left its mark at the lexical level in three forms: loanwords, loan translations, and semantic loans. Of these, semantic borrowing is the most significant, but it is also subtle and sometimes unconscious. Specialized theological vocabulary often consists of semantic loans.

Semitic Influence in the Syntax of the Septuagint. Even when the words themselves are native Greek, the way they are put together may reflect Hebrew influence. It is not always easy to distinguish syntactic Semitisms in the strict sense from lexical or stylistic features. Some of the Greek translators were very sensitive to Greek idiom, but others were not.

Translation Technique. Describing a translation as literal or free is not very precise; several different criteria need to be used. The study of translation technique is closely related to the tasks of textual criticism. Several methods have been developed to distinguish translation documents from native Greek compositions.

As we have noticed repeatedly in earlier chapters, what we call *the* LXX[1] is in effect a collection of documents produced by a variety of translators who had differing gifts and backgrounds and who worked in diverse places over a long period. Nowhere is this pluriformity more

1. Hereafter we will normally use the common abbreviation LXX when referring to the OG version(s) of the Hebrew Bible (i.e., in contrast to the later versions and revisions, such as *Kaige*-Theodotion, Aquila, and Symmachus). In ambiguous contexts, the abbreviation OG may be used.

evident than in the character of the language used by them. Although one often comes across statements about "the language of the LXX" or general descriptions of "Biblical Greek," such phrases can be misleading. To be sure, nothing is intrinsically wrong with them, and in some contexts the convenience of using a general label may outweigh the disadvantages. From time to time, however, such terms reflect a naive understanding or a careless handling of the linguistic data, and the effects can be unfortunate.

Even specialists sometimes fall into this trap. The very first issue of *Vetus Testamentum* many years ago carried an article by a prominent scholar who argued that the LXX was composed in a "Jewish Greek" dialect that reflected the language of Jews in Alexandria.[2] Because this article failed, among other things, to include the necessary caveats, it gave the distinct impression that the Greek of the LXX was a homogeneous language and that it made sense only to readers who spoke a similar, peculiar form of Greek. To make matters worse, some scholars subsequently appealed to this article in support of their view that the NT too was written in a Jewish Greek dialect.[3]

What then can be said about the Greek of the LXX as a whole? In the first place, it may be described as Hellenistic Greek. The term *Hellenistic* is not used in precisely the same way by all scholars. Classicists, for example, employ it primarily as a chronological label, bracketing the period from Alexander the Great's conquests to the establishment of the Roman Empire. Biblical scholars tend to use the label Hellenistic Greek broadly, more or less equivalent to Koine (Common) Greek, that is, a particular form of the language that contrasted with the many different dialects characterizing the earlier classical period.

Though it developed from the dialect spoken in Attica (including the city of Athens), the Koine avoided many of the peculiarities of that region, while at the same time being influenced by other cultures in the Mediterranean world. Its Attic character is evident from many basic features, such as the presence of long η where other Greek dialects have α (e.g., Attic φήμη ["fame"] for the more general φάμα), the ab-

2. Henry S. Gehman, "The Hebraic Character of Septuagint Greek," *Vetus Testamentum* 1 (1951): 81–90. See the critiques in Moisés Silva, "Bilingualism and the Character of Palestinian Greek," *Biblica* 61 (1980): 198–219, esp. 210; repr. in *The Language of the New Testament: Classic Essays*, ed. Stanley E. Porter (Journal for the Study of the New Testament Supplement 60; Sheffield: JSOT Press, 1991), 205–26; and G. H. R. Horsley, *New Documents Illustrating Early Christianity*, vol. 5: *Linguistic Essays* (Sydney: Macquarrie University Press, 1989), chap. 1: "The Fiction of 'Jewish Greek.'"

3. See especially Nigel Turner, "The Unique Character of Biblical Greek," *Vetus Testamentum* 5 (1955): 208–13. In a later work, *Christian Words* (Edinburgh: Clark, 1980), Turner goes so far as to suggest that the NT's Jewish-Christian Greek helps explain the nature of glossolalia. See the review by Moisés Silva in *Trinity Journal* n.s. 3 (1982): 103–9.

sence of digamma (i.e., the letter Ϝ, which represented the sound *w*), and so forth. On the other hand, such distinctive Attic features as the combination -ττ- (e.g., θάλαττα) and the word λεώς were abandoned in favor of the corresponding pan-Hellenic forms (-σσ- and λαός). Also, as is true of most languages, Greek tended to simplify grammatical forms (e.g., some -μι verbs became -ω verbs: δείκνυμι → δεικνύω). Contact with non-Greek cultures had little effect on the grammar, but the vocabulary was enriched with many new terms.[4]

In the second place, it would be appropriate to describe the language of the LXX as *Jewish* Hellenistic Greek—but only for the same reasons that it is appropriate to use such labels as *Stoic Greek* or *journalistic English*. These terms do not suggest that the "dialects" in question possess a unique grammatical structure and that they should be isolated from their respective languages as a whole. Rather, we are merely recognizing that a given group has formed a community of sorts sharing distinctive interests and that these interests are sometimes reflected in its vocabulary (including idioms) and style.

Similarly, "Biblical Greek" is Jewish Hellenistic for the simple reason that it was written by Jews who lived in the Hellenistic era. These writers shared a faith in the God of Israel and practiced Hebrew customs. Inevitably, therefore, their vocabulary reflected those common interests. In the case of some Jewish Hellenistic writers, that is about all we can say about the distinctiveness of their language, since they do not otherwise betray foreign influence. In the case of others, the Semitic imprint is much stronger, primarily for reasons having to do with translation technique, as we shall see later in this chapter.

Semitic Influence in the Vocabulary of the Septuagint

The most noticeable, but also the most superficial, evidence of Semitic influence consists of loanwords, such as the Greek term for "Passover," πάσχα (from Aramaic פַּסְחָא, Hebrew פֶּסַח).[5] Like the word *sombrero*—which is immediately recognized by English speakers as a foreign term, but which tells us nothing about those speakers' competence in Spanish—the presence of πάσχα and similar words in the LXX merely reflects the contact two cultures have with each other.

4. See Leonard R. Palmer, *The Greek Language* (The Great Languages; Atlantic Heights, N.J.: Humanities, 1980), especially chap. 3 on the Greek dialects and chap. 6 on postclassical Greek. For greater detail on the Hellenistic and Roman periods, see Robert Browning, *Medieval and Modern Greek*, 2d ed. (Cambridge: Cambridge University Press, 1983), chap. 2; and more recently Geoffrey Horrocks, *Greek: A History of the Language and Its Speakers* (London/New York: Longman, 1997), chaps. 4–6.

5. For the material in this section, see Moisés Silva, *Biblical Words and Their Meaning: An Introduction to Lexical Semantics*, rev. ed. (Grand Rapids: Zondervan, 1994), 86–94, which includes greater detail and further bibliographical information.

This phenomenon has no greater linguistic significance than does the presence of such words as δηνάριον (from Latin *denarius*) or βάϊον ("palm branch," from Coptic *bai*) in the NT.

More significant is the use of loan translation, that is, the adoption of a foreign phrase by translating its constituent parts rather than by rendering the meaning of the whole phrase. The English term *skyscraper* has been treated in this way by other modern languages, such as Spanish (*rascacielos*) and, more modestly, German (*Wolkenkratzer* ["cloudscraper"], though *Hochhaus* ["tall house"] is also available). In this example, the metaphor is transparent and so the meaning can be readily understood, but that is not always the case. One of the best-known examples in the LXX is the Hebrew idiom נָשָׂא פָּנִים (lit., "to lift [someone's] face"), a metaphorical way of expressing various ideas, such as "to favor" (Gen. 32:21). In a negative sense, it indicates an action that shows partiality toward someone (Lev. 19:15; Ps. 82:2). Some of the LXX translators, instead of choosing a Greek verb or expression that conveyed the sense of the whole phrase, opted for translating the constituent parts, that is, using the verb λαμβάνω and the noun πρόσωπον. The resulting combination must have appeared odd or even confusing to Greek readers, but it became common among Greek-speaking Jews, including the early Christians (Luke 20:21; Galatians 2:6), who even made up such new words as προσωπολημπτέω and its derivatives (Acts 10:34; James 2:1, 9).

From a linguistic viewpoint, however, the most important type of foreign influence on the vocabulary is the phenomenon known as semantic borrowing (also referred to as calque), which takes place when the degree of bilingual competence in a community is relatively high. French-speaking Canadians, for example, under the influence of the English expression *to introduce a person to someone else*, began to use the verb *introduire* ("to bring in") in this metaphorical sense, even though French already had *présenter* for such contexts. The process is fairly clear: speakers first notice some semantic correspondence between a word in their language and a similar word in the foreign language, then proceed to bring the usage (i.e., the distribution) of the two closer together.[6] Another way of looking at this phenomenon is to regard it as a case of semantic extension: if we view the semantic areas covered by the terms as two overlapping circles, semantic borrowing

6. The process is usually unconscious and most frequently affects the speaker's use of the word in the foreign language, especially if he or she is not proficient in it. In such cases the use is typically regarded as an anomaly or a mistake and does not spread to other native speakers of the foreign language. When the process affects the speaker's own language, as in the case of *introduire*, the resulting change often spreads to the speaker's community, probably because (consciously or unconsciously) the foreign language enjoys a measure of prestige.

involves extending the area covered by one word so that the overlap becomes greater or even complete.

Semantic borrowing typically takes place (a) when the native and foreign terms have phonetic resemblance, as in the example of *introduire*, or (b) if the semantic change involved is relatively minor. Given the characteristic morphology of the Semitic languages, and that Greek belongs to a different family (Indo-European), one rarely comes across a word in Greek that sounds like a corresponding word in Hebrew (or Aramaic). Accordingly, one might not expect to find many examples of semantic loans developing as a result of oral communication among speakers of these two languages.[7] But as the level of sophistication in bilingual settings increases, the opportunity for semantic borrowing becomes greater. The reason is that the speakers continue to come across precise or otherwise useful terms in one language that are absent in the other, and a natural way of filling the gap is to take an available, corresponding term and extend its use.

Such a practice becomes even more common when speakers and writers must translate from one language to another, so we are not surprised to find many examples of this type in the LXX. Sometimes the semantic change involved must have been unconscious and perhaps barely noticed, as when the Greek translators used ἄρτος ("bread") in the general sense of "food" under the influence of Hebrew לֶחֶם. At other times the process no doubt was quite deliberate, although one is not always sure whether the readers would have perceived what was happening to the Greek word.

The classic example of a semantic loan in the LXX is the specialized use of νόμος ("law"), which the translators chose as the rendering of Hebrew תּוֹרָה.[8] More than likely, this choice was not original with them; such a lexical correspondence may have predated the LXX by a century, if not longer. Greek-speaking Jews in Alexandria (or elsewhere) would have naturally, and perhaps without much thought, used νόμος when they needed to refer to the Mosaic legislation. Limited to legal contexts, such a rendering would have had little effect on the Greek language. The Hebrew term, however, had a greater semantic range, including both a broader sense of "instruction" and a specific reference to (what we now call) the Pentateuch. Having adopted the initial lexical correspondence, the translators continued to use νόμος consistently to render תּוֹרָה, even when the Hebrew term occurred

7. One interesting possibility is the use of θάλασσα ("sea") rather than λίμνη in reference to a lake (Matthew 8:24), under the influence of Aramaic יַמָּא. While the Greek and Aramaic terms have no phonetic resemblance, the semantic shift from "sea" to "[large] lake" is relatively slight.

8. See above, chap. 4, p. 88, for further discussion of this lexical choice as evidence of interpretation on the part of the translators.

in contexts where a different Greek word might have been preferable. In some passages, Greek readers must have found the word odd, but it would not take long for them to make sense of the respective passages, recognizing that the word meant "more" in a Jewish context than it did among the Greeks. Of course, basically the same thing has happened with the English word *law*, which in Jewish and Christian circles is just as "semitized" as was νόμος.

Another interesting example of semantic borrowing is the use of δόξα, which in Classical Greek meant "opinion" or, in its passive sense, "reputation" (i.e., the opinion others have of a person). In the NT, of course, the word commonly has quite a different sense: "radiance, glory." How can we account for such a substantial semantic shift? The explanation is that the LXX translators chose this word to render Hebrew כָּבוֹד ("weight"), which was commonly used in the figurative sense of "importance, distinction" (cf. English *weighty*), then more specifically of divine manifestations. It is possible that in the Hellenistic period δόξα, because of its sense of "(good) reputation," was already used with reference to the renown of kings and others in authority.[9] If so, one can more easily understand why the LXX translators would have used this term in passages such as Exodus 24:17; 40:34; Ezekiel 1:28; and many others. But whatever the precise reasons for such use, it remains a striking instance of the effect that Hebrew had on the vocabulary of the Greek Bible.

Semitic Influence in the Syntax of the Septuagint

F. C. Conybeare and St. George Stock, after giving a summary of the morphology of LXX Greek, introduce the next section of their grammar with the following statement:

> In treating of Accidence we have been concerned only with dialectical varieties within the Greek language, but in turning to syntax we come unavoidably upon what is not Greek. For the LXX is on the whole a literal translation, that is to say, it is only half a translation—the vocabulary has been changed, but seldom the construction. We have therefore to deal with a work of which the vocabulary is Greek and the syntax Hebrew.[10]

9. See Matthew 6:29 with reference to Solomon. Extrabiblical references are ambiguous; the passages listed in BAGD 204 (s.v. δόξα 3) are not convincing, with the possible exception of Polyaenus 8 Prooem.: δόξα ἀθάνατος ("eternal renown"). Some argue that the original use of the term, possibly continued in colloquial speech, was "appearance" or even "radiance."

10. F. C. Conybeare and St. George Stock, *Selections from the Septuagint* (Boston: Ginn, 1905), part 2, §38. This work has been reprinted as *Grammar of Septuagint Greek: With Selected Readings, Vocabularies, and Updated Indexes* (Peabody, Mass.: Hendrickson, 1995).

Although this way of putting the matter is both an overgeneralization and an overstatement, it helps explain why some scholars conclude that LXX Greek is a unique Jewish language. Even the great scholar Henry Barclay Swete, for example, argues that one could not adequately account for the Greek of the LXX by simply pointing out that the document is a translation. In fact, he claims,

> the manner of the LXX. is not Greek, and does not even aim at being so. It is that of a book written by men of Semitic descent, who have carried their habits of thought into their adopted tongue. The translators write Greek largely as they doubtless spoke it; they possess a plentiful vocabulary and are at no loss for a word, but they are almost indifferent to idiom, and seem to have no sense of rhythm. Hebrew constructions and Semitic arrangements of the words are at times employed, even when not directly suggested by the original.[11]

Few today endorse Swete's description, but all Greek scholars recognize that LXX syntax displays numerous unusual features.

First Reigns (1 Samuel) 3:19–4:2 helps us identify some of the peculiarities that distinguish "LXX Greek" from other Greek literature. A nearly word-for-word translation is included for easier reference (illustration 12).[12] In this passage, as in most LXX books, one notices a relative absence of traits that are characteristic of typical Greek documents. In particular, we rarely if ever find in the LXX long, involved sentences formed by an abundant use of participles or subordinating conjunctions or both. Rather, following the pattern of Hebrew sentences, LXX Greek is characterized by parataxis, that is, the chaining of independent clauses through a coordinating conjunction (most frequently καί). From a semantic viewpoint, the context sometimes suggests that a given clause functions as a subordinate thought, while another clause conveys the main idea. Notice in 4:2c–d, for example, the two clauses, καὶ ἔκλινεν ὁ πόλεμος and καὶ ἔπταισεν ἀνὴρ Ισραηλ, which may be fairly translated, "And *when* the battle took an unfavorable turn, the Israelites fell." In some cases, the LXX translator will use a subordinating conjunction in the first clause and, surprisingly, retain the coordinating conjunction in the second.[13]

11. Henry Barclay Swete, *An Introduction to the Old Testament in Greek*, 2d ed. (Cambridge: Cambridge University Press, 1914; repr. Peabody, Mass.: Hendrickson, 1989), 299.

12. Lines 21c–h are absent in the MT. That section in the LXX may well reflect a different Hebrew *Vorlage*, but the originality of the material is disputed.

13. See Josh. 4:1: Καὶ ἐπεὶ συνετέλεσεν πᾶς ὁ λαὸς διαβαίνων τὸν Ιορδάνην, καὶ εἶπεν κύριος τῷ Ἰησοῖ ("and *when* all the people finished crossing the Jordan, *and* the Lord said to Joshua"). Conybeare and Stock refer to this passage in *Selections from the Septuagint*, §40; they also point out, however, similar examples from Homer.

12. 1 Reigns (1 Samuel) 3:19–4:2

19a	Καὶ ἐμεγαλύνθη Σαμουηλ,	And Samuel grew up,[a]
b	καὶ ἦν κύριος μετ' αὐτοῦ,	and the Lord was with him,
c	καὶ οὐκ ἔπεσεν ἀπὸ πάντων	and there did not fall (one) from all
d	τῶν λόγων αὐτοῦ ἐπὶ τὴν γῆν.	his words upon the ground.
20a	καὶ ἔγνωσαν πᾶς Ισραηλ ἀπὸ Δαν	And all Israel knew from Dan
b	καὶ ἕως Βηρσαβεε ὅτι πιστὸς Σαμουηλ	even to Beersheba that Samuel was faithful
c	εἰς προφήτην τῷ κυρίῳ.	as a prophet to the Lord.
21a	καὶ προσέθετο κύριος δηλωθῆναι ἐν Σηλωμ,	And the Lord appeared again[b] in Selom,
b	ὅτι ἀπεκαλύφθη κύριος πρὸς Σαμουηλ·	for the Lord was revealed to Samuel;
c	καὶ ἐπιστεύθη Σαμουηλ προφήτης γενέσθαι	and Samuel was credited to be a prophet
d	τῷ κυρίῳ εἰς πάντα Ισραηλ ἀπ' ἄκρων	of the Lord to all Israel from the ends
e	τῆς γῆς καὶ ἕως ἄκρων.	of the land even to the (other) ends.
f	καὶ Ηλι πρεσβύτης σφόδρα, καὶ οἱ υἱοὶ αὐτοῦ	And Eli was very old, and his sons
g	πορευόμενοι ἐπορεύοντο	continued what they were doing,[c]
h	καὶ πονηρὰ ἡ ὁδὸς αὐτῶν ἐνώπιον κυρίου.	and their way was evil before the Lord.
1a	Καὶ ἐγενήθη ἐν ταῖς ἡμέραις ἐκείναις	And it happened in those days
b	καὶ συναθροίζονται ἀλλόφυλοι εἰς πόλεμον	that[d] the Philistines[e] assemble(d) for war
c	ἐπὶ Ισραηλ· καὶ ἐξῆλθεν Ισραηλ	against Israel; and Israel went out
d	εἰς ἀπάντησιν αὐτοῖς εἰς πόλεμον	to meet them for war
e	καὶ παρεμβάλλουσιν ἐπὶ Αβενεζερ,	and encamp(ed) in Abenezer,
f	καὶ οἱ ἀλλόφυλοι παρεμβάλλουσιν ἐν Αφεκ.	and the Philistines encamp(ed) in Aphek.
2a	καὶ παρατάσσονται οἱ ἀλλόφυλοι	And the Philistines line(d) up
b	εἰς πόλεμον ἐπὶ Ισραηλ·	for war against Israel;
c	καὶ ἔκλινεν ὁ πόλεμος,	and the war declined,[f]
d	καὶ ἔπταισεν ἀνὴρ Ισραηλ	and the men[g] of Israel stumbled
e	ἐνώπιον ἀλλοφύλων,	before the Philistines,
f	καὶ ἐπλήγησαν ἐν τῇ παρατάξει	and there were smitten in the line of battle
g	ἐν ἀγρῷ τέσσαρες χιλιάδες ἀνδρῶν.	in the field four thousand men.

a. lit., and Samuel was made great
b. lit., and the Lord added to be manifested
c. lit., going were going
d. lit., and
e. lit., foreigners (similarly in the rest of this passage)
f. that is, the battle turned against Israel
g. lit., and a man

sources: Greek = Alfred Rahlfs, *Septuaginta* (Stuttgart: Deutsche Bibelgesellschaft, 1935), 1.508; English = Jobes and Silva.

Among features found in the LXX but not in typical Greek documents, one of the most striking is the frequency with which the phrase καὶ ἐγένετο (or ἐγένετο δέ; also the passive form ἐγενήθη) introduces a new sentence, clearly in imitation of Hebrew וַיְהִי. Our passage contains one example of this construction: Καὶ ἐγενήθη ἐν ταῖς ἡμέραις ἐκείναις καὶ συναθροίζονται ἀλλόφυλοι (4:1a–b). Notice that the second καί appears to function (awkwardly) as something like a subordinating conjunction—thus our translation *that*. Elsewhere in the LXX, the second καί is omitted altogether.

Other interesting peculiarities include the following:

1. Instead of using the adverb πάλιν ("again"), the LXX often imitates the Hebrew construction וַיֹּסֶף לְ־ by using the verb προστίθημι + infinitive, as in the clause καὶ προσέθετο κύριος δηλωθῆναι (3:21a), which could also be translated, "and the Lord continued to manifest himself."
2. The expression καὶ οἱ υἱοὶ αὐτοῦ πορευόμενοι ἐπορεύοντο (3:21f–g) reflects two Hebrew traits:[14] (a) the use of the verb πορεύομαι ("to walk") in the sense of "to conduct oneself," like Hebrew הָלַךְ, and (b) the use of the same verb in its participial form (like Hebrew הֹלֵךְ) to express the progress of the action signaled by the main verb.[15] This combination must have sounded quite odd to Greek speakers.
3. In the latter part of the passage, the verbs describing the movements of the armies are in the present tense even though they have a past reference: συναθροίζονται . . . παρεμβάλλουσιν . . . παρεμβάλλουσιν . . . παρατάσσονται (4:1b–2a). This use of the so-called historic present is very common in the LXX, but it is not evenly distributed among the books and it does not correspond to the Hebrew syntax.
4. The passage contains several other literal translations that do not conform to normal Greek usage (e.g., 3:19a).

One could list a very large number of additional "syntactic" features throughout the LXX that reflect its strong Semitic background. Most of the examples, however, would not belong in the category of syntax strictly understood. Many of them, such as the use of καὶ ἐγένετο and προστίθημι discussed above, are idiomatic expressions that can just as easily be viewed as lexical phenomena. Others, such as the use of parataxis and of the historic present, are found in native Greek compositions and thus need to be regarded as stylistic features. Part of our difficulty is that the line between syntax and style is not clearly drawn in most discussions. At any rate, most of the "syntactic Semitisms"

14. As already mentioned, the MT does not include these words, and one must leave open the possibility that the clause does not translate a Hebrew text but is rather an original Greek composition in Semitic style.

15. A close parallel is 1 Sam. 17:41: וַיֵּלֶךְ הַפְּלִשְׁתִּי הֹלֵךְ וְקָרֵב אֶל־דָּוִד ("and the Philistine went going and approaching [i.e., kept coming closer to] David"). This verse, though missing from the OG, is translated literally in the Hexaplaric and Lucianic traditions: καὶ ἐπορεύθη ὁ ἀλλόφυλος πορευόμενος καὶ ἐγγίζων πρὸς Δαυιδ.

found in the LXX do not affect the structure of Greek syntax in a substantive way.

To put it differently, the Semitisms of the Greek Bible are largely to be explained on the basis of translation technique. It is evident that most of the LXX translators attempted to preserve the linguistic form of the Hebrew. Some of them, apparently, did not much care if this approach violated normal Greek idiom, while others—with varying degrees of success—sought to strike a balance.

Translation Technique

Because the LXX is a translation, not an original composition, the character of its Greek is determined by the translator's method, which may not have been carefully worked out. When the translation was intended to be very literal, the resulting Greek would naturally show more influence of Hebrew syntax and word order than when a free, dynamic approach was taken. The apparent translation technique, which can be inferred only by studying the resulting character of the Greek, varies from book to book, reflecting the different methods used by different translators. For instance, the Greek Pentateuch, Joshua, and Isaiah are as a whole moderately literal translations of the Hebrew (though Genesis and Exodus are characterized by a freer method than Leviticus–Deuteronomy). In contrast, some sections of Reigns, Jeremiah, Song of Songs, and Lamentations are extremely literal, often producing very awkward Greek; while the translations of Esther, Job, and Proverbs are much freer.[16]

The characterization of a translation as literal or free, however, is not sufficiently precise to be useful to scholars who wish to compare the texts of two or more books. In a seminal 1979 monograph, James Barr attempts to bring precision to the term *literal* by identifying six categories that are "distinguishable modes of difference between a more literal and a less literal rendering of a Hebrew text."[17] He also makes the important point that "there are different ways of being literal and of being free, so that a translation can be literal and free at the same time but in different modes or on different levels."[18]

16. See the chart in Henry St. John Thackeray, *A Grammar of the Old Testament in Greek according to the Septuagint*, vol. 1: *Introduction, Orthography and Accidence* (Cambridge: Cambridge University Press, 1909), 13. Some of Thackeray's assessments need revision in the light of more recent work.

17. James Barr, *The Typology of Literalism in Ancient Biblical Translations* (Mitteilungen des Septuaginta-Unternehmens 15; Göttingen: Vandenhoeck & Ruprecht, 1979), 294 (offprint p. 20).

18. Ibid., 280 (offprint p. 6).

At about the same time as Barr's work, Emanuel Tov sought to provide a more precise definition of the categories *literal* and *free* by proposing the following five criteria:[19]

1. internal consistency, such as lexical stereotyping
2. representation of the constituents of Hebrew words
3. preservation of Hebrew word order in the Greek
4. quantitative representation (correspondence between the number of elements in the Greek and the number of elements in the Hebrew)
5. linguistic adequacy of Greek lexical choices

Tov is interested in determining the value of the LXX for the textual criticism of the Hebrew Bible. Before determining if a reading in the Greek of a particular book reflects a Hebrew *Vorlage* different from the MT, the overall character of the translation must be ascertained. A given word, phrase, or verse in the Greek is more likely to reflect its Hebrew parent text if the translation overall is a literal rendering. Therefore, the first step in determining the value of a Greek text for reconstructing its *Vorlage* must be to discover to what extent and in what ways the translation is literal or free.

As Anneli Aejmelaeus points out, the use of the LXX for the textual criticism of the Hebrew Bible is closely and mutually related to the textual criticism of the LXX itself (we need to work with the original Greek text rather than with later modifications) and to the study of translation technique.[20] Aejmelaeus represents a distinct approach to the study of characterizing translation technique. She differentiates between translation technique understood as an object of study (as if "the Septuagint translators had a technique or a method of translation that can be discovered and described") and translation technique "regarded as a question of method followed in the study of linguistic phenomena in the translation."[21] Selecting one syntactic feature of the

19. See Emanuel Tov, *The Text-Critical Use of the Septuagint in Biblical Research*, 2d ed. (Jerusalem: Simor, 1997), 20–24. The first edition of this important work appeared in 1981. For a more detailed analysis, see Emanuel Tov and Benjamin G. Wright, "Computer-Assisted Study of the Criteria for Assessing the Literalness of Translation Units in the LXX," *Textus* 12 (1985): 149–87.

20. Aejmelaeus discusses these complexities and mutual dependencies in her article "What Can We Know about the Hebrew *Vorlage* of the Septuagint?" *Zeitschrift für die alttestamentliche Wissenschaft* 99 (1987): 58–89, included in Anneli Aejmelaeus, *On the Trail of the Septuagint Translators* (Kampen: Kok Pharos, 1993), 77–115.

21. Aejmelaeus, *Trail of the Septuagint Translators*, 1–3. This distinction is not totally clear. Her objection to the former approach is that "abstract percentages of literalness" may not reliably describe what the translators were doing intuitively. The aim of the latter approach "is to follow the trail of the Septuagint translators, to understand their way of working, the problems they met and how they solved them, and to describe and explain the result of their work on the basis of these premises."

Greek text, she seeks to characterize the extent to which that particular feature reflects a corresponding item of Hebrew syntax. In one particular study she concludes that LXX texts, when they translate causal כִּי, contain a peculiarly high frequency of ὅτι clauses (in contemporary Greek, causal clauses were usually introduced by γάρ); the causal use of ὅτι, therefore, is a special LXX feature that "must be considered a Hebraism and is probably a novelty" introduced by the translators.[22]

Because the Greek of the LXX results from translation work, it has linguistic features that would not occur in texts composed in Greek. In 1974 Raymond Martin developed a method called "syntax criticism" that attempts to characterize translation Greek and distinguish it from composition Greek.[23] Martin studied selections from both the LXX and Greek texts composed in the Hellenistic era (e.g., Josephus, Epictetus, Polybius, and Plutarch). He identified syntactic features that he believed could be used to distinguish the two, namely, seventeen criteria based on Hebrew constructions and the Semitic arrangements of words.[24]

In theory, one could examine a Greek text using Martin's criteria and determine whether it was translation Greek or composition Greek. Subsequent scholars question whether Martin's criteria actually do the job as advertised because the occurrence patterns of some of the criteria that Martin identified as distinctively translation Greek occur also in papyri that are known to have been composed in Greek.[25] For instance, the frequency of copulative καί with respect to postpositive δέ in selected Egyptian papyri indicates composition Greek, as would be expected. However, the relative frequency of the same criterion in both Greek translations of Esther indicates composition Greek even more strongly than do the papyri. Evidently, Martin's criteria examine Greek style, not necessarily syntactic differences between translation and composition. Nevertheless, syntax criticism is useful for comparing the syntax of two or more Greek texts, even

22. Ibid., 24–25.

23. Raymond A. Martin, *Syntactical Evidence of Semitic Sources in Greek Documents* (SBLSCS 3; Cambridge, Mass.: Society of Biblical Literature, 1974).

24. Simply stated, these criteria are the following: (1–8) the frequency of eight prepositions relative to the preposition ἐν; (9) the frequency of καί copulative relative to postpositive δέ; (10) the frequency of articles separated from their substantive; (11–12) the frequency and position of dependent genitives; (13) the frequency of the genitive personal pronoun dependent on anarthrous substantives; (14–15) the frequency and position of attributive adjectives; (16) the frequency of adverbial participles; and (17) the frequency of words in the dative case without the preposition ἐν.

25. See E. C. Maloney's review of Martin's *Syntax Criticism of the Synoptic Gospels* (Lewiston, N.Y.: Mellen, 1987) in *Catholic Biblical Quarterly* 51 (1989): 378–80. For a more comprehensive critique of Martin's methodology see Karen H. Jobes, *The Alpha-Text of Esther: Its Character and Relationship to the Masoretic Text* (Society of Biblical Literature Dissertation Series 153; Atlanta: Scholars Press, 1996), 29–47.

though his criteria probably cannot be used to prove conclusively that the Greek text resulted from translation or composition.

Karen Jobes reworked Martin's methodology by quantifying the relative frequency of occurrence of his criteria such that the syntactic profile of a Greek text can be graphically represented. This allows the profiles of two or more Greek texts to be directly compared, whether of the same book (e.g., OG Daniel and Theodotion Daniel) or of different books (e.g., Alpha-Text of Esther and OG Daniel).[26] The use of syntax criticism to profile Greek texts allows for easier, direct comparison and may also help to identify textual families, isolate recensional strata, and perhaps even point to a geographical provenance.

Although there may be various approaches to the study of translation technique, whatever methodology is used must examine the linguistic character of the text throughout the book as a whole. It is insufficient to identify individual phrases in isolation and then draw generalizations from them. The danger of interpreting an isolated syntactic construction without considering the overall style of the translator can be easily illustrated. Charles T. Fritsch, for example, appealed to LXX Deuteronomy 32:10 as evidence that the Greek translation was anti-anthropomorphic. In his view, the omission of the possessive pronoun ("an eye" for "his eye" in reference to God) indicated that the translator was making God less personal and more distant.[27] Fritsch was faulted on this particular point for failing to notice that the omission of the personal pronoun was not restricted to the so-called anti-anthropomorphic passages, but was characteristic of the translator's style throughout. The omission of the possessive personal pronoun is often found in idiomatic Greek, especially in reference to body parts, where the implied possession is obvious.[28] The moral of the story is that any single reading—whether to be used for textual criticism or for studying the exegesis and theology of the translators—must be evaluated in light of the overall character of the Greek vocabulary, syntax, and style of the book under study.

To Continue Your Study

Henry Barclay Swete's *Introduction to the Old Testament in Greek*, 2d ed. (Cambridge: Cambridge University Press, 1914; repr. Peabody, Mass.: Hendrickson, 1989), includes a chapter entitled "The Greek of the Septuagint" (pp. 289–314); and chapter 10 of Sidney Jellicoe's *Sep-*

26. Jobes, *Alpha-Text of Esther*, chap. 1. See also below, chap. 12, pp. 271–72.

27. Charles T. Fritsch, *Anti-anthropomorphisms of the Greek Pentateuch* (Princeton: Princeton University Press, 1943), 11. See also above, chap. 4, p. 95.

28. T. Wittstruck, "So-called Anti-anthropomorphisms in the Greek Text of Deuteronomy," *Catholic Biblical Quarterly* 38 (1976): 29–34, esp. 30.

tuagint and Modern Study (Oxford: Clarendon, 1968) updates the material, though unsystematically. Especially useful are Natalio Fernández Marcos, *Introducción a las versiones griegas de la Biblia*, 2d ed. (Textos y Estudios "Cardenal Cisneros" 23; Madrid: Consejo Superior de Investigaciones Científicas, 1998) = *The Septuagint in Context: Introduction to the Greek Version of the Bible*, trans. Wilfred G. E. Watson (Leiden: Brill, 2000), chapter 1; and Marguerite Harl, Gilles Dorival, and Olivier Munnich, *La Bible Grecque des Septante: Du judaïsme hellénistique au christianisme ancien*, 2d ed. (Initiations au christianisme ancien; [Paris]: Cerf/Centre National de la Recherche Scientifique, 1994), 223–66.

On the Trail of the Septuagint Translators by Anneli Aejmelaeus (Kampen: Kok Pharos, 1993) includes essays addressing translation technique in general and specific cases of how Hebrew syntax was rendered in the LXX, especially the Pentateuch.

Emanuel Tov's book, *A Classified Bibliography of Lexical and Grammatical Studies on the Language of the Septuagint* (Jerusalem: Academon, 1980), is a valuable resource for specialized research.

6

Establishing the Text of the Septuagint

The Aims of Textual Criticism. Recent scholarship has questioned the work of restoring the original text of biblical documents. ***Should the Autograph Receive Priority?*** Philosophical and theological objections to this principle may be based on false dichotomies. ***Is the Goal Unreachable?*** Substantial progress has been made, and in any case we should make every effort to come as close to this goal as possible. ***How Is the Textual Criticism of the Septuagint Different?*** While some important correspondences exist between the textual criticism of the LXX and that of other Greek literature, such as the NT, the differences are significant. Both of these aspects need to be taken into account.

Assessing Internal Evidence. When evaluating internal evidence, attention must be paid to two different criteria. ***Intrinsic Probability*** seeks to determine what the author was most likely to have written. ***Transcriptional Probability*** seeks to determine which of the variants was most likely to have come from a copyist. At times, these two principles appear to be in tension.

Assessing External Evidence. Before making a final decision among textual variants, we must have a solid knowledge of the documents where these variants appear. Manuscripts need to be evaluated both as individual witnesses and as parts of larger groups. This evidence should be supplemented by data from the daughter versions and from the citations of ancient writers.

Scholars have long recognized that the LXX is of great value for the textual criticism of the Hebrew Bible, and this topic will be discussed in the next chapter. While it is certainly legitimate to use the LXX for this purpose and others, we should point out again that such tasks must be preceded by the attempt to analyze and study the LXX on its own terms. In the present instance, the reason is especially clear. Before we can use the LXX to help us determine the Hebrew text, we need to establish the Greek text itself. Unfortunately, the textual transmission of the LXX and later Greek versions is a uniquely complex topic, so we must devote a whole chapter to this question.

The Aims of Textual Criticism

The time-honored and most usual understanding of the task of textual criticism is typically formulated thus: "To follow back the threads of transmission and try to restore the texts as closely as possible to the form which they originally had."[1] This approach, however, is becoming increasingly controversial in biblical scholarship, and it is sometimes argued that the identification of the original text should be viewed at best as a subsidiary task and at worst as an impractical, misguided goal. Here we will deal with some of the questions most frequently raised.

Should the Autograph Receive Priority?

In the first place, we are told that it is no longer feasible to give preferential treatment to the autograph as opposed to later forms of the text. This argument may be formulated in various ways.

For some scholars, the problem is primarily theological. Traditional theories of biblical inspiration and infallibility, they claim, are to blame for attributing excessive authority to the original form of the text. In their opinion, the textual forms adopted by later communities are just as important, if not more so.[2]

For others, the real issue is one of philosophy of interpretation. Unhappy with the dominance of historical exegesis during the modern period, these scholars downplay—to a greater or lesser degree—the

1. L. D. Reynolds and N. G. Wilson, *Scribes and Scholars: A Guide to the Transmission of Greek and Latin Literature*, 2d ed. (Oxford: Clarendon, 1974), 186. See also E. J. Kenney's formulation in *New Encyclopedia Britannica* (15th ed.): "The technique of restoring texts as nearly as possible to their original form is called textual criticism" (20.164; this contribution is part of the larger article, "History, Study of").

2. Note, for example, David C. Parker, *The Living Text of the Gospels* (Cambridge: Cambridge University Press, 1997), who begins his book with this novel definition: "Textual criticism is in essence the act of understanding what another person means by the words that are laid before me" (p. 1). In his concluding chapter he states that even if we could recover the original form of the Gospels, "the ambiguity of the definitive text would not be at an end. . . . Theologically, there would be no resolution of the central problem. For the heart of the matter is that the definitive text is not essential to Christianity, because the presence of the Spirit is not limited to the inspiration of the written word" (p. 211).

significance of authorial meaning and adopt some form of "reader-response" theory. Even apart from theological concerns, they argue that how subsequent readers understand a document is of greater moment than what the original author might have meant.[3] If so, the recovery of the original form of the text can recede into near-oblivion.

Still other scholars are motivated not by weighty theological or philosophical commitments but by the simple reality of textual transmission as such and thus seek to understand that phenomenon on its own terms. In their view, excessive attention to the original form of the text has led to ignoring how much can be learned from scribal practices, especially as they illumine the history of biblical interpretation.[4]

In response, it should be stressed that the most influential scholars in the history of textual criticism, while asserting the priority of recovering the original text, have at the same time fully appreciated the value of understanding the scribal tradition—even in cases where the variants produced by that tradition have no claim to being part of the original text.[5] Indeed, if we pay attention only to the variants that have such a claim, we end up with a truncated picture of the manuscript tradition and thus jeopardize the very goal we seek to reach.

In other words, one should studiously avoid false dichotomies when addressing this question. The analysis of the manuscript tradition for its own sake does not undermine the task of recovering the autographa; on the contrary, such an analysis is an indispensable prerequisite if we hope to make reliable decisions regarding original readings. (Conversely, we can hardly describe in a meaningful way the textual history of a book unless we know which original text that history is a deviation *from*. This mild paradox may be regarded as one more instance of the so-called hermeneutical circle.)

Similarly, one needs to avoid misleading dichotomies when assessing hermeneutical and theological problems. Historical criticism, for example, has to a large extent ignored the role of the reader in interpretation. As a result, we have at times been somewhat naive in as-

3. For a more detailed description and critique of this viewpoint, see Moisés Silva, "Contemporary Theories of Biblical Interpretation," in *The New Interpreter's Bible*, ed. Leander Keck et al. (Nashville: Abingdon, 1994), 1.107–24.

4. See the brilliant application of these concerns by Bart D. Ehrman, *The Orthodox Corruption of Scripture: The Effect of Early Christological Controversies on the Text of the New Testament* (New York/Oxford: Oxford University Press, 1993).

5. As an aside, it should be pointed out that the study of secondary readings has often opened up new exegetical vistas. The alteration of the text can reflect interpretative options faced (consciously or unconsciously) by scribes, thus prompting us to consider questions that otherwise might not have occurred to us. Note also Kenney's comment: "For the advanced student the criticism and editing of texts offers an unrivalled philological training and a uniquely instructive avenue to the history of scholarship; it is broadly true that all advances in philology have been made in connection with the problems of editing texts" (*New Encyclopedia Britannica* 20.614).

suming that we can discover the pure and true meaning of the biblical text, untainted by the hosts of assumptions we bring with us. Reader-response critics have helpfully reminded us that human interpretations, grounded as they are in our own personal and cultural relativities, are hardly free of ambiguities.

But to deduce from these facts that the search for historical meaning is secondary or unimportant—let alone that it is fatuous and hopeless—flies in the face of every human instinct. And that includes the instinct of the most radical reader-response critics themselves, who presumably make every effort to understand authorial meaning if they happen to receive, say, a warning from their landlord, threatening to evict them if they do not pay their rent fairly soon. The whole of our social intercourse is predicated on the assumption that we will be courteous enough to avoid, insofar as that is possible, interpreting what someone says in ways not intended by that speaker.

In the case of ancient texts, it should go without saying (but unfortunately it does not) that, *mutatis mutandis*, the same principle applies.[6] For example, when Thucydides (*History* 2.67) tells us about a Spartan embassy sent to the King of Persia, does it matter whether the name of one of the messengers was Stratodemus, as two important manuscripts indicate, or Patrode(a)mus, as most of the other documents have it? Or will we argue that both names have equal validity? One can hardly take seriously the suggestion that what really matters is how readers understand the text and so what Thucydides actually wrote and meant (here or elsewhere) is at best an interesting but irrelevant question.

This example also helps us to answer the objection based on theological considerations. No one argues that Thucydides was a divinely inspired author, yet over the centuries scholars have rightly expended considerable effort determining the original form of his text (as well as his intended meaning). The definition of textual criticism quoted at the beginning of this section was deliberately chosen from a book devoted primarily to the transmission of nonbiblical literature. On the question of whether the biblical text has distinctive religious authority, different people will come to different conclusions. But even if what the prophet Jeremiah or the apostle John said (and meant) were regarded as having no such authority, it would still be crucially important to distinguish what they actually wrote from what later scribes and readers represented them as saying.

6. This is not to deny that literary works, and poetry in particular, may allow for—or actually invite—multiple readings not consciously intended by the writer. But again, some balance is needed here. We need not reject one truth just because we have accepted another. See Silva, "Contemporary Theories of Biblical Interpretation," 121.

Is the Goal Unreachable?

The second argument offered against the traditional text-critical task of recovering the autograph is that such a goal is beyond our reach. The primary reason for this skepticism lies in the undeniable fact that many of the significant corruptions found in ancient texts were introduced prior to the earliest time for which we have documentary evidence. The editor of Aeschylus in the Loeb Classical Library, for example, tells us that the earliest surviving manuscript of the tragedian's plays goes back only to about the year 1000 of our era, that is, almost fifteen centuries later than the autograph. Although able to remove most minor corruptions in the manuscripts, modern scholarship "is obliged to confess that the actual words of the poet are often beyond all hope of successful restoration. The gravest disturbances of the textual tradition antedate any period for which satisfactory testimony can be produced."[7]

The transmission of the biblical text was not immune to this process. Even in the case of the NT, for which manuscript evidence is extraordinarily rich and early, textual critics reach something of an impasse prior to the year 200 of our era. Many important variants were surely introduced during the second century, yet the evidence for that period is quite fragmentary. The problem is more serious in the case of the Hebrew Bible. While the Masoretic tradition is astonishingly uniform and trustworthy, the earlier transmission of the text was not as careful.[8] In addition, it is sometimes difficult to determine what the word *autograph* might mean. If the Hebrew Book of Jeremiah, for example, existed in both a longer and a shorter "edition," as many believe, which of the two qualifies as the original text?

The LXX has its own set of problems. Although the number of surviving Greek manuscripts approaches two thousand, the transmission of the text has been far from pure. Recensional activity, which probably began not too long after the translation of all the books was completed, continued for several centuries. Subsequent scribal work resulted in extensive cross-pollination, so that the vast majority of surviving manuscripts contain not one form of the text but a complex textual mixture. The work of reconstructing the various recensions has

7. Herbert W. Smyth, *Aeschylus*, 2 vols. (Loeb Classical Library; Cambridge: Harvard University Press, 1922), 1.xxxvii. It is worth noting that even in the extreme case of Aeschylus, we are able today to read his plays in translation without even being aware of these textual problems. When one takes the larger context into account, it is only rarely that such problems prevent us from understanding the text.

8. Surviving manuscripts of the MT go as far back as the ninth century of our era, and the Masoretic scribes had been at work for several centuries before that. The evidence suggests that, as a whole, the MT is for all practical purposes the same Hebrew text that was standardized late in the first century of our era, but that still leaves a significant temporal gap between the earliest form of the text and the period of standardization.

been the primary immediate goal of LXX textual criticism for over a century. Some doubt whether that goal will ever be fully reached. And even if it is reached, we are still left with the gap between those recensions and the original form of the translation.[9]

Should we then give up the task of recovering the original text of the LXX? While it is very important not to minimize the problems faced by LXX textual critics, neither should we become overly pessimistic. Consider, for example, that the Septuaginta-Unternehmen in Göttingen has already produced a reliable critical edition of the whole Pentateuch, all the prophets, most deuterocanonicals, and other books.[10] To be sure, a great deal of work still remains, and some of the books yet to be edited (such as Judges, 1–4 Reigns, and Psalms) present serious challenges. Moreover, many unresolved questions will occupy scholars for a long time. But the work of the Septuaginta-Unternehmen proves that the goal is not illusory. Although the text of the Göttingen edition is hardly infallible, no one would dispute its basic trustworthiness, and that level of confidence is at least sufficient to provide a secure base for further work.

Perhaps a simple illustration will help clarify the nature of the enterprise. Water-treatment plants should ideally provide water that is 100% pure, but this is not feasible. That obstacle, however, is no reason to stop treating water altogether or to consider such a task to be of secondary importance. Since we are able to determine safe, attainable levels of contamination, it is right and necessary to make those levels our goal.

Similarly, the concern that we may never succeed in fully reconstructing the original LXX is no argument to slacken our efforts. The authors of this book concur with Albert Pietersma when he states bluntly: "The primary focus in LXX text-criticism must always remain on the reconstruction of the original text."[11] Readers of this book, however, are not asked to agree with such a strong formulation, but only to recognize that the task of establishing the earliest form of the LXX text is a legitimate and necessary enterprise.

How Is the Textual Criticism of the Septuagint Different?

Many of those who begin their study of the LXX have already had some exposure to the textual criticism of Greek literature in general and of the NT in particular. Naturally, they often wonder what may be the points of contact between the text of the NT and that of the LXX. After reviewing the scholarly literature one is likely to conclude, "Not

9. Our discussion here assumes the validity of Paul de Lagarde's view that there was one such original translation. See above, chap. 1, pp. 35–36.

10. See above, chap. 3, p. 75.

11. Albert Pietersma, "Septuagint Research: A Plea for a Return to Basic Issues," *Vetus Testamentum* 35 (1985): 296–311, quotation from 297.

much!" The textual transmission of the LXX is so distinctive that scholars in this field tend to emphasize the differences and thus to isolate their work from that of their NT counterparts.[12] This situation is understandable, and the reasons for it will shortly become plain. In our view, however, careful integration of the two fields could be very beneficial, and so we begin by pointing out the correspondences between the textual criticism of the LXX and that of the NT:

1. Most obviously, both fields deal with the transmission of Greek documents. It would indeed be very surprising if the traits that characterize the transmission of the LXX books were unparalleled in other Greek literature—and in fact no one makes that claim. But if we can find parallels, then the broader the base of our research, the more likely we are to make responsible decisions.
2. The LXX has strong affinities with the NT in matters of character and style. That is only to be expected. We cannot forget that most NT authors, like the LXX translators, were Jews writing in Greek about their religion. So we would also expect to find special points of contact in the transmission of these two groups of books, even beyond what we may find in Greek literature more generally.
3. More important still, the LXX was adopted by Greek-speaking Christians as their Bible, and it continued in that function even after it began to lose prestige among the Jews. In other words, the people who read and made copies of the Greek NT were to a large extent the same people who read and made copies of the Greek OT. This factor alone suggests that much can be learned from analyzing the transmission of these two works in tandem.
4. In particular, some of the most significant LXX manuscripts—such as codices Sinaiticus, Vaticanus, and Alexandrinus—also contain the NT. It is evident that scribal patterns would be very similar for both sets of documents.[13]

These four factors are of great weight and need to be taken seriously. On the other hand, it would be a grave mistake to assume a one-

12. There have been some eminent exceptions, however. In the nineteenth century, for example, NT scholar Friedrich von Tischendorf produced an edition of the LXX. NT textual critics such as Eberhard Nestle and Bruce M. Metzger devoted considerable attention to LXX studies. Well-known paleographer Frederick G. Kenyon published in 1936 his important work, *The Text of the Greek Bible*, 3d ed. rev. by A. W. Adams (London: Duckworth, 1975), a title that reflects the author's interest in dealing with LXX and NT manuscripts as an integrative whole.

13. Paleographers have been able to determine, for example, that Codex Sinaiticus was produced by three scribes. One of them (referred to as scribe A) was responsible for almost the whole of the NT and also for most of the historical and poetic books of the OT. See H. J. M. Milne and T. C. Skeat, *Scribes and Correctors of the Codex Sinaiticus* ([London]: British Museum, 1938), 29.

to-one correspondence between the textual transmission of the LXX and that of the NT. The differences are substantial:

1. The LXX is mostly translation literature, and the inextricable connection it has with its parent Hebrew (or Aramaic) text puts it in quite a different category from that of the NT. As we shall see, textual decisions about the Greek text of the LXX are almost always dependent on knowledge of the *Vorlage*. This factor has the effect of neutralizing (at least partially) some other factors that might play a major role in establishing the text of other Greek documents, including the NT.
2. During the early history of the LXX, when many of the most significant variants would have been created, Christians were not even around, so at that crucial stage the question of its connection with the NT does not arise at all.
3. Even after the Christian era, individual books (or groups of books) of the LXX were often copied independently, so their own transmission did not necessarily parallel that of the NT books in every respect.

In view of these two sets of considerations, it might appear that we are at something of a stalemate. The art of textual criticism, however, requires the ability to keep in balance a variety of apparently conflicting principles. It's just that in the case of the LXX, the tensions are greater than usual—both in number and in difficulty.

Assessing Internal Evidence

When evaluating textual variants, perhaps the most perplexing tension is that which often arises between intrinsic probability and transcriptional probability. Before we can fully appreciate this problem, however, it is necessary to define our terms and to review recent scholarly discussion.

Intrinsic Probability

The concept of intrinsic probability can be simply defined by means of an exegetical question: What is the author most likely to have written? A more concrete way of formulating the question is: Which of the variants best fits the context? The word *context* here needs to be understood rather broadly, so as to include the following considerations:

1. *The immediate context*. This is of course the most frequent use of the term, and it lies at the heart of the exegetical task. When we face one or more variants in the manuscript tradition, we should give preference to the variant that least disturbs the sentence and

paragraph in question. Another way of putting it (though seldom articulated in this fashion) is to say that we are looking for the most redundant variant.[14]

2. *The larger literary context*. Good exegetes avoid tunnel vision. They keep in mind everything that a writer has said up to and subsequent to the passage being analyzed. Textual variants sometimes arise because a copyist is influenced by features close at hand, even though the author's thought may be guided by broader concerns that surface elsewhere in the book.
3. *The style of the author.* We cannot limit ourselves to the particular document being studied but must expand our research to other works by the same author, if they are available. At this stage we are looking for patterns in vocabulary and syntax.[15] If a certain variant conforms to the author's usage as a whole, it is reasonable to give preference to that variant over one that is inconsistent with such usage.
4. *The thought of the author.* We must also move beyond the strictly linguistic realm to that of thought. What Plato, for example, says in his *Republic* is part of the conceptual context that must be taken into account in the process of interpreting the *Apology* or some other work of his. No textual critic, therefore, will ignore such data when a decision must be made between two variants, either of which may otherwise appear reasonable.
5. *The broader historical and literary setting*. Everything else being equal—and this is an important qualification, as we shall see—preference should generally be given to textual variants that conform to the community of which the author is a part and to the probable literary connections of the work in question. The interpretation of the Gospel of Matthew, for example, and therefore the text-critical work linked to that interpretation, cannot exclude consideration of matters such as the Jewish setting of the gospel story (including language and thought), the literary relationship between Matthew and the other Synoptic Gospels, and the role of the early Christian church in the transmission of the traditions about Jesus.

14. On the principle of "maximal redundancy," see Moisés Silva, *Biblical Words and Their Meaning: An Introduction to Lexical Semantics*, rev. ed. (Grand Rapids: Zondervan, 1994), 153–56. The term *redundant* does not have a pejorative meaning in communication theory. Every language has a large amount of built-in redundancy that serves to neutralize the many ways in which communication suffers disturbance (such as a typographical blur, a speaker's mispronunciation, a sneeze in the audience, or just plain daydreaming).

15. Strictly speaking, orthography and morphology also come under purview. For purposes of this book, we confine our attention to substantive variants, that is, variants that have semantic import (keeping in mind, however, that even semantic differences cannot always be represented when the text is translated into English or another language).

In the case of the LXX, unfortunately, questions of intrinsic probability are complicated by the nature of translation literature. It is obviously not sufficient to determine whether, for example, the translator of Genesis typically uses a particular construction. One must first check whether the Hebrew construction it translates also follows a pattern. Moreover, as we saw in the previous chapter, one must have sufficient knowledge of the translator's technique to determine how concerned the translator was to represent the Hebrew usage consistently. Although the degree of correspondence between the Greek and Hebrew texts varies dramatically from book to book, at no point can the LXX textual critic afford to discount that relationship.

Transcriptional Probability

In contrast with intrinsic probability, the criterion known as transcriptional probability asks the obverse question: What is a scribe most likely to have done? More specifically: Which of the variants is more likely to have originated, consciously or unconsciously, in the work of a copyist? Scholars who study manuscripts are aware that textual alterations follow certain patterns. Rarely, we may have access to the master copy from which a manuscript was produced; in such a case, we have direct evidence of the kinds of changes introduced. More frequently, we need to look for a manuscript's singular (or otherwise exceptional) readings that are clearly not original.

It does not take long to discover that such secondary readings are, as a rule, "easier" to make sense of than the competing variants. And thus arises a basic canon or principle of textual criticism: A reading that would have appeared difficult to a scribe is more likely original than an easy reading. Now, when one variant is shorter than another, we usually find that the longer variant makes the passage more intelligible. And so we can formulate a more specific canon: Give preference to the shorter reading (but see below). Similarly, we should be suspicious of variants that appear to harmonize the text with another passage. And so on.

In addition, numerous variants arise as a result of mechanical errors, but in these cases too we need to ask which reading is most likely the result of the scribe's carelessness. Suppose, for example, that a passage has two variants, one of which includes a whole phrase while the other one does not. Suppose further that the phrase in question ends with the same combination of letters found immediately preceding that phrase. It would be reasonable to infer that the phrase was original, and that a scribe inadvertently omitted it when his eye jumped from the first combination of letters to the second one.

Several difficulties unfortunately arise in the use of the traditional canons of textual criticism:

1. Students tend to ignore all the *likely*s and *probably*s that pepper any discussion of these canons. One can never forget that such rules are only general principles of scribal proclivities and that therefore they can never be applied automatically.
2. Specific qualifications are necessary. We need to remember that the classic formulations of these canons, especially those by NT text critic Johann J. Griesbach, have been carefully nuanced. An excellent example is the canon of the shorter reading. Griesbach did not simply say that the shorter reading is to be preferred. Rather, he specified five different situations where such a reading is likely to be original, and then he went on to make clear that, on the other hand, *the longer reading is to be preferred* in half-a-dozen situations, for example, when what "is lacking could be lacking without harming the sense or the structure of the sentence, as for example incidental, brief propositions, and other matter the absence of which would be scarcely noticed by the scribe when re-reading what he had written."[16]
3. Finally, attention needs to be paid to the individual "profile" of each scribe. In the Pauline Epistles, for example, it is easy to show that the canon of the shorter reading, as Griesbach defined it, is generally reliable, but further qualifications are necessary. If we focus on Codex Alexandrinus, we notice that the difference in frequency between adding and omitting function words (such as prepositions, articles, conjunctions) is not significant; in the case of 𝔓[46], Sinaiticus, Vaticanus, and 33 the difference is considerable, with all four of these important manuscripts being three times more likely to omit a function word than to add one. (It is also important to note that the omission of a verb is so rare as to be an irrelevant consideration.)[17] At this point in the argument, however, we have really begun to move into the area of external evidence, which will occupy us shortly.

At any rate, the fact that the canons of textual criticism are often misused leads some scholars to minimize their importance and even to suggest that they should be jettisoned. This would be a serious mistake. It is true that general probability does not tell us what a particular scribe will do in a particular passage, but that is no reason to neglect relevant data. A life insurance company cannot tell when any

16. As translated by Bruce M. Metzger, *The Text of the New Testament: Its Transmission, Corruption, and Restoration*, 3d ed. (New York: Oxford University Press, 1992), 120. The reader is encouraged to study the whole formulation of this canon and to reflect carefully on its implications.

17. This material is based on a fresh collation of Philippians and Galatians by Moisés Silva. Some of the results were presented under the title "Scribal Tendencies in the Pauline Corpus: A Computer-Assisted Report," a paper read at the November 1989 Annual Meeting of the Society of Biblical Literature in Anaheim, California.

particular individual will die, but the actuarial (life-expectancy) tables they use make it possible for them to maintain a profitable business. Similarly, although we have no guarantee that such-and-such a manuscript will add rather than omit a word in such-and-such a passage, a responsible text-critical decision must take into account the likelihood that the manuscript may do so.

The matter needs to be put even more strongly: no aspect of text-critical work is more important than the proper evaluation of transcriptional probability. After all, unless we can give a reasonable explanation why the variant we reject arose in the first place, our choice of variants is indefensible. This way of putting it, by the way, helps us see that the most fundamental canon of transcriptional probability—indeed, of textual criticism as a whole—is this: choose the variant that best explains the competing variant(s). This is not simply one principle, or even the primary principle, among others. Every other canon is the application of this criterion to a specific situation. Thus, the reason we give preference to a difficult reading is that we can convincingly show how a scribe might have come up with an alternate easier reading if the difficult reading was indeed original (while it is seldom possible to explain why a scribe would alter a clear and simple reading into one that makes the text harder to understand).

The distinctive character of the LXX, unfortunately, throws a monkey wrench into the discussion. In some respects, the principles we have considered are even more clearly relevant to the LXX. Since most books of the Hebrew Bible were translated quite literally, the reader is constantly faced with awkward or difficult Greek. When evaluating variants, therefore, the easy ones are suspect, especially if the difficult variant appears to represent the Hebrew literally. The problem, however, is that sometimes the Greek text was altered on the basis of the Hebrew.[18] The extent to which such revisions may have taken place is a matter of some controversy, but one cannot in principle exclude the possibility that the original translation of a certain passage was free and easy to understand and that subsequently a reviser altered it by rendering the passage literally and thus producing a more difficult Greek text. In Isaiah 21:9, for example, the Hexaplaric recension repeats the word πέπτωκε in conformity with the MT, even though such a change introduces some stylistic awkwardness.

18. The resulting variants are often referred to as Hexaplaric because most of them can be traced back to the Hexapla produced by Origen. The term *Hexaplaric* often has a pejorative connotation, since it may indicate a corruption of the OG (as such, it is contrasted with the term *pre-Hexaplaric*, which is applied to variants or whole documents that escaped Origen's influence). Confusingly, this term can also be used with reference to the later versions (Aquila, Symmachus, and Theodotion) and to readings peculiar to them, since those versions were included in Origen's Hexapla.

Intrinsic Probability and Transcriptional Probability in Tension

Scholars who minimize the value of the traditional text-critical canons typically argue that we are dependent on the context, which is to say, preference should be given to intrinsic probability.[19] This approach, however, faces two severe difficulties. In the first place, intrinsic probability is strongly ambiguous in character: time and time again, competent scholars draw diametrically opposed conclusions as to which reading is most appropriate to the context. We must be able to appeal to additional data.

The second difficulty is even more acute. A moment's reflection makes it clear that context was the primary motive for scribal alteration. In other words, the principles of intrinsic probability that a modern textual critic uses today were the very factors that created variants in the first place! We must therefore have some kind of criterion to distinguish between two types of contextually appropriate readings: those that are original and those that are secondary. The answer, as Fenton J. A. Hort expressed it brilliantly, is that we can usually distinguish readings that to the scribe may have had the appearance of excellence from those that are excellent in reality.[20] But the only way to achieve this goal is to become familiar with scribal activity, to establish its patterns, and to evaluate "the relative fitness of each [reading] for explaining the existence of the others."[21]

Assessing External Evidence

Even after we have carefully weighed both intrinsic probability and transcriptional probability, we often hit an impasse. What do we do if the conclusion reached by the former conflicts with the one reached by the latter? We must be able to appeal to a different, indeed "higher," level of evidence, and that evidence is provided by the quality of the

19. See Emanuel Tov, *The Text-Critical Use of the Septuagint in Biblical Research*, 2d ed. (Jerusalem: Simor, 1997), 231: "The quintessence of textual evaluation is the selection from the different transmitted readings of the one reading which is the *most appropriate to its context*" (emphasis added). In view of such a general and subjective formulation, it is puzzling that Tov repeatedly minimizes the value of the canons on the basis that they are subjective.

20. Brooke Foss Westcott and Fenton J. A. Hort, *The New Testament in the Original Greek*, 2 vols. (1881; repr. Graz, Austria: Akademische Verlag, 1974), 2.26–30. It is generally acknowledged that Hort was responsible for volume 2, which consists primarily of an extensive introduction to the principles and methods used to edit the text. Hort's exceptional analytical powers and acumen are very much evident in this material.

21. Ibid., 2.22. For further discussion of this matter, see Moisés Silva, "Internal Evidence in the Text-Critical Use of the LXX," in *La Septuaginta en la investigación contemporánea (V Congreso de la IOSCS)*, ed. Natalio Fernández Marcos (Textos y Estudios "Cardenal Cisneros" 34; Madrid: Consejo Superior de Investigaciones Científicas, 1985), 151–67.

manuscripts themselves. As Hort expressed it, "Knowledge of documents should precede final judgment upon readings."[22]

To use a helpful analogy: before we reach a final verdict we must, like members of a jury, take into account the reliability of the witnesses. If a witness in a trial is color-blind, for example, we will not have great confidence in that person's testimony when it involves identifying the color of a car used in a crime (which is not to say that such a testimony is necessarily false). Similarly, suppose that a particular manuscript shows a propensity for confusing the divine names; in that case, we should of course become suspicious if in a particular passage it has the word κύριος when the rest of the witnesses have θεός (even though we cannot totally exclude the possibility that this manuscript alone preserved the original reading).

For most manuscripts, unfortunately, that kind of detailed information is not readily available to students. Instead, the scholarly literature describes witnesses in general terms as more or less reliable. A broad description like this does have value, being based partly on the age of the manuscripts, but more significantly on their relative quality, which is not that difficult to determine.[23] What is more difficult to do is to apply such an assessment to individual cases if one does not know in what specific respects a manuscript is reliable. To use again the analogy of the courtroom: a witness who is trustworthy in recalling visual details may be undependable when it comes to aural memory. To be sure, if a significant number of manuscripts that are considered (for different reasons) generally reliable agree on a particular reading, that agreement itself offsets our difficulty to some degree. It would be better, however, if information were readily available concerning the specific strengths and weaknesses of individual manuscripts. Until it becomes available, special caution is necessary.

In addition to taking into account the reliability of individual witnesses relative to each other, attention must be given to the comparative weight of families of witnesses. Careful collation of manuscripts against each other soon reveals patterns of readings that are shared by some and not others. Establishing textual affinities among manuscripts is particularly convincing and clear when they are based on

22. Westcott and Hort, *New Testament in the Original Greek*, 2.31.

23. Aside from forming an initial impression regarding the care with which the scribe worked (an impression that may be superficial and misleading), one needs to assess the text that lies, as it were, beneath the text produced by the particular scribe. This assessment involves (a) choosing representative passages with substantive textual variation but where a decision is fairly easy, (b) noting how frequently the manuscript appears to reflect the original text, and (c) comparing the results with the same kind of data for other manuscripts. One thus arrives at a rather general, but not unreliable, assessment of the quality of the manuscript—though a quality that is only relative to that of the other witnesses. See Westcott and Hort, *New Testament in the Original Greek*, 2.32–35.

secondary (nonoriginal) readings.[24] And once we have managed to identify groups of related witnesses, we can proceed to evaluate the age and quality of each group relative to the other groups.

Early in the history of NT textual criticism, it was noticed that, in addition to very close connections within small clusters of manuscripts, witnesses seemed to group themselves into two major families, one of which could be regarded as generally eastern and the other as western. Further refinements resulted in the identification of at least three groups: (a) Egyptian or Alexandrian, widely regarded as very ancient and reliable; (b) Western, also very old but erratic; and (c) Syrian or Antiochene, a somewhat later textual form with which the name of Lucian of Antioch (died 312) is often associated.

A comparable but not identical division has been identified among LXX manuscripts, based in part on Jerome's complaint that in his day the world was in conflict over three forms of the text.[25] Setting aside for a moment the controversy over the specifics of Jerome's characterization, one can hardly deny that by the fourth century most LXX books could be found in more than one textual form and that each form was associated (if only loosely) with a geographical area.

Thus, to take a specific example, Joseph Ziegler's detailed examination of the Greek manuscripts of Isaiah for his critical edition of this book in the Göttingen LXX (illustration 15 on p. 142) yielded four broad groups:[26]

1. The Alexandrian text, found especially in codices Alexandrinus (A) and Marchalianus (Q),[27] four minuscules, and the citations of Cyril; partial witnesses for this text-type are manuscript 965 (a fragmentary papyrus in the Chester Beatty collection, dated in the early third century of our era), Codex Sinaiticus (S), a dozen minuscules, the Coptic version, and the citations of the early Latin fathers. The antiquity and relative purity of this text are confirmed by the early evidence of manuscript 965 and by the absence of distinctive Hexaplaric readings, especially additions.[28]

24. Just as it is easier to prove that a student has cheated in an exam if an unusually large number of *wrong* multiple-choice answers coincide with those of another student.

25. See above, chap. 2, p. 47.

26. For the discussion in this section we are dependent on Joseph Ziegler's introductory material in *Isaias*, 3d ed. (Septuaginta 14; Göttingen: Vandenhoeck & Ruprecht, 1983).

27. The special affinity between A and Q is established by several readings that are found exclusively in these two manuscripts. For example, in Isa. 19:22 the rest of the textual tradition has the verb εἰσακούσεται (except that the first hand of Sinaiticus has this verb in the third-person plural), but A and Q have ἐπακούσεται, a reading rejected as secondary by both Rahlfs and Ziegler.

28. For example, in Isa. 44:5 the Alexandrian text reads, καὶ ἕτερος ἐπιγράψει Τοῦ θεοῦ εἰμι ("and another one will write, I am God's"), which is almost certainly the original reading. Most of the other witnesses, however, include the phrase (τῇ) χειρὶ αὐτοῦ

2. The Hexaplaric recension, found in codices Vaticanus (B) and Venetus (V), three minuscules, two Syriac versions (the Syro-Hexaplar and the Syro-Palestinian), and the citations of Eusebius, Basil, and Jerome. The church fathers sometimes tell us directly that a particular variant, usually originating in one or more of the later Greek versions, was used by Origen for his fifth (i.e., LXX) column.[29] Moreover, a few manuscripts retain the Hexaplaric signs (asterisk, obelus, metobelus), which indicate the same phenomenon. By inference, it is then possible to identify additional variants of a similar type, when they appear to reflect an adjustment toward the Hebrew text.[30]
3. The Lucianic recension, found in over twenty minuscules, the corrections of Sinaiticus and of three additional minuscules, the Syro-Lucianic version, and the commentaries of Chrysostom and Theodoret. These witnesses, which can be further subdivided into several groups, share with the Hexaplaric recension a large number of variants (especially additions) that reflect an adjustment toward the Hebrew text. Many other features, however, unite these witnesses over against both the Alexandrian and the Hexaplaric text-types. In particular, the Lucianic recension is characterized by numerous changes of a grammatical or stylistic nature that are not at all motivated by differences in the Hebrew text.
4. The Catena group, found in some ten minuscules. The name derives from the presence of this type of text in the medieval *catenae*, that is, "chains" or collections of fragments from ancient Christian exegetes. Though recognizably different from the other text-types, this one is difficult to characterize; sometimes it aligns itself with the Alexandrian text, sometimes with the Hexaplaric recension.

A comparable analysis of the manuscript tradition can be found in Ziegler's edition of the other prophetic books. In contrast, however, John W. Wevers's edition of the Pentateuch for the Göttingen LXX (illustration 16 on p. 144) recognizes neither an Alexandrian text as

("with his hand") after the verb ἐπιγράψει, in conformity with the MT. In Q, 88, and the Syro-Hexaplar, this phrase is marked with an asterisk, indicating that the later translations (Aquila and Theodotion in this case) had the phrase and that Origen correspondingly adjusted the LXX column of the Hexapla so that it would represent more accurately the Hebrew text available to him.

29. For example, Theodoret's commentary on Isa. 63:11 identifies the variant ἀπὸ θαλάσσης as Origenic (the original LXX reading is ἐκ τῆς γῆς).

30. For example, in Isa. 29:1 the Alexandrian text has Δαυιδ ἐπολέμησε, whereas the manuscripts identified as Hexaplaric transpose the two words, in accordance with the MT (חָנָה דָוִד). Although we have no external confirmation (either patristic comments or Hexaplaric signs) that this was the reading in Origen's fifth column, it is reasonable to suppose that Origen indeed inverted the words so as to bring the Greek translation into closer correspondence with his Hebrew text.

such[31] nor a Lucianic recension. Wevers does refer to the Hexaplaric recension (for which he uses the siglum *O*) and to the Catena group (*C*); he further identifies as many as eight smaller groups (each composed of between two and eight manuscripts). This different textual picture between the prophets and the Pentateuch reminds us that what may be true for one book (or group of books) in the LXX may not be true for another. Notice in particular that Codex Vaticanus, which clearly preserves an ancient and excellent text for most books, is a primary representative of the Hexaplaric recension in Isaiah.

Evidence from the Greek manuscripts is supplemented by the daughter versions (i.e., secondary translations from the Greek into other languages) and by citations from ancient writers.[32] This type of evidence is often ambiguous and more difficult to apply, but it occasionally sheds important light on the text.

One fascinating example is the textual transmission of 2 Samuel 13:39. The MT here reads as follows: וַתְּכַל דָּוִד הַמֶּלֶךְ לָצֵאת אֶל־אַבְשָׁלוֹם ("and David the king longed[33] to go out to Absalom"). Vaticanus, Alexandrinus (with a minor word-order change), and the Hexaplaric recension have a literal translation: καὶ ἐκόπασεν ὁ βασιλεὺς Δαυιδ τοῦ ἐξελθεῖν πρὸς Αβεσσαλωμ ("and David the king ceased to go out to Absalom"). In the Lucianic manuscripts, however, the subject of the verb is τὸ πνεῦμα τοῦ βασιλέως Δαυιδ. This reading (without Δαυιδ) is supported by the rest of the manuscripts and was chosen by Alfred Rahlfs as the original Greek.[34] Curiously, one OL manuscript reads, "et requietus est iratus regis" ("and the anger of the king ceased"). At first blush, this translation seems unexplainable, but Eugene Ulrich rightly sees that *est iratus* must have originally read ESTSPIRITUS ("the *spirit* of the king ceased"), which was then corrupted to ESTIRITUS; since this reading did not make sense, the sequence IRITUS was subse-

31. It should be noted, however, that codices Alexandrinus and Vaticanus, along with some papyri and versions, function in Wevers's edition similar to the way that "Alexandrian text" functions in Ziegler's work. Wevers's description of the various textual groups is found not in the introduction of each volume in his edition of the Pentateuch, but in detailed separate volumes. Note, e.g., *The Text History of Genesis* (Göttingen: Vandenhoeck & Ruprecht, 1974), esp. the summary on 228–30.

32. On the use of the secondary versions, see also below, chap. 13, pp. 278–80. On the use of quotations from later writers, much that is applicable to the LXX can be found in the articles by Gordon D. Fee (Greek Fathers), J. Lionel North (Latin Fathers), and Sebastian P. Brock (Syriac Fathers) in *The Text of the New Testament in Contemporary Research: Essays on the Status Quaestionis—A Volume in Honor of Bruce M. Metzger*, ed. Bart D. Ehrman and Michael W. Holmes (Studies and Documents 46; Grand Rapids: Eerdmans, 1995), 191–236. On quotations in the NT, see also below, chap. 9, pp. 190–92.

33. This rendering assumes a Qal stem; the MT points it as Piel, "to cease."

34. Moreover, it has now been confirmed that such a translation reflects a Hebrew *Vorlage*, for 4QSam[a] reads ח המלך . . . , which certainly should be reconstructed as רוּחַ הַמֶּלֶךְ.

quently changed to IRATUS ("anger").[35] Thus, even readings that appear useless can provide evidence for the original text.

As is the case with other aspects of textual criticism, external evidence cannot be applied mechanically. If an individual witness (or group of witnesses) can be shown in general to be more reliable than another one, it would be ill-advised to ignore its readings or to give them relatively less weight. On the other hand, it would be just as unwise to disregard the evidence of less reliable witnesses. It is well known that late and otherwise untrustworthy manuscripts do occasionally preserve original readings. But to accept the testimony of a less reliable witness, one must have substantive reasons that in effect neutralize the value of the more reliable documents.

Moreover, one must allow for the possibility that the original reading has not been preserved in any of our witnesses. The need for conjectural emendation is acute in the case of ancient writings for which we have few and poor manuscripts. The LXX books, in contrast, are attested by a large number of witnesses, some quite excellent, and it is therefore likely that the original reading in any one problem passage has indeed survived somewhere.

But "likely" is not the same as "certain." In Isaiah 53:2, for example, all Greek manuscripts, supported by the versions and the fathers, read, ἀνηγγείλαμεν ἐναντίον αὐτοῦ ὡς παιδίον ("we brought a report before him as a child"). This reading not only makes poor sense, but it is also unexplainable as a translation of the Hebrew: וַיַּעַל כַּיּוֹנֵק לְפָנָיו ("and he grew up like a plant before him"). Since the word יוֹנֵק can mean "infant," the rendering παιδίον is understandable, but the verb עָלָה (lit., "to go up") is extremely common, and the translator of Isaiah elsewhere renders it correctly (see especially 55:13). Once we remember, however, that the verb ἀναγγέλλειν is sometimes confused with the similar verb ἀνατέλλειν,[36] the answer becomes obvious. The original translator rendered וַיַּעַל with ἀνέτειλε μέν, but at a very early stage in the transmission, under the influence of the context (v. 1 speaks of a report, ἀκοῇ), a scribe confused ANETEIΛEMEN with ANHΓΓEIΛAMEN, and this variant spread throughout the whole tradition.

We should reiterate, in summary, that responsible use of the LXX requires careful attention to the complicated history of its transmission. Too many scholars in the past have consulted the editions of Rahlfs or Swete as though they were more or less identical with the original text. Conclusions reached on that basis can hardly inspire confidence.

35. Eugene C. Ulrich Jr., *The Qumran Text of Samuel and Josephus* (Harvard Semitic Monographs 19; Missoula, Mont.: Scholars Press, 1978), 106–7.

36. For examples in Isaiah, see Ziegler, *Isaias*, 99.

To Continue Your Study

On pages 138–45 we reproduce four pages from standard critical editions of the Septuagint (presented in chronological order). To assist students in learning how to use these editions, we identify the major sections found in each edition (labeled with capital letters) and highlight a few elements (labeled with arabic numerals). The key on the page facing each Septuagint page includes instructive comments about each of these elements.

Almost as an afterthought, the last chapter in Henry Barclay Swete's *Introduction to the Old Testament in Greek*, 2d ed. (Cambridge: Cambridge University Press, 1914; repr. Peabody, Mass.: Hendrickson, 1989), 478–97, is devoted to textual problems in the LXX. Not only this work, but most other introductions, seem to assume that the reader has some prior training in the textual criticism of Greek literature, presumably from the study of the classics or of the NT. Indeed, to gain familiarity with textual transmission, scribal practices, and methodological issues, it is almost essential that the student be familiar with introductory textbooks like Bruce M. Metzger, *The Text of the New Testament: Its Transmission, Corruption, and Restoration*, 3d ed. (New York: Oxford University Press, 1992); and Frederick G. Kenyon, *The Text of the Greek Bible*, 3d ed. rev. by A. W. Adams (London: Duckworth, 1975).

Responsible use of the LXX, however, requires systematic study of the special problems that arise in the transmission of this document. In the absence of a textbook on the textual criticism of the LXX, the student should consult essays that address this topic along general lines (e.g., Harry M. Orlinsky, "On the Present State of Proto-Septuagint Studies," *Journal of the American Oriental Society* 61 [1941]: 81–91) and specialized articles that discuss concrete textual problems (e.g., Henry S. Gehman, "Some Types of Errors of Transmission in the LXX," *Vetus Testamentum* 3 [1953]: 397–400).

Special note should be made of Peter Katz, author of the magisterial essay, "Septuagintal Studies in the Mid-Century: Their Links with the Past and Their Present Tendencies," in *The Background of the New Testament and Its Eschatology: In Honour of Charles Harold Dodd*, ed. W. D. Davies and David Daube (Cambridge: Cambridge University Press, 1956), 176–208, reprinted in *Studies in the Septuagint: Origins, Recensions, and Interpretations*, ed. Sidney Jellicoe (New York: Ktav, 1974), 21–53. More technical, but indispensable for specialized research, is Katz's posthumous work, *The Text of the Septuagint: Its Corruptions and Their Emendation*, ed. David W. Gooding (Cambridge: Cambridge University Press, 1973).

13. Larger Cambridge Septuagint

ΓΕΝΕΣΙΣ

XXXI 3

38 ὃ ἐλέπισεν ποικίλον.¶ [38]καὶ παρέθηκεν τὰς ῥάβδους ἃς ἐλέπισεν ἐν ταῖς ληνοῖς τῶν ποτιστηρίων (A) 1
τοῦ ὕδατος, ἵνα ὡς ἂν ἔλθωσιν τὰ πρόβατα πιεῖν, ἐνώπιον τῶν ῥάβδων καὶ ἐλθόντων αὐτῶν εἰς (¶ L) 2
39 τὸ πιεῖν, ἐνκισσήσωσιν (39)τὰ πρόβατα εἰς τὰς ῥάβδους. [39]καὶ ἔτικτον τὰ πρόβατα διάλευκα
40 καὶ ποικίλα καὶ σποδοειδῆ ῥαντά. [40]τοὺς δὲ ἀμνοὺς διέστειλεν Ἰακώβ, καὶ ἔστησεν ἐναντίον
τῶν προβάτων κριὸν διάλευκον καὶ πᾶν ποικίλον ἐν τοῖς ἀμνοῖς· καὶ διεχώρισεν ἑαυτῷ ποίμνια
A 41 καθ' ἑαυτόν, καὶ οὐκ ἔμιξεν αὐτὰ εἰς τὰ πρόβατα Λαβάν. [41]ἐγένετο δὲ ἐν τῷ καιρῷ ᾧ ἐνεκίσσων
τὰ πρόβατα ἐν γαστρὶ λαμβάνοντα, ἔθηκεν Ἰακὼβ τὰς ῥάβδους ἐναντίον τῶν προβάτων ἐν ταῖς
42 ληνοῖς, τοῦ ἐνκισσῆσαι αὐτὰ κατὰ τὰς ῥάβδους· [42]ἡνίκα γὰρ ἔτεκον τὰ πρόβατα, οὐκ ἐτίθει·
43 ἐγένετο δὲ τὰ ἄσημα τοῦ Λαβάν, τὰ δὲ ἐπίσημα τοῦ Ἰακώβ. [43]καὶ ἐπλούτησεν ὁ ἄνθρωπος
σφόδρα σφόδρα· καὶ ἐγένετο αὐτῷ κτήνη πολλὰ καὶ βόες καὶ παῖδες καὶ παιδίσκαι καὶ κάμηλοι
καὶ ὄνοι.
XXXI 1 [1]Ἤκουσεν δὲ Ἰακὼβ τὰ ῥήματα τῶν υἱῶν Λαβὰν λεγόντων Εἴληφεν Ἰακὼβ πάντα τὰ τοῦ
2 πατρὸς ἡμῶν, καὶ ἐκ τῶν τοῦ πατρὸς ἡμῶν πεποίηκεν πᾶσαν τὴν δόξαν ταύτην. [2]καὶ εἶδεν
3 Ἰακὼβ τὸ πρόσωπον Λαβάν, καὶ ἰδοὺ οὐκ ἦν πρὸς αὐτὸν ὡς ἐχθὲς καὶ τρίτην ἡμέραν. [§3]εἶπεν (§ d_2) 3

B 38 ελεπεισεν E | αυτων] αυτον E* (ω suprascr Eᵃ) | εκκισσησωσιν E 39 σποδοειδη] δη suprascr A¹ ᶠᶜᵗ 41 εν 2°] ν sup ras Aᵃ | εγκισσησαι E XXXI 1 πατρος 1°] π rescr Aᵈ | εκ των sup ras Aᵃ 2 ειδεν] ειδ sup ras (6) A¹: ιδεν E

C E(L)M a–xc_2(d_2) 𝔄𝔅ℭᶜ𝔈𝔏ʳ 4 5 6

D 38 om και 1° m | τας 1°—ελεπισεν] om 𝔈ᵖ: om ας ελεπισεν 𝔈ᶜᶠ | ελεπτυσεν n | εν—υδατος] *in alueis aquaris in quibus adaquabantur oues* 𝔏 | om εν c_2 | ταις] τοις bfmnpquvw Chr | των ποτιστηριων] των ποτηριων ej(txt)w: του ποτιστηριου l | του υδατος] *ouium* 𝔅ᵖ: om ℭ: +*ouium* 𝔅ˡʷ | ελθωσιν] ελθη dp | om τα προβατα 1° 𝔏 | πιειν 1°] πινειν egjn | om ενωπιον—πιειν 2° c𝔅 | ενωπιον των ραβδων] *coram eis essent uirgae* 𝔈 | και 2°—ενκισσησωσιν] ενκισσησωσιν ελθοντων αυτων εις το πιειν afkmoxc_2𝔄 [[ενκισσ.] pr και f: εγκισσωσιν a: ενκισησουσιν m | ελθοντων] +δε fm]] | om και 2°—πιειν 2° ℭ | om και 2° EMb deg–jln–x𝔏 Chr Cyr | ελθοντων αυτων] *ubi uenerunt oues* 𝔈 | ⟨om εις το 25⟩ | πιειν 2°] πινειν dkp | ενκισσησωσιν] εγκισσησουσι l: εγγισωσι d: ενεκισσον i*: om c | τα προβατα 2°] pr ενεκισσησεν km: pr και ενεκισσων f𝔄: pr και ενεκισσησεν aco (-σαν)xc_2: pr τα προβατα εις τας ραβδους και ενεκισσων Mgj𝔅ˡʷ Chr: pr τα προβατα εις τας ραβδους και ελθοντων εις το πιειν ενεκισσων E(εκισσησαν)iᵃrsᵗˣᵗ⁺ᵐᵍ(om και): *oues ad uirgas et ubi uenerunt oues bibere conceperunt* ℭ: *ad similitudinem uirgarum et ubi uenerunt et biberunt conceperunt* 𝔈ᶜᶠ: om 𝔈ᵖ | τας 2°] τους v

39 om και 1° 𝔈ᵖ | τα προβατα] om p: om τα Cyr-cod: +ποικιλα E | διαλευκα—ραντα] *subalba et maculosa et uaria* 𝔄 | διαλευκα] pr τα c: *albas* 𝔏 | om και ποικιλα 𝔅ᵖ | ποικιλα—ραντα] *coloris cinerei et uaria* 𝔈

40 τους δε] και τους h Chr: om δε Ej | εστησεν] εθηκεν a–do ps(txt)twc_2𝔏 Cyr-ed | εναντιον—κριον] *eas coram arietibus* 𝔈 | κριον] pr *et* 𝔄: om c_2: +*et* 𝔏 | παν—αμνοις] *coloris fusci* 𝔈ᵖ: *coloris albi* 𝔈ᶜ: om 𝔈ᶠ | παν ποικιλον] παμποικιλον efgj: om παν m | αμνοις] +λαβαν achᵇmxc_2: +του λαβαν o | εαυτω] αυτω finorsc_2: αυτοις a: om 𝔈 | ποιμνιον ir(uid)x Chr | καθ εαυτον] καθ εαυτην l: ⟨κατα μονας 32⟩: om 𝔅 | λαβαν] pr του Cyr-ed

41 καιρω] +εκεινω dfhmnpt | ω] pr εν ⟨25⟩ Chr: ως mn: ως αν dp: om fi*(uid) | ενεκισσων] ενεκισσησαν o: ενεκισσησε acmtxc_2: εκισσησε d: εγγυσσησον p(γγυ ex corr) | προβατα] +τα c_2 | (εθηκεν] pr και f: εστησεν j(mg): +δε Eb) 7 | ενωπιον ir | om εν ταις ληνοις Chr | ταις] τοις bfmpw | ληνοις] αρνοις m | om του mc_2 | αυτα] αυτας m: ⟨αυτω 25⟩: *oues* 𝔅 | om κατα w | ⟨τας ραβδους 2°] των ραβδων 20⟩ 8

42 ηνικα γαρ] (*et cum* 𝔄𝔈𝔏) | γαρ A] δε E*(uid)dkpt𝔅ᵖℭ: δαν EᵃM rell Chr Cyr: om 𝔅ˡʷ | ετεκον τα προβατα] *coepissent oues parere* 𝔏 | ετεκον AEbhimrw] ετικτεν dfkpt𝔄 Chr: ετεκεν M rell Cyr | ουκ] ουκετι m | ετεθη i* | εγενετο δε] και ην Org r | τα ασημα—ιακωβ] *omnia in quibus signum Iacob et in quibus non signum Laban* 𝔈 | του 1°] pr τα n*: τω El: om m | τα δε επισημα] *et notate* 𝔏 | του 2°] τω El

43 ο ανθρωπος] ο ανηρ fir: *Iacob* 𝔈 | σφοδρα 2°] σφοδρως ⟨20⟩ Chr: om fhmnc_2ℭ Cyr-ed ½ | εγενοντο bhnpw Cyr-ed | om αυτω m | και βοες] post παιδισκαι k: om και E𝔏: +*et oues* 𝔈ᵖ | και παιδες] παιδες τε Cyr ½: om και Mhjln–qtu𝔄-ed | παιδισκαι και παιδες acmx | om και 6°—ονοι Chr | om και 6° Mdeg hjln–qs–v𝔄 Cyr ½ | ονοι] +και ημιονοι bw Cyr-ed ½

XXXI 1 om τα ρηματα fir | om λαβαν e | λεγοντων] +τα ρηματα ταυτα fir | ειληφεν] pr οτι v𝔄(uid): + δε n* | om τα 2° Edps Cyr-cod ½ | και—ημων 2°] om d𝔏(hab *et* int lin): om εκ—ημων lm | εκ των] *ex omnibus* 𝔅: om των Efpvx* | πεποιηκεν] εποιησεν Edfipr: ⟨πεπλουτηκε 32⟩: +εαυτω k𝔄ℭ | om πασαν Cyr-cod | ταυτην] om egj: +εκειθεν l

2 om το προσωπον n𝔈 | το] ⸸ +ras (1) b | λαβαν] pr το aq*u: pr του bcegj–oqᵃ¹twxc_2 | και ιδου] οτι E𝔅𝔈: om ιδου f | προς αυτον] pr *facies eius* 𝔈: προσωπον αυτου j(mg)qs(mg)u: το προσωπον αυτου v Cyr ½: om Cyr-cod ½ | ως] ωσει qu: καθως Cyr ½ | εχθες AEMaiors] χθες rell

E 38 ινα—ενκισσησωσιν] σ' οπως ερχομενων των βοσκηματων πιειν αντικρυς ωσιν των βοσκηματων και εγκισσηση ελθοντα πιειν M

41 εν τω—ραβδους 1°] σ' παντοτε οταν ενεκισσων τα βοσκηματα πρωιμα ετιθει ιακωβ τας ραβδους Msv [[om σ' sv | εκισσων s | βοσκ. πρωιμα] προβατα s | ραβδους] +τας χλωρας v]] | εν γαστρι λαμβανοντα] α' αντι του πρωιμα καταδεδεμενοις M(indice ad (42) επισημα posito)s(sine nom)

42 ηνικα—ετιθει] σ' οποτε (αποτε js) δε ην οψιμα τα βοσκηματα ουκ ετιθει Mjsv(sine nom) | ηνικα γαρ ετεκον] α' και εν δευτερογονοις Mjs | (ασημα] α' οψιμα Mjs: σ' δευτερογονα M(pr τα)js(sine nom)) 9

83 II—2

source: Alan E. Brooke and Norman McLean, *The Old Testament in Greek according to the Text of Codex Vaticanus*, vol. 1: *The Octateuch*, part 1: *Genesis* (Cambridge: Cambridge University Press, 1906), 83.

Key to Illustration 13 (Genesis 30:37–31:3)

Major Sections

A the Greek text of Genesis, based on a principal manuscript (in this case, Codex Alexandrinus)

B spelling variations (itacisms), minor errors, and scribal corrections in the principal manuscript and a few other uncials; also readings of the principal manuscript that were not adopted in the text

C a list of witnesses quoted in the apparatus for this page; parentheses indicate that a witness is extant for only part of the text printed on the page

D main apparatus, listing substantial variants from the uncials, numerous cursives, daughter versions, and ancient writers (Philo, Josephus, and important Christian writers)

E secondary apparatus, listing the readings of the Hexaplaric versions as preserved in the margins of some manuscripts and in the Syro-Hexaplar

Notes

1. The letter A at the top of the margin indicates that Codex Alexandrinus is the principal manuscript, that is, the manuscript that supplies the text for this page.
2. Manuscript L ends (indicated by ¶) at this point: for this page, this fragmentary manuscript contains only the last words of 30:37 (however, it contains text for subsequent parts of the book).
3. Manuscript d_2 begins (indicated by §) at this point: for this page, this fragmentary manuscript contains only the first word of 31:3 (however, it contains text for previous parts of the book).
4. Uncials are indicated with capital letters.
5. Cursives are indicated with lowercase letters; in the Larger Cambridge edition, a dash indicates inclusiveness (here, all manuscripts between a and x).
6. Ancient versions are indicated with Gothic letters.
7. In 30:41, cursive f has και εθηκεν; the margin of cursive j has εστησεν; uncial E and cursive b have εθηκεν δε.
8. The evidence of the ancient versions is often given in Latin.
9. In 30:42, according to marginal notations in uncial M and cursives j and s, Aquila has οψιμα instead of ασημα; according to M, Symmachus has τα δευτερογονα at this point (j and s give δευτερογονα without attributing this rendering to a specific name).

14. Rahlfs's Septuagint

627 **REGNORUM III** 2 1—11

1Καὶ ἤγγισαν αἱ ἡμέραι Δαυιδ ἀποθανεῖν αὐτόν, καὶ ἐνετείλατο 2
τῷ Σαλωμων υἱῷ αὐτοῦ λέγων 2Ἐγώ εἰμι πορεύομαι ἐν ὁδῷ πά- 2
σης τῆς γῆς· καὶ ἰσχύσεις καὶ ἔσῃ εἰς ἄνδρα 3καὶ φυλάξεις τὴν 3
φυλακὴν κυρίου τοῦ θεοῦ σου τοῦ πορεύεσθαι ἐν ταῖς ὁδοῖς αὐτοῦ φυλάσσειν τὰς ἐντολὰς αὐτοῦ καὶ τὰ δικαιώματα καὶ τὰ κρί-
ματα τὰ γεγραμμένα ἐν νόμῳ Μωυσέως, ἵνα συνίῃς ἃ ποιήσεις
κατὰ πάντα, ὅσα ἂν ἐντείλωμαί σοι, 4ἵνα στήσῃ κύριος τὸν λόγον 4
αὐτοῦ, ὃν ἐλάλησεν λέγων Ἐὰν φυλάξωσιν οἱ υἱοί σου τὴν ὁδὸν
αὐτῶν πορεύεσθαι ἐνώπιον ἐμοῦ ἐν ἀληθείᾳ ἐν ὅλῃ καρδίᾳ αὐτῶν
καὶ ἐν ὅλῃ ψυχῇ αὐτῶν, λέγων Οὐκ ἐξολεθρευθήσεταί σοι ἀνὴρ
ἐπάνωθεν θρόνου Ισραηλ. 5καί γε σὺ ἔγνως ὅσα ἐποίησέν μοι 5
Ιωαβ υἱὸς Σαρουιας, ὅσα ἐποίησεν τοῖς δυσὶν ἄρχουσιν τῶν δυνά-
μεων Ισραηλ, τῷ Αβεννηρ υἱῷ Νηρ καὶ τῷ Αμεσσαϊ υἱῷ Ιεθερ,
καὶ ἀπέκτεινεν αὐτοὺς καὶ ἔταξεν τὰ αἵματα πολέμου ἐν εἰρήνῃ
A καὶ ἔδωκεν αἷμα ἀθῷον ἐν τῇ ζώνῃ αὐτοῦ τῇ ἐν τῇ ὀσφύι αὐτοῦ
καὶ ἐν τῷ ὑποδήματι αὐτοῦ τῷ ἐν τῷ ποδὶ αὐτοῦ· 6καὶ ποιήσεις 6
κατὰ τὴν σοφίαν σου καὶ οὐ κατάξεις τὴν πολιὰν αὐτοῦ ἐν εἰρήνῃ εἰς ᾅδου. 7καὶ τοῖς υἱοῖς Βερζελλι τοῦ Γαλααδίτου ποιήσεις 7
ἔλεος, καὶ ἔσονται ἐν τοῖς ἐσθίουσιν τὴν τράπεζάν σου, ὅτι οὕτως
ἤγγισάν μοι ἐν τῷ με ἀποδιδράσκειν ἀπὸ προσώπου Αβεσσαλωμ
τοῦ ἀδελφοῦ σου. 8καὶ ἰδοὺ μετὰ σοῦ Σεμεϊ υἱὸς Γηρα υἱὸς τοῦ 8
Ιεμενι ἐκ Βαουριμ, καὶ αὐτὸς κατηράσατό με κατάραν ὀδυνηρὰν
τῇ ἡμέρᾳ, ᾗ ἐπορευόμην εἰς Παρεμβολάς, καὶ αὐτὸς κατέβη εἰς
ἀπαντήν μου εἰς τὸν Ιορδάνην, καὶ ὤμοσα αὐτῷ ἐν κυρίῳ λέγων
Εἰ θανατώσω σε ἐν ῥομφαίᾳ· 9καὶ οὐ μὴ ἀθῳώσῃς αὐτόν, ὅτι 9
ἀνὴρ σοφὸς εἶ σὺ καὶ γνώσῃ ἃ ποιήσεις αὐτῷ, καὶ κατάξεις τὴν
πολιὰν αὐτοῦ ἐν αἵματι εἰς ᾅδου. 10καὶ ἐκοιμήθη Δαυιδ μετὰ τῶν 10
πατέρων αὐτοῦ καὶ ἐτάφη ἐν πόλει Δαυιδ. 11καὶ αἱ ἡμέραι, ἃς ἐβα- 11
σίλευσεν Δαυιδ ἐπὶ τὸν Ισραηλ, τεσσαράκοντα ἔτη· ἐν Χεβρων
ἐβασίλευσεν ἔτη ἑπτὰ καὶ ἐν Ιερουσαλημ τριάκοντα τρία ἔτη. 1

2 1 αυτον > *O* | ενετειλ.] απεκρινατο B*O*† | τω > B || 3 την > B† | κυ- 2
ριου του] > B†, του > *O* | δικαιωμ.] + αυτου *O*† | κριματα] + ※και τα μαρ-
τυρια αυτου *O* | νομω] pr. τω *OL*† | συνιης *O*] συνησεις B* (Bc -σης) | αν > *O* 3
|| 4 ελαλ.] + περι εμου *OL* | αυτων $2^0 \frown 3^0$ B | θρονου] pr. του *OL* ||
5 εποι. μοι] tr. A† | τω 1^0 > B† | αμεσσαι (cf. II 17 25)] -σσαια B†, αμμεσα A†
| εν ειρ. και εδ. αιμα αθ.] > B, in *O* sub ※ || 6 ου] συ B, > Orig. (Rahlfs
B Sept.-Stud. 1 [1904], p. 78) || 7 με > A || 8 ιεμεινει B†: cf. 35^1 | βαουριμ
compl.] βαθουρ. A, βααθουρ. B; γαβααθουρ. $L^{p\dagger}$: cf. 35^1 | απαντησιν *OL* ||
11 εν ιερουσ.] + εβασιλευσεν *O*, + εβασιλευσεν επι ισραηλ *L*† | τρια] pr. και *OL*
| fin.] + και σολομων εκαθισεν επι του θρονου δαυιδ του πατρος αυτου *L*†
(superaddit $L^{127\dagger}$ ετων δωδεκα: cf. 12): haec sunt prima uerba tertii Regnorum libri iuxta *L*† ab III 2 12 incipientis. cf. Regn. I subscr. et Regn. II
subscr.; post haec uerba hab. $L^{127\dagger}$ subscriptionem βασιλειων β′, ante 12
habent omnes editionis Luciani codices inscriptionem βασιλειων γ′

source: Alfred Rahlfs, *Septuaginta* (Stuttgart: Deutsche Bibelgesellschaft, 1935), 1.627.

Key to Illustration 14 (3 Reigns [1 Kings] 2:1–11)

Major Sections

A the Greek text of 3 Reigns, critically reconstructed by the editor (Alfred Rahlfs) based on the three great uncials: Vaticanus, Sinaiticus, and Alexandrinus

B brief apparatus, limited mainly to noting variations among the three great uncials and the major recensions

Notes

1. In 2:1, Vaticanus and Origen's recension have απεκρινατο instead of ενετειλατο; the superscript dagger indicates that, at the most, one additional minuscule may support this reading.
2. In 2:4, Vaticanus omits the words και εν ολη ψυξη αυτων through haplography (i.e., between the second and third occurrences of αυτων).
3. In 2:5, Vaticanus and Origen's recension (the latter marked by an asterisk) omit the clause εν ειρηνη και εδωκεν αιμα αθωον.

15. Göttingen Isaiah

52_{13}—53_{3} ΗΣΑΙΑΣ 320

A

13 [13]Ἰδοὺ συνήσει ὁ παῖς μου καὶ ὑψωθήσεται καὶ δοξασθήσεται
14 σφόδρα. [14]ὃν τρόπον ἐκστήσονται ἐπὶ σὲ πολλοί, οὕτως ἀδοξήσει
ἀπὸ ἀνθρώπων τὸ εἶδός σου καὶ ἡ δόξα σου ἀπὸ τῶν ἀνθρώπων,
15 [15]οὕτως θαυμάσονται ἔθνη πολλὰ ἐπ' αὐτῷ, καὶ συνέξουσι βασιλεῖς
τὸ στόμα αὐτῶν· ὅτι οἷς οὐκ ἀνηγγέλη περὶ αὐτοῦ, ὄψονται, καὶ οἳ
1 οὐκ ἀκηκόασι, συνήσουσι. **53** [1]κύριε, τίς ἐπίστευσε τῇ ἀκοῇ ἡμῶν;
2 καὶ ὁ βραχίων κυρίου τίνι ἀπεκαλύφθη; [2]ἀνέτειλε μὲν ἐναντίον αὐτοῦ
ὡς παιδίον, ὡς ῥίζα ἐν γῇ διψώσῃ, οὐκ ἔστιν εἶδος αὐτῷ οὐδὲ δόξα·
3 καὶ εἴδομεν αὐτόν, καὶ οὐκ εἶχεν εἶδος οὐδὲ κάλλος· [3]ἀλλὰ τὸ εἶδος

B

534 Tht.; *προ προσωπον* S Just. ⊙: cf. 𝔐 | *ὑμῶν*] *ημ.* 311′-86^{c}; *υπερ ημων* 36 | *κύριος*1⁰] pr. *ο* 62 | om. *καί* 87* 534 | om. *ὁ*1⁰ 22-93 *C* Cyr.^{lem} | *συναγων* S* Q 407 Eus.ecl. Cyr.; *επισυναγαγων* 456 534 | om. *ὑμᾶς* V | om. *κύριος*2⁰ *O''* L'^{n-36}-233-456 *C* 403′ 407 449′ 534 538 544 Eus.comm.et ecl. Tht. Hi. = 𝔐 | om. *ὁ*2⁰ *O''* 147-233-456 534 538 544 Eus.comm.et ecl. Tht. **13** om. *μου* 49* | *ὑψωθήσ.* et *δοξασθήσ.*] tr. 309* Syp | *δοξασθήσεται* Just.] +(※ 449′) *και μετεωρισθησεται* 106 V-88-*oII* L'^{n}-86^{c}-233 *C* 239′ 403′ 407 449′ Syp(post *σφόδρα* tr.) Or.I 105 Eus.comm.et ecl. Tht. = 𝔐↓ **14** *ἐπὶ σὲ/ πολλοί*] tr. L'^{n}-233 449′ Just. Tht. Tert.III 404; *επι σοι π.* 26 V 407 Eus. ecl. Cyr.; *επι με π.* Syp | *οὕτως*]-*τος* 36 91; > Syp | *αδοξασουσιν* 544 | *ἀνθρώπων*1⁰] pr. *των* 311′ C^{-91} 403′ | *σου*1⁰] *αυτου* Syp = 𝔐 | om. *καὶ ἡ δόξα σου* Syp | *τῶν ἀνθρώπων*] pr. *των* (> 86 88 Tht.) *υιων* 86-106 V-*oI* L^{n}-147 -233-456 *cII* 403′ 407 449′ 538 Syp Eus. Tht. Hi. = 𝔐: cf. 53_{3}; *υιων ανθρ.* *oII* *C* 239′ **15** *αὐτῷ*]-*τον* 86* | *συναξουσι(ν)* A *oI* 410 | *βασιλεῖς*] + *επ αυτω* Syp | *ακοασι(ν)* V 22

53 1 *τίνι*] pr.(※) *επι* 88 = 𝔐↓ | *απεκαλυφη* S* **2** *ἀνέτειλε μέν* scripsi: cf. praef. p. 99] *ανηγγειλαμεν* codd.gr.et verss.et traditio patristica | *ἐναντίον* (*ενωπιον* Eus.dem. Tht.) *αὐτοῦ / ὡς π.* Just. Tert.III 244.404 Cypr.] tr. *O''* *C* 403′ 407 Syp(pr. *αυτον*) Eus.comm.et ecl. Hi. = 𝔐 | *παιδίον*] *πεδιον* S* 86*-106 *oII* 48^{c}-51^{c}-90-36 87-91^{c}-309-764 Cyr. ○; *pueri* Cypr. | *ὡς*2⁰] *εν* 763 | *ριζαν* 565 | *οὐκ*1⁰] pr. *et* Tert. Cypr. | *εἶδος αὐτῷ*] tr. Q Syp ⊙; *ειδ. αυτου* 407 456 Eus.ecl. Tert. Cypr.: cf. 3 | *οὐδέ*1⁰] *ουτε* S Cyr.^{lem} ⊙ | om.

1

2

C

σεσθε Q | *ἐπισυνάγων*] *α′ συλλεγων* 86 **13** *Ἰδού — μου*] *εβρ′ ιννη ιεσχι⟨λ⟩ αβδι* Chr.; *α′ ιδου επιστημονισθησεται δουλος μου* (*σ′ δουλος μου* Pr.) Eus. Chr. | *δοξασθήσεται*] *α′σ′θ′ επαρθησεται και μετεωρισθησεται* 86; *οι γ′* + ※ *και μετεωρισθησεται* Q Chr. **14** *ὃν τρόπον — πολλοί*] *θ′ ον τροπον εθαυμασαν* (*α′ admirati sunt σ′ stupefacti sunt* Chr.) *πολλοι επ αυτον* Eus. | *οὕτως ἀδοξήσει*] *οι λ′ sic corrupta est* Chr. | *τὸ εἶδος — σου* 2⁰] *α′ ορασις αυτου και μορφη αυτου* 86 | *ἀπὸ τῶν ἀνθρ.*] *σ′ παρα τους υιους των ανθρωπων* 86 **15** *θαυμάσονται*] *α′θ′ ραντισει σ′ αποβα[λ]λει* 86 | *συνέξουσι — αὐτῶν*] *α′ συντελεσουσιν* (leg. *συστελουσιν* ?) 86; *α′ tegent* βασιλεις στομα αυτων Chr.

53 1 *τίνι*] *θ′ επι* (*α′θ′* ※ *επι* Q, Syh sub *α′σ′*) *τινα* 86 **2**] *α′ και αναβησεται* (*αναρρηθησεται* Eus. dem.) *ως τιθιζομενον* (*α′ ως τιτθ.* Q) *εις προσωπον αυτου και ως ριζα απο γης αβατου* (*α′ invia* Hi.; *α′ ως ρ. απο γης αβ.* Tht.) Eus. comm. et dem. p. 103sq. Chr.; *α′* ου μορφη αυτω και ου διαπρεπεια (*α′ διαπρεπεια* 86) Chr.; *σ′ και ανεβη ως κλαδος* (*σ′ ramus* Hi.) *ενωπιον αυτου* (*σ′* init. — αυτου Chr.) *και ως ριζα απο γης διψωσης ουκ ειδος αυτω ουδε αξιωμα* (*σ′* ουδε αξ. Chr.) *ινα ιδωμεν αυτον ουδε θεωρια ινα επιθυμησωμεν αυτον* 86 (om.

3

source: Joseph Ziegler, *Isaias*, 3d ed. (Septuaginta 14; Göttingen: Vandenhoeck & Ruprecht, 1983), 320.

Key to Illustration 15 (Isaiah 52:13–53:3)

Major Sections

A the Greek text of Isaiah, critically reconstructed by the editor (Joseph Ziegler)
B main apparatus, listing substantial variants from virtually all extant witnesses
C secondary apparatus, listing the readings of the Hexaplaric versions as preserved in the margins of some manuscripts, in the Syro-Hexaplar, and in ancient citations

Notes

1. In 52:14, three variations are recorded for the reading επι σε πολλοι:
   a. The following witnesses have the transposition πολλοι επι σε: the Lucianic tradition, 449′ (= mixed manuscripts 449 and 770), and three Christian writers. The symbol *L*′'` indicates the agreement of the major Lucianic group (*L*, five manuscripts) and three Lucianic subgroups (*lI*, two manuscripts; *lII*, three manuscripts; *lIII*, three manuscripts); manuscript 233 is an additional Lucianic witness not included within any of those groups.
   b. Instead of σε, the following witnesses have σοι: cursive 26, uncial V, cursive 407, and two Christian writers. The order in the listing of the Greek manuscripts reflects their respective importance, according to the editor.
   c. Instead of σε, the Syropalestinian has με.
2. Also in 52:14, two variations are recorded for the reading των ανθρωπων:
   a. The following witnesses have των υιων των ανθρωπων in conformity with the Masoretic Text (possibly influenced by 53:3): the closely related cursives 86 and 106 (note that the hyphen, in distinction from the Larger Cambridge edition, does *not* indicate all manuscripts between those numbers); uncial V and a closely related subgroup of the Hexaplaric tradition (*oI*); a large part of the Lucianic tradition (*L* '`); a subgroup of the Catena recension (*cII*); a number of cursives that have a mixed text; the Syropalestinian; and three Christian writers. Note, however, that cursives 86 and 88, as well as Theodoret, have υιων instead of των υιων.
   b. A subgroup of the Hexaplaric tradition (*oII*), the main group of the Catena recension (*C*), and 239′ (= 239 + 306) have υιων ανθρωπων.
3. In 52:13, cursive 86 records that Aquila, Symmachus, and Theodotion have επαρθησεται και μετεωρισθησεται instead of δοξασθησεται; according to uncial Q and Chrysostom, however, "the Three" (οι γ′) have δοξασθησεται και μετεωρισθησεται (the asterisk indicates that this reading is explicitly marked as an addition to Origen's text in conformity with the Hebrew).

16. Göttingen Genesis

95 *ΓΕΝΕΣΙΣ* **3**24—**4**4

Ἀδὰμ καὶ κατῴκισεν αὐτὸν ἀπέναντι τοῦ παραδείσου τῆς τρυφῆς, καὶ
ἔταξεν τὰ χερουβὶμ καὶ τὴν φλογίνην ῥομφαίαν τὴν στρεφομένην φυ-
λάσσειν τὴν ὁδὸν τοῦ ξύλου τῆς ζωῆς.
4 [1]*Ἀδὰμ δὲ ἔγνω Εὔαν τὴν γυναῖκα αὐτοῦ, καὶ συλλαβοῦσα ἔτεκεν* 1
A *τὸν Κάιν, καὶ εἶπεν Ἐκτησάμην ἄνθρωπον διὰ τοῦ θεοῦ.* [2]*καὶ προσέ-* 2
θηκεν τεκεῖν τὸν ἀδελφὸν αὐτοῦ τὸν Ἅβελ. καὶ ἐγένετο Ἅβελ ποιμὴν
προβάτων, Κάιν δὲ ἦν ἐργαζόμενος τὴν γῆν. [3]*καὶ ἐγένετο μεθ᾽ ἡμέρας* 3
ἤνεγκεν Κάιν ἀπὸ τῶν καρπῶν τῆς γῆς θυσίαν τῷ κυρίῳ, [4]*καὶ Ἅβελ* 4 — 1
ἤνεγκεν καὶ αὐτὸς ἀπὸ τῶν πρωτοτόκων τῶν προβάτων αὐτοῦ καὶ ἀπὸ

B A(DL)M (911) *O*′(376-) *C*′′ *bdf* 75 *styz* al verss (Ach Pal) Sa

C **24** *καί* 1°⌒2° Aeth^{C} Sa^{20} | *ἐξέβαλεν*] -*βαλλε* 646; + *κς ο θς* 53′-56^{mg} Chr VII 152 Aeth^{G}; + *ο θς* 72 129 392 Sa^{20} | *ἐξέβαλεν τόν*] *iactus est* Bo^{K}; *exivit* Bo^{L} | *κατῴκισεν*] -*κησεν* 15′-72-135*-426 16-18-422′-551-615*-646 *d* 129-246 75 *s* 74*-134*-799 121-318-527 *z*$^{-31}$ 55 59 319 | om *αὐτόν* 75 318 120′ 59 730 Phil I 170.1 | *τοῦ παραδείσου / τῆς τρυφῆς*] tr *C*′′$^{-16\ 18\ 78txt\ 79\ 128}$ *d* 56*-246 75 71-527 120′ 55 730 | om *τῆς τρυφῆς* L | *ἔταξεν / τὰ χερουβίμ*] tr 911(vid) | *τὰ χερουβίμ*] *krwba* Barh; om *τά* Bo^{K} | *χερουβειμ* M 135-400*-426 343-344* 121-424 122 55 = Ald; *χαιρουβημ* 75; *χεροβιμ* 664; [*χερου*]*βεῖ* 911; -*βιν* A Bo^{K} Sa; -*βειν* 17 | *ῥομφαίαν τήν*] tr 911(vid) | *τήν* 2°] *μετα* 55 | om *τὴν στρεφομένην* 121-424 31′ 54 | *φυλάσσειν*] *και φυλασσουσαν* Or I 33 (sed hab II 121) | om *τὴν ὁδόν* 130(spat 5 litt relict) | *εισοδον* Chr VII 152^{ap}

4 1 *εγνω δε Αδαμ* 346 319 BasSel 68 Epiph I 29 II 76 Or IV 302bis XII fragm 4 | *Εὔαν*] *εβαν* 664; > 72 77-569 130 Phil I 179.24 La^{E} (sed hab Ambr passim Chr III 908 Lib geneal 16ss^{te} Or *Matth* 55 Ruf *Rom* V 9 VII 8 Vulg) | *συλλαβοῦσα*] *συνελαβε(ν) και* A 129 318 Phil I 179.24 | *τὸν Κάιν*] pr *υιον* 314 Bo^{K}(+ *vocavit nomen eius*) ^{Lat}Ambr *Exh virg* 36 IulEcl in Aug *Nupt* II 17 FirmMat *Consult* III 5; *υιον* Anast 1069; om *τόν* Procop 233 | *εκτισαμην* 426 569 314 56-246* 54* | *ἄνθρωπον*] *υιον* Epiph II 76 | *τοῦ*] *κῦ* Epiph II 76

2 *καί* 1°] + *ως* 246 | *προσέθηκεν*] -*θετο* (-*θητο* 55*) 911 *O*′$^{-135}$ 18-128-413 *b d f*$^{-129}$ *t* 392′-424 31 54 55 59 Chr VII 154 | om *τόν* 2° 82 77 31 | *ἐγένετο*] + *ο* 527; *ην* Epiph II 401 | om *ἦν* 79 107 370* Epiph II 401 | om *τὴν γῆν* 422(|) — 2

3 om init — (*s*) fin 31^{txt}(c pr m) | *μετα* 426 | *ἤνεγκεν*] pr *και* 64^{c}-707 16 246 *s* | *του καρπου* Phil I 223.1^{ap} La^{E} (sed hab Ambr passim ClemR 4 Lib geneal 20) Arm | om *τῆς γῆς* BasSel 69 | *θυσίαν*] *δωρον* Phil I 223.2^{ap} | *τῷ*] pr *κῶ* 72 | *κῶ*] *θῶ* 72 422-551 125 129 121 122 509 Phil I 223.2^{UF} BasSel 69 ClemR 4 Ach Arm Sa ^{Lat}Tert *Adv Iud* 5 = Ald

4 om *καὶ αὐτός* Arab ^{Lat}ClemR 4 Lib geneal 20 Vulg | *προβατων των πρωτοτοκων* 527 | om *τῶν* 2° 78-569 76 | om *αὐτοῦ* 1° ClemR 4 ^{Lat}Ruf *Rom*

D **24** *τὰ χερουβίμ*] *α′* (inc) *ἑβρ′ χεροουι* 130 (vid); *τὸ ἑβρ′ ακχερουβιν* 400^{cat}; *α′ ἑβρ′ χερουβ* 344′

4 1 *ἔγνω*] *ἐπέγνω καὶ συνετίσθη* 130-344′ | *ἐκτησάμην* — fin] *ὁ ἑβρ′ ὁ συρ′ ἐκτησάμην ανον ἐν θῶ ὡς ἀνατιθέντος τὸν πρωτότοκον* (+ *τω* 135) *θῶ* 17-135^{cat}(s ind); *σ′ ἐκτησάμην ἄνθρωπον σὺν κυρίῳ ἕτερος· ἐκτησάμην ἄνθρωπον κύριον* Anast 1072 — 3

2 *προσέθηκεν τεκεῖν*] *σ′ πάλιν ἔτεκε(ν)* M 130 (s nom vid)-344′

source: John W. Wevers, *Genesis* (Septuaginta 1; Göttingen: Vandenhoeck & Ruprecht, 1974), 95.

Key to Illustration 16 (Genesis 3:24–4:4)

Major Sections

A the Greek text of Genesis, critically reconstructed by the editor (John W. Wevers)

B a list of the witnesses appearing on this page; parentheses indicate that a witness is extant for only part of the text printed on the page; note that this information does not appear in the earlier volumes of the Göttingen Septuagint (1–3 Maccabees, Psalms, the Prophets)

C main apparatus, listing substantial variants from virtually all extant witnesses

D secondary apparatus, listing the readings of the Hexaplaric versions as preserved in the margins of some manuscripts, in the Syro-Hexaplar, and in ancient citations

Notes

1. Lowercase italic letters indicate groups of closely related Greek manuscripts; e.g., *z* = cursives 31, 120, 122, and 407.
2. In 4:2, the following witnesses have προσεθετο instead of προσεθηκεν: the very important papyrus 911, the Origenic recension (with the exception [indicated by –, a minus sign] of cursive 135), a significant number of other cursives (including several groups), and Chrysostom; note that the original hand (indicated by *) of cursive 55 spells the verb προσεθητο.
3. In 4:1, according to Anastasius and cursive 1072, Symmachus gives Eve's words as συν κυριω (rather than δια του θεου), while another, unnamed translator renders κυριον as the predicate accusative of the verb.

7

Using the Septuagint for the Textual Criticism of the Hebrew Bible

The Transmission of the Hebrew Text. In spite of the remarkably accurate work of the Masoretes, scribal changes prior to the standardization of the Hebrew text need to be identified and evaluated. The LXX is our primary source for such data, and in some biblical books it may contain a significant number of textual variants that would have been present in its parent text. Scholars often disagree, however, about the value of the evidence.

The Septuagint versus the Masoretic Text. Assuming that the MT should function as our starting point, under what circumstances should we abandon one of its readings in favor of a variant in the LXX? Several important conditions need to be met before we can use the LXX to emend the MT.

The Greek Text of Samuel–Kings. The LXX books known as 1–4 Reigns present some peculiar problems that help to illustrate text-critical principles. The so-called *Kaige* sections of these books preserve a different translation from what we find in the other sections. Moreover, the Lucianic manuscripts offer an additional, distinctively different Greek text for the whole of 1–4 Reigns.

For the work of OT scholarship, the LXX can serve several purposes. One of them is philological: occasionally, the Greek translator's rendering can shed light on a rare Hebrew word or construction. Another function is more broadly exegetical: the LXX may be regarded as the earliest surviving interpretation of the Bible, and the exegesis of the translators, even when wrong, can be very valuable in our own exegetical process. By far the greatest significance of the LXX, however, has been its extensive use by scholars in the textual criticism of the Hebrew Bible. Why is this so?

The Transmission of the Hebrew Text

For the many students who have first developed familiarity with the NT text, the field of OT textual criticism can prove somewhat disorienting. In the case of the NT, we are delighted (even if sometimes overwhelmed) by the immense number of textual variants preserved in thousands of Greek manuscripts, to say nothing of the additional evidence from ancient versions, church fathers, and lectionaries. Although the transmission of the Greek NT was stabilized as early as the fourth century, leading to its standardization in a form known as the Byzantine Text, extensive (and not always rigorous) copying prior to that time gave rise to a multitude of competing readings. Even during the late medieval period, when most scribal activity had become much more disciplined, new variants continued to appear.

In striking contrast—if we leave aside for a moment the discoveries in Qumran and elsewhere in the Judean Desert—substantive variants among manuscripts of the Hebrew Bible are rare. These manuscripts, the earliest of which dates only to the ninth century, were produced by the Masoretes,[1] extraordinarily disciplined copyists whose scribal practices can be traced back to about the year 500 of our era. It is generally agreed that even earlier, by the second century, the whole text of the Hebrew Bible had reached a high level of standardization. This text is often referred to as pre-Masoretic not only because it preceded the work of the Masoretes but primarily because it already exhibited the basic form that we have come to identify as the MT.

Although detailed analysis of the Masoretic manuscripts reveals subtle differences and even groupings among them, the evidence consists almost exclusively of orthographic peculiarities (including vocalization), the presence or absence of the conjunction *wāw*, and other features that have no effect on the meaning of the text.[2] The remarkably faithful work of the Masoretes assures us that the form of their text takes us as far back as the late first century of our era, that is, the

1. From מָסַר, a verb meaning "to hand over, transmit."

2. See Moshe H. Goshen-Gottstein, "Hebrew Biblical Manuscripts: Their History and Their Place in the HUBP Edition," *Biblica* 48 (1967): 243–90; repr. in *Qumran and the History of the Biblical Text*, ed. Frank M. Cross and Shemaryahu Talmon (Cambridge: Harvard University Press, 1975), 42–89. On p. 278 he comments that the large number of readings in medieval manuscripts "melt into nothing, and the huge mass of variations does not finally yield a single variant which is significantly, decisively and undoubtedly connected with a pre-medieval tradition."

very beginnings of rabbinic Judaism as that movement developed after the destruction of Jerusalem in the year 70.

Wonderful as this picture of textual transmission is, however, it still leaves us with some crucial gaps where they count the most. It is well known that many significant variants typically arise in the first few generations of copyings, before readers realize how many changes are being introduced. From the time that, say, the prophecies of Isaiah were written down to the time of rabbinic standardization, more than eight centuries transpired. It is only reasonable to assume that competing forms of the Book of Isaiah would have existed during that long stretch. But where to find evidence of textual variation? Some can be found in rabbinic citations, yet such variants are scant and often late. The primary source consists of the ancient versions, and inasmuch as the LXX was the only translation of the whole Bible produced prior to the standardization of the pre-Masoretic Text,[3] it takes on unique importance.

Consider, for example, the Greek translator of Isaiah. Since he probably produced his translation during the second century B.C.E., the Hebrew manuscript (or manuscripts) he used had to be at least a millennium older than the oldest Masoretic manuscripts available to us, which means that this manuscript was produced at least three centuries prior to the rabbinic standardization of the text. This earlier manuscript was not identical to the MT available to us, and so the differences would be reflected in the Greek translation.

Comparison of MT Isaiah with LXX Isaiah does in fact reveal a large number of differences. Before we can use them to reconstruct the Hebrew text of Isaiah, however, we have to remove those that appear to be the result of the translator's own method of work. And as it turns out, the vast majority of the differences in Isaiah do *not* seem to have resulted from the use of a Hebrew parent text at variance with the MT.

But some are at least worth considering. In Isaiah 5:17, for instance, the MT says: "And sheep will graze as in their pasture, and in the ruins of the rich,[4] strangers [גָּרִים] will eat." The LXX translator, who had problems with this difficult verse, rendered the last phrase as ἄρνες φάγονται ("lambs will eat"), and on that basis many scholars reconstruct the Hebrew substantive as גְּדָיִם, from גְּדִי, which indeed means "kid, lamb." Three decisions—all of them reasonable but also

3. For the Pentateuch, of course, the Samaritan evidence is also available. Here again we are leaving out of account, momentarily, some recent discoveries, such as the Targum of Job in Qumran. It should also be noted that, among the other ancient versions, the Syriac (Peshitta) is of special value. In addition, we can often profit from quotations of the Bible in sources such as Philo, Josephus, the Book of Jubilees, and others.

4. Hebrew מֵחִים ("fatlings"); several interpretations of this passage have been proposed.

debatable—are involved in this reconstruction: (a) the LXX rendering is not the result of the translator's technique or imagination; (b) the translator's Hebrew manuscript had the consonant ד rather than ר—in other words, it was not merely a matter of the translator's misreading of the Hebrew; and (c) ד in the translator's Hebrew manuscript represented the original rather than a secondary reading.

For books other than Isaiah, the LXX translation offers a larger proportion of genuine variants, that is, readings that very likely reflect a *Vorlage* different from the MT. Unfortunately, scholars do not always agree on how much weight should be placed on the evidence of the LXX for the textual criticism of the Hebrew Bible. Many attribute these differences, in general, to the translation technique or creative work of the translator as he more or less deliberately deviated from his Hebrew parent text, which is presumed to have been a direct ancestor copy of the MT. For instance, John W. Wevers, editor of the Göttingen Pentateuch, writes:

> One should not automatically presuppose a different parent text when differences between the Greek and the Hebrew obtain; rather one should first seek for and pursue other explanations. It is only through such details that a picture of the attitudes, the theological prejudices, as well as of the cultural environment of these Jewish translators can emerge.[5]

Other scholars explain many of the differences between the Greek and Hebrew texts as deviations of the translator's Hebrew *Vorlage* from the MT that has come down to us. For instance, Anneli Aejmelaeus, director of the Septuaginta-Unternehmen in Göttingen, writes:

> The scholar who wishes to attribute deliberate changes, harmonizations, completion of details and new accents to the translator is under the obligation to prove his thesis with weighty arguments and also to show why the divergences cannot have originated with the *Vorlage*. That the translator *may* have manipulated his original does not mean that he necessarily did so. All that is known of the translation techniques employed in the Septuagint points firmly enough in the opposite direction.[6]

Of course, all LXX scholars recognize that the differences between the Hebrew and Greek texts derived almost certainly from a combination of (a) a variant *Vorlage*, (b) the deliberate work of the translator, and (c) transmission errors that occurred when both the Hebrew and

5. John W. Wevers, *Notes on the Greek Text of Deuteronomy* (SBLSCS 39; Atlanta: Scholars Press, 1995), xxii.

6. Anneli Aejmelaeus, *On the Trail of the Septuagint Translators* (Kampen: Kok Pharos, 1993), 92–93.

Greek texts were repeatedly copied. Competent scholars, however, disagree about how individual differences should be explained.

For instance, both Wevers and Aejmelaeus examine the variation between the Greek and Hebrew of Exodus 2:22 and arrive at different explanations. The MT says simply וַתֵּלֶד בֵּן ("and she bore a son"), while the Greek has a much fuller sentence, ἐν γαστρὶ δὲ λαβοῦσα ἡ γυνὴ ἔτεκεν υἱόν ("and after she conceived in her womb, the woman bore a son"). Wevers explains the added phrase as an embellishment originating with the translator's "fine biological logic."[7] Aejmelaeus, on the other hand, argues that the Greek preserves the original text of its *Vorlage* and that the Hebrew words corresponding to the additional Greek phrase were accidentally dropped from the MT.[8]

While a given scholar may tend toward one general explanation over the other, scholars in both camps recognize that each difference must be evaluated individually in light of the textual nature of the book in which it occurs. With frustrating frequency, even the most capable scholar will be unable to decide with certainty whether a given reading in the Greek is due to a variant parent text or to the work of the translator. Generally speaking, if a difference between the Hebrew and Greek can be easily explained by one of the several frequent types of mechanical errors scribes were known to make in copying the texts, that explanation is to be preferred over translation technique or literary creativity. On the other hand, if the difference is consistent with the translator's method of work, as evidenced in the book as a whole, then one would need weighty reasons to posit a variant parent text.

One must keep in mind that a Hebrew variant due to mechanical transmission errors is quite a different concept from a Hebrew *Vorlage* that reflects a different stage of literary development. In the former case, the variant is isolated to a specific reading. Even if a manuscript has many transmission errors, they arose more or less independently of each other (although sometimes one corrupt reading led a scribe to "fix" the text elsewhere). The corrected Hebrew text can be reconstructed from what is known about the kinds of errors scribes typically made when copying either the Hebrew or the Greek.

If, however, by a variant Hebrew *Vorlage* we mean a different literary stage of the book or the literary development of the book at the time it was translated into Greek, then the situation is much more complicated. The principles for identifying a variant Hebrew text due to deliberate lit-

7. John W. Wevers, *Notes on the Greek Text of Exodus* (SBLSCS 30; Atlanta: Scholars Press, 1990), 22.

8. Aejmelaeus, *Trail of the Septuagint Translators*, 102–3. For a different example of disagreements on this issue, see Martin Rösel, "The Text-Critical Value of Septuagint-Genesis," *BIOSCS* 31 (1998): 62–70, and the responses to this article by Ronald S. Hendel and William P. Brown in *BIOSCS* 32 (1999): 31–39.

erary development are not so clearly known. The deliberate revision of a biblical text introduces a discontinuity that breaks the genetic lineage of a text. In other words, if a variant reading came about by scribal error, the correct reading obviously preceded the error, and the error can be explained in a direct relationship to the original reading (e.g., transposition of letters, haplography, etc.). A reviser, on the other hand, may create new readings by paraphrasing the text or by omitting or adding to it in such a way that the resulting text cannot be so easily distinguished from or explained by the original reading.[9]

What needs to be appreciated, in any case, is the unique value of the LXX as a source of Hebrew textual variants. It would be fair to say that, in the majority of passages in the Hebrew Bible where a textual variant is suspected, the question comes down to a decision between the MT and the LXX. This is easily confirmed by noting the frequent use of LXX evidence in the apparatus to editions of the Hebrew Bible. The question then becomes, How do we decide between the readings of the MT and the variants reflected in the LXX?

The Septuagint versus the Masoretic Text

In the attempt to establish the text of the Hebrew Bible, most scholars use the MT as their point of departure. Some argue that such a method prejudges the issue, and that the problem is aggravated by the reality that all modern publications of the Hebrew Bible, timidly bowing to tradition, consist of diplomatic editions (i.e., they simply reproduce a specific manuscript) instead of providing an eclectic, critically reconstructed text.[10] According to these scholars, we should start from scratch and use all potential variants—and perhaps even conjectures unsupported by the documents—as having an equal claim to the text.

This proposal has serious theoretical problems, but even if we accepted the principles behind it, we would face too many practical obstacles. It may be partly true that the weight of tradition has played a role in the practice of publishing diplomatic editions of the Hebrew Bible, but a more fundamental reason is the number of serious difficulties involved in

9. For a good example of the complexities of explaining the differences between the Greek and Hebrew texts, see Dominique Barthélemy, David W. Gooding, Johan Lust, and Emanuel Tov, *The Story of David and Goliath: Textual and Literary Criticism: Papers of a Joint Research Venture* (Orbus biblicus et orientalis 73; Fribourg: Éditions Universitaires/Göttingen: Vandenhoeck & Ruprecht, 1986). See also below, chap. 8, pp. 177–82.

10. Up until the third edition of *Biblia hebraica*—when for the first time a printed edition was based on an actual manuscript, Leningrad Codex B19$_A$—the reigning text had been the 1525 Venice edition of Jacob ben Hayim. It has been reprinted as *Biblia rabbinica*, with an important introduction by Moshe H. Goshen-Gottstein (Jerusalem: Makor, 1972). This *textus receptus* was (to use Goshen-Gottstein's language) a subcrystallization of the Tiberian MT, that is, Aaron ben Asher's text.

producing an eclectic edition.[11] At any rate, for most biblical books the MT has preserved a demonstrably good text, and given its long lineage and uniformity, it can serve us well as the point of departure.

But even if we agree to use the MT as our starting point, just how much weight should be given to it? One finds a perplexing breadth of opinions on this issue. At one end are scholars who abandon the readings of the MT in favor of a LXX variant only as a matter of last recourse. Though they do not claim that the Masoretic tradition is perfect,[12] they place a very heavy burden of proof on those who support an alternate text. We should not be too quick to dismiss this approach, which is often motivated by scholarly integrity. In the view of these scholars, it is lazy and sloppy work to abandon a reading because it is difficult to understand; every effort should be made to solve the problem before concluding that it reflects a textual corruption. It can hardly be denied, however, that the proposed solutions sometimes give the appearance of grasping at straws. The principle at work seems to be, "Retain the MT reading if at all possible," but such an approach cannot be easily defended, and it is likely to lead us astray.

At the other end of the spectrum are scholars who treat the MT as an inferior, unreliable text and who are ready to abandon it at the slightest provocation. If the MT reading presents any kind of interpretative challenge, they readily adopt an easier variant reflected in the LXX or some other ancient version.[13] But even when the MT makes perfectly good sense, they are disposed to adopt a variant or even to conjecture a reading that, in their judgment, enhances the literary quality of the text. This approach was all the rage in the first half of the twentieth century; it has since become less common, but hardly extinct.

Between the two extremes, most OT textual critics today, it is probably safe to say, claim to assign equal weight to the MT and the LXX, thus avoiding preferential treatment. While such a formulation has the appearance of objectivity, it is, however, too vague to be of much value. Before it can be used at all, several conditions would have to be met:

11. See Emanuel Tov, *The Text-Critical Use of the Septuagint in Biblical Research*, 2d ed. (Jerusalem: Simor, 1997), 3–5. Tov, however, overestimates the differences between the textual criticism of the Hebrew Bible and that of other writings. Just because eclectic editions of a particular classical work have been successfully published, we should not infer that its text is more secure than the Hebrew Bible text.

12. Even in the view of the most theologically conservative scholars, whether Jewish or Christian, divine inspiration applies to the original writing of the Scriptures and does not extend to scribal activity. One can hardly deny, however, that belief in the divine preservation of Scripture has often—and not always in a salutary way—influenced text-critical decisions.

13. Often such decisions contradict the principle that variants typically arise to make the text easier (see above, chap. 6, pp. 128–31). When we reject a reading in the MT because it is difficult, we have the accompanying responsibility to give a reasonable explanation of why the MT reading arose.

- We need to assure ourselves that the LXX reading is not the result of interpretative thought or of carelessness in the process of translation.
- The proposed retroversion (i.e., the translation of the Greek back to the presumed Hebrew or Aramaic that lies behind it) should conform to rigorous criteria.[14]
- We should have good reason to believe that the presumed Hebrew/Aramaic reading truly existed in a manuscript and not only in the mind of the translator (whether by a mistake or by a conscious emendation).[15]
- If we decide that we are indeed dealing with a genuine variant, we ought to make a general assessment regarding the textual quality of both the MT and the LXX's *Vorlage* for that particular book.

This last point requires special emphasis. The viewpoint that claims to assign equal value to the MT and the LXX gives the impression of impartiality and objectivity, but it could just as easily reflect a failure to make a much-needed judgment on the available evidence. Suppose that, of one hundred selected genuine variants in the books of Samuel, seventy appear to be secondary readings in the MT over against the LXX, and that many of these are easily explained as omissions due to haplography. Does it make sense to give equal weight to both textual witnesses in other passages where the MT has a shorter text? Patently not. The unwillingness on the part of some scholars to take into account the general quality of textual witnesses may lead to atomistic, even haphazard, decisions on individual cases.[16]

Now for most books of the OT, the situation is quite different from what we find in Samuel. Generally speaking, the MT can be shown to

14. For this difficult matter, see especially Tov, *Text-Critical Use of the Septuagint*, chap. 3.

15. Scholars seldom reflect on how difficult it is to make such a determination. Others dismiss it as an unimportant question (Aejmelaeus, *Trail of the Septuagint Translators*, 87). The issue is, however, crucial if we wish to make a decision regarding the original form of the Hebrew. To use the example of Isa. 5:17, discussed earlier: it is wholly reasonable to suppose that the *Vorlage* had ר (גָּרִים) and that the translator either (a) made a visual mistake, thinking ר was really ד, or (b) decided that his *Vorlage* was wrong and in his mind emended it. One's determination must be based on thorough familiarity with the translator's propensities. In the case of Greek Isaiah, which often treats the text quite freely, one ought to be especially careful.

16. Some scholars argue that, while statistics regarding textual witnesses may have some general validity, such information is not relevant for the evaluation of individual readings. But how can statistical information be valid if it cannot be used? If a doctor tells a patient that his or her chances of surviving a disease are 20% with medicine but 80% with surgery, should that information not influence the patient's decision? The truth is that almost every decision we make every day of our lives—such as whether to hold a picnic in view of a 95% probability of rain—is (rightly) influenced by some sort of statistical information.

reflect a text superior to that of the LXX's parent text, meaning that in a majority of demonstrable cases, the readings of the LXX appear to be secondary. This is no proof, of course, that in any one particular case the LXX reading must be secondary. What it does mean is that our various documents have not preserved equally good texts and that the general, relative quality of the witnesses should therefore play a role—and a significant role at that—in individual decisions.

The likelihood that a difference in the LXX represents a genuine variant increases significantly if we can verify the reading in a Hebrew manuscript. Retroversions are always hypothetical,[17] and even though in some cases they are probably reliable (especially if the translation for the particular book is very literal and uniform), one feels much more confident if they can be confirmed by actual Hebrew texts. For example, MT Isaiah 29:3 reads, "And I will encamp like a circle about you." The word *circle* translates Hebrew דוּר, a rare word of uncertain meaning. The LXX at this point reads Δαυιδ = דָּוִד, a reading attested in two medieval Hebrew manuscripts and accepted, for instance, by the NRSV: "And like David I will encamp against you." While the evidence of the medieval manuscripts does not prove that the *Vorlage* of the LXX also had the name David,[18] it certainly strengthens the argument.

The discoveries in the Judean Desert, to be discussed in the next chapter, have provided even stronger confirmation in many cases. A clear example is Deuteronomy 31:1, where the MT has וַיֵּלֶךְ מֹשֶׁה וַיְדַבֵּר ("and Moses went and spoke"). The LXX, however, reads, συνετέλεσε Μωυσης λαλῶν ("Moses finished speaking"), which suggests that the translator read the first word as וַיְכַל.[19] Before reaching a conclusion on this variant, it may be helpful to review, in checklist fashion, the questions to be considered:

1. *Ascertain the Greek text itself*. If we consult the apparatus in Wevers's edition of Deuteronomy for the Göttingen LXX, we find

17. Eminent LXX scholar Max L. Margolis went so far as to state, "As a matter of fact, in passages wanting in the Hebrew, all attempts at retroversion are unscientific"; see his article, "Complete Induction for the Identification of the Vocabulary in the Greek Versions of the Old Testament with Its Semitic Equivalents: Its Necessity and the Means of Obtaining It," *Journal of the American Oriental Society* 30 (1910): 301–12, quotation from 302–3.

18. The reading καὶ κυκλώσω ("and I will surround") for וְחָנִיתִי ("and I will encamp") in the same verse makes us suspicious that something else is going on. Léo Laberge calls it a "double lecture" influenced by 29:1 and 28:21; see *La Septante d'Isaïe 28–33: Étude de tradition textuelle* (Ottawa: Chez l'auteur, 1978), 23. At any rate, it is quite possible that the correction from ר to ד could have taken place independently in the various witnesses.

19. The difference involves a simple transposition of כ and ל; in the Hebrew script at the time of the translation, כ had the same form in medial or final position. This example is treated briefly by Tov, *Text-Critical Use of the Septuagint*, 62.

that the text is secure. We have no evidence for the use of ἐπορεύθη (or some other verb that might correspond to וַיֵּלֶךְ), and moreover the whole tradition confirms συνετέλεσε as original.[20]

2. *Inquire whether the Greek translator's method of work can account for a change in this passage*. Is there any exegetical concern, principle of translation, or stylistic trait that might have given rise to the reading συνετέλεσε? No such reason is apparent, and thus we conclude that the change is likely due to the translator's having "read" a different Hebrew text (at this point we leave open the question whether such a Hebrew text existed only in the translator's mind).
3. *Determine whether the equivalence is merely possible or likely.* Hatch and Redpath's *Concordance to the Septuagint* shows that the συντελέω ≈ כָּלָה equivalence is in fact a standard correspondence, especially in the Pentateuch, which as a whole evinces a moderately literal style of translation.[21]
4. *Evaluate the internal evidence*. (a) Intrinsic probability supports the LXX reading, since the similar phrase וַיְכַל מֹשֶׁה לְדַבֵּר occurs in Deuteronomy 32:45. The sequence וַיֵּלֶךְ מֹשֶׁה וַיְדַבֵּר, on the other hand, is not found elsewhere in the Pentateuch (though it occurs twice in Judges). (b) With regard to transcriptional probability, the evidence is a bit ambiguous. It is certainly possible that a scribe might have harmonized 31:1 with 32:45. On the other hand, a scribal change from וַיְכַל to וַיֵּלֶךְ is more likely than the reverse, since the latter form is extremely common; indeed, we have convincing evidence for this corruption in Joshua 19:49 and 19:51, where an original וַיְכַלּוּ (supported by the Targum and Peshitta) was misread by the Greek translator, who has ἐπορεύθησαν.
5. *Determine whether the LXX variant is supported by other witnesses*. Prior to the discovery of the Dead Sea Scrolls, the LXX was the only evidence for this variant, and thus one might plausibly argue that the reading וַיְכַל did not actually exist in a Hebrew manuscript but was only in the translator's mind. As it turns out, however, a Hebrew fragment found in Qumran (1QDeut[a] 13.ii.4) has the reading reflected in LXX: ויכל משה לדבר.[22] Although it is not impossible that

20. One manuscript has the simple form ἐτέλεσε. In addition, a handful of medieval manuscripts omit λαλῶν.

21. The Hebrew verb can be translated with several Greek verbs, depending on the context (e.g., in Gen. 21:15, וַיִּכְלוּ הַמַּיִם מִן־הַחֵמֶת ["and the water was gone from the skin"], the verb συντελεῖν would have been inappropriate, and so the LXX renders ἐξέλιπεν δὲ τὸ ὕδωρ ἐκ τοῦ ἀσκοῦ). However, of some two dozen occurrences of συντελεῖν in the Pentateuch, about twenty translate כָּלָה.

22. See Dominique Barthélemy and J. T. Milik, *Qumran Cave 1* (Discoveries in the Judaean Desert 1; Oxford: Clarendon, 1955), 59. Incidentally, this fragment also includes the word כל, which is absent in MT but found in many medieval manuscripts and reflected in the LXX and most ancient versions.

this variant arose independently in both documents, such a scenario does seem quite unlikely. One would have to have a very good reason to deny that the *Vorlage* of LXX had this reading.

6. *Choose between the two competing readings*. Internal evidence, as noted, suggests the originality of the reading וַיְכַל. External evidence does as well: the Qumran document—though too fragmentary for us to make a general assessment of the quality of its text—is obviously ancient and, as far as we can tell, independent of the *Vorlage* of the LXX. As we noted earlier, the MT in general witnesses to a better text than LXX, but the agreement of LXX with Qumran shifts the balance. Since internal and external evidence agree, the variant reflected in LXX is probably original; it follows that the MT witnesses to a subsequent, though early, metathesis of the two consonants, which in turn led to the further change of לְדַבֵּר to וַיְדַבֵּר. It should be added, however, that even if we did not have the evidence from Qumran, we might still conclude reasonably on the basis of internal evidence that the LXX reading should be preferred.

Retroversion is also used to reconstruct entire sentences found in the Greek but missing from the MT. For example, 2 Samuel 14:30 ends with the words,

> וַיַּצִּתוּ עַבְדֵי אַבְשָׁלוֹם אֶת־הַחֶלְקָה בָּאֵשׁ
> "and Absalom's servants set the field on fire"

The LXX, however, goes on to say:

> καὶ παραγίνονται οἱ δοῦλοι Ιωαβ πρὸς αὐτὸν διερρηχότες τὰ ἱμάτια αὐτῶν καὶ εἶπαν Ἐνεπύρισαν οἱ δοῦλοι Αβεσσαλωμ τὴν μερίδα ἐν πυρί.
> "And Joab's servants came to him with their clothes torn and said, 'Absalom's servants have set the field on fire.'"

This sentence can be retroverted according to the usual translation equivalents found elsewhere.[23] So scholars propose that the corresponding Hebrew sentence must have read:

> ויבאו עבדי יואב אליו קרועי בגדיהם ויאמרו הציתו עבדי אבשלום את־החלקה באש

They argue that the sentence had fallen out of the Hebrew text because of the scribal error of homoeoteleuton, which occurs when the endings of two sentences are so similar (in this case עַבְדֵי אַבְשָׁלוֹם אֶת־הַחֶלְקָה בָּאֵשׁ) that the scribe's eye skips from the first to the second phrase, inadvertently dropping the words in between.

23. See Tov, *Text-Critical Use of the Septuagint*, 66–67.

The value of such a retroversion was viewed with skepticism before the discovery of the Dead Sea Scrolls; after all, the simple fact that one could translate the Greek back into Hebrew was hardly a conclusive reason to believe that a Hebrew text containing that reading ever actually existed. One of the fragments from Qumran, however (4QSam^{c}), contains in substance the additional sentence at 2 Samuel 14:30. This proof that some of the readings retroverted from the Greek did at one time exist in the Hebrew gives the Greek version greater weight for the textual criticism of the Hebrew Bible and for reconstructing the *Vorlage* from which the Greek had originally been translated.[24]

One might think that the discovery of a Hebrew sentence in 4QSam^{c} that corresponds to the additional sentence in LXX 2 Samuel 14:30 would settle the question of how the Hebrew text originally read. It would be easy to conclude that the sentence was in fact original and had dropped out in the Hebrew tradition, probably after the Greek translation was made. However, even this new manuscript evidence is open to interpretation because it merely offers a second Hebrew reading. Which reading was in fact original is still open to debate. For instance, Stephen Pisano argues that the Hebrew text of the Qumran scroll was corrected to agree with the Greek version of Samuel and that therefore the shorter text in MT is the original reading here.[25]

This example of 2 Samuel 14:30 shows how frustratingly difficult it is to reach a firm conclusion about the Hebrew *Vorlage* of the Greek. Recovery of the parent text of the LXX remains a hypothetical ideal, even with possession of the Qumran scrolls, and therefore the value of the LXX for the textual criticism of the Hebrew text remains indirect. Anneli Aejmelaeus prefaces her article "What Can We Know about the Hebrew *Vorlage* of the Septuagint?" with this reminder:

> The use of the Septuagint in textual criticism of the OT is essentially concerned with tracing the Hebrew text underlying the translation, i.e., the *Vorlage* of the translators, and comparing it with the MT. The *Vorlage* is thus presupposed to be somehow within our reach. Nevertheless, *it is a text that is lost to us for good and all.* The rich discoveries of the past decades have not brought to light any text that could be identified as the

24. It is important to note that both this example and the previous one, Deut. 31:1, can be explained by common scribal errors as the Hebrew was copied.

25. Stephen Pisano, *Additions or Omissions in the Books of Samuel: The Significant Pluses and Minuses in the Massoretic, LXX and Qumran Texts* (Orbus biblicus et orientalis 57; Freiburg: Universitätsverlag; Göttingen: Vandenhoeck & Ruprecht, 1984), 232–36. He suggests that the LXX (or its *Vorlage*) "has inserted a plus designed to show the reaction of Joab's servants to the burning of his field, and to make the report of the event to Joab, while MT's shorter text left this up to the reader. The plus has been inserted in such a way that it has created a text in which the repetition of one word at the beginning and end of the insertion has led some to blame its absence from MT on a textual accident due to homeoteleuton" (p. 236).

Vorlage, nor can this be expected to happen in the future. All we know about the *Vorlage* is thus in fact secondhand knowledge, and that is the problem.[26]

The Greek Text of Samuel–Kings

The Greek variant at 2 Samuel 14:30 raises once again a question we have commented on previously, namely, the peculiar problems presented by the books of Samuel and Kings, known in the LXX as 1–4 Reigns (or 1–4 Kingdoms). It will be useful to devote special attention to this topic, not only because of its intrinsic interest and importance, but also because it helps to illustrate text-critical principles that have broader relevance.

To begin with, we need to review the origins and transmission of the Greek text of Reigns, and our point of departure must be Henry St. John Thackeray's famous Schweich Lectures, delivered in 1920.[27] In the first lecture he argued that while the Jewish-Egyptian pioneers in Alexandria (whom he wittily referred to as JE!) executed the translation of the Pentateuch and the Latter Prophets, there were some gaps left in the Former Prophets and these were filled by the Asiatic-Palestinian school (P).

Taking Codex B as our basis, the evidence is as follows: beginning with 2 Samuel 11 and extending to 1 Kings 2:11, the Hebrew word גַּם is consistently translated with καίγε (about thirty times). Moreover, this pattern resurfaces beginning with 1 Kings 22 and extending through 2 Kings. These two *Kaige* sections of the narrative (designated by Thackeray as βγ and γδ, and together as βδ) are characterized by other patterns of translation, such as the avoidance of the historic present—which in the other sections occurs about two hundred times—and the rendering of the first-person personal pronoun אָנֹכִי with the perplexing phrase ἐγὼ εἰμί. It should also be added that these sections are much closer to our Hebrew text than are the non-*Kaige* sections (although this matter was not part of Thackeray's main concern).

Thackeray noticed that the material in these sections did not present Hebrew history in a positive light, and so his interpretation of the evidence zeroed in on their content. In his view, the original translators stopped with 2 Samuel 9, after having shown David as favored by God (chap. 7), victorious (chap. 8), and generous (chap. 9). The latter part of this book, omitted by the original translator, focuses on David's adultery and murder plus the ensuing trouble in his family (interestingly, Codex B omits "save only in the matter of Uriah the Hittite" at 1 Kings 15:5).

26. Aejmelaeus, *Trail of the Septuagint Translators*, 77 (emphasis added).

27. Henry St. John Thackeray, *The Septuagint and Jewish Worship: A Study in Origins*, 2d ed. (London: Oxford University Press, 1923).

The translator picked up the narrative again with the accession of Solomon in 1 Kings 2:12 but laid down his pen at 21:44, "leaving Israel victorious over Syria."[28] By omitting the period of the divided monarchy, the translator succeeded in presenting a more favorable picture of Jewish history. Some time later, an Asiatic-Palestinian translator came along and filled in the gap (using, however, a Hebrew text much closer to the MT than the text used by the original translators). Thackeray identified this subsequent translator as Ur-Theodotion—pioneer of the literal school and predecessor of Aquila—whose text-type is also reflected in Josephus.

Thackeray, however, did not address a distinct (and, as it turns out, related) problem, namely, the peculiar text found in manuscripts boc_2e_2 in these books. Alfred Rahlfs had earlier succeeded in identifying the text in those manuscripts as the Lucianic recension for Reigns.[29] He found that this text was characterized by two opposing tendencies: on the one hand, Lucian seems to have corrected the OG toward the Hebrew text of his time (which was virtually the same as the later MT), but on the other hand he freely revised the style away from the Hebrew. Since, however, many of the variants reflected in these manuscripts are also found in early sources, Rahlfs spoke of Proto-Lucianic variants.[30] This evidence in turn suggests that Lucian, rather than changing the OG according to the standardized Hebrew text (he probably did not know Hebrew), simply used a Greek text that had earlier been brought into conformity with a proto-Masoretic Hebrew text.

Such was the situation before the discoveries in the Judean Desert. In 1952, however, Dominique Barthélemy published an article entitled "Rediscovery of a Missing Link in the History of the Septuagint,"[31] which was a preliminary announcement of the Greek Minor Prophets Scroll, found in Naḥal Ḥever (sometimes called the "Cave of Horror") and dated before 70 C.E. He noted that the scroll showed some striking agreements with Justin Martyr, Aquila, Symmachus, and Quinta. It

28. Ibid., 20. Thackeray notes that 21:43 has the last instance of the historic present.

29. Alfred Rahlfs, *Septuaginta Studien*, vol. 3: *Lucians Rezension der Königsbücher* (Göttingen: Vandenhoeck & Ruprecht, 1911). The Cambridge manuscripts in question, boc_2e_2, bear the respective Göttingen (Rahlfs) numbers 19, 82, 93, and 127; in addition, it should be noted that Cambridge siglum b (in roman type) includes manuscript *b* (in italic), which bears the Göttingen number 108.

30. This last point seemed confirmed in 1936 with the publication of Rylands 458 (Göttingen 957), dated around the Maccabean era, which was thought to contain a Lucianic text, but more recent work disputes this identification.

31. Dominique Barthélemy, "Redécouverte d'un chaînon manquant de l'histoire de la Septante," *Revue biblique* 60 (1953): 18–29. Further information on Barthélemy's ideas will be included in chaps. 8 and 13 below.

was clearly a literal recension of the Greek, characterized by the use of καίγε and other features.

The same year that Barthélemy's article was published, several hundred fragments of Samuel were discovered in Qumran Cave 4. Frank M. Cross published a preliminary report in which he announced that a Hebrew text of Samuel corresponding to the LXX *Vorlage* had been found.[32] Actually, three manuscripts were identified, the most important of which are 4QSam[a] (first century of our era, relatively well preserved) and 4QSam[b] (older but poorly preserved). Cross goes on to argue that 4QSam[a] contains many Proto-Lucianic readings and that boc_2e_2 reflect a twofold revision of OG: first a textual revision (Proto-Lucianic) toward a Hebrew text like 4QSam[a], then the historical Lucian's stylistic corrections. Cross also set these ideas within a larger and ambitious theory of local texts.[33]

This brief description of a very complicated problem needs to be understood and kept in mind if we hope to use LXX 1–4 Reigns responsibly for Hebrew text-critical purposes. For example, it is apparent that the "LXX" of these books consists of two very different translations, depending on what section is in view. If we are considering a textual problem in 1 Samuel, the first part of 2 Samuel, or most of 1 Kings (from 2:11 to the end of chap. 21), we need to remember that here the Greek translation in Rahlfs's LXX (a) is based on a Hebrew text somewhat different from the MT and (b) uses a method of translation that can be characterized as literal in general, but not in every respect.[34] The Greek of the *Kaige* sections, on the other hand, (a) is based on a Hebrew text very close to the MT and (b) uses a more consistent and distinctively literal method of translation. Of course, one

32. Frank M. Cross, "A New Qumran Biblical Fragment Related to the Original Hebrew Underlying the Septuagint," *Bulletin of the American Schools of Oriental Research* 132 (1953): 15–20. The fragment included 1 Sam. 1:22b–2:6 and 2:16–25. "In virtually every variant where we can reconstruct the Hebrew of 4Q with certainty, the reading of the Egyptian recension [i.e., as reflected in the LXX] is followed" (p. 24).

33. In spite of some problems, Cross's theory is impressive for breadth (it integrates many areas of study), depth (it is built on minute analysis of Hebrew scripts), and clarity of formulation. For semipopular expositions, see his well-known book, *The Ancient Library of Qumran*, 3d ed. (Biblical Seminar 30; Sheffield: Sheffield Academic Press, 1995), chap. 4; and "Problems of Method in the Textual Criticism of the Hebrew Bible," in *The Critical Study of Sacred Texts*, ed. Wendy Doniger O'Flaherty (Berkeley Religious Studies Series; Berkeley: Graduate Theological Union, 1979), 31–54. More technical but still readable are "The History of the Biblical Text" and "The Evolution of a Theory of Local Texts," both in *Qumran and the History of the Biblical Text*, ed. Frank M. Cross and Shemaryahu Talmon (Cambridge: Harvard University Press, 1975), 177–95, 306–20.

34. See the passage discussed above in chap. 5, pp. 111–13. A good example of excessively literal translation is the odd rendering of בִּי (an idiomatic formula to open conversation with a superior, often translated in English as "please") with ἐν ἐμοί. One also finds, however, a tendency to make brief additions that fill out the sense, such as καὶ εἶπεν Σαμουηλ πρὸς Σαουλ for a simple וַיֹּאמֶר שְׁמוּאֵל (1 Sam. 15:17).

can find additional features that distinguish *Kaige* and non-*Kaige* from one another. All this means that the use of the LXX for the textual criticism of the Hebrew Bible must take such differences into account. An approach that works in 1 Samuel and most of 1 Kings may be invalid in most of 2 Samuel and in 2 Kings.

Further complicating our work is the question of what to do with the Lucianic or Antiochene recension (the text in manuscripts boc_2e_2), which offers a distinctively different Greek text for the whole of Samuel–Kings. Since this text, whose final form took place in the fourth century, is attested by a very small number of manuscripts, scholars in the past have not held it in high regard. And indeed one can point to numerous passages that are evidently secondary in character. One important piece of evidence consists in its so-called double renderings. For example, the text of 1 Samuel 11:5 reads, וְהִנֵּה שָׁאוּל בָּא אַחֲרֵי הַבָּקָר ("and behold, Saul came after [i.e., behind] the cattle"). The original Greek translator, however, wrongly vocalized the last word (*bāqār*, "cattle") as *bōqer* ("morning"), rendering the clause, καὶ ἰδοὺ Σαουλ ἤρχετο μετὰ τὸ πρωΐ ("and behold, Saul came after the early morning"). This is indeed the reading of most Greek manuscripts. The Antiochene text, on the other hand, reads, καὶ ἰδοὺ Σαουλ ἤρχετο πρωῒ κατόπισθεν τῶν βοῶν ("and behold, Saul came early in the morning behind the cattle"), obviously a secondary conflation.

During the last several decades, however, increasing attention has been given to the Lucianic manuscripts of 1–4 Reigns. Barthélemy, for example, points out that they alone had escaped the revisions associated with the *Kaige* movement. Moreover, the Hebrew fragments of 4QSam[a] reportedly show a significant measure of agreement with the Lucianic manuscripts in the *Kaige* section of 2 Samuel.[35] Even apart from its value for reconstructing either the OG or the original Hebrew, the Lucianic recension is important in that it represents the LXX as it was known in large parts of ancient Christianity.

We can best appreciate the significance of this discussion by analyzing a specific passage. Careful study of 3 Reigns 2:1–5 reveals interesting and useful details (illustration 17). It is quickly apparent, for example, that the Lucianic recension is characterized by stylistic revisions. Some are relatively innocuous, such as the preference for the middle voice of φυλάσσω in line 4c or the use of ὅπως instead of ἵνα in lines 3g and 4a. In line 2a, the odd ἐγώ εἰμι becomes simply ἐγώ, while in line 5a καί γε becomes καί.[36] Some of the stylistic changes move the Greek away from the Hebrew text, as in lines 3b–c. Other changes suggest that the Greek has been

35. Natalio Fernández Marcos, *Scribes and Translators: Septuagint and Old Latin in the Books of Kings* (Vetus Testamentum Supplement 54; Leiden: Brill, 1994), 35, with reference to Eugene C. Ulrich's work.

36. Or καὶ νῦν. The latter word possibly reflects a misreading of Hebrew אתה as עתה.

adjusted *toward* the Hebrew text: in line 3f, for example, καθὼς γέγραπται represents Hebrew כַּכָּתוּב more exactly than does τὰ γεγραμμένα.[37]

17. 3 Reigns (1 Kings) 2:1–5

	Masoretic Text	Codex Vaticanus	Lucianic Text
1a	וַיִּקְרְבוּ יְמֵי־דָוִד לָמוּת	Καὶ ἤγγισαν αἱ ἡμέραι Δαυεὶδ ἀποθανεῖν αὐτόν,	Καὶ ἐγένετο μετὰ ταῦτα, καὶ ἀπέθανε Δαυὶδ καὶ ἐκοιμήθη μετὰ τῶν πατέρων αὐτοῦ.
b	וַיְצַו אֶת־שְׁלֹמֹה בְנוֹ לֵאמֹר׃	καὶ ἀπεκρίνατο Σαλωμὼν υἱῷ αὐτοῦ λέγων	καὶ ἐνετείλατο τῷ υἱῷ αὐτοῦ Σολομῶντι ἔμπροσθεν τοῦ θανάτου αὐτοῦ λέγων
2a	אָנֹכִי הֹלֵךְ בְּדֶרֶךְ כָּל־הָאָרֶץ	Ἐγώ εἰμι πορεύομαι ἐν ὁδῷ πάσης τῆς γῆς·	Ἐγὼ πορεύομαι ἐν ὁδῷ πάσης τῆς γῆς,
b	וְחָזַקְתָּ וְהָיִיתָ לְאִישׁ׃	καὶ ἰσχύσεις καὶ ἔσῃ εἰς ἄνδρα·	καὶ κραταιωθήσῃ καὶ ἔσῃ εἰς ἄνδρα δυνάμεως·
3a	וְשָׁמַרְתָּ אֶת־מִשְׁמֶרֶת יְהוָה אֱלֹהֶיךָ	καὶ φυλάξεις φυλακὴν θεοῦ σου	καὶ φυλάξῃ τὴν φυλακὴν Κυρίου τοῦ Θεοῦ Ἰσραήλ,
b	לָלֶכֶת בִּדְרָכָיו	τοῦ πορεύεσθαι ἐν ταῖς ὁδοῖς αὐτοῦ,	τοῦ πορεύεσθαι ἐνώπιον αὐτοῦ,
c	לִשְׁמֹר חֻקֹּתָיו	φυλάσσειν τὰς ἐντολὰς αὐτοῦ	φυλάσσειν τὴν ὁδὸν αὐτοῦ καὶ τὰ προστάγματα αὐτοῦ,
d	מִצְוֹתָיו וּמִשְׁפָּטָיו	καὶ τὰ δικαιώματα καὶ τὰ κρίματα	ἀκριβάσματα αὐτοῦ καὶ τὰ κρίματα αὐτοῦ,
e	וְעֵדְוֹתָיו		ἐντολὰς αὐτοῦ καὶ τὰ μαρτύρια αὐτοῦ,
f	כַּכָּתוּב בְּתוֹרַת מֹשֶׁה	τὰ γεγραμμένα ἐν νόμῳ Μωυσέως,	καθὼς γέγραπται ἐν τῷ νόμῳ Μωσῆ,
g	לְמַעַן תַּשְׂכִּיל	ἵνα συνήσεις	ὅπως εὐοδωθῇ
h	אֵת כָּל־אֲשֶׁר תַּעֲשֶׂה	ἃ ποιήσεις κατὰ πάντα	πάντα ἃ ποιήσεις,
i	וְאֵת כָּל־אֲשֶׁר תִּפְנֶה שָׁם׃	ὅσα ἂν ἐντείλωμαί σοι·	καὶ πανταχῇ οὗ ἐὰν ἐπιβλέψῃς ἐκεῖ,
4a	לְמַעַן יָקִים יְהוָה אֶת־דְּבָרוֹ	ἵνα στήσῃ Κύριος τὸν λόγον αὐτοῦ	ὅπως στήσῃ Κύριος τὰ ῥήματα αὐτοῦ
b	אֲשֶׁר דִּבֶּר עָלַי לֵאמֹר	ὃν ἐλάλησεν λέγων	ἃ ἐλάλησε περὶ ἐμοῦ λέγων
c	אִם־יִשְׁמְרוּ בָנֶיךָ אֶת־דַּרְכָּם	Ἐὰν φυλάξωσιν οἱ υἱοί σου τὴν ὁδὸν αὐτῶν	Ἐὰν φυλάξωνται τὰ τέκνα σου τὰς ὁδοὺς αὐτῶν,
d	לָלֶכֶת לְפָנַי בֶּאֱמֶת	πορεύεσθαι ἐνώπιον ἐμοῦ ἐν ἀληθείᾳ	τοῦ πορεύεσθαι ἐνώπιόν μου ἐν ἀληθείᾳ
e	בְּכָל־לְבָבָם וּבְכָל־נַפְשָׁם	ἐν ὅλῃ καρδίᾳ αὐτῶν,	καὶ ἐν ὅλῃ καρδίᾳ αὐτῶν καὶ ἐν ὅλῃ τῇ ψυχῇ αὐτῶν,

37. Some knowledge of the Hebrew text may also be reflected in the change from the verb συνίημι to εὐοδόω in line 3g (the verb שָׂכַל can mean both "to understand" and "to be successful").

f	לֵאמֹר לֹא־יִכָּרֵת לְךָ	λέγων Οὐκ ἐξολοθρευθήσεταί σοι	οὐκ ἐξαρθήσεταί σοι
g	אִישׁ מֵעַל כִּסֵּא יִשְׂרָאֵל׃	ἀνὴρ ἐπάνωθεν θρόνου Ἰσραήλ.	ἀνὴρ ἀπὸ τοῦ θρόνου Ἰσραήλ.
5a	וְגַם אַתָּה יָדַעְתָּ אֵת אֲשֶׁר־עָשָׂה לִי	καί γε σὺ ἔγνως ὅσα ἐποίησέν μοι	καὶ νῦν σὺ οἶδας ἃ ἐποίησέ μοι
b	יוֹאָב בֶּן־צְרוּיָה אֲשֶׁר עָשָׂה	Ἰωὰβ υἱὸς Σαρουίας, ὅσα ἐποίησεν	Ἰωὰβ υἱὸς Σαρουία, καὶ ἃ ἐποίησε
c	לִשְׁנֵי־שָׂרֵי צִבְאוֹת יִשְׂרָאֵל	τοῖς δυσὶν ἄρχουσιν τῶν δυνάμεων Ἰσραήλ,	τοῖς δύο ἀρχιστρατήγοις Ἰσραήλ,
d	לְאַבְנֵר בֶּן־נֵר	Ἀβεννὴρ υἱῷ Νὴρ	τῷ Ἀβεννὴρ υἱῷ Νὴρ
e	וְלַעֲמָשָׂא בֶן־יֶתֶר	καὶ τῷ Ἀμεσσαιὰ υἱῷ Ἰέθερ,	καὶ τῷ Ἀμεσσὰ υἱῷ Ἰεθὲρ ἀρχιστρατήγῳ Ἰούδα,
f	וַיַּהַרְגֵם	καὶ ἀπέκτεινεν αὐτοὺς	καὶ ἀπέκτεινεν αὐτοὺς
g	וַיָּשֶׂם דְּמֵי־מִלְחָמָה	καὶ ἔταξεν τὰ αἵματα πολέμου	καὶ ἐξεδίκησεν αἷμα πολέμου
h	בְּשָׁלֹם וַיִּתֵּן דְּמֵי מִלְחָמָה		ἐν εἰρήνῃ καὶ ἔδωκεν αἷμα ἀθῷον
i	בַּחֲגֹרָתוֹ	ἐν τῇ ζώνῃ αὐτοῦ	ἐν τῇ ζωῇ μου
j	אֲשֶׁר בְּמָתְנָיו	τῇ ἐν τῇ ὀσφύι αὐτοῦ	καὶ ἐπὶ τῇ ζώνῃ τῆς ὀσφύος μου
k	וּבְנַעֲלוֹ אֲשֶׁר בְּרַגְלָיו׃	καὶ ἐν τῷ ὑποδήματι αὐτοῦ τῷ ἐν τῷ ποδὶ αὐτοῦ.	καὶ ἐν τῷ ὑποδήματί μου τῷ ἐν τῷ ποδί μου.

See illustration 14 for Rahlfs's edition of this passage.

sources: MT = *Biblia hebraica stuttgartensia*, 560–61; Vaticanus = Henry Barclay Swete, *The Old Testament in Greek according to the Septuagint*, vol. 1: *Genesis–IV Kings*, 3d ed. (Cambridge: Cambridge University Press, 1901), 673; Lucian = Natalio Fernández Marcos and José Ramón Busto Saiz, *El texto antioqueno de la Biblia griega*, vol. 1: *1–2 Samuel* (Textos y Estudios "Cardenal Cisneros" 50; Madrid: Consejo Superior de Investigaciones Científicas, 1989), 171–72. Note: in this edition of the Lucianic text, this passage appears as 2 Samuel 26:1–5.

The very first verse contains an interesting textual variant. In the MT as well as in most LXX manuscripts, David's death is not reported until verse 10. The Lucianic text, however, begins with the statement, "It happened after these things that David died and slept with his fathers" (line 1a). As it has been argued, this feature may be evidence that at some stage in the tradition a form of the text circulated that did not include "David's testament" (vv. 2–9); later, when the passage was introduced, it became necessary to include the qualification ἔμπροσθεν τοῦ θανάτου ("before his death") in line 1b.

Special attention should be given to the textual problem raised by line 5h.[38] The MT for lines 5f–i can be translated literally as follows:

> 5f and he killed them
> 5g and he placed [i.e., shed] the blood of battle

38. The discussion that follows is fairly involved, but the student should make a special effort to understand it, since it illustrates some important principles in the field.

5h in [time of] peace, and he put the blood of battle
5i in his belt

Codex B, supported by two other uncials (M and N), half a dozen cursives, and some versional evidence, omits line 5h completely. The rest of the witnesses—A, a dozen cursives (including the Lucianic manuscripts), and three ancient versions—include the line, but with an important variation: instead of the expected πολέμου ("battle") for מִלְחָמָה as in line 5g, we find ἀθῷον. The adjective ἀθῷος means "unpunished" or "not deserving punishment," so we should translate, "he put innocent blood (on his belt)."

Rahlfs includes clause 5h in his edition of the LXX, and on the basis of this evidence many scholars emend the difficult MT reading. Alfred Jepsen, for example, in his edition of 1–2 Kings for *Biblia hebraica stuttgartensia*, suggests (with a question mark) that we read דָּם נָקִי; others prefer דְּמֵי חִנָּם, as in verse 31.[39] How does one then explain the MT reading? C. F. Burney responds: "Doubtless . . . the corruption arose through the previous דְּמֵי מִלְחָמָה standing directly above דְּמֵי חִנָּם in the MS. from which the copy was made."[40] This is a plausible interpretation of the evidence, and if in fact the change was accidentally caused by an error of sight, we would not need to insist on the principle that the more difficult reading is preferable.

What this emendation does not explain, however, is why line 5h is missing in the best Greek tradition. It is true that the words in question are found in Codex Alexandrinus, but this witness often shows signs of Hexaplaric influence. Moreover, cursive c_2 and the Syro-Hexaplar have these words marked with the Origenic asterisk. We have thus every reason to believe that they were missing from the LXX text common in the second century. The words are also missing from a handful of medieval Hebrew manuscripts, and James A. Montgomery rightly believes that the omission was caused by ancient haplography.[41] The reason we divided the parallel texts as we did was to show

39. Note, however, that in 2:31 the Greek does not translate with ἀθῷος, but instead renders ὃ δωρεάν. A useful parallel is 1 Sam. 19:5, וְלָמָּה תֶחֱטָא בְּדָם נָקִי לְהָמִית אֶת־דָּוִד חִנָּם ("and why will you sin against innocent blood by killing David without cause?"), rendered καὶ ἵνα τί ἁμαρτάνεις εἰς αἷμα ἀθῷον θανατῶσαι τὸν Δαυιδ δωρεάν;

40. C. F. Burney, *Notes on the Hebrew Text of the Books of Kings* (Oxford: Clarendon, 1903), 16. In addition, Burney (followed by other scholars) accepts the Lucianic reading ἐξεδίκησεν in 5g and emends the Hebrew from וַיָּשֶׂם to וַיִּקֹּם, yielding the smooth translation, "And he avenged in time of peace blood shed in war, and put innocent blood on his belt." James A. Montgomery objects, however, that an original וַיִּקֹּם, a perfectly intelligible reading, would not likely be corrupted to וַיָּשֶׂם; see *A Critical and Exegetical Commentary on the Books of Kings*, ed. Henry S. Gehman (International Critical Commentary; Edinburgh: Clark, 1951), 98. For other objections to Burney and some interesting proposals, see W. T. Koopmans, "The Testament of David in 1 Kings ii 1–10," *Vetus Testamentum* 41 (1991): 429–49.

41. Montgomery, *Kings*, 98.

how easy it would have been for line 5h to be skipped if indeed two consecutive lines ended with the words דְּמֵי מִלְחָמָה.[42] If, on the other hand, the first line ended with מִלְחָמָה, but the second with either נָקִי or חִנָּם, it is not clear what could have caused the omission.[43]

It seems more reasonable to assume that (a) the MT preserves the original reading, (b) the line in question was omitted either in the Hebrew copy that served as the Greek translator's *Vorlage* or in the mind of the translator, and (c) the missing words were supplied by Origen and preserved in most witnesses, including the Lucianic manuscripts. Our solution, to be sure, labors under another difficulty, namely, we know of no apparent reason that might have led Origen to use the Greek term ἀθῴον (rather than πολέμου) at this point. Possible answers to this question would be purely conjectural.

In the absence of additional data, we reach an impasse, and our final judgment comes down to a question of deciding which scenario seems less unlikely: (a) that a line was dropped for no apparent reason, or (b) that Origen would have chosen ἀθῴον for no apparent reason. The evidence that the line in question may be Hexaplaric tips the scales in favor of the MT.

We conclude by encouraging the reader to go over this particular textual problem until it is clearly understood. In spite of—indeed, because of—its complexities, it serves as a most useful test case for appreciating the nature of LXX textual criticism.

To Continue Your Study

Natalio Fernández Marcos, *Introducción a las versiones griegas de la Biblia*, 2d ed. (Textos y Estudios "Cardenal Cisneros" 23; Madrid: Consejo Superior de Investigaciones Científicas, 1998) = *The Septuagint in Context: Introduction to the Greek Version of the Bible*, trans. Wilfred G. E. Watson (Leiden: Brill, 2000), devotes chapter 5 to assessing the value of the LXX for the study of the Hebrew text. Marguerite Harl, Gilles Dorival, and Olivier Munnich, *La Bible Grecque des Septante: Du judaïsme hellénistique au christianisme ancien*, 2d ed. (Initia-

42. Even if the line was broken at a different point, the repetition of the phrase could readily have caused the omission. Alternatively (but less likely), haplography could have taken place in the transmission of the Greek if the original translation repeated the phrase τὰ αἵματα πολέμου.

43. Presumably, one would have to posit an additional, parallel series of steps. (a) After an original נָקִי was changed to מִלְחָמָה by mistake, (b) some scribe omitted the line, a mistake preserved in a few medieval manuscripts as well; (c) this new corrupted text was used by the original Greek translators, so that (d) a Greek text without the line in question was preserved in pre-Hexaplaric witnesses; (e) Origen, whose Hebrew text preserved the original נָקִי, introduced the line with ἀθῴον into his fifth column, and (f) this new reading spread to the majority of witnesses. Possible, but speculative.

tions au christianisme ancien; [Paris]: Cerf/Centre National de la Recherche Scientifique, 1994), devote a chapter (pages 201–22) to the divergences between the LXX and the MT, but much of it is concerned with deliberate changes on the part of the translators.

Countless individual articles deal with the issues treated in the present chapter. Especially helpful is John W. Wevers's critique of the apparatus for Deuteronomy in *Biblia hebraica stuttgartensia*; see "Text History and Text Criticism of the Septuagint," in *Congress Volume: Göttingen 1977* (Vetus Testamentum Supplement 29; Leiden: Brill, 1978), 392–402. Note also the perceptive essay by Moshe H. Goshen-Gottstein, "Theory and Practice of Textual Criticism: The Text-Critical Use of the Septuagint," *Textus* 3 (1963): 130–58. It should be noted, however, that recent scholars are less skeptical than Wevers and Goshen-Gottstein regarding the value of the LXX for the textual criticism of the Hebrew Bible.

Pride of place goes to Emanuel Tov, *The Text-Critical Use of the Septuagint in Biblical Research*, 2d ed. (Jerusalem Biblical Studies 8; Jerusalem: Simor, 1997). Systematically and in painstaking detail, Tov identifies and evaluates virtually every concept that is relevant to this difficult endeavor. Although not all of his judgments command universal assent, it would be difficult to find a more sober and reliable guide.

8

The Judean Desert Discoveries and Septuagint Studies

The Greek Biblical Texts. Although few and fragmentary, the Greek biblical manuscripts found in the Judean Desert are of great importance. Among the fragments from the ***Greek Pentateuch***, some previously unknown variant readings have been identified, but scholars disagree as to whether any of these represent the original Greek text. Special importance attaches to the ***Greek Minor Prophets Scroll***, which preserves an early recension of the OG.

The Hebrew Biblical Texts. Numerous Hebrew manuscripts of the Bible have been discovered in the Judean Desert, some of which affect directly the study of the Greek versions. Two of the ***Jeremiah Fragments***, for example, provide a Hebrew text that closely matches that of the Greek Jeremiah, raising new questions about the textual and literary history of this book. Much discussion surrounds the ***Text of Samuel at Qumran***. It has been argued that one of the Samuel fragments provides a distinct Hebrew text-type. Some of its variant readings coincide with the Greek evidence, while others are unique.

The manuscripts discovered in Qumran and elsewhere in the Judean Desert, popularly called the Dead Sea Scrolls, have enormous significance for biblical studies in general and for LXX studies in particular. In previous chapters we have had occasion to comment on the importance of these discoveries, but a more systematic discussion is needed.

When Bedouin shepherds found seven ancient scrolls in a cave at Qumran near the Dead Sea in 1947, they discovered among other things texts of Scripture that had last been read about two thousand years ago.[1] Over the next decade additional finds were made in other caves at the site of the original discovery and in several other locations

1. For the story of the original and subsequent discoveries, see the clear description in James C. VanderKam, *The Dead Sea Scrolls Today* (Grand Rapids: Eerdmans, 1994).

in the Jordan River valley. These scrolls are of great value because they are a millennium older than the best manuscripts of the Hebrew Bible previously available, such as the Aleppo Codex and Codex Leningradensis (both early eleventh century). The few Greek biblical texts found in the Judean Desert are as much as five hundred years older than the great uncials of the fourth and fifth centuries.

Because these scrolls were untouched for almost two thousand years, they provide a snapshot of what Hebrew and Greek biblical texts looked like at the time they were hidden, around the time of the Jewish revolts in the years 70 and 135 of our era. Moreover, many of the scrolls were already quite old at the time they were hidden, some even dating back to the period during which the Greek translations of some books of the Hebrew Bible were being made. Thus the scrolls provide crucial evidence for the history of the biblical text.[2]

The Greek Biblical Texts

In comparison with the large number of Hebrew and Aramaic manuscripts so far discovered in the Judean Desert, only a small amount of material written in Greek has been found. These Greek biblical manuscripts, however, are obviously of great importance to LXX studies because they can be compared directly to the Greek text preserved in the oldest codices (Sinaiticus, Vaticanus, Alexandrinus). The Greek biblical manuscripts from the Judean Desert, along with the Egyptian papyri described in chapter 2, provide a representation of the text as it appeared before the work of Origen in the third century of this era. Furthermore, the great uncials have the Greek OT bound with the NT, indicating that the text was transmitted in the Christian tradition. The Judean Desert texts, on the other hand, were hidden by a Jewish community and provide a sample of the Greek biblical texts before they were adopted by the church and possibly edited by Christian scribes.

Qumran and the Greek Pentateuch

Unfortunately, the Greek biblical texts found in Qumran are fragmentary. Caves 4 and 7 at Qumran yielded fragments of two copies of Greek Leviticus, one of Numbers, two of Exodus, one of Deuteronomy, and several fragments of unidentified Greek texts. We have no reason to believe that all of the fragments are of the same age. Paleography

2. The scrolls are published in the ongoing series Discoveries in the Judaean Desert (Oxford: Clarendon, 1955–). See also the important collection of essays, *The Dead Sea Scrolls after Fifty Years: A Comprehensive Assessment*, 2 vols., ed. Peter W. Flint and James C. VanderKam (Leiden: Brill, 1998–99), which includes an article by Leonard J. Greenspoon entitled "The Dead Sea Scrolls and the Greek Bible" (1.101–27).

dates them to the first century B.C.E. or somewhat later. The Qumran Pentateuch fragments of major significance are the following:[3]

Rahlfs No.	DJD Sigla	Biblical Text
801	4Q119 *or* 4QLXXLev[a]	Leviticus 26:2–16
802	4Q120 *or* 4QpapLXXLev[b]	Leviticus 2–5 with lacunae
803	4Q121 *or* 4QLXXNum	Numbers 3:30–4:14 with lacunae
805	7Q1 *or* 7QpapLXXExod	Exodus 28:4–7
819	4Q122 *or* 4QLXXDeut	Deuteronomy 11:4

There were no major surprises when these Greek texts were compared to the uncials, such as Vaticanus. According to Emanuel Tov, the Qumran texts of Leviticus and Numbers have a common background with the texts of those books in the uncials.[4] He believes that the Qumran documents may represent an older form of the Greek version, while the uncial tradition reflects at times a later revision. Although differences with the later tradition may be found, we find no substantial pluses or minuses.

Some of the variants found in the Greek fragments of the Pentateuch are unique.[5] The twenty-eight fragmentary lines of 4QLXXLev[a] contain as many as fifteen variant readings, seven of which are not found in any other extant Greek witness. They are typically synonymous substitutions. For instance, Leviticus 26:12 in the Qumran fragment reads μοι εθν[ος] where the other Greek manuscripts have μου λαός. Both are semantically acceptable translations of the phrase found at that place in the MT, לִי לְעָם, and therefore provide no evidence of a different Hebrew *Vorlage*.

However, the appearance of the noun ἔθνος in the Qumran fragment presents what Tov calls a "remarkable lexical discrepancy" between this text and that of the uncials that "probably characterizes the relation between the two texts best."[6] The main LXX textual tradition, as preserved for example in Vaticanus, usually reads λαός when He-

3. The fragments labeled 4Q are published in Patrick W. Skehan, Eugene C. Ulrich Jr., and Judith E. Sanderson, *Qumran Cave 4*, vol. 4: *Palaeo-Hebrew and Greek Biblical Manuscripts* (Discoveries in the Judaean Desert 9; Oxford: Clarendon, 1992). The Exodus fragment, 7Q1, was published earlier in M. Baillet, J. T. Milik, and Roland de Vaux, *Les "Petites Grottes" de Qumrân* (Discoveries in the Judaean Desert 3; Oxford: Clarendon, 1962).

4. Emanuel Tov, "The Greek Biblical Texts from the Judean Desert," in *The Bible as Book: The Transmission of the Greek Text*, ed. S. McKendrick and O. A. O'Sullivan (London: British Library, 2003), 97–122.

5. The following examples and others are found in Eugene C. Ulrich Jr., "The Septuagintal Manuscripts from Qumran: A Reappraisal of Their Value," in *Septuagint, Scrolls and Cognate Writings*, ed. George J. Brooke and Barnabas Lindars (SBLSCS 33; Atlanta: Scholars Press, 1992), 49–80.

6. Tov, "Greek Biblical Texts from the Judean Desert," 108.

brew עַם refers to Israel as the chosen people, but ἔθνος when the reference is to peoples other than Israel. This lexical distinction is picked up later by the NT writers. In Tov's opinion, the Qumran fragment "does not reflect this later standard vocabulary and therefore probably reflects the OG." He also observes that dative μοι in the Qumran fragment represents Hebrew ל more closely than does genitive μου in the other witnesses.

A second example from the same fragment shows that even when the Qumran variant is semantically equivalent to the reading found in other witnesses, the difference between them can provide valuable insight into the history of the text. On the basis of the Qumran reading at Leviticus 26:4, τον ξυλινον καρ[πον], Eugene Ulrich infers that the clause read, "the land will give its produce and arboreal fruit."[7] The main textual tradition, however, has a longer reading: "the land will give its produce, *and the trees of the field will give their fruit*" (καὶ τὰ ξύλα τῶν πεδίων ἀποδώσει τὸν καρπὸν αὐτῶν, which reflects a Hebrew text like MT, וְעֵץ הַשָּׂדֶה יִתֵּן פִּרְיוֹ). The Qumran text uses an adjective where Vaticanus uses a fuller expression that has a similar meaning; in other words, the Qumran reading may be a free translation of the same Hebrew text. On the other hand, the Qumran rendering may be evidence for a variant parent text that read simply עץ פרי. While that question must remain undecided, according to Tov the use of the Greek adjective ξύλινος is consistent with older Greek style, indicating that the text preserved in the Qumran fragment is earlier than that preserved in the great uncials.

These and similar variant readings are quite significant for tracing the history of the text, but they do not present evidence for either an alternate Greek translation of the Pentateuch (independent from that found in the uncials) or a Hebrew *Vorlage* that is significantly different from the MT. Overall, the Greek biblical texts from Qumran reflect either a freer rendering of the Hebrew text that later became the MT or a literal translation of a slightly different Hebrew text.

Where these Qumran texts differ from the later codices, both Ulrich and Tov judge many of the Qumran readings to be the original Greek translation, but not all LXX scholars agree. When John W. Wevers produced the critical Greek text of Leviticus for the Göttingen edition, he did not choose even one of the Qumran readings as original.[8] In Ulrich's opinion, Wevers assumed that the Hebrew reading found in the MT was in fact the *Vorlage* of the original Greek, and thus he chose the readings of the uncials because they render the MT more literally than do the Qumran texts. Ulrich and Tov believe that the less literal readings found at Qumran are in fact characteristic of the original Greek

7. Ulrich, "Septuagintal Manuscripts from Qumran," 54.
8. Ibid., 65.

translation. If so, the original Greek translation was later revised toward the MT, resulting in the text found in the codices of the fourth and fifth centuries.

Barthélemy and the Greek Minor Prophets Scroll

In July 1952, Bedouins offered for sale in Jerusalem a scroll of uncertain provenance that contained large portions of a Greek version of the Minor Prophets. Almost ten years later, in the spring of 1961, an expedition entered a cave in Naḥal Ḥever, one of the wadis that empty into the Dead Sea south of Qumran. Among many skeletons in the cave (sometimes called the "Cave of Horror"), they found small fragments of a Greek text that proved to be pieces broken off the Minor Prophets scroll previously purchased in Jerusalem in 1952. A large cache of the personal letters of Bar Kokhba was also found in the cave, dating the massacre to the second Jewish revolt in the years 132–35 of our era.

Of all the Greek biblical texts found in the Judean Desert, none has made a greater impact on LXX studies than this Minor Prophets scroll, designated 8ḤevXIIgr or 8Ḥev1 (Rahlfs 943; not to be confused with MurXII [or Mur88], a Hebrew Minor Prophets scroll found at Wadi Murabbaʿat). Dated no later than the first century of our era,[9] it preserves twenty-four fragmentary columns (much more text than the Pentateuch fragments found at Qumran), written in the hand of two different scribes. Moreover, the text it preserves has distinctive characteristics that set it apart from the main LXX tradition. The order of the twelve prophets apparently follows the sequence of the MT, not the LXX codices. Extant fragments contain verses from Jonah, Micah, Nahum, Habakkuk, Zephaniah, and Zechariah. This scroll therefore provides an important link in the textual history of the Greek version.

To appreciate the significance of this scroll, we must go back to 1963, when Dominique Barthélemy published an edition of the scroll in a monograph that had the suggestive title "The Precursors of Aquila."[10] Scholars had earlier noted the distinctive translation of the Hebrew particle גַּם(וְ) by καίγε in various books such as Judges, Ruth, sec-

9. The date of the copy was narrowed by paleographer Peter J. Parsons, who concluded that the scroll was written in the last half of the first century B.C.E. (The date a translation or recension was produced must not be confused with the date of the manuscript preserving it.) The official publication of this scroll is by Emanuel Tov, with the collaboration of Robert A. Kraft and a contribution by Peter J. Parsons, *The Greek Minor Prophets Scroll from Naḥal Ḥever (8ḤevXIIgr)* (Discoveries in the Judaean Desert 8; Oxford: Clarendon, 1990). Parsons's discussion of the script and the date is on pp. 19–26.

10. Dominique Barthélemy, *Les devanciers d'Aquila: Première publication intégrale du texte des fragments du Dodécaprophéton* (Vetus Testamentum Supplement 10; Leiden: Brill, 1963).

tions of Samuel–Kings, and Lamentations.[11] Barthélemy argued, however, that eight other translational features are also characteristic of this *Kaige*-group, to which should be added Song of Songs, the Theodotionic version of Daniel, the additions to Job attributed to Theodotion, certain anonymous additions to Jeremiah, and the Quinta text of the Psalms.[12] Some of these distinctive features also appear in texts attributed to Aquila, whose translation is characterized by additional peculiarities, such as the use of the preposition σύν to render the Hebrew direct object marker אֵת. What is the connection among Theodotion (or Proto-Theodotion), Aquila, and the *Kaige*-group?[13] The Greek Minor Prophets scroll provides evidence relevant to this important question.

Barthélemy found that the Greek Minor Prophets scroll from Naḥal Ḥever contains some of the features characteristic of the *Kaige*-group, but not those features peculiar to Aquila. The evidence indicates that this text does not represent an independent translation, but rather a Jewish Palestinian recension of the Greek version found in the main LXX tradition, and so Barthélemy used the siglum R to refer to this text. Moreover, he argued that this recension brought the Greek closer to the Hebrew; that it was used by Justin Martyr (*Dialogue with Trypho*, about 135 C.E.); that it was chosen by Origen as the seventh column (i.e., the fifth translation, or Quinta) for the Hexapla; that it became the basis for Aquila's work (which brought to its culmination this method of revision, linked to rabbinic hermeneutics); and that it has nothing to do with "Theodotion's" translation of the Minor Prophets (which is really a late, eclectic, and pseudepigraphic work).[14]

The evidence, to be sure, is not decisive. Determining which Greek text was used as the basis for each later recension remains one of the central pursuits of LXX scholarship. Among the Greek fragments found in the Judean Desert, the Minor Prophets scroll yields evidence that is especially useful for understanding the history of the Greek ver-

11. See above, chap. 7, pp. 158–61. Outside the Greek Bible, καί and γέ (which in combination usually have an epexegetical function) are almost always separated by several intervening words. Editions of the LXX, such as Rahlfs's, treat these particles as two separate words, but in the modern literature they are typically treated as one. It should also be noted that the surviving Greek translation of Ecclesiastes, also characterized by the use of καίγε, is generally regarded to have been produced by Aquila.

12. Barthélemy, *Les devanciers d'Aquila*, 47. The additional characteristics of the group, treated by him in chap. 3, include such features as the rendering of distributive אִישׁ with ἀνήρ (instead of the more appropriate ἕκαστος), the avoidance of the historic present, and the use of ἐγώ εἰμι for אָנֹכִי.

13. See above, chap. 1, pp. 41–42.

14. For these and other conclusions, see Barthélemy, *Les devanciers d'Aquila*, chap. 11.

sions. It provides an early recension of the Greek that formed an intermediate stage between the original translation and the mixed text that resulted from Origen's work.

The Hebrew Biblical Texts

Most of the discussion concerning the relationship of the Qumran Hebrew texts to the Greek LXX texts has focused on the books of Jeremiah and Samuel. The Qumran fragments of both books appear to present a Hebrew text different from the MT and possibly closer to the *Vorlage* of the Greek versions of Jeremiah and Samuel. It is important, however, to understand the nature of the Qumran evidence in order to appreciate the conclusions inferred from it.

The Jeremiah Fragments

Differences between the LXX and the MT are not limited to individual variant readings, for the Greek and Hebrew texts of some books exhibit substantial differences in the content and sequence of the material. For instance, the Greek version of Jeremiah is significantly shorter than MT Jeremiah. Moreover, the contents of the Greek form of the book are found in a sequence quite different from the more familiar sequence of the Hebrew version.[15] It has long been thought that the Greek version of Jeremiah was translated from a Hebrew text that also contained these substantial differences, although no Hebrew manuscript supported such a claim.

The discovery of some fragments of Jeremiah at Qumran, however, has now provided a Hebrew text that closely matches the Greek version of Jeremiah. It appears to reflect the long minuses and the sequence of material found in the Greek. In addition, the Qumran text agrees in characteristic details with the Greek version, making it probable that the translator's *Vorlage* was quite similar to a Hebrew text that had remained unknown for two thousand years. Emanuel Tov writes:

> Two of the three fragments that have been previously labeled 4QJer[b], and which we now name 4QJer[b] and 4QJer[d], display a very close relation with the Hebrew *Vorlage* of the LXX. In fact, no other Qumran text is as close to the LXX as these two fragments.[16]

15. See above, chap. 3, pp. 78–79.

16. Emanuel Tov, "The Contribution of the Qumran Scrolls to the Understanding of the LXX," in *Septuagint, Scrolls and Cognate Writings*, ed. George J. Brooke and Barnabas Lindars (SBLSCS 33; Atlanta: Scholars Press, 1992), 28. For a more extensive discussion of Greek Jeremiah, see Tov's *Textual Criticism of the Hebrew Bible* (Minneapolis: Fortress, 1992), 319–27.

Since 4QJer[b] (also called 4Q71) and 4QJer[d] (also called 4Q72a) are the best representatives of a Hebrew *Vorlage* of the LXX text that differs from the MT, it is worth considering in more detail the nature of these fragments and how such a conclusion was reached. The texts in question consist of three small fragments (see illustration 18). When they were first discussed in the literature, all three were given the single siglum 4QJer[b] on the assumption that they came from the same scroll. That assumption is challenged by Tov, who assigns each fragment a separate siglum: 4QJer[b], 4QJer[d], and 4QJer[e] (also called 4Q72b). (4QJer[c] had been previously assigned to another scroll.) Tov believes that a different scribe wrote each of the three fragments, but that 4QJer[b] and 4QJer[d] are nevertheless fragments from the same scroll.[17]

18. 4QJer[b,d,e]; first century B.C.E.–first century C.E.

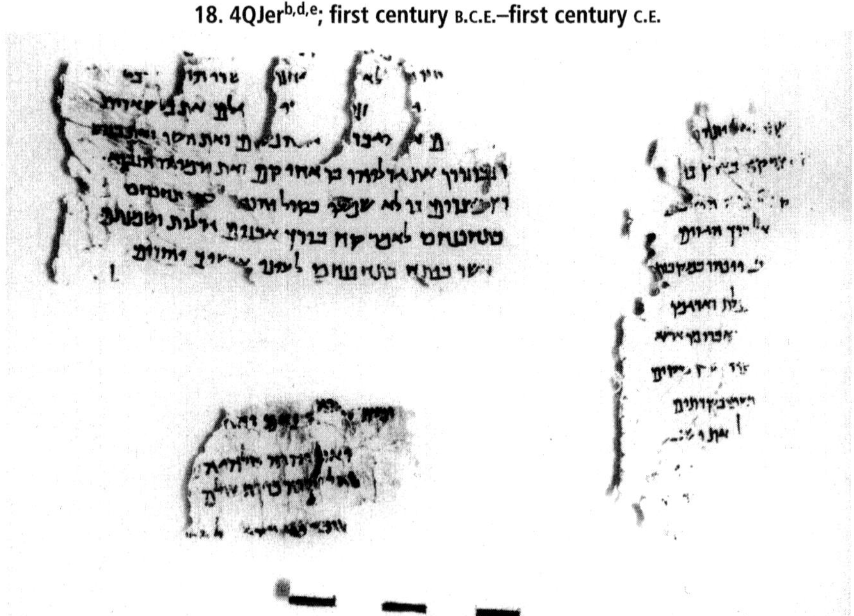

The Jeremiah fragments from Qumran provide manuscript evidence for the existence of a shorter Hebrew version of Jeremiah, which was attested only by Greek Jeremiah prior to the Qumran discovery.

source: Israel Antiquities Authority and Ancient Biblical Manuscript Center; PAM #43.078

The three fragments contain a total of about three hundred Hebrew letters, so the amount of material for examination is quite slim. Because the three fragments are broken, they contain no complete verse

17. Emanuel Tov, "The Jeremiah Scrolls from Qumran," *Revue de Qumran* 14 (1989): 191, 195. Tov points out, however, that Frank M. Cross and Joseph Naveh take all three fragments as belonging to one scroll produced by one scribe.

of Jeremiah, just sections of several lines from Jeremiah 9:22–10:21; 43:3–9; 50:4–6. This means that reconstruction of the text is necessary. Fortunately, the left margin is partially preserved, which facilitates reconstruction. Among the Hebrew words preserved in the fragments, one finds the short name formula, which is also characteristic of the Greek Jeremiah.[18] In Jeremiah 10:4, where the MT reads "nails and hammers," 4QJer^{b,d} agrees with the order of the Greek phrase against the MT by placing "hammers" before "nails."[19]

One must remember, however, that the conclusions offered by scholars rest on a very small sample of actual Hebrew text and a great deal on a reasonable, but nonetheless hypothetical, reconstruction. Furthermore, although these fragments of Jeremiah contain readings that agree with the LXX against the MT, they also contain several readings that agree with the MT against the LXX. It is not, therefore, as if what little Hebrew text survives in 4QJer^{b,d} exactly matches the corresponding Greek text of Jeremiah.

The evidence that 4QJer^{b,d} reflects the Hebrew *Vorlage* of LXX Jeremiah is stronger when the sequence of its verses is considered. The Greek text omits 10:6–8, and 4QJer^{b,d} also omits these verses. Moreover, verse 9 in the Greek is placed in the same location as it is in the Qumran fragment. The agreement in omissions and displacements constitutes impressive evidence that the Hebrew text of 4QJer^{b,d} is closer to the *Vorlage* of the Greek Jeremiah than is the MT. Moreover, if we reconstruct the missing text in 4QJer^{b,d} and then count the resulting number of Hebrew characters per line, the total corresponds more closely to the translator's *Vorlage* (as retroverted from the Greek) than to the extant MT.[20]

Tov argues that the Book of Jeremiah existed in two distinct Hebrew forms: a shorter edition from which the extant Greek was translated, and an expanded edition that became the MT. He proposes that the shorter text of Jeremiah—reflected by 4QJer^{b,d} and the Greek version—is the older edition of Jeremiah.[21] Fragments of both the shorter and longer Hebrew texts were found at Qumran. The oldest of the Jeremiah fragments, 4QJer^{a} (also called 4Q70)—as well as 2QJer (also called 2Q13) and 4QJer^{c} (also called 4Q72)—reflects the MT tradition

18. For example, יוחנן ("Johanan") in 43:4, 5, where the MT has יוֹחָנָן בֶּן־קָרֵחַ ("Johanan son of Kareah"). See Tov, "Contribution of the Qumran Scrolls," 28.

19. Todd S. Beall, "4QJer^{b} and the Text of Jeremiah," paper read at the Evangelical Theological Society Eastern Regional Meeting, 29 March 1996.

20. Because the fragments contain one margin of the text, it is possible to estimate how many letters and spaces comprised the missing portion of the lines, though we must keep in mind that the legible text comprises only about 10%–15% of each line. For full details see Emanuel Tov, "Three Fragments of Jeremiah from Qumran Cave 4," *Revue de Qumran* 15 (1992): 531–41.

21. Tov, *Textual Criticism of the Hebrew Bible*, 321.

and is thought to date from approximately 200 B.C.E., while 4QJer^{b,d} is dated somewhat later, to the first half of the second century B.C.E.[22] Because the age of a given manuscript must not be confused with the age of the text it contains, this evidence does not refute Tov's theory. It does, however, confirm that the expanded Hebrew text of Jeremiah already existed by 200 B.C.E.

Only by appreciating the condition of the preserved fragments and the nature of the reconstruction can one understand the tentativeness of any conclusion about the relationship of 4QJer^{b,d} to the Greek Jeremiah and the MT. And one should keep in mind that since 4QJer^{b} is the *best* evidence from Qumran for a variant Hebrew *Vorlage*, conclusions about other books involves even greater uncertainty.

Similar differences in length and the sequence of content are found in the Greek versions of Joshua and Ezekiel and in one of the Greek versions of Esther. Certain chapters of other books show analogous patterns of shorter length and a different sequence of material in the Greek. For instance, the story of David and Goliath in 1 Samuel in Greek contains only thirty-nine of the eighty-eight verses found in the MT. Differences in sequence are found in the Greek versions of Genesis, Proverbs, and Kings. The discoveries at Qumran have not proven that these books were also translated from a different Hebrew edition, but the evidence offered by the two Hebrew texts of Jeremiah increases the probability that other books were translated into Greek from a shorter, different Hebrew edition that is no longer extant. As Tov suggests,

> Textual features recognized for one biblical book may have existed also for other ones, even if they have not been preserved. Thus, even though the number of Qumran texts closely related to the LXX is very small, it stands to reason that at one time all books of the Bible existed in a Hebrew form which is now represented in Greek.[23]

The few Qumran texts that differ from the MT have deservedly received much scholarly attention. However, only about 5% of the Qumran manuscripts could be argued to reflect a Hebrew text-type close to the LXX. About 40% of the Hebrew biblical texts from Qumran contain the consonantal text of MT.[24] Tov describes the remaining texts as

22. Tov, "Jeremiah Scrolls from Qumran," 197.

23. Ibid., 190.

24. In *Textual Criticism of the Hebrew Bible*, 115, Tov specifies 60%, but has since revised his estimate; see his recent and important article, "The Significance of the Texts from the Judean Desert for the History of the Text of the Hebrew Bible: A New Synthesis," in *Qumran between the Old and New Testaments*, ed. F. H. Cryer and Thomas L. Thompson (Journal for the Study of the Old Testament Supplement 290; Copenhagen International Seminar 6; Sheffield: Sheffield Academic Press, 1998), 277–309, esp. 296.

"nonaligned" because their agreements and disagreements with the major textual traditions "follow an inconsistent pattern."[25] It is clear from the Hebrew texts found at Qumran that the MT, on which modern English translations of the OT are based, is indeed an ancient text that was already stable before the time of Jesus. The great Isaiah scroll (1QIsa[a]) and the Hebrew Minor Prophets scroll (MurXII) contain essentially the same Hebrew text as found in Codex Leningradensis dating from about a thousand years later. Many other finds from Qumran confirm the antiquity of the text preserved in the MT. But the discoveries in the Judean Desert also show that the Hebrew text that has come down to us in the MT was not the only Hebrew edition of at least some of the books. The extant Greek version of such books may have been based on a Hebrew text edition significantly different from the MT.

The Text of Samuel at Qumran

The Qumran fragment labeled 4QSam[a] (also called 4Q51) deserves special consideration. Even before the discovery of this document, the relationship between the Greek and Hebrew of Samuel was difficult to sort out. For example, as pointed out in the previous chapter, the differences between the two texts are significant. Moreover, the main Greek tradition of Samuel (and Kings) includes large sections that contain a *Kaige*-type translation based on a Hebrew text different from what served as the basis for the non-*Kaige* sections. In addition, some Greek manuscripts preserve the Lucianic recension, which likewise reflects a different Hebrew text. The new evidence presented by 4QSam[a] is difficult to interpret, but it clearly shows either that MT Samuel is severely corrupted by haplography or that a second Hebrew edition of the book once circulated.

The many agreements between 4QSam[a] and the "LXX" of Samuel against the MT are used to argue that the Qumran scrolls represent a distinct Hebrew text-type. In particular, Frank M. Cross proposed in the 1960s that the Samuel manuscripts found at Qumran preserve a Palestinian text-type different from the MT (which he considered a Babylonian text-type) but close to the *Vorlage* of the Greek Samuel (which he considered an Egyptian text-type).[26] Subsequently, his student Eugene Ulrich carried this theory further by arguing that the Qumran fragments of Samuel and other books represent a second literary edition. Ulrich defines the phenomenon as

> a literary unit—a story, pericope, narrative, poem, book, and so forth—appearing in two (or more) parallel forms in our principal textual witnesses,

25. Tov, *Textual Criticism of the Hebrew Bible*, 116.
26. See above, chap. 7, p. 160.

> which one author, major redactor, or major editor completed and which a subsequent redactor or editor intentionally changed to a sufficient extent that the resultant form should be called a revised edition of that text.[27]

Perhaps the best example of such a literary unit is the story of David and Goliath, which exists in two different forms, a short one in the OG and a fuller one in the MT.[28] The question then becomes which—if either—of the versions is supported by the fragments at Qumran. The OG story is 44% shorter than the MT, for it excludes the doublets present in the MT, such as David's being twice introduced to Saul, twice appointed as an officer in Saul's army, and twice offered one of Saul's daughters in marriage.[29]

The story of Hannah in 1 Samuel 1–2 also exists in two different forms in the OG as compared to the MT, but the relationship between these two literary forms is different from that of the David and Goliath story, which further complicates a reconstruction of the textual history of Samuel as a whole. Evidence of literary development of the biblical books is not limited to Samuel. Such evidence is also found when the OG and MT are compared for Exodus, Jeremiah, and Daniel. Were these developments introduced in the Hebrew text or in the Greek version? Scholars look to the Hebrew fragments from Qumran to shed light on this question.

Ulrich argues that because of the impressive number of agreements between 4QSam[a] and the Greek Samuel, the Qumran fragments must represent a shorter Hebrew text from which the Greek translation was made. He infers that a later literary edition developed in the Hebrew, culminating with the form preserved in the MT. But even if one agrees that the double literary editions developed in the Hebrew and that the Greek translator was simply translating the *Vorlage* before him, it is

27. Eugene C. Ulrich Jr., "Double Literary Editions of Biblical Narratives and Reflections on Determining the Form to be Translated," in *Perspectives on the Hebrew Bible*, ed. James L. Crenshaw (Macon, Ga.: Mercer University Press, 1988), 101–16, quotation from 102. This article builds on his important dissertation, *The Qumran Text of Samuel and Josephus* (Harvard Semitic Monographs 19; Missoula, Mont.: Scholars Press, 1978), summarized in "4QSam[a] and Septuagintal Research," *BIOSCS* 8 (1975): 24–39.

28. For other examples, see Zipora Talshir, "The Contribution of Diverging Traditions Preserved in the Septuagint to Literary Criticism of the Bible," in *VIII Congress of the International Organization for Septuagint and Cognate Studies: Paris 1992*, ed. Leonard J. Greenspoon and Olivier Munnich (SBLSCS 41; Atlanta: Scholars Press, 1995), 21–41. See also Tov, *Textual Criticism of the Hebrew Bible*, chap. 7.

29. For further details, including a chart summarizing the texts in parallel, see Tov, *Textual Criticism of the Hebrew Bible*, 334–36. The reader is also referred to *The Story of David and Goliath: Textual and Literary Criticism; Papers of a Joint Research Venture*, by Dominique Barthélemy, David W. Gooding, Johan Lust, and Emanuel Tov (Göttingen: Vandenhoeck & Ruprecht, 1986). These four scholars, each with different specializations and approaches to the text, present their explanations of the development of the David and Goliath story, critique each other's views, and then attempt to synthesize the results.

still debatable whether the Qumran fragments of Samuel actually represent that earlier, shorter edition.

Tov, for example, calls the conclusion that a distinct text-type is represented in the agreements between the Qumran scrolls and the Greek Samuel an "optical illusion presented by the evidence."[30] In his opinion, the evidence proves only that the Hebrew text of Samuel that has come down to us as the MT apparently experienced significant textual corruption after the Greek translation was made. Moreover, as we have seen, the textual transmission of the Greek translation itself is very complicated.

Greek Samuel and 4QSam[a] contain a few common readings that are clearly errors.[31] This evidence indicates that the Greek was translated from a Hebrew *Vorlage* that already contained these errors. Since the MT does not have these readings, that text has come to us on a separate transmission path. However, to balance these distinctive agreements, it needs to be pointed out that 4QSam[a] also disagrees with the Greek in ways that make it difficult to conclude that the scroll represents the Hebrew *Vorlage* from which the Greek was translated.

Of even greater interest, 4QSam[a] contains a narrative that is found in neither the Greek nor the MT![32] Between 1 Samuel 10:27 and 11:1, the scroll includes a unique episode about King Nahash of the Ammonites. Comparison of the NIV, which follows the MT, and the NRSV, which accepts the Qumran reading, displays the difference:

NIV	**NRSV**
They despised him and brought him no gifts. But Saul kept silent.	They despised him and brought him no present. But he held his peace. Now Nahash, king of the Ammonites, had been grievously oppressing the Gadites and the Reubenites. He would gouge out the right eye of each of them and would not grant Israel a deliverer. No one was left of the Israelites across the Jordan whose right eye Nahash, king of the Ammonites, had not gouged out. But there were seven thousand men who had escaped from the Ammonites and had entered Jabesh-gilead. About a month later,
Nahash the Ammonite went up and besieged Jabesh Gilead.	Nahash the Ammonite went up and besieged Jabesh-gilead.

30. Tov, "Contribution of the Qumran Scrolls," 31.

31. Ibid., 32.

32. This variation has been discussed in various publications. See, for example, T. L. Eves, "One Ammonite Invasion or Two? 1 Sam 10:27–11:2 in the Light of 4QSam[a]," *Westminster Theological Journal* 44 (1982): 308–26.

The NRSV translators apparently believe that the additional material in the Qumran text more adequately introduces the siege of Jabesh Gilead by providing a motivation for it. On the other hand, although Nahash and his siege of the city are introduced rather abruptly in the MT, it is not obvious that something is missing. Even though the motivation for the attack is not given, the text reads smoothly enough. While the additional section found in 4QSam[a] gives the reason Nahash attacked the city, one must ask whether this paragraph provides evidence of literary development or of haplography.

Earlier Hebrew readers may have felt that a reason for the attack was needed, even if modern readers do not, and the paragraph could have been a deliberate addition to the Hebrew text. Alternatively, the paragraph could have been deliberately dropped from the text for unknown political or sociological reasons that developed over time. Haplography may also explain the omission, because the phrases immediately before and after the omitted paragraph have a similar form.

What is particularly interesting about this example is that no trace of this paragraph is found in any of the Greek manuscripts of Samuel.[33] This indicates that the paragraph was not in the Hebrew *Vorlage* from which the Greek translation was made. A further implication is either that the paragraph quite early dropped out of the Hebrew text that became the MT or that it was added to the Hebrew text after the Greek translation was made (and that the Greek was never corrected to the fuller edition of the Hebrew). 4QSam[a] raises more questions than it answers about the textual history of Samuel.

Tov and Ulrich agree that the Greek version of Samuel represents a literary edition of the Hebrew distinct from the MT, though they disagree whether the Qumran fragment 4QSam[a] represents that edition. The shorter edition reflected in the Greek is thought to be a faithful translation of an abridged Hebrew text (contrast the situation of Jeremiah, where the shorter Greek text is thought to translate an early Hebrew edition from which the expanded edition was later produced). Questions about the relationship of the Hebrew *Vorlage* of the Greek Samuel to the MT and whether there was a second Hebrew edition of Samuel remain unsettled.[34]

For similar reasons, claims have been made about the close relationship of LXX Leviticus, Numbers, and Deuteronomy to fragments

33. Note, however, that the phrase "about a month later" in 11:1 is found in the Greek (καὶ ἐγενήθη ὡς μετὰ μῆνα) and corresponds to the last phrase of 10:27 in the MT: "and he was silent" (וַיְהִי כְּמַחֲרִישׁ; the translator's *Vorlage* must have read וַיְהִי כְּמוֹ חֹדֶשׁ, as does 4QSam[a]). The NRSV apparently assumes that the original Hebrew text originally had both these phrases and that their similarity led to haplography.

34. For an excellent discussion of both approaches, see Barthélemy et al., *Story of David and Goliath*.

of the Hebrew texts found at Qumran. In these cases, only a small amount of Hebrew text was preserved at Qumran, from which it is difficult to make generalizations. Some argue that the agreement of individual readings between the scrolls and the LXX against the MT in those books is evidence of a different Hebrew edition. This appears to be a rash conclusion based on the existence of a second Hebrew text of Jeremiah that apparently follows the sequence and content of the Greek version.

Tov describes the methodological issues in determining the relationship of the Qumran scrolls and the LXX as problematic in almost every respect:[35]

1. The reconstruction of the *Vorlage* of the LXX is tentative.
2. Only fragments have been preserved of the Qumran scrolls.
3. The published statistics of the relationship between the LXX and the scrolls are incomplete.
4. Different types of readings common to the LXX and the scrolls must be distinguished.
5. Agreements in readings common to the scrolls, the LXX, and additional sources are less persuasive than agreements shared only by the scrolls and the LXX.
6. The generally accepted view of the relationship between the scrolls, the LXX and MT, and in particular the use of the term *text-type*, must be revised.

Therefore, although the Qumran scrolls provide invaluable data for understanding the history of the biblical texts, they also present complex methodological issues that should caution us against drawing generalized conclusions.

The existence of different kinds of variations between the Greek version(s) and the MT, and the possibility that some of these differences group together to form a pattern that reshapes the biblical text, suggests that a distinction must be made between textual criticism and literary criticism. Individual variant readings independently introduced by countless scribes over centuries of time are of a fundamentally different nature than changes to the text resulting from a deliberate, thorough reworking of an entire book at some point in its history. In practice, it has proven difficult for scholars to identify criteria that would clearly distinguish the

35. Emanuel Tov, "Determining the Relationship between the Qumran Scrolls and the LXX: Some Methodological Issues," in *The Hebrew and Greek Texts of Samuel: 1980 Proceedings IOSCS, Vienna*, ed. Emanuel Tov (Jerusalem: Academon, 1980), 46. With regard to Tov's skepticism about the label *text-types*, see the important response by Frank M. Cross, *The Ancient Library of Qumran*, 3d ed. (Sheffield: Sheffield Academic Press, 1995), 177–81.

two. How many accumulated scribal errors would it take before one text-type appears to be transformed into some other?

Moreover, although a revision would have been made with a deliberate purpose in mind, that purpose remains unknown to us. For instance, a reviser might simply update the language, replacing words with their more contemporary synonyms and revising the syntax. Or a revision might be done to form a new literary edition by adding and deleting material that substantially changes the content. Scribes also added and deleted material accidentally. How many changes would constitute a new literary edition?[36]

The biblical scrolls from Qumran are too fragmentary to help us answer those questions conclusively. They have nevertheless added greatly to our knowledge of the biblical text during the Second Temple period and have thus changed the complexion of the scholarly debate. No attempt to identify the *Vorlage* of the LXX or to use the LXX for the textual criticism of the Hebrew Bible can succeed without taking seriously into account the evidence from the Judean Desert.

To Continue Your Study

For a clear, sober, and up-to-date survey of the Dead Sea Scrolls, see James C. VanderKam, *The Dead Sea Scrolls Today* (Grand Rapids: Eerdmans, 1994). Much can still be learned from Frank M. Cross's classic popularization, *The Ancient Library of Qumran*, 3d ed. (Sheffield: Sheffield Academic Press, 1995); this latest edition includes an additional chapter in which the author interacts with criticisms of his work. The most comprehensive bibliography, with many features helpful to students and researchers, is Joseph A. Fitzmyer, *The Dead Sea Scrolls: Major Publications and Tools for Study*, rev. ed. (Society of Biblical Literature Resources for Biblical Study 20; Atlanta: Scholars Press, 1990). See also the comprehensive list of scrolls compiled by Emanuel Tov in *The SBL Handbook of Style: For Ancient Near Eastern, Biblical, and Early Christian Studies*, ed. Patrick H. Alexander et al. (Peabody, Mass.: Hendrickson, 1999), 176–233.

Several collections of essays are of special value. See, for example, *The Dead Sea Scrolls after Fifty Years: A Comprehensive Assessment*, ed. Peter W. Flint and James C. VanderKam (Leiden: Brill, 1998), especially the article by Leonard J. Greenspoon on "The Dead Sea Scrolls and the Greek Bible." Note also *Septuagint, Scrolls, and Cognate Writings: Papers Presented to the International Symposium on the Septuagint and Its Relations to the Dead Sea Scrolls and Other Writings (Manchester, 1990)*, ed. George J. Brooke and Barnabas Lindars (SBLSCS 33; Atlanta: Scholars Press, 1992), especially the surveys by Emanuel Tov and Eugene Ulrich.

36. For a more complete discussion of textual criticism versus literary criticism, we again refer the reader to Tov, *Textual Criticism of the Hebrew Bible*, chap. 7.

9

Septuagint and New Testament

Language. The importance of LXX Greek for understanding the language of the NT is widely acknowledged, although the influence of the former on the latter has sometimes been exaggerated. Septuagintalisms in the NT do not characteristically affect the structure of the language.

Text. The numerous quotations from the LXX by NT writers provide information useful for text-critical purposes. In the first place, we can view the ***New Testament as a Source for the Textual Criticism of the Septuagint***, since the quotations at times preserve very early readings, some of which may reflect the original LXX text. Second, we can use the ***Septuagint as an Aid for the Study of the New Testament Text***, although the data must be used with caution.

Interpretation. The LXX is of special value for the light it sheds on the hermeneutics of the NT writers. ***Quotations:*** the ways in which the apostles quote the OT raise some important problems of interpretation, particularly when they follow the LXX rather than the Hebrew form of the passages. ***Theological Terms:*** the use of specialized theological vocabulary under the influence of the LXX reveals significant aspects of apostolic thought. ***Allusions:*** although less obvious than direct quotations, allusions demonstrate how pervasive has been the impact of the LXX on the authors of the NT.

When the LXX is discussed in scholarly literature or used by students, much of the time the purpose in view is to enhance our understanding of the NT. Such studies can be valuable. However, when a literary work is used predominantly for purposes other than the understanding of the work itself, the potential for misuse is great. Theological seminaries, in the rare instances that they offer a course on the LXX, typically include it not among the offerings in the OT department, but rather as a NT course, for which Hebrew might not even be a prerequisite. Such courses are sometimes strictly linguistic in character, aiming at little more than increasing the student's proficiency in Greek. At other times they focus primarily on the quotations found in the NT. In either case, the student is not able to develop a comprehensive view of the field.

We have deliberately placed the present chapter after our discussion of the more technical problems related to LXX studies. Responsible analysis of the material covered here requires patience: the effort must be made to understand the Greek OT on its own terms before using it for something else. Having said that, however, we may readily acknowledge that the relationship between the LXX and the NT constitutes a legitimate, important, and exciting field of research.

Language

The importance of the LXX as a source for our knowledge of Koine is widely recognized. On that basis alone, students of the Greek NT would have plenty of reason to become as familiar as possible with the language of the Greek OT. In addition, these two bodies of literature share numerous linguistic and conceptual features not found in other documents representative of Koine Greek, such as the *Histories* of Polybius, the *Discourses* of Epictetus, and the nonliterary papyri discovered in Egypt. It is thus not altogether inappropriate to bring the language of the LXX and of the NT together under the rubric of "Biblical Greek"—although we must continually remind ourselves that this literature is characterized by much linguistic diversity.

An additional consideration, however, brings the LXX and the NT even closer together, namely, the indisputable fact that the NT writers knew and used the OT in its Greek form. In other words, we are not dealing with two bodies of literature that merely happen to use the same type of Greek or that cover similar subject matter in isolation from each other. An important question then arises regarding the influence of the LXX on the NT writers. Later in this chapter we shall discuss the effect of the Greek OT on apostolic thought and theology. Here, however, we are interested only in its influence on the NT language. What was the nature and extent of this influence? Widely differing answers have been given to this question.[1]

One influential approach was that of Edwin Hatch, who argued in 1889 that Biblical Greek is "a language which stands by itself. What we have to find out in studying it is what meaning certain Greek words

1. The paragraphs that follow summarize material in Moisés Silva, *Biblical Words and Their Meaning: An Introduction to Lexical Semantics*, rev. ed. (Grand Rapids: Zondervan, 1994), 56–68.

conveyed to a Semitic mind." In his opinion, the main difference between Classical Greek and NT Greek is that the latter was written by "men whose thoughts were cast in a Semitic and not in a Hellenic mould." In fact, "the great majority" of words in the NT reflect this Semitic background and therefore must "be examined in the light of the cognate documents which form the LXX." These words "are so numerous, and a student is so frequently misled by his familiarity with their classical use, that it is a safe rule to let no word, even the simplest, in the N.T. pass unchallenged."[2]

Within two years, however, T. K. Abbott published a sound rebuttal of this position. To begin with, he questioned the view that NT Greek is heavily semitized: "Expressions characterized as Hebraisms may in not a few instances be paralleled in classical writers, the difference being in their frequency." He then argued that a comparison of LXX Greek with the language of the NT reveals a striking "unlikeness." Relatively few "biblical meanings" are common to both, while the NT contains numerous words and meanings not found in the LXX. "Such facts as these show that the influence of the Septuagint version on the vocabulary of the NT was not predominant, and that to make the usage of the former determine the interpretation of the latter, except in the case of terms of Hebrew theology, is quite out of the question."[3]

Further evidence supporting Abbott came from unexpected quarters. H. A. A. Kennedy, who had been inspired by the work of Hatch and on whose conclusions he had depended, undertook an extensive study of this topic. But "the further the inquiry was pushed, the more decidedly was [the author] compelled to doubt those conclusions, and finally to seek to establish the connection between the language of the LXX and that of the New Testament on a totally different basis." After a thorough analysis of terms common only to the LXX and the NT, he readily admits that in the case of theological and religious terms (and to a lesser extent those denoting Jewish customs), the influence of the LXX on the NT has been direct and therefore Hatch's maxims are applicable. As a whole, however, this influence "must not be exagger-

2. Edwin Hatch, *Essays in Biblical Greek* (Oxford: Clarendon, 1889), 10, 11, 34. His method for determining the meaning of such words was based on two "self-evident" principles: (1) if a word is used uniformly in the LXX to translate the same Hebrew word, that Greek word has the same meaning as the Hebrew word; and (2) if several Greek words are used interchangeably to translate one Hebrew word, those Greek words have "an allied or virtually identical meaning" (p. 35). In fact, both of these criteria are debatable and misleading.

3. T. K. Abbott, *Essays, Chiefly on the Original Texts of the Old and New Testaments* (London: Longmans, Green, 1891), 66, 71. A detailed evaluation of the very examples Hatch used led Abbott to conclude that whenever Hatch "tries to apply to the N.T. a signification peculiar to the LXX, or ascertained according to the maxims he lays down, he is in no one instance successful" (p. 98).

ated," and caution is needed when using the evidence from the LXX. "When we consider the exceptional importance of the Greek Bible to the New Testament writers, the astonishing fact is that its influence on their vocabulary is not incomparably greater than it is found to be."[4]

The papyrological discoveries during the last decades of the nineteenth century served to confirm that NT Greek is best understood not as a peculiar semitized dialect but as a true representative of living Koine Greek.[5] No scholar was more vocal about this issue than Adolf Deissmann. Without denying the existence of Semitisms in the NT, he argued that these "are merely birthmarks" and therefore do not constitute "sufficient reason for scholars to isolate the language of the sacred texts" from cosmopolitan Greek. This conviction naturally led Deissmann to oppose Hatch's views regarding the meaning of LXX words. That ἱλαστήριον, for example, is used to translate Hebrew כַּפֹּרֶת does not prove that the Greek word means "lid"; the papyri show that ἱλαστήριον means "propitiation," so the LXX translators must have replaced the Hebrew concept by another one that "brings out the purpose of the lid." Moreover, although Deissmann affirmed the importance of the LXX for understanding the NT and spoke of the "hundreds of threads" uniting the two sets of documents, he viewed the LXX language as largely artificial in character and thus quite different from NT Greek.[6]

Deissmann's basic position—though opposed by a handful of scholars and modified by others—was certainly on target. What are its implications for our present purposes? A distinction needs to be made between the influence of the LXX on NT thought (to be discussed later in this chapter) and its influence on NT language. And with regard to the latter, a further distinction needs to be made between matters that affect the structure of the language and those that do not.

4. H. A. A. Kennedy, *Sources of New Testament Greek: The Influence of the Septuagint on the Vocabulary of the New Testament* (Edinburgh: Clark, 1895), v, 108, 165.

5. With specific reference to Paul's vocabulary, note especially Theodor Nägeli, *Der Wortschatz des Apostels Paulus: Beitrag zur sprachgeschichtlichen Erforschung des Neuen Testament* (Göttingen: Vandenhoeck & Ruprecht, 1905), which includes a discussion of Paul's dependence on the LXX.

6. Adolf Deissmann, *The Philology of the Greek Bible* (London: Hodder & Stoughton, 1908), 13, 65, 92. A fine synthesis of Deissmann's views may be found in his article "Hellenistisches Griechisch" (1899), now available in English translation: "Hellenistic Greek with Special Consideration of the Greek Bible," in *The Language of the New Testament: Classic Essays*, ed. Stanley E. Porter (Journal for the Study of the New Testament Supplement 60, Sheffield: JSOT Press, 1991), 39–59. For further defense of this position, see Moisés Silva, "Bilingualism and the Character of Palestinian Greek," *Biblica* 61 (1980): 198–219 (repr. in *Language of the New Testament*, ed. Porter, 205–26), and G. H. R. Horsley, *New Documents Illustrating Early Christianity*, vol. 5: *Linguistic Essays* (Sydney: Macquarrie University Press, 1989), esp. chap. 1.

Literary monuments, such as the King James Version, affect later stages of the language at the stylistic level (especially when a minister is trying to evoke biblical associations!), but seldom if ever do they interfere with natural developments in the structure of the language. Thus, for example, when Luke uses the expression καὶ ἐγένετο (= וַיְהִי = "and it came to pass" in the King James Version), it would be pointless to deny that, under the influence of the LXX, he is imitating the biblical style. But this is a matter of phraseology rather than syntax in the strict sense.

What we do *not* find in NT Greek is, for instance, the use of ἀνήρ in place of ἕκαστος for the distributive meaning "each," a usage common in some LXX books in imitation of the use of אִישׁ in the Hebrew Bible. Similarly, the NT authors never—except when quoting the OT directly—use the peculiar combination of a finite verb with a participle of the same (or similar) verb in imitation of the Hebrew infinitive absolute construction, such as πληθύνων πληθυνῶ ("increasing I will increase" = הַרְבָּה אַרְבֶּה; Gen. 3:16).[7]

James H. Moulton was quite right that, characteristically, Semitisms in the NT consist in the overuse of terms or idioms that were "correct enough as Greek, but which would have remained in comparatively rare use but for the accident of their answering to Hebrew or Aramaic phrases."[8] We should be careful, however, not to minimize the significance of this phenomenon, for changes in frequency can indeed affect linguistic structure. Notice, for example, the following set of equivalents:

δίδωμι = נָתַן ("to give")
τίθημι = שִׂים ("to set")
ποιέω = עָשָׂה ("to make")

One finds a very large measure of semantic (or more precisely, distributional) correspondence between each of these Greek verbs and its

7. The Hebrew construction is often rendered in the LXX with a finite verb preceded by a cognate noun in the dative case (e.g., περιτομῇ περιτμηθήσεται = הִמּוֹל יִמּוֹל; Gen. 17:13). This approach would have seemed less strange to a Greek reader (BDF §198.6) and is used in the NT, especially by Luke. See also below, chap. 12, pp. 268, 270.

8. James H. Moulton, *A Grammar of New Testament Greek*, vol. 1: *Prolegomena*, 3d ed. (Edinburgh: Clark, 1908), 11. Even with regard to the LXX Pentateuch (and other LXX books of like character), Thackeray argues that its Hebraic character "consists in the *accumulation* of a number of just tolerable Greek phrases, which nearly correspond to what is normal and idiomatic in Hebrew. If we take these phrases individually, we can discover isolated parallels to them in the papyri, but in no document outside the Bible or writings directly dependent upon it do we find them in such profusion." See Henry St. John Thackeray, *A Grammar of the Old Testament in Greek according to the Septuagint*, vol. 1: *Introduction, Orthography and Accidence* (Cambridge: Cambridge University Press, 1909), 29.

matching Hebrew verb; in the majority of cases, therefore, the use of these standard renderings by the LXX translators is unremarkable. The three Hebrew verbs, however, have greater semantic overlap than do the Greek verbs. From the perspective of English or Greek, one could say that both נָתַן and עָשָׂה encroach on the meaning of שִׂים. Thus, for example, we find in Exodus 31:6, "And I have *appointed* with him [i.e., with Bezalel] Oholiab"; the Hebrew has נָתַתִּי אִתּוֹ אֵת אָהֳלִיאָב, rendered by LXX with δέδωκα [variant ἔδωκα] αὐτὸν καὶ τὸν Ελιαβ, where the verb τίθημι might have been more natural. And in 1 Kings 12:31, "*He also made* houses on high places, *and appointed* priests from among all the people," both of the italicized English phrases represent Hebrew וַיַּעַשׂ, translated in the LXX with καὶ ἐποίησεν.

From time to time, the Greek translators abandon the standard equivalent for the sake of a more idiomatic rendering. In 2 Chronicles 32:6, "He *appointed* combat commanders over the people," the Hebrew verb is וַיִּתֵּן, rendered by the LXX with καὶ ἔθετο. As a whole, however, the tendency to maintain the standard equivalents causes a significant increase in the frequency of certain lexical uses that were, at best, rare in native Greek compositions.

What needs to be appreciated is that such a frequency shift has indeed had an effect on linguistic structure. To the extent that δίδωμι and ποιέω have encroached on the semantic area normally occupied by τίθημι, to that extent we may say that the lexical *system* has been reorganized. Moreover, this change is reflected in NT Greek, at least in the case of δίδωμι.[9] Once again, the clearest evidence comes from the Lucan material (e.g., Luke 19:23; Acts 13:20), but other possible instances are Ephesians 1:22; 4:11; Revelation 3:8–9; 17:17.

A more obvious example is the use of καρδία with reference to the seat of the mental faculties, in imitation of לֵב. Although some ancient Greek evidence supports such a meaning, the word was not especially common in the Hellenistic and Roman periods,[10] and for all practical purposes it no longer occupied the semantic field of "mind," for which Greek had a rich supply of terms (e.g., γνώμη, διάνοια, νοῦς, φρήν). These other terms are used from time to time in the LXX, but there they are eclipsed by καρδία, which occurs more than 960 times. With regard to this semantic field, the influence of the LXX on the NT is ap-

9. With regard to ποιέω, note Mark 3:12, καὶ ἐποίησεν δώδεκα ("and he appointed twelve"), which some regard as a Septuagintalism. Since Mark's language is not especially affected by the LXX, however, perhaps Aramaic עֲבַד ("to make, do") is the source of this use. See Matthew Black, *An Aramaic Approach to the Gospels and Acts*, 3d ed. (Oxford: Clarendon, 1967), 140–41.

10. Polybius and Epictetus both use it only once. Plutarch, however, uses it with some frequency.

parent. While the proportions are not as dramatic,[11] καρδία occurs in the NT more than 160 times and clearly dominates the field.

These examples of δίδωμι and καρδία, however, could be viewed as exceptions that prove the rule, since one cannot find many changes in the linguistic system of NT Greek (whether in the vocabulary or in the syntax) that have been caused by the language of the LXX. In the end, we have to recognize that the influence of the Greek OT on the language of the early Christians was, on the whole, limited to the use of technical or semitechnical terms distinctive of Hebrew theology or Jewish customs.[12] But that means that the influence in question is primarily extralinguistic (cultural or conceptual) in nature. We shall therefore need to return to these terms later in this chapter, when we deal with the area of interpretation.

Text

With regard to textual criticism, the relationship between the LXX and the NT surfaces in passages where the NT writers quote (or directly allude to) the OT. These quotations have long intrigued scholars. Around the middle of the nineteenth century, for example, a writer by the name of D. M. Turpie made an extensive study of 275 NT passages and concluded that the NT, the LXX, and the Hebrew text all agree in only about 20% of the quotations. Of the 80% where some disagreement occurs, less than 5% agree with the Hebrew against the LXX, while about a third of the quotations agree with the LXX against the Hebrew.[13]

Although other scholars give somewhat different figures, these proportions indicate how heavily the NT writers used the Greek version of the OT. The remaining quotations agree with neither the Hebrew nor the LXX, so the NT authors must have either paraphrased the passages or perhaps used a variant Greek text that has not survived. Later

11. For example, the ratio of καρδία to νοῦς is about 33:1 in the LXX, but about 6:1 in the NT. It should be emphasized, moreover, that almost all uses of νοῦς in the NT are found in the Pauline Epistles.

12. Of course, many of these terms, such as the loanword πάσχα or the semantic loan νόμος for "Jewish religion," would doubtless have been used among Jewish and Jewish-Christian Greek speakers even if a Greek version of the OT had never been produced.

13. See D. M. Turpie, *The Old Testament in the New* (London: Williams & Norgate, 1868), 267–69. A recent and useful manual is Gleason L. Archer and G. C. Chirichigno, *Old Testament Quotations in the New Testament: A Complete Survey* (Chicago: Moody, 1983), which includes the three texts in parallel columns as well as evaluative comments (which must, however, be used with caution). For the Pauline letters in particular, see Moisés Silva, "Old Testament in Paul," in *Dictionary of Paul and His Letters*, ed. Gerald F. Hawthorne and Ralph P. Martin (Downers Grove, Ill.: InterVarsity, 1993), 630–42, esp. the chart on 631. See also Hans Hübner, *Vetus Testamentum in Novo*, vol. 2: *Corpus Paulinum* (Göttingen: Vandenhoeck & Ruprecht, 1997).

in this chapter we shall examine the hermeneutical implications of this material. Here we focus on the text-critical question.

The textual relationship between the LXX and the NT can be looked at in one of two ways. From the viewpoint of the LXX scholar, the NT—along with other writers that quote the OT in Greek, such as Philo, Josephus, and the church fathers—provides information regarding the LXX text in the early centuries of our era and therefore helps us establish that text in its original form. From the viewpoint of the NT scholar, knowledge of the LXX's textual tradition can occasionally help establish the original NT text; moreover, it can shed light on why the NT is often distinctive.

The New Testament as a Source for the Textual Criticism of the Septuagint

If the NT text is secure at a point where the OT is quoted, the NT provides important evidence for the text of the Greek OT—evidence that antedates the great uncials by three or four centuries. For example, Paul quotes Isaiah 28:16 in Romans 9:33 (cf. 10:11): καὶ ὁ πιστεύων ἐπ' αὐτῷ οὐ καταισχυνθήσεται ("and he who believes in him will not be ashamed"). Some LXX manuscripts, including Codex Vaticanus and Codex Venetus, as well as the Syro-Hexaplar, omit the phrase ἐπ' αὐτῷ in accordance with the MT. Since we can establish on other grounds that these witnesses are representatives of the Hexaplaric recension in Isaiah, the omission of the phrase in them is immediately suspect. And since the words in Romans 9:33 are textually secure,[14] Paul provides the earliest available evidence for the original text of LXX Isaiah 28:16.

Things are not usually so simple, however. The last clause of Hosea 1:10 (LXX 2:1), according to Rahlfs's text, is ἐκεῖ κληθήσονται υἱοὶ θεοῦ ζῶντος ("there they will be called sons of the living God"). This reading, which we shall refer to as LXX^{A}, is found in Codex Alexandrinus, Codex Venetus, and many minuscules (mainly belonging to the Lucianic recension), with some versional and patristic support. The other witnesses, however, including Codex Vaticanus, Codex Marchalianus, and the Catena recension, read: κληθήσονται καὶ αὐτοὶ υἱοὶ θεοῦ ζῶντος ("they too [*or,* even they] will be called sons of the living God"). (Codex Sinaiticus is missing the Book of Hosea.) This second reading, which we will refer to as LXX^{B}, is closer to the Hebrew; and it has stronger external support, which is probably why Joseph Ziegler chose it as representing the original text.[15]

14. That is, NT manuscripts display no variants for this particular phrase (although we do find variants for other parts of the quotation).

15. Joseph Ziegler, *Duodecim Prophetae*, 3d ed. (Septuaginta 13; Göttingen: Vandenhoeck & Ruprecht, 1984), 148. This reading, like the Hebrew, does not have the word *there*. It should be kept in mind, however, that in another (less significant) respect, the Hebrew is unlike this second reading, since it does not have any element that corresponds to the adverbial use of καί (indeed, a few Greek witnesses omit καί as well).

Paul quotes this verse in Romans 9:26 in the form LXX[A], and the passage is textually secure (i.e., the NT manuscripts have no competing variants). In other words, Romans 9:26 must be added to the list of witnesses in support of the first variant. But how much weight should be given to this Pauline evidence? Can we simply assume that the reading in question was already present in a document used by Paul? Or is it possible that this variant originated with Paul himself and that subsequent manuscripts of the LXX were affected by what he had done? We need to remember that the scribes who copied the surviving manuscripts of the LXX were by and large Christians who would have been familiar with the NT writings. When, in the process of producing a LXX manuscript, they came to a passage that was quoted in the NT, they sometimes adjusted the text, either inadvertently (because of their memory of the NT form) or purposely (because they assumed the NT form was correct).

We may approach this matter, first, by considering intrinsic probability. Given the simple Hebrew יֵאָמֵר לָהֶם (lit., "it will be said to them"; i.e., "they will be called"), what is more likely: that the original LXX translator rendered the phrase κληθήσονται καὶ αὐτοί or ἐκεῖ κληθήσονται? Both renderings involve a slight alteration that highlights this clause (over against the previous clause), and both might have been motivated by the context. In other words, the addition of ἐκεῖ could have been motivated by the previous reference to a place (ἐν τῷ τόπῳ), while the addition of καὶ αὐτοί could have served to heighten the contrast with the Israelites' prior condition. Since variant LXX[A] (the addition of ἐκεῖ) is the more substantive change, for which no clear parallel can be adduced in the Greek Minor Prophets, we may tentatively view reading LXX[B] as original.

Transcriptional probability also supports LXX[B]. If we assume that ἐκεῖ was original, we know no obvious reason that would have led a Greek scribe to change it.[16] On the other hand, if we assume that καὶ αὐτοί was in fact original and that Paul was responsible for reading LXX[A], we can easily explain what caused its change to ἐκεῖ in LXX manuscripts: scribes may well have been influenced by the form in which Paul quoted the passage.[17]

16. Someone wishing to adjust the Greek toward the Hebrew would have simply omitted ἐκεῖ rather than replacing it with καὶ αὐτοί.

17. If we assume that Paul was not responsible for reading LXX[A], however, it is more difficult to make a decision on this matter. For further discussion, see Dietrich-Alex Koch, *Die Schrift als Zeuge: Untersuchungen zur Verwendung und zum Verständnis der Schrift bei Paulus* (Beiträge zur historischen Theologie 69; Tübingen: Mohr Siebeck, 1986), 174, who argues that Paul's text already had LXX[A], but who believes nevertheless that it is easier to understand how that reading originated from LXX[B] than vice versa (unfortunately, Koch does not explain why he thinks that this is the case).

But how do we go about deciding whether Paul was indeed the one who made the change? The answer depends on our ability to detect Paul's hermeneutical concerns in this passage. Some commentators attempt to find a reason that might have led Paul to add ἐκεῖ, but most are skeptical.[18] Of course, if we knew for sure that Paul was responsible for this change, then we might be more inclined to detect a hermeneutical motive.

At any rate, note that evidence in the NT for a particular variant can be a double-edged sword. If we have good reason to believe that the variant is an innovation on the part of the NT author, then the evidence is decisively negative in character, that is, such a variant could not have been the original LXX reading. If, on the other hand, the presence of this variant in the NT suggests that it was already in existence, then it would count as strongly positive external evidence, since the NT provides exceptionally early witness. Even then, however, a final decision regarding its originality depends on other text-critical factors.[19]

The Septuagint as an Aid for the Study of the New Testament Text

Frequently, OT quotations in the NT present textual problems. If we revisit Romans 9:33, we find that the reading καὶ ὁ πιστεύων is attested in the earliest witnesses, but that the majority of NT manuscripts have καὶ πᾶς ὁ πιστεύων ("and everyone who believes"). In this case, the LXX text, which does not have πᾶς, is secure: only manuscript 407, a ninth-century minuscule, includes the word.

For the NT textual critic, it is helpful to know that Paul's Bible—that is, the text of the Greek OT available to him—did not include the word. This information, however, is of only limited value in establishing the text of the NT. In the case of Romans 9:33, text-critical principles lead us to accept the text without πᾶς even if the original LXX text had included it. The reason is that Paul frequently modifies his OT quotations to highlight exegetical interests.

But this fact, in turn, helps us appreciate that attention to textual differences can shed light on the distinctiveness of the NT writers. As it turns out, Paul quotes Isaiah 28:16 again in Romans 10:11, a verse that certainly includes πᾶς, since at this point the NT manuscripts display no textual variants. Moreover, one can readily see that the univer-

18. Incidentally, it is sobering to realize that some of the best NT commentators (C. E. B. Cranfield, Joseph A. Fitzmyer, James D. G. Dunn) show no awareness of Ziegler's edition at this point. They simply assume that Rahlfs's text reflects the original, then mention that some manuscripts have καὶ αὐτοί.

19. For a different set of examples, see the useful survey by Kenneth J. Thomas, "The Old Testament Citations in Hebrews," *New Testament Studies* 11 (1964–65): 303–25; repr. in *Studies in the Septuagint: Origins, Recensions, and Interpretations*, ed. Sidney Jellicoe (New York: Ktav, 1974), 507–29.

sality of salvation was important for the apostle in this particular context. He goes on to affirm: "For there is no difference between Jew and Gentile, for the same Lord [is Lord] of all, being generous to all who call upon him." The chain of events is fairly evident: (a) Paul modified the quotation to highlight his hermeneutical point; (b) subsequently, a scribe altered Romans 9:33 under the influence of the parallel in 10:11; (c) finally, the scribe of LXX manuscript 407, influenced by Romans, added the word to his copy of Isaiah.

In short, solid knowledge of the textual tradition of both the LXX and the NT, as well as close familiarity with the relationship between the two, is important not only for text-critical purposes but also for the task of NT exegesis more generally. Thus we turn our attention more directly to the value of the LXX for NT interpretation.

Interpretation

The influence of the LXX on the hermeneutics of the NT writers can be readily seen in their quotations from the OT, in their use of theological terms, and in their allusions to concepts formed in the LXX.

Quotations

The Gospels and Acts

The use of the LXX in the Gospels and Acts raises the interesting question of whether Jesus and the early church leaders themselves used the Greek Bible. This is a complicated issue that has occupied the attention of many scholars.

Richard N. Longenecker observes that in the Gospels, when Jesus quotes Scripture, the quotation most often follows the LXX reading, although it is not certain that Jesus himself taught in Greek. Even if he did teach in Greek at times, he probably more often spoke in his native tongue, Aramaic. Longenecker points out that even in the Gospel of Matthew, where the evangelist's own quotations of the OT usually follow the Hebrew reading, the citations by Jesus "are strongly Septuagintal."[20]

Robert Gundry's work on the use of the OT in Matthew shows that this is indeed an intricate problem that eludes easy generalizations. Of approximately eighty formal and allusive quotations of the OT in this Gospel, about thirty clearly follow the LXX reading, and most of these instances happen to be in the direct speech of Jesus and John the Baptist.[21] Of particular interest are cases when the Gospel writers have

20. See Richard N. Longenecker, *Biblical Exegesis in the Apostolic Period*, 2d ed. (Grand Rapids: Eerdmans, 1999), 48.

21. Robert H. Gundry, *The Use of the Old Testament in St. Matthew's Gospel: With Special Reference to the Messianic Hope* (Novum Testamentum Supplement 18; Leiden: Brill, 1967), 147–50.

Jesus quoting the Greek version even though it differs in substance from the original Hebrew. For the point the evangelist is making, the LXX form is often more suitable than a literal translation of the Hebrew.

In Luke 4:18, for instance, Jesus is reported to have quoted Isaiah 61:1. While this citation is textually complicated, one thing is certain: the LXX phrase "recovering sight to the blind" is used instead of the Hebrew reading, "opening of the prison to those who are bound." The LXX reading was consistent with the healing miracles Jesus was performing. Did Jesus himself quote LXX Isaiah 61 to give prophetic fulfillment to his healing of the blind? Or did Luke see that the Greek reading was more appropriate to Jesus' ministry than the Hebrew reading? Or did Luke perhaps use LXX Isaiah simply because it was the only version of Isaiah he could read, and thus he was unaware that it was more apt than the Hebrew?

In the Book of Acts, Luke records sermons and speeches by Peter, Stephen, Philip, James, and Paul. When Luke records them quoting Scripture, the quotations are primarily from the LXX, though, again, it is not always likely that they were speaking in Greek.[22] The case of James's quotation of Amos 9:11–12 during the Jerusalem Council is a good example (Acts 15:13–18). Was the council conducted in Aramaic or Greek? Since it was held in Jerusalem, Aramaic would seem likely. But since there were people at the council from Antioch, a Greek-speaking city, Greek may have been used in consideration of them.

Moreover, regardless of the language used in the council, when James quoted Scripture, did he personally quote the Hebrew text or the Greek version? One of the differences between the two is that MT Amos 9:12 reads, לְמַעַן יִירְשׁוּ אֶת־שְׁאֵרִית אֱדוֹם וְכָל־הַגּוֹיִם ("so that they may *possess* the remnant of *Edom* and all the nations"). The LXX, however, reads, ὅπως ἐκζητήσωσιν οἱ κατάλοιποι τῶν ἀνθρώπων καὶ πάντα τὰ ἔθνη ("so that the remnant of *men* and all the nations may *seek* [me]").[23] It is clear that the translator read or interpreted the Hebrew verb יִירְשׁוּ (from יָרַשׁ, "to inherit, take possession of") as יִדְרְשׁוּ (from דָּרַשׁ, "to seek"), then ignored the direct object marker אֶת (allowing him to take שְׁאֵרִית as the subject), and finally took the name אֱדוֹם ("Edom") as אָדָם ("man"), a collective. Acts 15 clearly follows the LXX, although it makes the object of the verb explicit by adding τὸν κύριον.[24]

22. Longenecker, *Biblical Exegesis in the Apostolic Period*, 83.

23. The pronoun με is in fact found in the Lucianic recension and in several daughter versions and church fathers.

24. Acts 15 also adds the particle ἄν after ὅπως. Both of these additions are found in the LXX of Codex Alexandrinus and its allies, probably under the influence of Acts.

On the basis of the LXX, supported as it is by Acts, some propose to emend the MT to לְמַעַן יִדְרְשׁוּ אִתּוֹ אָדָם וְכָל־הַגּוֹיִם.[25] We have, however, little reason to posit a different Hebrew *Vorlage* here. Since the Hebrew preserved in the MT is not particularly difficult, we may consider the possibility that the LXX translator—whether or not he made a mistake in reading the Hebrew characters—was primarily motivated by hermeneutical concerns. Elsewhere in the Minor Prophets (Hos. 9:6; Amos 2:10; Obad. 17, 19, 20; Mic. 1:15; Hab. 1:6; Zech. 9:4), the Hebrew verb יָרַשׁ is represented with κληρονομέω ("to inherit") or one of its cognates, but such a rendering may have appeared to the translator less appropriate here. Possibly inspired by the parallel concept of "all the nations," he in effect harmonized "Edom" to the context, an instance of the part for the whole, that is, one pagan nation representing all nations. In line with the spiritual thrust of the rest of the verse ("upon whom my name is called"), the translator then expressed the concept of possessing Edom in terms of human response to God.

In any event, these two changes made the Greek reading more fitting to the debate at the Jerusalem Council as to whether those Gentile peoples who stood outside the covenant nation of Israel could receive the spiritual blessings without submitting to circumcision. We may not be able to determine whether James himself used the Greek reading because it best suited his point. The fact remains that it is Luke, the Greek, who provides us with his interpretative report of the Jerusalem Council.

The Epistles

The interface between textual and exegetical issues is nowhere more evident than in the Epistle to the Hebrews. Of particular interest is 10:5–7, in which the author quotes Psalm 40:6–8a (MT 40:7–9a; LXX 39:7–9a). As is well known, the quotation differs from the Hebrew in one important respect. In the MT, the second clause of verse 7 reads אָזְנַיִם כָּרִיתָ לִּי ("ears you have dug for me"), usually interpreted to mean, "you have opened my ears," that is, "you have properly instructed me" (in contrast to the first clause: "Sacrifice and offering you did not desire"). In Hebrews 10:6, however, we read σῶμα δὲ κατηρτίσω μοι ("but you prepared a body for me"), which is the reading found in virtually the whole LXX tradition.

It was long ago suggested that the original LXX translation had ὠτία, corresponding to Hebrew אָזְנַיִם, but that at a very early stage of transmission, the two letters TI were read as the one letter M, a confusion aided by the final *sigma* of the previous word (ἠθέλησας). Thus an

25. See Archer and Chirichigno, *Old Testament Quotations*, 155.

original ΗΘΕΛΗΣΑΣΩΤΙΑ was copied as ΗΘΕΛΗΣΑΣΣΩΜΑ.[26] Few scholars are persuaded by this solution, however. The most common approach is well expressed by F. F. Bruce:

> The Greek translator evidently regarded the Hebrew wording as an instance of *pars pro toto* [the parts used for the whole]; the "digging" or hollowing out of the ears is part of the total work of fashioning a human body. Accordingly he rendered it in terms which express *totum pro parte*. The body which was "prepared" for the speaker by God is given back to God as a "living sacrifice," to be employed in obedient service to Him.[27]

Since throughout the Epistle to the Hebrews the author depends on the LXX and appears not to have made use of the Hebrew text, it would follow that he seized on the LXX's defensible paraphrase to present a messianic interpretation of the Psalm.

This popular solution assumes that the Psalms text used by the author read σῶμα—an assumption shared by virtually all Hebrews commentators, many of whom seem not to have even considered the possibility that his LXX text had ὠτία. Indeed, one could read several of the standard commentaries without so much as learning that Rahlfs, both in his handy edition of the LXX and in his critical edition of the Psalms for the Göttingen LXX, accepted ὠτία as the original translation. Because the sole textual basis for this decision is the Latin rendering *aures* ("ears"), found in the Gallic Psalter and OL manuscript G,[28] NT commentators either express surprise at Rahlfs's judgment[29] or ignore it altogether. But given the generally literal character of LXX Psalms, Rahlfs must have (rightly) deduced that the use of σῶμα as a rendering of אָזְנַיִם was out of character for the Greek translator.

Now if ὠτία was the original translation, then at what point in the textual tradition would σῶμα have been inserted? As we attempt to answer this question, it is important to note that the author of Hebrews introduced several other changes in his quotation:

26. This explanation (though without reference to the preceding *sigma*) is preferred by Masséo Caloz, *Étude sur la LXX origénienne du Psautier* (Orbus biblicus et orientalis 19; Fribourg: Éditions Universitaires/Göttingen: Vandenhoeck & Ruprecht, 1978), 383–84. Caloz also thinks that this corruption may have been related to a messianic interpretation of the passage.

27. F. F. Bruce, *The Epistle to the Hebrews: The English Text with Introduction, Exposition and Notes* (New International Commentary on the New Testament; Grand Rapids: Eerdmans, 1964), 232.

28. We do find ὠτία in Aquila, Symmachus, Theodotion, and other later versions that sought to give a more literal representation of the Hebrew.

29. Philip Edgcumbe Hughes, *A Commentary on the Epistle to the Hebrews* (Grand Rapids: Eerdmans, 1977), 396 n. 58.

1. The singular ὁλοκαύτωμα[30] ("burnt offering") has become plural ὁλοκαυτώματα.
2. The verb ᾔτησας ("you asked") has been changed to εὐδόκησας ("you were pleased with").
3. The last sentence in LXX Psalm 39:9, τοῦ ποιῆσαι τὸ θέλημά σου, ὁ θεός μου, ἐβουλήθην καὶ τὸν νόμον σου ἐν μέσῳ τῆς κοιλίας μου ("I wanted to do your will, my God, and your law [that is] in the midst of my belly"), has been rearranged and shortened to τοῦ ποιῆσαι ὁ θεὸς τὸ θέλημά σου, with the result that the infinitive becomes the complement of the earlier verb, ἥκω ("I have come . . . to do your will, O God").

It is evident that the last change cannot be characterized as a simple abbreviation of the LXX reading. Jesus, in contrast to the psalmist, is represented as not merely desiring to do God's will but as accomplishing it. "The variation comprised of transposition and truncation introduces an efficacy and finality to Christ's words that is appropriately lacking in David's."[31] Moreover, the first two changes may have been in part motivated by a desire for assonance: the last three syllables of ὁλοκαυτώματα parallel the sound of σῶμα δέ, and οὐκ εὐδόκησας pairs syllable-by-syllable with οὐκ ἠθέλησας. The choice of the verb εὐδοκέω has the additional advantage of possibly recalling the divine voice at Jesus' baptism and transfiguration.

In the light of these considerations, we have good reason to believe that the author of Hebrews had before him a Greek text of Psalms with the reading ὠτία and that therefore he is the one responsible for changing this word to σῶμα, which then spread through nearly the whole tradition.[32] In other words, it was he rather than the LXX translator who came up with the *pars pro toto* metonymy as a means of highlighting the messianic significance of the psalm. The context of the quotation (Hebrews 10:1–4, 8–18) stresses the value of Jesus' sacri-

30. This is almost certainly the original LXX reading; Codex Alexandrinus and many other manuscripts have the plural, but influence from Hebrews 10 is likely.

31. Karen H. Jobes, "The Function of Paronomasia in Hebrews 10:5–7," *Trinity Journal* n.s. 13 (1992): 181–91, esp. 189. See also Paul Ellingsworth, *The Epistle to the Hebrews: A Commentary on the Greek Text* (New International Greek Testament Commentary; Grand Rapids: Eerdmans, 1993), 501, although he believes that the other changes in this passage did not originate with the author of Hebrews. For greater detail on the material covered here, see Karen H. Jobes, "Rhetorical Achievement in the Hebrews 10 'Misquote' of Psalm 40," *Biblica* 72 (1991): 387–96.

32. We cannot be certain of this reconstruction. After all, if the Greek version of the Psalms available in the first century had ὠτία, it is difficult to explain why this reading was not preserved in the Greek manuscript tradition. Nevertheless, should the reading σῶμα (even if it was not original) have been already in existence for the author of Hebrews to use, this would not change the hermeneutical significance being suggested here.

ficial body over against that of animals. In contrast to David, whose obedience was faltering and certainly ineffective for others, Jesus' sacrificial obedience is both perfect and capable of saving completely those who come to God through him (7:25).

Not every quotation of the OT in the NT reflects a textual difference with the LXX, and among those that do, not all have theological import. But even when the quotation is exact, something can often be learned. Take, for instance, 1 Corinthians 2:16, where Paul quotes LXX Isaiah 40:13a, "Who has known the mind [νοῦς] of the Lord?" even though the Hebrew text has "spirit" (רוּחַ). The rendering of the LXX translator can perhaps be defended as an attempt to clarify the meaning of the original. But whatever we may think of the translator's technique, Paul could surely have changed νοῦς ("mind") to πνεῦμα ("spirit") if he had wanted. His choice not to do so was probably intentional, and it gives us an important insight into Paul's use of Scripture, namely, the role played by the LXX in his theological reflection.

In effect, 1 Corinthians 2 focuses on the Spirit as the one who makes it possible for us to know God (see especially v. 11). As Paul draws that discussion to a close, he appeals to Isaiah 40:13 and concludes with the statement, "But we have the mind of Christ." The use of the word *mind* here links this last comment with the LXX quotation, but the Hebrew original, as well as the context of Paul's discussion more generally, makes clear that what the apostle means is, "We have the Spirit of Christ and therefore we really know Christ." Could it be then that the LXX's interpretative rendering itself became a source for the development of Paul's teaching? This is surely the sort of thing that Adolf Deissmann had in mind when he spoke about the value of studying the LXX for understanding the Pauline Epistles.[33]

Not only the Pauline Epistles, however! Both Paul and Peter—perhaps reflecting an early Christian tradition—link two passages in Isaiah, namely, 8:14 with 28:16, presumably because the word λίθος occurs in those two passages (see Romans 9:33 and 1 Peter 2:6–7). But there is more. LXX Isaiah 8:14 begins with the clause καὶ ἐὰν ἐπ' αὐτῷ πεποιθὼς ᾖς ("and if you put your confidence in him"), for which no corresponding text is found in the Hebrew. The translator evidently took his cue from the last clause of verse 17 (καὶ πεποιθὼς ἔσομαι ἐπ' αὐτῷ = וְקִוֵּיתִי־לוֹ) and used it to give a surprising interpretation of verse 14.[34] In addition, he provided a closer link between 8:14 and 28:16 by

33. See above, introduction, p. 23. On the importance of Isaiah for Paul's thought, see now the extensive study by Florian Wilk, *Die Bedeutung des Jesajabuch für Paulus* (Forschungen zur Religion und Literatur des Alten und Neuen Testaments 179; Göttingen: Vandenhoeck & Ruprecht, 1998).

34. MT Isa. 8:14 is a warning that God will be a trap and a stone that causes stumbling, but the Greek translator assures the readers that if they have faith, God will not

adding the words ἐπ' αὐτῷ to the latter passage. It is clear that the Greek translator's own reflection on the message of Isaiah had a significant impact on early Christian theology.

Theological Terms

As emphasized in the first section of this chapter, when terms are used in a specialized sense to designate new entities or ideas, the study of such terms is only to a limited extent linguistic in character. Once we have identified the extralinguistic referents to which they point, any further discussion becomes cultural or conceptual.

For example, the noun ἄγγελος in Classical Greek meant "messenger" in a fairly general sense. When the LXX translators used it to represent Hebrew מַלְאָךְ, which often specifically designated a (superhuman) messenger sent by God, a new acceptation or definition was created.[35] The use of this specialized Greek term in the NT doubtlessly reflects the strong influence of the LXX. From the standpoint of language, however, such a new meaning can be seen as merely a semantic addition to the lexical inventory, necessitated by the appearance of a new "thing." Any explanations of what this thing is belong not to linguistic description but rather extralinguistic—in this case, theological.[36]

But to say that the effect of such changes on linguistic structure is relatively small and superficial is not to suggest that, with respect to them, the influence of the LXX on NT thought is unimportant. Any time that a NT writer uses a term that is common in the LXX and that is closely associated with Hebrew theology, we may safely assume that what is said about that term's referent in the LXX would have significantly affected Christian reflection.

Thus, for example, when Paul describes the law as having been ordained through angels (Galatians 3:19; cf. Acts 7:53 and Hebrews 2:2), we should take into account LXX Deuteronomy 33:2, which speaks about the Lord's coming from Sinai σὺν μυριάσιν Καδης, ἐκ δεξιῶν αὐτοῦ ἄγγελοι μετ' αὐτοῦ ("with myriads of Cades, [and] on his right hand his angels were with him"). The Hebrew text does not have the

---

be a cause of stumbling for them. Since the NT writers consciously reject that interpretation, it is evident that their adoption of LXX renderings was hardly uncritical.

35. Note that in the phrase ἄγγελος κυρίου (e.g., Gen. 16:7) this semantic change has not yet taken place. It is only when the noun is used by itself to represent the meaning of the phrase (e.g., Gen. 48:16) that the technical specialization occurs. Note further that the translators had the option of simply transliterating the Hebrew term and using it as a loanword (as they did with πάσχα for פֶּסַח, "Passover"; an additional option was to coin a new word, such as ἀπερίτμητος for עָרֵל, "uncircumcised"). In fact, English translations typically translate both מַלְאָךְ and ἄγγελος not with "messenger" but with the Greek loanword "angel."

36. See Silva, *Biblical Words and Their Meaning*, 80–81, 105–8.

word מַלְאָךְ at all,[37] and the last clause is very problematic. It is likely that the Greek translator was simply stumped by that clause and came up with a statement conceptually parallel to the previous clause so as to disturb the context as little as possible.[38] For Paul, as well as for other Greek-speaking Jews who used the LXX, this passage would have contributed to the belief (suggested elsewhere, perhaps Ps. 68:17) that angels were involved in the giving of the Mosaic law. (Note again, however, that to describe an angelic function is quite different from discussing the meaning of the word ἄγγελος.)

Many terms used in the NT—such as δικαιοσύνη, κληρονομία, νόμος, πνεῦμα, to mention a small sample—refer to concepts that cannot be adequately understood without careful attention to their Hebrew counterparts as mediated through the LXX. One of the clearest examples is διαθήκη, which meant "last will, testament" in Classical Greek. When confronted by the need to render Hebrew בְּרִית ("covenant"), the LXX translators could have used συνθήκη ("agreement"), and such a choice would have been adequate in many contexts. In passages where God establishes a covenant, however, he alone sets the conditions, so that the rendering συνθήκη would have been inaccurate or at least misleading. Although διαθήκη too is misleading for a different reason (God's death is hardly required to make the arrangement operative!), it probably seemed more adequate to the translators, since this word preserves the unilateral element distinctive of God's covenants.

Inevitably, this choice occasioned a significant semantic shift in the Greek word. In the first place, the element of the death of the testator is suppressed; and, second, the meaning becomes specialized, for the word now refers specifically to the distinctive arrangements that God establishes with human beings.[39] Any attempt to understand the use of διαθήκη in the NT on the basis of nonbiblical rather than LXX Greek will get us nowhere. The matter becomes complicated, however, by the importance that Jesus' death has for the NT writers. When we are told (Luke 22:20) that at the last supper Jesus said to his disciples, Τοῦτο τὸ ποτήριον ἡ καινὴ διαθήκη ἐν τῷ αἵματί μου τὸ ὑπὲρ ὑμῶν ἐκχυννόμενον ("this cup is the new covenant in my blood, which is poured out for

37. For the first clause, the MT apparently says, "he came from myriads of holy ones" (אָתָה מֵרִבְבֹת קֹדֶשׁ); the LXX vocalized the last word as referring to Kadesh, and on that basis many scholars further revocalize and read, "he came from Meribath-Kadesh," but several other reconstructions have been proposed.

38. See John W. Wevers, *Notes on the Greek Text of Deuteronomy* (SBLSCS 39; Atlanta: Scholars Press, 1995), 540. In his own way, the translator was using the principle of maximal redundancy (see Silva, *Biblical Words and Their Meaning*, 153–54).

39. This is not to deny that the word is also used by the translators in contexts where God is not one of the parties involved. The Greek term became a standard equivalent of the corresponding Hebrew term, without apparent consideration of the differing contexts in which the latter appears.

you"), it is impossible to dissociate the Hebrew concept expressed by בְּרִית from the death of the one who is establishing this new covenant.

The resulting lexical difficulty becomes especially acute in Hebrews 9:16–17. Up to that point, it is evident that the author has used the term διαθήκη in the OT sense of "covenant." In these verses, though, he states that "in the case of a διαθήκη, the death of the one who made it needs to be demonstrated, for a διαθήκη takes effect at death, since it is not in force while the one who made it lives" (ὅπου γὰρ διαθήκη, θάνατον ἀνάγκη φέρεσθαι τοῦ διαθεμένου· διαθήκη γὰρ ἐπὶ νεκροῖς βεβαία, ἐπεὶ μήποτε ἰσχύει ὅτε ζῇ ὁ διαθέμενος). Understandably, most commentators argue that here the meaning of διαθήκη shifts back to "testament."[40] Others, just as understandably, find it difficult to believe that in the middle of his argument the author would change the meaning of such a key word.[41]

Verse 15, however, makes clear an association between God's διαθήκη and death. The role of animal sacrifices in the Sinaitic Covenant, as well as Jesus' linking of the new covenant with his death, may have suggested to the author that there was a special appropriateness in the use of διαθήκη to designate God's covenant. Whether the author in fact understood this term to include both ideas or whether he was only exploiting semantic associations is difficult to decide.[42] In either case, it is clear that his argument would have been impossible if the LXX translators had not chosen διαθήκη as their default translation of בְּרִית.

Allusions

Although the dependence of the NT writers on the LXX is most obvious in their OT quotations and in their use of theological terms, one could argue that the deepest and most pervasive impact of the LXX is to be found elsewhere.[43] Philippians, for example, is conspicuously absent from the standard lists of explicit citations, but it would be a grave mistake to infer that this letter shows no OT influence. Fairly obvious dependence on the OT may be seen in the way Paul describes the monetary gifts he received from the Philippian church: "They are a

40. See especially Ellingsworth, *Epistle to the Hebrews*, 462–63.

41. See William L. Lane, *Hebrews 9–13* (Word Biblical Commentary 47b; Dallas: Word, 1991), 242–43.

42. See Harold W. Attridge, *The Epistle to the Hebrews* (Hermeneia; Philadelphia: Fortress, 1989), 256: "It must simply be admitted that he plays on two different senses of the term, thus assimilating two different legal and religious forms." Jesus "does not simply serve as the arbitrator or messenger of God's contract with God's people as did Moses. Rather, because the covenant/testament requires the testator's death, and the 'living God' (9:14) cannot, by definition, die, that is the mediator's role" (p. 213).

43. What follows is taken from Silva, "Old Testament in Paul," 634–35, to which readers are referred for more detail.

fragrant offering, an acceptable sacrifice, pleasing to God" (4:18). This language, of course, comes from various ceremonial passages, such as Exodus 29:18; moreover, a figurative shift is already present in Ezekiel 20:41: "I will accept you as fragrant incense when I bring you out from the nations." This detail must be understood against a larger theological framework, for Paul elsewhere uses priestly language to describe Christian service (cf. λειτουργία ["service"] and related words in Philippians 2:17, 25, 30). In effect, the ceremonial system of Israel is viewed as having been transformed and then transferred to the Christian church, which properly fulfills the significance of that system. A few scholars even suggest that Paul sees himself as the priest who, serving in the church as the true temple of God, receives the Christian's offerings.

Another well-known allusion is Philippians 2:9–11, where Paul states that the purpose of Christ's exaltation is that "every knee should bow . . . and every tongue confess that Jesus Christ is Lord." In Isaiah 45:23, after God has repeatedly affirmed his oneness and uniqueness, he adds: "By myself I have sworn. . . . Before me every knee will bow; by me every tongue will swear" (the last verb is translated by the LXX with the same verb used by Paul: ἐξομολογήσεται, "will confess"). Although not an explicit or precise quotation, this use of Isaiah is especially significant because of its profound implications for Paul's conception of Jesus (this is true whether the so-called Christ-hymn was originally composed by Paul or someone else).

Close attention to the LXX reveals other interesting allusions to the OT in Philippians. A few verses later, Paul addresses the problem of grumbling and complaining (2:14), a theme reminiscent of the experience of the Israelites in the wilderness. That comment leads him to speak of the Philippians as "children of God without fault in a crooked and depraved generation" (2:15), a phrase that reproduces half a dozen words from LXX Deuteronomy 32:5. Since the OT passage (which is exegetically difficult) speaks of the Israelites themselves as a crooked people and thus *not* God's children, Paul here gives a provocative, possibly ironic, twist to the phrase in Deuteronomy: it is the Gentile Christians of Philippi, not the unbelieving Jews, who may be regarded as God's children, and therefore the Philippians need not be intimidated by the Jewish-based opposition they are experiencing (cf. 3:1–3).

Another allusion that is easy to miss unless one refers specifically to the LXX text is Philippians 1:19: "What has happened to me will turn out for my deliverance." The Greek here is τοῦτο μοι ἀποβήσεται εἰς σωτηρίαν ("this will lead to salvation for me"), a verbatim quotation from LXX Job 13:16. Most commentators, even if they notice the striking verbal correspondence, appear to see little significance in it. And, to be sure, it is possible that Paul has simply—and perhaps even unconsciously—borrowed the language of Job to express quite a different idea, namely, his hoped-for deliverance from prison (the connection would have been aided by the parallel between Job's accusers and the individuals Paul mentions in 1:17).[44] Much can be said, however, for the view that what Paul has in mind is the more profound issue of his relationship with God and thus his spiritual destiny. Since the context of Job 13:13–18 deals precisely with matters of eternal import, Paul's use of that passage may be more than a casual allusion.[45]

In other instances, conceptual rather than strict verbal correspondences suggest that Paul has an OT passage or theme in mind. For example, some scholars argue that the clause "made himself nothing" (ἑαυτὸν ἐκένωσεν; lit., "emptied himself") in Philippians 2:7a alludes to Isaiah 53:12, which says that the Servant of the Lord "poured out his life unto death." Since Paul definitely uses Isaiah later in the passage (2:10–11) and since he refers to Jesus as δοῦλος ("servant"; 2:7b), it may well be that the Suffering Servant motif played a role in the formulation of the Christ-hymn. If so, the allusion is rather subtle, and therefore one should be cautious about reading too much into the meaning of the phrase.

Even more subtle is the suggestion that Philippians 2:12, where Paul encourages his readers to continue their obedience regardless of whether he is present with them, may be an allusion to Moses' words in Deuteronomy 31:27: "If you have been rebellious against the Lord while I am still alive and with you, how much more will you rebel after I die!" Three verses later, as already noted, Paul certainly alludes to a statement in the close context of Moses' exclamation (Deut. 32:5); moreover, Paul seems to have his own death in mind at Philippians 2:17. The possibility that Deuteronomy 31:27 may have affected the apostle's writing can hardly be excluded, but it is difficult to determine whether the allusion was a conscious one and, if so, how much significance should be attached to it.

One reason for focusing on Philippians is to show that even a letter with no citations in the usual sense may reflect Paul's great dependence on the OT. In the case of letters that do include citations, readers usually concentrate on those citations to the exclusion of the less obvious ways in which Paul uses Scripture. A good case in point is 2 Corinthians 4:13, where Paul quotes Psalm 116:10 (LXX 115:1): "I believe; therefore I have spoken," in support of his own attitude to his apostolic ministry. Commentators usually fail to note, however, that Psalm 116 yields several references to humiliation and death, both of which are recurring themes in 2 Corinthians; that Psalm 118, which

44. See Richard B. Hays, *Echoes of Scripture in the Letters of Paul* (New Haven: Yale University Press, 1989), 21–24.

45. See Moisés Silva, *Philippians* (1988; repr. Grand Rapids: Baker, 1992), 76–78.

also has references to death, speaks of affliction (v. 5), God's power (vv. 15–16, LXX δύναμις; cf. 2 Corinthians 6:7), and discipline (v. 18, LXX ἐπαίδευσαν; cf. 2 Corinthians 6:9); and that some light parallels may be found in nearby Psalms. Several important allusions to other parts of Scripture are also present in 2 Corinthians. As Paul relates his ministry to the problems in Corinth, he shows

> that he has "lived in the Bible" to the point where the Bible has formed his whole outlook on how the world is and what his place in it might be. Those who idly suppose that Scripture is important only when Paul uses it in argument in Galatians and Romans have a superficial view of the situation.[46]

Conclusion

The present chapter has covered a fairly diverse group of issues surrounding the relationship of the LXX and the NT. And yet we have barely scratched the surface. While the examples included here are largely representative of the field as a whole, numerous important questions have been left untreated. Moreover, comparable issues arise in the study of patristic literature, an enormous field of investigation that lies beyond the scope of this book.

We hope, however, that our discussion will motivate readers to pursue this rich subject on their own. More important, we hope that when they do so, they will not underestimate the complexities involved but rather make every effort to do justice to the character of the Greek OT and its transmission.

To Continue Your Study

Most introductory works pay significant attention to the use of the LXX in the NT and in early Christian literature. See Henry Barclay Swete, *An Introduction to the Old Testament in Greek*, 2d ed. (Cambridge: Cambridge University Press, 1914; repr. Peabody, Mass.: Hendrickson, 1989), 381–432; Natalio Fernández Marcos, *Introducción a las versiones griegas de la Biblia*, 2d ed. (Textos y Estudios "Cardenal Cisneros" 23; Madrid: Consejo Superior de Investigaciones Científicas, 1998) = *The Septuagint in Context: Introduction to the Greek Version of the Bible*, trans. Wilfred G. E. Watson (Leiden: Brill, 2000), chapters 17, 21, and 22; Marguerite Harl, Gilles Dorival, and Olivier Munnich, *La Bible Grecque des Septante: Du judaïsme hellénistique au*

46. Frances Young and David F. Ford, *Meaning and Truth in 2 Corinthians* (Grand Rapids: Eerdmans, 1988), 63, though not all of the parallels mentioned on pp. 64–69 are convincing.

christianisme ancien, 2d ed. (Initiations au christianisme ancien; [Paris]: Cerf/Centre National de la Recherche Scientifique, 1994), chapters 7–8. It should be remembered that the commentaries in La Bible d'Alexandrie (see above, chap. 3, p. 77) have a special focus on the patristic use of the LXX. Note also the essays by H. F. D. Sparks, Kenneth J. Thomas, and Peter Katz reprinted in *Studies in the Septuagint: Origins, Recensions, and Interpretations*, ed. Sidney Jellicoe (New York: Ktav, 1974), 497–540. On matters of style, see David Tabachovitz, *Die Septuaginta und das Neue Testament: Stilstudien* (Lund: Gleerup, 1956).

Scholarly literature on the NT writers' use of the OT is vast. The most influential monographs are the following: Charles H. Dodd, *According to the Scriptures: The Sub-structure of New Testament Theology* (London: Fontana, 1952); Earle E. Ellis, *Paul's Use of the Old Testament* (Edinburgh: Oliver & Boyd, 1957; repr. Grand Rapids: Baker, 1981); Dietrich-Alex Koch, *Die Schrift als Zeuge des Evangeliums: Untersuchungen zur Verwendung und zum Verständnis der Schrift bei Paulus* (Beiträge zur historischen Theologie 69; Tübingen: Mohr Siebeck, 1986); Barnabas Lindars, *New Testament Apologetic: The Doctrinal Significance of the Old Testament Quotations* (Philadelphia: Westminster, 1961); Richard N. Longenecker, *Biblical Exegesis in the Apostolic Period*, 2d ed. (Grand Rapids: Eerdmans, 1999); Otto Michel, *Paulus und seine Bibel* (1929; repr. Darmstadt: Wissenschaftliche Buchgesellschaft, 1972); Christopher D. Stanley, *Paul and the Language of Scripture: Citation Technique in the Pauline Epistles and Contemporary Literature* (Society for New Testament Studies Monograph Series 69; Cambridge: Cambridge University Press, 1992). All of these works pay more or less attention to the LXX specifically, but the most reliable among them is the volume by Koch.

10

Interpreting the Septuagint

In this chapter, three passages from the LXX are examined as a way of bringing together and applying the principles and issues treated previously. The isolated examples in earlier chapters have their value as illustrative material, but only through the exegesis of running texts are we able to appreciate the character of the Greek translation and to handle problems responsibly.

For the first passage, **Genesis 4:1–8**, extensive, almost word-by-word, comments are provided. The discussion of a longer and important portion, **Isaiah 52:13–53:12**, is more selective, highlighting distinctive traits of that translation. Finally, a brief treatment of **Esther 5:1–2 with Addition D** focuses on the special problems raised by the existence of competing Greek translations and by the presence of Greek material not found in the Hebrew text.

Genesis 4:1–8

The Greek Book of Genesis as a whole—and the story of Cain and Abel in particular—consists of simple narrative material. The Semitic flavor of the text is evident, but only rarely does the translator fail to communicate the meaning of the Hebrew. For ease of reference, the MT and the LXX are displayed below in parallel columns.[1]

	MT	LXX
4:1	וְהָאָדָם יָדַע אֶת־חַוָּה אִשְׁתּוֹ וַתַּהַר וַתֵּלֶד אֶת־קַיִן וַתֹּאמֶר קָנִיתִי אִישׁ אֶת־יְהוָה׃	Ἀδὰμ δὲ ἔγνω Εὔαν τὴν γυναῖκα αὐτοῦ, καὶ συλλαβοῦσα ἔτεκεν τὸν Κάιν, καὶ εἶπεν Ἐκτησάμην ἄνθρωπον διὰ τοῦ θεοῦ.
	Now the man knew his wife Eve, and she conceived and bore Cain, saying, "I have produced a man with the help of the Lord."	Now Adam came to know Eve his wife, and she, having conceived, bore Cain and said, "I have obtained a man through God."

1. Sources: MT = *Biblia hebraica stuttgartensia*, 6; LXX = John W. Wevers, *Genesis* (Septuaginta 1; Göttingen: Vandenhoeck & Ruprecht, 1974), 95–97; English translation

Ἀδὰμ δέ = וְהָאָדָם. In the first few chapters of Genesis, the translator seems to reserve the conjunction δέ to represent Hebrew *wāw* disjunctive, especially if a topical shift occurs in the narrative (e.g., ἡ δὲ γῆ = וְהָאָרֶץ in 1:2; see also 2:6, 10; 3:1; etc.). Beginning with 4:9, however, he uses it frequently to render *wāw* consecutive as well. The conjunction καί is used to render both (e.g., καὶ σκότος = וְחֹשֶׁךְ in 1:2; but καὶ εἶπεν = וַיֹּאמֶר in 1:3).

ἔγνω = יָדַע. Because the English word *knew* suggests a state rather than an action, it does not satisfactorily represent the force of the Greek; thus our rendering, "came to know." The use of the verb γινώσκω with reference to sexual intercourse is usually regarded as a lexical Semitism. Such a meaning is in fact attested in nonbiblical Greek, but only rarely (aside from Plutarch).[2] This use of the verb illustrates a more general principle: many LXX/NT "Semitisms" consist of linguistic features that are acceptable Greek, and what lends a distinct flavor to the style is their unexpected presence or frequency.

καὶ συλλαβοῦσα ἔτεκεν = וַתַּהַר וַתֵּלֶד. A literal translation of the Hebrew would be καὶ συνέλαβεν καὶ ἔτεκεν, which is in fact the reading of a handful of witnesses, including Codex Alexandrinus (doubtless a later adjustment toward the Hebrew).[3] The use of the participle here, which makes for a more pleasing Greek style, demonstrates the translator's sense of freedom to depart occasionally from a strict representation of Hebrew syntax. In this particular case, he may have also been motivated by the desire to specify the change of subject: in the first clause Adam is the subject, but in this clause, by using a participle (which is declined for gender), the reference to Eve becomes grammatically explicit.[4]

Ἐκτησάμην = קָנִיתִי. This is an accurate rendering of the Hebrew verb, which most frequently means "to obtain, acquire," although some commentators on Genesis prefer here the meaning "to create, produce." The Hebrew also exhibits a wordplay with Cain's name, קַיִן, a feature that may have influenced the choice of the Greek word (which includes the sounds *k* and *n*).

διὰ τοῦ θεοῦ = אֶת־יְהוָה. The standard equivalent of יְהוָה is of course κύριος (θεός normally renders אֱלֹהִים), but most of the Greek translators are not totally consistent; often, as here and in verse 4, no clear reason lies behind the choice. In view of this fact, we have no good

of MT = NRSV; English translation of LXX = Jobes and Silva. For this passage, the text in Wevers's edition is identical to that printed in Rahlfs's *Septuaginta* except for some differences in punctuation. See also illustration 16 in chap. 6 above, p. 144.

2. See BAGD 161 s.v. γινώσκω 5. On Semitisms, see also above, chap. 9, pp. 184–89.

3. Cf. 4:17, which has the participial construction without attested variants; this construction also occurs in 4:25; 21:2; 30:17, 23; 38:3—even when the Hebrew omits the first verb.

4. See John W. Wevers, *Notes on the Greek Text of Genesis* (SBLSCS 35; Atlanta: Scholars Press, 1993), 51.

reason to suspect a different Hebrew *Vorlage*. It should also be noted that the interchange of the divine names is a particularly common problem in the transmission of biblical Greek texts, both LXX and NT. A more significant question is the rendering of Hebrew אֶת־, which a few scholars understand as the object marker: "I have obtained a man, namely, the Lord."[5] The LXX is our earliest evidence for the interpretation that the Hebrew particle should be understood as a preposition: "I have obtained a man with [the help of] the Lord."[6]

4:2	וַתֹּסֶף לָלֶדֶת אֶת־אָחִיו אֶת־הָבֶל וַיְהִי־הֶבֶל רֹעֵה צֹאן וְקַיִן הָיָה עֹבֵד אֲדָמָה׃	καὶ προσέθηκεν τεκεῖν τὸν ἀδελφὸν αὐτοῦ τὸν Ἅβελ. καὶ ἐγένετο Ἅβελ ποιμὴν προβάτων, Κάιν δὲ ἦν ἐργαζόμενος τὴν γῆν.
	Next she bore his brother Abel. Now Abel was a keeper of sheep, and Cain a tiller of the ground.	And next she bore his brother Abel. And Abel became a shepherd of sheep, but Cain used to work the land.

καὶ προσέθηκεν τεκεῖν = וַתֹּסֶף לָלֶדֶת ("and she added [i.e., proceeded] to bear"). This stereotypical rendering of the Hebrew construction (which is used to indicate repetition or continuation) could have been translated more smoothly with καὶ πάλιν ἔτεκεν (this is in fact the way Symmachus rendered the clause here). It is not clear why the LXX translators as a whole chose to render this construction, and not others, so literally. Perhaps this rendering sounded quaint rather than awkward to Greek ears. Moreover, one cannot totally exclude the possibility that it had earlier become part of the speech among Greek-speaking Jews; if so, its use in the translation would not have been perceived as a novelty.[7]

ποιμὴν προβάτων = רֹעֵה צֹאן. Although in Homer the word ποιμήν (like Hebrew רֹעֶה) meant generally "herdsman" and could be applied to a keeper of oxen as well as of sheep, later it was specialized so that it meant only "shepherd." The literal translation of the phrase here (but not the original Hebrew) is therefore redundant.

5. Anastasius Sinaita reports that "another" (ἕτερος) Greek translation rendered the clause with ἐκτησάμην ἄνθρωπον κύριον. On that basis, Anastasius links this verse with Thomas's confession in John 20:28. See Frederick Field, *Origenis Hexaplorum quae supersunt sive veterum interpretum graecorum in totum Vetus Testamentum fragmenta*, 2 vols. (Oxford: Oxford University Press, 1875), 1.17.

6. Although the Hebrew preposition does mean "with," some scholars doubt that it can be used in the sense "with the help of." See Claus Westermann, *Genesis 1–11: A Continental Commentary*, trans. John J. Scullion (Minneapolis: Fortress, 1994), 291.

7. It is suggestive that this construction appears to be the only Hebraism used by Josephus. See Henry St. John Thackeray, *A Grammar of the Old Testament in Greek according to the Septuagint*, vol. 1: *Introduction, Orthography and Accidence* (Cambridge: Cambridge University Press, 1909), 53 and note. In the NT, the construction is found in Luke 20:11–12 (cf. 19:11) and Acts 12:3.

Κάιν δὲ = וְקַיִן. Notice again the use of δέ to represent disjunctive *wāw*, which clearly has an adversative function here.

ἦν ἐργαζόμενος = הָיָה עֹבֵד. It would have been possible to take the Hebrew participle as a substantive (in parallel with רֹעֵה) and to translate with the noun ἐργάτης or the like, but such a use of עֹבֵד is not common. The translator may have felt that a literal rendering of the participial form, which presents an action in progress, was more faithful to the text.[8]

4:3	וַיְהִי מִקֵּץ יָמִים וַיָּבֵא קַיִן מִפְּרִי הָאֲדָמָה מִנְחָה לַיהוָה׃	καὶ ἐγένετο μεθ' ἡμέρας ἤνεγκεν Κάιν ἀπὸ τῶν καρπῶν τῆς γῆς θυσίαν τῷ κυρίῳ,
	In the course of time Cain brought to the LORD an offering of the fruit of the ground,	And it happened after some time [that] Cain brought from the fruits of the land an offering to the Lord.

καὶ ἐγένετο . . . ἤνεγκεν = וַיָּבֵא . . . וַיְהִי. The translator does not reproduce the second *wāw*, a repetition that may have sounded awkward to Greek ears, although we find it in verse 8 and often elsewhere, especially in the later historical books.[9]

μεθ' ἡμέρας = מִקֵּץ יָמִים. The Hebrew phrase may be translated literally as "from the end of days." The translator wisely chose an idiom that, while retaining the word *days*, is perfectly good Greek (cf. Demosthenes, *Orations* 21.168: μεθ' ἡμέρας δύο; Diodorus Siculus, *History* 1.41.7: μεθ' ἡμέρας τίνας).

θυσία = מִנְחָה. The same correspondence is found in verse 5 (and frequently in Leviticus), but in verse 4 the translator uses δῶρον, which is what we find elsewhere in Genesis (e.g., 32:14 [= MT 32:13]; 33:10; 43:11).

4:4	וְהֶבֶל הֵבִיא גַם־הוּא מִבְּכֹרוֹת צֹאנוֹ וּמֵחֶלְבֵהֶן וַיִּשַׁע יְהוָה אֶל־הֶבֶל וְאֶל־מִנְחָתוֹ׃	καὶ Ἅβελ ἤνεγκεν καὶ αὐτὸς ἀπὸ τῶν πρωτοτόκων τῶν προβάτων αὐτοῦ καὶ ἀπὸ τῶν στεάτων αὐτῶν. καὶ ἐπεῖδεν ὁ θεὸς ἐπὶ Ἅβελ καὶ ἐπὶ τοῖς δώροις αὐτοῦ,

8. Philo begins his work *On Husbandry* (*De agricultura*) by quoting Gen. 9:20: Καὶ ἤρξατο Νῶε ἄνθρωπος γεωργὸς γῆς ("and Noah began to be a husbandman"). Later, in §21, he interprets Gen. 4:2 as evidence that Cain did not merit to be called a γεωργός. We have no reason to think that the translators saw such significance. For this and other references to Philo's use of the LXX, see Marguerite Harl, *La Genèse* (La Bible d'Alexandrie 1; Paris: Cerf, 1986), passim.

9. For some valuable statistics, see Thackeray, *Grammar of the Old Testament in Greek*, 51. Another possible way of representing the Hebrew would be to use an infinitive for the second verb (this option is found in the Lucan writings, especially in Acts, but in the LXX only as a variant in 3 Reigns 11:43).

and Abel for his part brought of the firstlings of his flock, their fat portions. And the LORD had regard for Abel and his offering,	And Abel too brought [an offering to the Lord] from the firstborn of his sheep and from their fat. And God looked favorably on Abel and on his gifts.

ἤνεγκεν = הֵבִיא. Contrary to English usage, neither Hebrew nor Greek requires that the object of a verb be made explicit if that object is evident from the context. In this case, the Greek reader would assume that the object of the verb is θυσίαν ("offering"), mentioned in the immediately preceding clause.

καὶ αὐτός = גַם־הוּא. The rendering and position of this clause represents the Hebrew literally. Nevertheless, the resulting Greek is unexceptional (cf. Thucydides, *History* 4.78.4: ἔλεγε δὲ καὶ αὐτὸς Βρασίδας, "but Brasidas himself said"; Polybius, *Histories* 5.86.3: ἠναγκάσθη καὶ αὐτὸς εἰσελθεῖν, "he was compelled to enter [the city] himself also").

καὶ ἀπὸ τῶν στεάτων αὐτῶν = וּמֵחֶלְבֵהֶן. The Hebrew probably means "namely, the fatty portions,"[10] and perhaps a Greek reader would have understood the translation that way. The plural στεάτων is found in some medical texts (e.g., Soranus Ephesius, *Gynaeciorum libri* 4.3.14.3), but the singular στέαρ would have been more idiomatic in the present context.

καὶ ἐπεῖδεν ὁ θεὸς ἐπὶ Ἅβελ = וַיִּשַׁע יְהוָה אֶל־הֶבֶל. The Greek is a skillful translation of the Hebrew. The verb שָׁעָה ("to look") when used with either אֶל or עַל seems always to include the positive connotation of a favorable attitude. Greek ἐφοράω (with a simple accusative rather than with the preposition ἐπί) occurs in a broad range of contexts, but when used of the gods, it too has strong positive overtones. The Persian Harpagus, in a message sent inside a hare, said to Cyrus: "The gods watch over you [σὲ γὰρ θεοὶ ἐπορῶσι], for without them you would not have been so fortunate" (Herodotus, *Histories* 1.124).

καὶ ἐπὶ τοῖς δώροις αὐτοῦ = וְאֶל־מִנְחָתוֹ. The translator uses the plural δώροις for grammatical consistency with the referent (τῶν πρωτοτόκων . . . τῶν στεάτων). His choice of the word δῶρον rather than θυσία, which he had used in verse 3, shows again that he felt no compulsion to represent the Hebrew consistently. In this case, the decision may have been motivated by a desire to mark a qualitative difference between the two offerings, but it is difficult to under-

10. See *Gesenius' Hebrew Grammar*, ed. Emil Kautzsch, trans. A. E. Cowley (Oxford: Clarendon, 1910), §154a n. 1 (b).

stand what the nature of that difference might be, since both terms have positive associations elsewhere in the Pentateuch.[11]

4:5	וְאֶל־קַיִן וְאֶל־מִנְחָתוֹ לֹא שָׁעָה וַיִּחַר לְקַיִן מְאֹד וַיִּפְּלוּ פָּנָיו׃	ἐπὶ δὲ Κάιν καὶ ἐπὶ ταῖς θυσίαις αὐτοῦ οὐ προσέσχεν. καὶ ἐλύπησεν τὸν Κάιν λίαν, καὶ συνέπεσεν τῷ προσώπῳ.
	but for Cain and his offering he had no regard. So Cain was very angry, and his countenance fell.	But he did not pay attention to Cain and to his offerings. And [this] grieved Cain very much, and his countenance fell.

προσέσχεν = שָׁעָה. Once again, the translator introduces a lexical variation not in the Hebrew. This one can be explained only on stylistic grounds.[12] Often used with πρός or εἰς, not with ἐπί, the verb προσέχω means "to bring to." With the object νοῦν, it takes on the figurative meaning of "to turn the mind to, pay attention to," but the verb by itself can also be used with such a meaning.

καὶ ἐλύπησεν τὸν Κάιν = וַיִּחַר לְקַיִן. The Hebrew verb חָרָה, with the noun אַף expressed or implied, is used with reference to the burning of anger, so a literal rendering would be, "And [anger] kindled to Cain."[13] The verb λυπέω, on the other hand, is not as strong: "to give pain to, distress, annoy." For example, at the end of Plato's *Apology* (41E), Socrates says: "When my sons are grown, Gentlemen, exact a penalty of them; give pain to them exactly as I gave pain to you [ταὐτὰ ταῦτα λυποῦντες ἅπερ ἐγὼ ὑμᾶς ἐλύπουν]."[14] It would have been more appropriate to render the Hebrew with ὠργίσθη, as the translator would do later in 31:36, and as Symmachus does here in 4:5.

11. For a detailed study of the rendering of מִנְחָה by the Greek translators, see the important monograph by Suzanne Daniel, *Recherches sur le vocabulaire du culte dans la Septante* (Études et commentaires 61; Paris: Klincksieck, 1966), chap. 9. With reference to Genesis 4, she states—but without persuasive evidence—that while θυσία was a commonplace term for sacrifice and would not suggest an offering of particular importance, δῶρον could evoke the splendid gifts given to persons of high rank (p. 210). Notice that in the NT (Hebrews 10:4) both terms are used to refer to Abel's offering.

12. Daniel (*Recherches sur le vocabulaire du culte*, 209) asserts that the variation highlights the drama of the story because it accentuates the difference in the divine response: God pays no attention to Cain's offering but looks for a long time ("longuement") at Abel's. There may be some truth to this observation, although her paraphrase goes beyond the textual data.

13. Nahum M. Sarna, *Genesis* (JPS Torah Commentary; Philadelphia: Jewish Publication Society, 1989), 33, states that without אַף the verb חָרָה indicates depression rather than anger, but he gives no evidence for this view.

14. Translation from R. E. Allen, *The Dialogues of Plato* (New Haven: Yale University Press, 1984), 1.104.

καὶ συνέπεσεν τῷ προσώπῳ = וַיִּפְּלוּ פָּנָיו. Since the Hebrew expression is "his face [lit., faces] fell" (i.e., he was downcast), one would expect πρόσωπον to be the subject, which is in fact what we find in verse 6 (cf. also 1 Sam. 1:18). Why the translator chose the dative here (a construction not attested elsewhere) is difficult to understand,[15] but the contrast between verse 5 and verse 6 is further evidence that he was not troubled by this sort of inconsistency if it did not alter the message. In any case, the expression should be regarded as a Hebraism; the translator may have chosen the verb συμπίπτω because it is sometimes used in the context of ailments (cf. LSJ 1683 s.v. συμπίπτω II), but the extant parallels are not exact.

4:6	וַיֹּאמֶר יְהוָה אֶל־קָיִן לָמָּה חָרָה לָךְ וְלָמָּה נָפְלוּ פָנֶיךָ׃	καὶ εἶπεν κύριος ὁ θεὸς τῷ Κάιν Ἵνα τί περίλυπος ἐγένου, καὶ ἵνα τί συνέπεσεν τὸ πρόσωπόν σου;
	The LORD said to Cain, "Why are you angry, and why has your countenance fallen?	And the Lord God said to Cain, "Why have you become sad, and why has your countenance fallen?

κύριος ὁ θεός = יְהוָה. Again, we should not infer that the translator had a different *Vorlage* that read יְהוָה אֱלֹהִים; note the inconsistencies in 2:4–9.

ἵνα τί = לָמָּה. A common equivalence. Other frequent renderings are διὰ τί (but not in Genesis) and simple τί.

περίλυπος ἐγένου = חָרָה לָךְ. The use of the adjective here (as opposed to the verb λυπέω in the previous verse) is one more instance of stylistic variation.

4:7	הֲלוֹא אִם־תֵּיטִיב שְׂאֵת וְאִם לֹא תֵיטִיב לַפֶּתַח חַטָּאת רֹבֵץ וְאֵלֶיךָ תְּשׁוּקָתוֹ וְאַתָּה תִּמְשָׁל־בּוֹ׃	οὐκ, ἐὰν ὀρθῶς προσενέγκῃς, ὀρθῶς δὲ μὴ διέλῃς, ἥμαρτες; ἡσύχασον· πρὸς σὲ ἡ ἀποστροφὴ αὐτοῦ, καὶ σὺ ἄρξεις αὐτοῦ.
	If you do well, will you not be accepted? And if you do not do well, sin is lurking at the door; its desire is for you, but you must master it."	Have you not sinned if you have brought [an offering] rightly but have not rightly divided it? Be still: he will return to you, and you will rule over him."

The Hebrew of the first half of Genesis 4:7 is quite difficult, and scholars often appeal to the Greek in an effort to make sense of the passage. But it is plain that the translator himself was in trouble, and his rendering is not likely to be of great help to reconstruct the He-

15. Wevers's view (*Notes on the Greek Text of Genesis*, 54) that it "places the emphasis on Cain" is not persuasive.

brew. (As a general rule, it is a bad idea to emend the MT on the basis of the LXX or another version, if it appears that the translator was struggling with the text.) We may begin by lining up the texts in a way that helps us figure out how the translator analyzed the original:

οὐκ ("not") הֲלוֹא ("not")
ἐὰν ὀρθῶς ("if correctly") אִם־תֵּיטִיב ("if you do well")
προσενέγκῃς ("you bring") שְׂאֵת ("lifting")
ὀρθῶς δὲ μή ("but correctly not") וְאִם לֹא תֵיטִיב ("and if you do not do well")
διέλῃς ("you divide") לַפֶּתַח ("to the door")
ἥμαρτες ("you have sinned") חַטָּאת ("sin")
ἡσύχασον ("be quiet") רֹבֵץ ("crouches")

The Hebrew, as it stands in the MT, consists of two separate conditional sentences (each with one protasis and one apodosis) and appears to mean, "If you do what is right, will not your countenance be lifted? But if you do not do what is right, sin is crouching at the door." If we assume that the Greek translator was working with a Hebrew manuscript that had the same reading as the MT, it is quite possible to understand how he would have come up with his rendering. First, he was perplexed by שְׂאֵת (infinitive of נָשָׂא), which functions as the apodosis of the first condition. The translator interpreted it as a perfect-tense second-person singular, and that led him to take the verb as part of the protasis. As a result of this decision, the Greek, instead of having two conditional sentences, consists of one conditional sentence with a complex protasis ("if you have brought rightly but have not rightly divided") and one apodosis (οὐκ . . . ἥμαρτες;). To make sense of the passage, he further (a) represented the finite verb תֵּיטִיב with the adverb ὀρθῶς; then (b) interpreted the noun פֶּתַח ("opening, door") as a verb ("to make an opening") or perhaps read it as the verb נָתַח ("to cut in pieces"); and finally (c) vocalized the verb רָבַץ as an imperative, interpreting the idea "to lie down, crouch" as a reference to being quiet.

Part of the translator's motivation, undoubtedly, was a desire to understand why God should be upset with Cain for bringing an offering that is approved in the Mosaic legislation. His rendering may be evidence of an ancient interpretation to the effect that the reason Cain's offering was defective was that he failed to follow the proper cultic ritual (notice that the verb διαιρέω is used in Gen. 15:10).

πρὸς σὲ ἡ ἀποστροφὴ αὐτοῦ = וְאֵלֶיךָ תְּשׁוּקָתוֹ. The rest of the verse is also difficult. The Hebrew seems to mean "its desire is toward you," that is, sin (already personified as crouching at the door) wishes to capture Cain. It is difficult to determine the meaning of ἀποστροφή here (similarly in 3:16), which some think reflects the Hebrew root שׁוּב. Earlier English translations of the LXX rendered the Greek noun with "recourse" (Thomson) and "submission" (Brenton). An attractive solution is suggested by John Wevers: "'Sin' will keep coming back to you, but you should rule (i.e. overcome) it."[16]

4:8	וַיֹּאמֶר קַיִן אֶל־הֶבֶל אָחִיו וַיְהִי בִּהְיוֹתָם בַּשָּׂדֶה וַיָּקָם קַיִן אֶל־הֶבֶל אָחִיו וַיַּהַרְגֵהוּ׃	καὶ εἶπεν Κάιν πρὸς Ἅβελ τὸν ἀδελφὸν αὐτοῦ Διέλθωμεν εἰς τὸ πεδίον. καὶ ἐγένετο ἐν τῷ εἶναι αὐτοὺς ἐν τῷ πεδίῳ καὶ ἀνέστη Κάιν ἐπὶ Ἅβελ τὸν ἀδελφὸν αὐτοῦ καὶ ἀπέκτεινεν αὐτόν.
	Cain spoke to his brother Abel. And when they were in the field, Cain rose up against his brother Abel, and killed him.	And Cain said to Abel his brother, "Let us go into the field." And it happened that while they were in the field, Cain rose against Abel his brother and killed him.

The phrase διέλθωμεν εἰς τὸ πεδίον has no corresponding phrase in the MT but is attested in the Samaritan Pentateuch, the Peshitta, and the Vulgate. Since Hebrew וַיֹּאמֶר normally introduces the content of what is being said, most scholars posit that the translator's *Vorlage* included the words נלכה השדה, that this was the original reading, and that it was accidentally omitted very early in the Hebrew tradition. A few scholars point out, in response, that in at least three other passages וַיֹּאמֶר is used without express mention of what was said (Exod. 19:25; 2 Chron. 1:2; 32:24—although these do not provide exact parallels). We should therefore leave open the possibility that, as the more difficult reading, the MT is to be considered original and that the Greek translator (perhaps relying on an earlier tradition) introduced the statement to fill out the meaning.[17]

καὶ ἐγένετο . . . καί ἀνέστη = וַיְהִי . . . וַיָּקָם. See the comments above on 4:3.

ἐν τῷ εἶναι αὐτούς = בִּהְיוֹתָם. Classical Greek uses the articular infinitive extensively in a variety of ways, but this temporal use with the preposition ἐν should be regarded as a Semitism (found often in the NT, especially in Luke). Note, however, that although the construction must have sounded unusual to Greek ears, it cannot be regarded as ungrammatical. We could say that here, and elsewhere, the translators

16. *Notes on the Greek Text of Genesis*, 56. Unfortunately, the implied subject would be ἁμαρτία, which is feminine, reflecting a corresponding grammatical switch in the Hebrew. It seems unlikely that either the translator or his readers would have referred αὐτοῦ to ἁμαρτία. In light of the succeeding context, αὐτοῦ could refer to Abel, who is about to be overcome by Cain, but this interpretation too is not totally satisfactory (see Wevers's objections, ibid., 55).

17. See the thorough discussion by Ronald S. Hendel, *The Text of Genesis 1–11: Textual Studies and Critical Edition* (Oxford: Oxford University Press, 1998), 46–47.

succeeded in representing the Hebrew quite literally by exploiting the normal resources of the Greek language.

Isaiah 52:13–53:12

Because both the Hebrew original and the Greek translation of Isaiah are difficult, we have divided the texts clause by clause for easier reference.[18] Throughout the Book of Isaiah, the Greek translator uses a variety of approaches. Some of his renderings are very literal and at times unintelligible, but he can also be creative and skillful. In this passage he struggled bravely to represent in meaningful Greek a text he did not always understand.

Isaiah 52:13–15

See, my servant shall prosper;	הִנֵּה יַשְׂכִּיל עַבְדִּי	**13a**	Ἰδοὺ συνήσει[19] ὁ παῖς μου	Behold, my servant will understand,
he shall be exalted and lifted up, and shall be very high.	יָרוּם וְנִשָּׂא וְגָבַהּ מְאֹד׃	**b**	καὶ ὑψωθήσεται καὶ δοξασθήσεται σφόδρα.	and he will be exalted and glorified greatly.
Just as there were many who were astonished at him	כַּאֲשֶׁר שָׁמְמוּ עָלֶיךָ רַבִּים	**14a**	ὃν τρόπον ἐκστήσονται ἐπὶ σὲ πολλοί,	Just as many will be astounded at you—
—so marred was his appearance, beyond human semblance,	כֵּן־מִשְׁחַת מֵאִישׁ מַרְאֵהוּ	**b**	οὕτως ἀδοξήσει ἀπὸ ἀνθρώπων τὸ εἶδός σου	for[20] your appearance will receive no glory from men
and his form beyond that of mortals—	וְתֹאֲרוֹ מִבְּנֵי אָדָם׃	**c**	καὶ ἡ δόξα σου ἀπὸ τῶν ἀνθρώπων,	and your glory [will be absent] from men—
so he shall startle many nations;	כֵּן יַזֶּה גּוֹיִם רַבִּים	**15a**	οὕτως θαυμάσονται ἔθνη πολλὰ	thus will many nations marvel

18. Sources: MT = *Biblia hebraica stuttgartensia*, 758–60; LXX = Joseph Ziegler, *Isaias*, 3d ed. (Septuaginta 14; Göttingen: Vandenhoeck & Ruprecht, 1983), 320–23; English translation of MT = NRSV; English translation of LXX = Jobes and Silva. The only substantial difference between Ziegler and Rahlfs is at 53:2a. On the passage as a whole, see the useful notes by Richard R. Ottley, *The Book of Isaiah according to the LXX (Codex Alexandrinus)*, 2 vols. (London: Cambridge University Press, 1904–6), 2.344–48. See also illustration 4 on p. 60 and illustration 15 on p. 142 above.

19. The verb συνίημι is a fairly standard LXX equivalent for שָׂכַל Hiphil, which most often means "to understand," though the extended sense of "to have success" is common and preferred by many commentators and translators in this verse. William L. Holladay suggests "act w. (religious) insight, devotion, piety"; see *A Concise Hebrew and Aramaic Lexicon of the Old Testament* (Grand Rapids: Eerdmans, 1971), 352.

20. Lit., "thus."

kings shall shut their mouths because of him;	עָלָיו יִקְפְּצוּ מְלָכִים פִּיהֶם	**b**	ἐπ᾽ αὐτῷ, καὶ συνέξουσι βασιλεῖς τὸ στόμα αὐτῶν·	at him, and kings will shut their mouth:
for that which had not been told them they shall see,	כִּי אֲשֶׁר לֹא־סֻפַּר לָהֶם רָאוּ	**c**	ὅτι οἷς οὐκ ἀνηγγέλη περὶ αὐτοῦ, ὄψονται,	because those to whom it was not reported about him will see,
and that which they had not heard they shall contemplate.	וַאֲשֶׁר לֹא־שָׁמְעוּ הִתְבּוֹנָנוּ׃	**d**	καὶ οἳ οὐκ ἀκηκόασι, συνήσουσι.	and those who have not heard will understand.

In verse 13, the phrase καὶ ὑψωθήσεται καὶ δοξασθήσεται σφόδρα corresponds to a fuller expression in the MT, which has three verbs, יָרוּם וְנִשָּׂא וְגָבַהּ מְאֹד (note that Hebrew has no initial *wāw* corresponding to καί). Not surprisingly, important witnesses to the Hexaplaric recension, especially manuscripts V and 88, and the whole of the Lucianic recension add καὶ μετεωρισθήσεται ("and will be raised high"), which reflects an adjustment to the MT.[21] It is unclear, however, why the original translator would have omitted one of the verbs. In the Hebrew, but not in the Greek, one notices a direct allusion to Isaiah's vision recorded in 6:1, since two of the three verbs (רָם וְנִשָּׂא, translated ὑψηλοῦ καὶ ἐπηρμένου)[22] are used there to describe the Lord seated on his throne. It is difficult to believe that the translator was unaware of this lexical inconsistency, yet one is at a loss to explain why he would have deliberately obscured the parallel.

The meaning of the Greek in the second part of verse 14 is doubtful; a literal translation certainly makes little sense ("your appearance will be disreputable from men and your reputation from the men"). We must keep in mind the semantic development of δόξα (and cognates) from its usual classical senses—the active "opinion" and the passive "reputation"—to its semitized sense of "glory."[23] This passage in fact

21. Two Lucianic witnesses (449 and 770) preserve the Origenic asterisk that marks this addition. It is difficult—and probably a fruitless exercise—to determine whether the original Greek translator omitted יָרוּם (so *Biblia hebraica stuttgartensia*) or גָּבַהּ ("by general agreement," according to Ottley, *Book of Isaiah*, 2.344). An additional minor question is whether the Hebrew adverb מְאֹד modifies all three verbs or (as in the NRSV rendering) only the last one—an ambiguity present also in the Greek.

22. Nowhere else does LXX Isaiah use ἐπαίρω with reference to God. In 33:10, where God speaks about himself, the same combination of Hebrew verbs is translated as in 52:13: δοξασθήσομαι . . . ὑψωθήσομαι. Isaac L. Seeligmann, *The Septuagint Version of Isaiah: A Discussion of Its Problems* (Leiden: Brill, 1948), 29, 116, points out that the Greek translators, and especially Isaiah, have a penchant for this lexical combination. The frequency of these two terms in LXX Isaiah may in part account for their recurring use in the Gospel of John with reference to Jesus' exaltation.

23. See above, chap. 5, p. 110.

well illustrates the transition from one meaning to the other: the verb δοξασθήσεται in verse 13 certainly carries the Semitic nuance, while in verse 14 ἀδοξέω ("to have a low opinion of [someone]," often intransitive/passive: "to be held in no esteem") preserves the classical sense. As a result, ἡ δόξα in the following clause is a little ambiguous (perhaps deliberately). It should be noted that the equivalent Hebrew term, כָּבוֹד, does not actually appear in these verses. The translator, on his own, has imaginatively exploited the new associations of δόξα in order to draw a sharp contrast between verse 13 and verse 14; this feature can be preserved in English only by the use of the term *glory*, as in the translation above.

An important difference between the Greek and the MT is the clause θαυμάσονται ἔθνη πολλὰ ἐπ' αὐτῷ in verse 15, which corresponds to יַזֶּה גּוֹיִם רַבִּים ("he will sprinkle many nations"). Because the Hebrew text is difficult, most commentators and modern translations emend the verb (e.g., to יִרְגְּזוּ, from רָגַז, "to quiver") on the basis of the Greek. As pointed out before, however, it is not wise to depend on the LXX translators for textual emendations when they too were struggling with the meaning of the Hebrew. The translator of Isaiah in particular often harmonizes the text to its context, especially if parallelism is involved.[24] Having already used the verb ἐξίστημι (for שָׁמַם) at the beginning of verse 14, which is the protasis (the "just as" clause) of a comparative sentence, it would have seemed natural to assign a similar meaning to the verb in the apodosis (the "so also" clause).[25] By the same token, it seems unlikely that the MT reading (*lectio difficilior*) would have arisen if the original Hebrew text had been as easy as suggested by the Greek translation.[26]

24. For example, MT Isa. 66:15 reads, "For behold, the Lord will come *in* fire [בָּאֵשׁ], and his chariots *like* a whirlwind [כַּסּוּפָה]." One would expect the corresponding prepositions ἐν and ὡς to be used, but the translator opted for ὡς in both cases. In 63:5, the Hebrew reads, "And I looked [אַבִּיט, properly translated ἐπέβλεψα], but there was no helper; and I was appalled [אֶשְׁתּוֹמֵם, translated προσενόησα ("I observed")!], but there was no one to lean on." See also David A. Baer, *When We All Go Home: Translation and Theology in LXX Isaiah 56–66* (Hebrew Bible and Ancient Versions 1; Sheffield: Sheffield Academic Press, 2000).

25. The syntax of the Greek, which reflects an ambiguity in the Hebrew, is difficult. Both Brenton and Thomson assume that v. 14b–c is the apodosis (in which case οὕτως in v. 15 begins a new and independent clause, but still logically tied to v. 14). Rahlfs encloses v. 14b–c within dashes, however, suggesting that v. 15 constitutes the apodosis, with the intervening words forming a parenthetical comment that explains why many will be astounded at the servant (the translation above follows this approach).

26. Other minor differences between the Greek and the Hebrew are the following: (a) In v. 14, the expression בְּנֵי אָדָם ("sons of man") is translated with simple τῶν ἀνθρώπων, but this is an appropriate rendering; the more literal translation, (τῶν) υἱῶν τῶν ἀνθρώπων, found in Hexaplaric and Lucianic manuscripts, must be an adjustment to the Hebrew. (b) Also in v. 14, the third-person of the MT (מַרְאֵהוּ וְתֹאֲרוֹ, "his appearance and his semblance") is changed to the second-person (τὸ εἶδός σου καὶ ἡ δόξα σου) as a con-

In spite of some ambiguities, the thrust of the Greek passage as a whole is comprehensible. God's servant will in the end be highly exalted. Though God himself anticipates that his servant will be rejected, the work he is about to do will draw universal amazement: even kings will be speechless! Why? Because those who could not have been expected to know about God's work or about his servant are in fact the ones who will understand. In line with remarkable passages such as Isaiah 19:19–25, it may be that the Greek translator understood this prophecy as a reference to the salvation of the Gentiles.

Isaiah 53:1–3

Who has believed what we have heard?	מִי הֶאֱמִין לִשְׁמֻעָתֵנוּ	**1a**	κύριε, τίς ἐπίστευσε τῇ ἀκοῇ ἡμῶν;	Lord, who has believed our report?
And to whom has the arm of the LORD been revealed?	וּזְרוֹעַ יְהוָה עַל־מִי נִגְלָתָה׃	**b**	καὶ ὁ βραχίων κυρίου τίνι ἀπεκαλύφθη;	And to whom has the arm of the Lord been revealed?
For he grew up before him like a young plant,	וַיַּעַל כַּיּוֹנֵק לְפָנָיו	**2a**	ἀνέτειλε μὲν[27] ἐναντίον αὐτοῦ ὡς παιδίον,	He grew up before him like a child,
and like a root out of dry ground; he had no form or majesty	וְכַשֹּׁרֶשׁ מֵאֶרֶץ צִיָּה לֹא־תֹאַר לוֹ וְלֹא הָדָר	**b**	ὡς ῥίζα ἐν γῇ διψώσῃ, οὐκ ἔστιν εἶδος αὐτῷ οὐδὲ δόξα·	like a root in a parched land. There is no form to him nor glory:
that we should look at him, nothing in his appearance that we should desire him.	וְנִרְאֵהוּ וְלֹא־מַרְאֶה וְנֶחְמְדֵהוּ׃	**c**	καὶ εἴδομεν αὐτόν, καὶ οὐκ εἶχεν εἶδος οὐδὲ κάλλος·	when[28] we saw him, he had no form or beauty.
He was despised and rejected by others;	נִבְזֶה וַחֲדַל אִישִׁים	**3a**	ἀλλὰ τὸ εἶδος αὐτοῦ ἄτιμον ἐκλεῖπον παρὰ πάντας ἀνθρώπους,	But his form was without honor, failing in comparison to[29] all men.

textual adjustment to σέ at the beginning of the verse. *Biblia hebraica stuttgartensia*, following two Hebrew manuscripts, the Peshitta, and the Targum, suggests reading עָלָיו rather than עָלֶיךָ at the beginning of the verse.

27. The reading ἀνέτειλε μέν is a widely accepted conjectural emendation (see above, chap. 6, p. 136). All surviving manuscripts, followed by Rahlfs, have ἀνηγγείλαμεν ("we have announced"), which does not yield good sense in context. Brenton's solution: "We brought a report as of a child."

28. Lit., "and."

29. Or, "failing more than."

a man of suffering and acquainted with infirmity;	אִישׁ מַכְאֹבוֹת וִידוּעַ חֹלִי	**b**	ἄνθρωπος ἐν πληγῇ ὢν καὶ εἰδὼς φέρειν μαλακίαν,	[He was] a man in calamity and experienced in[30] weakness,
and as one from whom others hide their faces	וּכְמַסְתֵּר פָּנִים מִמֶּנּוּ	**c**	ὅτι ἀπέστραπται τὸ πρόσωπον αὐτοῦ,	because his face was turned away,
he was despised, and we held him of no account.	נִבְזֶה וְלֹא חֲשַׁבְנֻהוּ׃	**d**	ἠτιμάσθη καὶ οὐκ ἐλογίσθη.	he was dishonored and not esteemed.

The addition of the word κύριε gives the Greek text of verse 1 a nuance not present in the Hebrew, which sounds rather like an exclamation. Otherwise, the rendering of this verse is a word-for-word representation of the Hebrew (note that no attempt is made to resolve the metaphor of "the arm of the Lord"). Ironically, however, this literal translation may have slanted the meaning of the original. The Hebrew noun שְׁמוּעָה means "the thing heard," therefore "news, message."[31] With the pronominal suffix, an ambiguity is created: the text may speak of a report that is either given ("who has believed our message?"; cf. NIV) or received ("who has believed what we have heard?"; cf. NRSV).[32] In the Greek text, on the other hand, only the former interpretation seems possible, and thus it becomes especially suitable for use by the NT writers (see John 12:38 and Romans 10:16, in both of which passages the word κύριε is included).

In verse 2, the noun παιδίον translates יוֹנֵק (from יָנַק, "to suck"). In a different context, this would have been an appropriate equivalent, but the phrase that follows should have alerted the translator that the Hebrew was speaking of a young plant or sapling (cf. יוֹנֶקֶת, "shoot, twig").

The phrase καὶ εἴδομεν αὐτόν is a possible translation of וְנִרְאֵהוּ, although modern scholars prefer to construe this Hebrew verb with what precedes (cf. NRSV: "he had no form or majesty that we should look at him"), thus providing a syntactic parallel with the construction at the end of the verse: וְנֶחְמְדֵהוּ ("[he had] no appearance that we should desire him"). The Greek translator, however, must have read this last verb as the noun חֶמְדָּה ("something desirable"), which he ren-

30. Lit., "and knowing [how] to carry."

31. In prophetic contexts—particularly here, where the second question suggests a parallel—the word may take on the nuance of "revelation" (cf. Isa. 28:9); so Holladay's *Concise Hebrew and Aramaic Lexicon*, 375, which paraphrases, "what we have heard (& must reveal)."

32. Unfortunately, no other examples exist of this noun with a pronominal suffix, and so (in spite of the assurance with which some commentators speak) it is difficult to prove one view over the other.

dered κάλλος ("beauty"). It is difficult to say whether this change was a mistake on his part or (perhaps more likely) an attempt to make sense of a clause he did not fully understand.

The first clause of verse 3 also gave the translator some difficulty. The Hebrew reads נִבְזֶה וַחֲדַל אִישִׁים, usually translated, "he was despised and rejected[33] by men." By starting the sentence with an addition, ἀλλὰ τὸ εἶδος αὐτοῦ, the translator changed the subject and connected this sentence more directly with the previous verse. The verb ἐκλείπω, when used intransitively as here, means "to cease, be wanting, fail" and thus corresponds closely to the Hebrew verb חָדַל; the translator may have taken the Hebrew word as a participle in construct with אִישִׁים, a relationship he expressed with the preposition παρά, which of course has a broad range of meaning. Finally, he intensified the statement by adding the adjective πάντας.[34]

The following construct phrase, אִישׁ מַכְאֹבוֹת ("a man of pains"), was rendered with an equivalent locution: ἄνθρωπος ἐν πληγῇ ὤν. The translator also avoided literalism in his handling of the passive participle יְדוּעַ ("acquainted") by using the active participle εἰδώς with the infinitive φέρειν. Finally, he must have felt stumped by the difficult Hebrew construction: וּכְמַסְתֵּר פָּנִים מִמֶּנּוּ (lit., "and as a hiding of face[s] from him/us"), that is, "as one who hides his face from us" or "as one from whom people hide their face." It appears that the translator (a) chose to take the first two letters as כִּי = ὅτι; (b) expressed the idea "to hide" with ἀποστρέφω ("to turn away"), a word that can imply disgust; (c) ignored the word מִמֶּנּוּ; and (d) interpreted the last word of the verse, חֲשַׁבְנֻהוּ (first-person plural active with third-person pronoun: "we esteemed him"), as third-person singular passive, thus rendered ἐλογίσθη.

Isaiah 53:4–5

Surely he has borne our infirmities	אָכֵן חֳלָיֵנוּ הוּא נָשָׂא	4a	οὗτος τὰς ἁμαρτίας ἡμῶν φέρει	This one carries our sins
and carried our diseases;	וּמַכְאֹבֵינוּ סְבָלָם	b	καὶ περὶ ἡμῶν ὀδυνᾶται,	and suffers pain for us,

33. While the first word is a Niphal verb, חֲדַל is actually an adjective meaning "ceasing" or "lacking"; the construction "lacking of [among] men" seems to convey the notion of being shunned or forsaken by others.

34. With the exception of manuscripts A, Q, and a few minuscules, which end the clause with ἀνθρώπους (for MT's אִישִׁים), virtually the whole Greek textual tradition reads (τοὺς) υἱοὺς τῶν ἀνθρώπων. Since the Hebrew textual tradition has no trace of the reading בְּנֵי אָדָם, this variant hardly reflects a different *Vorlage* but must have arisen early in stylistic imitation of the Semitic expression, which is otherwise common in the LXX.

yet we accounted him stricken,	וַאֲנַחְנוּ חֲשַׁבְנֻהוּ נָגוּעַ	c	καὶ ἡμεῖς ἐλογισάμεθα αὐτὸν εἶναι ἐν πόνῳ	and we realized that he underwent trouble,
struck down by God, and afflicted.	מֻכֵּה אֱלֹהִים וּמְעֻנֶּה׃	d	καὶ ἐν πληγῇ καὶ ἐν κακώσει.	calamity, and ill-treatment.[35]
But he was wounded for our transgressions,	וְהוּא מְחֹלָל מִפְּשָׁעֵנוּ	5a	αὐτὸς δὲ ἐτραυματίσθη διὰ τὰς ἀνομίας ἡμῶν	But he was wounded because of our transgressions
crushed for our iniquities;	מְדֻכָּא מֵעֲוֹנֹתֵינוּ	b	καὶ μεμαλάκισται διὰ τὰς ἁμαρτίας ἡμῶν·	and has been weakened because of our sins:
upon him was the punishment that made us whole,	מוּסַר שְׁלוֹמֵנוּ עָלָיו	c	παιδεία εἰρήνης ἡμῶν ἐπ' αὐτόν,	the punishment of our peace was upon him;
and by his bruises we are healed.	וּבַחֲבֻרָתוֹ נִרְפָּא־לָנוּ׃	d	τῷ μώλωπι αὐτοῦ ἡμεῖς ἰάθημεν.	by his bruise we were healed.

In verse 4a, the translator omitted the initial adverb (אָכֵן), unless οὗτος (rather than αὐτός, which is the expected equivalent of הוּא and which is a Hexaplaric variant here, attested in Q and the margin of the Syro-Hexaplar) was intended by him to capture some of the emphasis expressed by that adverb. Note moreover that (a) the translator uses the Greek (historic?) present tense, apparently construing the Hebrew verb as a participle; (b) the translator resolves the Hebrew metaphor of sickness by using the moral term ἁμαρτία; and (c) the translator, perhaps for stylistic reasons, avoids repeating the notion of "to bear/carry" and thus paraphrases the second clause.[36]

The rest of verse 4 reveals an even more significant difference between the Hebrew and the Greek. Where the LXX has simply ἐν πληγῇ, the MT has the remarkable phrase מֻכֵּה אֱלֹהִים ("smitten by God"; מֻכֵּה is a Hophal participle of נָכָה). This rendering is only one of several examples where the translator clearly avoids statements that attribute the servant's sufferings to God's action. Note also that the noun πόνος is a fairly weak rendering of the passive participle נָגוּעַ ("stricken").

In contrast, verse 5 is translated much better, with one exception.

35. A literal translation of lines 4c–d is "and we considered him to be in trouble and in blow and in ill-treatment."

36. Interestingly, the quotation of this statement in Matthew 8:17 follows the Hebrew more closely: αὐτὸς τὰς ἀσθενείας ἡμῶν ἔλαβεν καὶ τὰς νόσους ἐβάστασεν. Did the author of this gospel provide his own translation because he regarded the LXX reading as inadequate? Or did he have access to an alternate Greek translation current in his day? See above, chap. 9, pp. 190–92. See a fuller discussion of this quotation in Robert H. Gundry, *The Use of the Old Testament in St. Matthew's Gospel: With Special Reference to the Messianic Hope* (Novum Testamentum Supplement 18; Leiden: Brill, 1967), passim.

The choice of μαλακίζομαι ("to be softened, show weakness," sometimes alluding to effeminate behavior) reflects the use of this verb with reference to sickness (cf. Isa. 38:1, 9; 39:1). The corresponding Hebrew term, however, is much more forceful: מְדֻכָּא, Pual participle of דָּכָא ("to crush"). We may also note the very literal rendering παιδεία εἰρήνης ἡμῶν = מוּסַר שְׁלוֹמֵנוּ (NRSV: "the punishment that made us whole"). Perhaps the typical Greek reader would have struggled with the meaning of this phrase—but presumably not much more than the user of the King James Version: "the chastisement of our peace." The term παιδεία, incidentally, means "training, education" in nonbiblical Greek; the shift to "discipline, punishment" is a clear example of semantic borrowing from Hebrew (see above, chap. 5, pp. 108–10).

Isaiah 53:6–8

All we like sheep have gone astray;	כֻּלָּנוּ כַּצֹּאן תָּעִינוּ	**6a**	πάντες ὡς πρόβατα ἐπλανήθημεν,	We all have wandered like sheep,
we have all turned to our own way,	אִישׁ לְדַרְכּוֹ פָּנִינוּ	**b**	ἄνθρωπος τῇ ὁδῷ αὐτοῦ ἐπλανήθη·	[each] man has wandered in his own way;
and the LORD has laid on him the iniquity of us all.	וַיהוָה הִפְגִּיעַ בּוֹ אֵת עֲוֹן כֻּלָּנוּ׃	**c**	καὶ κύριος παρέδωκεν αὐτὸν ταῖς ἁμαρτίαις ἡμῶν.	and the Lord gave him over to our sins.
He was oppressed, and he was afflicted, yet he did not open his mouth;	נִגַּשׂ וְהוּא נַעֲנֶה וְלֹא יִפְתַּח־פִּיו	**7a**	καὶ αὐτὸς διὰ τὸ κεκακῶσθαι οὐκ ἀνοίγει τὸ στόμα·	And because of his affliction he does not open his mouth:
like a lamb that is led to the slaughter,	כַּשֶּׂה לַטֶּבַח יוּבָל	**b**	ὡς πρόβατον ἐπὶ σφαγὴν ἤχθη	like a sheep he was led to the slaughter,
and like a sheep that before its shearers is silent,	וּכְרָחֵל לִפְנֵי גֹזְזֶיהָ נֶאֱלָמָה	**c**	καὶ ὡς ἀμνὸς ἐναντίον τοῦ κείροντος αὐτὸν ἄφωνος	and as a lamb is silent before the one shearing it,
so he did not open his mouth.	וְלֹא יִפְתַּח פִּיו׃	**d**	οὕτως οὐκ ἀνοίγει τὸ στόμα αὐτοῦ.	so he does not open his mouth.
By a perversion of justice he was taken away.	מֵעֹצֶר וּמִמִּשְׁפָּט לֻקָּח	**8a**	ἐν τῇ ταπεινώσει ἡ κρίσις αὐτοῦ ἤρθη·	In [his] humiliation his [fair] judgment was taken away:
Who could have imagined his future?	וְאֶת־דּוֹרוֹ מִי יְשׂוֹחֵחַ	**b**	τὴν γενεὰν αὐτοῦ τίς διηγήσεται;	who will describe his generation?
For he was cut off from the land of the living,	כִּי נִגְזַר מֵאֶרֶץ חַיִּים	**c**	ὅτι αἴρεται ἀπὸ τῆς γῆς ἡ ζωὴ αὐτοῦ,	Because his life is being taken from the earth;

stricken for the transgression of my people.	מִפֶּשַׁע עַמִּי נֶגַע לָמוֹ׃	**d**	ἀπὸ τῶν ἀνομιῶν τοῦ λαοῦ μου ἤχθη εἰς θάνατον.	he was led to death because of the transgressions of my people.

In verse 6 we need comment on only two details. First, the translator used one and the same verb, πλανάω, to translate two Hebrew verbs: תָּעָה ("to wander") and פָּנָה ("to turn"). Second, the strong Hebrew expression "the Lord has struck[37] him with the iniquity of us all" is softened by means of the verb παραδίδωμι, a term that this translator uses at various times when he needs to get out of a difficulty (the force of the following dative construction, ταῖς ἁμαρτίαις, is not clear).

For no apparent reason, the Greek ignores the first word of verse 7: נִגַּשׂ ("he was oppressed"). Moreover, the causal construction διὰ τὸ κεκακῶσθαι is a less than successful attempt to interpret the simple Hebrew syntax: וְהוּא נַעֲנֶה ("and he was afflicted"), which may have rather a concessive force.[38] The last clause of verse 7 begins with οὕτως, a defensible "dynamic" rendering of Hebrew *wāw*.

Verse 8 is particularly difficult. Although the words are common and the syntax gives the appearance of simplicity, one wonders what it all means. The verse consists of four Greek clauses, each of which corresponds to a Hebrew clause:

a. The first clause in the Hebrew reads מֵעֹצֶר וּמִמִּשְׁפָּט לֻקָּח ("by oppression and judgment, he was taken away"; NIV), which the NRSV interprets to mean, "By a perversion of justice he was taken away."[39] Perhaps because of the difficulty of the Hebrew, the translator interpreted the first two words as though they read בעצר משפטו. In any case, the resulting Greek is not clear; Thomson renders it, "In this humiliation his legal trial was taken away."

b. The second clause, verse 8b, reflects a fairly literal translation, but commentators do not agree regarding the meaning of the Hebrew, which the NRSV renders, "Who could have imagined his future?" Moreover, scholars debate whether the clause is a complete question. According to some, the question continues into the next line, which begins with the ambiguous conjunction כִּי (cf. NIV note: "Yet who of his generation considered / that he was cut off from the land of the living?"). At any rate, the Greek may be understood in one of two dif-

37. Hebrew הִפְגִּיעַ (Hiphil of פָּגַע), "to cause to fall, to make (something) strike (someone)."

38. See Christopher R. North, *The Second Isaiah: Introduction, Translation and Commentary to Chapters xl–lv* (Oxford: Clarendon, 1964), 65, who translates the Hebrew, "He was harshly treated, though he submitted humbly and did not open his mouth."

39. Another possibility is North's translation (ibid., 65): "After arrest and sentence he was led away."

ferent ways: "Who can count his posterity?" or "Who can describe the [evil] generation of men among whom he lived?" (Thomson).

c. The word חַיִּים ("the ones living") in verse 8c was read by the translator as חיו ("his life"), though the resulting meaning is not substantially different. The main difficulty raised by the Greek, however, has to do with the logical relationship of this clause to its context. Our translation above takes the clause as an answer to the preceding question, or more precisely, as giving the reason why the preceding question was asked. If this interpretation is correct, the clause is syntactically unrelated to the following one, which simply repeats the idea with different words. It is also possible to take the third clause as subordinate to the following one, though the logical sense would be far from clear.[40]

d. In the last clause, the rendering ἀπὸ τῶν ἀνομιῶν τοῦ λαοῦ μου for מִפֶּשַׁע עַמִּי is literal but appropriate (the prepositions מִן and ἀπό can both be used causally). Unfortunately, the translator ran into trouble with the last two words: נֶגַע לָמוֹ ("a blow to him"; i.e., "he was stricken"). He may have felt confused by the word לָמוֹ, which more commonly has a plural reference (like לָהֶם); he may also have wanted to avoid, once again, the notion that God did violence to the servant. Be that as it may, the translator understood נֶגַע as a verb form, which can mean "to touch, reach, come" (but not "to lead"), and gave it a passive sense: ἤχθη. Then he read the last word as לַמָּוֶת and rendered it with εἰς θάνατον—almost certainly a case of assimilation to the context (see the references to death in vv. 9 and 12). Remarkably, not a few scholars accept לַמָּוֶת as the translator's *Vorlage* and as the original Hebrew text (cf. *Biblia hebraica stuttgartensia*). Considering the Greek translator's performance as a whole, one is tempted to view this curiosity as an example of the blind leading the blind.

Isaiah 53:9–12

They made his grave with the wicked	וַיִּתֵּן אֶת־רְשָׁעִים קִבְרוֹ	**9a**	καὶ δώσω τοὺς πονηροὺς ἀντὶ τῆς ταφῆς αὐτοῦ	And I will give the wicked for his burial
and his tomb with the rich,	וְאֶת־עָשִׁיר בְּמֹתָיו	**b**	καὶ τοὺς πλουσίους ἀντὶ τοῦ θανάτου αὐτοῦ·	and the rich for his death,
although he had done no violence,	עַל לֹא־חָמָס עָשָׂה	**c**	ὅτι ἀνομίαν οὐκ ἐποίησεν,	because he did not commit transgression,

40. Thomson, in what seems an act of despair, takes it as subordinate to v. 9 and views the fourth clause of v. 8 as parenthetical: "Because his life is taken from the earth—for the transgressions of my people he is led to death,—therefore I will appoint the wicked for his tomb."

and there was no deceit in his mouth.	וְלֹא מִרְמָה בְּפִיו׃	**d**	οὐδὲ εὑρέθη δόλος ἐν τῷ στόματι αὐτοῦ.	nor was deceit found in his mouth.
Yet it was the will of the LORD to crush him with pain.	וַיהוָה חָפֵץ דַּכְּאוֹ הֶחֱלִי	**10a**	καὶ κύριος βούλεται καθαρίσαι αὐτὸν τῆς πληγῆς·	And the Lord desires to cleanse him from the blow:
When you make his life an offering for sin,	אִם־תָּשִׂים אָשָׁם נַפְשׁוֹ	**b**	ἐὰν δῶτε περὶ ἁμαρτίας, ἡ ψυχὴ ὑμῶν	if you give [an offering] for sin, your soul
he shall see his offspring, and shall prolong his days;	יִרְאֶה זֶרַע יַאֲרִיךְ יָמִים	**c**	ὄψεται σπέρμα μακρόβιον·	will see a long-lived seed.
through him the will of the LORD shall prosper.	וְחֵפֶץ יְהוָה בְּיָדוֹ יִצְלָח׃	**d**	καὶ βούλεται κύριος ἀφελεῖν	Moreover, the Lord desires to take away
Out of his anguish he shall see light;	מֵעֲמַל נַפְשׁוֹ יִרְאֶה	**11a**	ἀπὸ τοῦ πόνου τῆς ψυχῆς αὐτοῦ, [41]δεῖξαι αὐτῷ φῶς	from the distress of his soul, to show him light,
he shall find satisfaction through his knowledge.	יִשְׂבַּע בְּדַעְתּוֹ	**b**	καὶ πλάσαι[42] τῇ συνέσει,	and to mold him with understanding—
The righteous one, my servant, shall make many righteous,	יַצְדִּיק צַדִּיק עַבְדִּי לָרַבִּים	**c**	δικαιῶσαι δίκαιον εὖ δουλεύοντα πολλοῖς,	to justify a righteous man who is serving many well;
and he shall bear their iniquities.	וַעֲוֺנֹתָם הוּא יִסְבֹּל׃	**d**	καὶ τὰς ἁμαρτίας αὐτῶν αὐτὸς ἀνοίσει.	and he himself will bear their sins.
Therefore I will allot him a portion with the great,	לָכֵן אֲחַלֶּק־לוֹ בָרַבִּים	**12a**	διὰ τοῦτο αὐτὸς κληρονομήσει πολλοὺς	Therefore, he will inherit many,[43]

41. Ziegler's edition and the translations by Thomson and Brenton begin v. 11 at this point.

42. It does not seem possible to account for πλάσαι (infinitive of πλάσσω, "to form, mold") as a rendering of the common verb שָׂבַע ("to be satisfied"), which elsewhere the translator represents properly with ἐμπίμπλημι (cf. Isa. 9:19; 44:16; 58:10–11; 66:11). The reading must be the result of inner-Greek corruption. Long ago Johann F. Schleusner (*Novus thesaurus philologico-criticus sive lexicon in LXX* [Leipzig: Weidmann, 1820], 4.554), with reference to earlier work, suggested the conjectural emendation πλῆσαι (infinitive of πίμπλημι), which is almost certainly correct, although neither Rahlfs nor Ziegler accepts it.

43. Alternatively, "he shall make many to inherit" (Ottley, *Book of Isaiah*, 1.279). Note that the subject of the Hebrew verb is first-person, which must have sounded abrupt to the translator, since the verbs preceding and following this clause are third-person.

and he shall divide the spoil with the strong;	וְאֶת־עֲצוּמִים יְחַלֵּק שָׁלָל	**b**	καὶ τῶν ἰσχυρῶν μεριεῖ σκῦλα,	and he will distribute the spoils of the powerful,
because he poured out himself to death,	תַּחַת אֲשֶׁר הֶעֱרָה לַמָּוֶת נַפְשׁוֹ	**c**	ἀνθ᾽ ὧν παρεδόθη εἰς θάνατον ἡ ψυχὴ αὐτοῦ,	because his soul was given over to death,
and was numbered with the transgressors;	וְאֶת־פֹּשְׁעִים נִמְנָה	**d**	καὶ ἐν τοῖς ἀνόμοις ἐλογίσθη·	and he was reckoned among the transgressors.
yet he bore the sin of many,	וְהוּא חֵטְא־רַבִּים נָשָׂא	**e**	καὶ αὐτὸς ἁμαρτίας πολλῶν ἀνήνεγκε	And he himself bore the sins of many,
and made intercession for the transgressors.	וְלַפֹּשְׁעִים יַפְגִּיעַ׃	**f**	καὶ διὰ τὰς ἁμαρτίας αὐτῶν παρεδόθη.	and because of their sins he was given over.

In these verses, again, the individual clauses seem simple to understand, but the sense of the whole is not exactly transparent. We should not be too hard on the translator, however, since the Hebrew text is challenging. Students are encouraged to examine the Hebrew carefully, identify the various exegetical options, and then evaluate the Greek translator's approach. Here we limit ourselves to discussing one interesting detail in each verse.

The reading εὑρέθη δόλος in verse 9d is probably original; it certainly is in keeping with the translator's tendency to use stylistically fuller expressions (the Hebrew has no verb). We should note, however, that the first hand of Sinaiticus, supported by Vaticanus, Venetus, and not a few minuscules, has the simple accusative δόλον (to be taken, with ἀνομίαν, as the object of ἐποίησεν). This looks like a Hexaplaric adjustment toward the Hebrew, but one must be open to the possibility that it is original and that the fuller rendering originated with 1 Peter 2:22, thereafter spreading through most of the textual tradition.

In verse 10a, the use of καθαρίσαι αὐτόν to represent דַּכְּאוֹ (Piel infinitive with pronominal suffix, "to strike him") is another instance of the translator's concern to avoid attributing to God the action of mistreating the servant. But how did he come up with this rendering? It may appear that he simply took ד as ז, since זָכָה indeed means "to cleanse." More likely, he may have been influenced by the corresponding term in Aramaic, דְּכָא (דְּכֵי).[44] Of course, we cannot tell whether he thought that the Hebrew term itself really had that meaning.

44. So Seeligmann, *Septuagint Version of Isaiah*, 50. The Proto-Semitic phoneme /d̲/ appears as ז in Hebrew, but as ד in Aramaic. For example, the Hebrew term for "gold," זָהָב, corresponds to Aramaic דְּהַב (it is possible that the phoneme /d̲/ was preserved in earlier Aramaic dialects, as it is in Arabic).

In verse 11a, where the Hebrew simply says "he will see" (יִרְאֶה), the translator understands the verb as a Hiphil, rendering it into Greek with a causative verb (δεῖξαι) and supplying both a direct object (φῶς) and an indirect object (αὐτῷ). On the basis of the Greek, many scholars and modern versions emend the MT to read יִרְאֶה אוֹר (cf. NRSV). Of all emendations suggested by the LXX renderings in Isaiah 53, this is the most persuasive one, since three distinct scrolls of Isaiah from Qumran have precisely this reading. To be sure, even here the evidence is not conclusive. The MT reading is more difficult, so we would need to assume an early accidental omission (such a scribal mistake is possible, but what could have caused it here?). Note also that elsewhere the Greek translator was quite capable of inserting a direct object to fill out the thought; especially interesting is 40:5, where the verb וְרָאוּ has no object but the Greek adds τὸ σωτήριον τοῦ θεοῦ. Moreover, we have some evidence that the translator had a theological preoccupation with the notion of light as knowledge.[45] Similarly, a case can be made that an ideological motivation lies behind the Qumran reading.[46] On balance, however, it seems likely that the LXX reading reflects a parent text different from MT and that this reading is original.

Finally, we note in verse 12 the translator's use, not once but twice, of one of his favorite terms, παραδίδωμι. The first time it corresponds to הֶעֱרָה (Hiphil of עָרָה): the Hebrew transitive construction "he poured out his soul [i.e., himself]" is turned into a somewhat banal passive expression: "his soul was delivered." The second instance is even less defensible. Failing to recognize here the meaning "to intercede" for Hiphil פָּגַע and having already in verse 6 avoided the other meaning of this Hebrew verb ("to strike"), once again the translator falls back on the rendering that he hopes will deliver him from all of his troubles. It is ironic that the very last word in this passage encapsulates the nature of his work as a whole—a remarkable combination of creativity and confusion.

Esther 5:1–2 with Addition D

In the previous two sections we closely compared the Greek text with the Hebrew. In this example we will briefly compare two distinct Greek versions of Esther, usually referred to as the LXX and the

45. See Seeligmann, *Septuagint Version of Isaiah*, 119. Besides, the concept of "seeing light" was ready at hand from Isa. 9:1.

46. See especially Jean Koenig, *L'herméneutique analogique du Judaïsme antique d'après les témoins textuels d'Isaïe* (Vetus Testamentum Supplement 33; Leiden: Brill, 1982), 274–83.

Alpha-Text (AT).[47] One of the distinctive traits of the Greek versions of Esther in comparison to the Hebrew is that both Greek versions contain six additional chapters, referred to as additions A–F. Five of these additional chapters were cleanly inserted as blocks in such a way that could be described in modern terms as cut-and-paste.[48]

Not so, however, with addition D, an expanded story of Esther's uninvited audience with the king. It is woven within the Greek verses translating the Hebrew text of 5:1–2, expanding these two Hebrew verses to sixteen in the Greek (illustration 19). The distinctive way in which addition D was integrated into the translation of the Hebrew verses suggests how the addition came to be included in both of the Greek versions.

The Hebrew text of Esther 5:1 is trisected at exactly the same place in both the LXX and the AT by the insertion of additional text (with minor variation), as indicated by the italic phrases:

5:1a And it happened on the third day,
as Esther ceased praying, she took off the garments of humility,
5:1b and put on her glory.
Then, when she had become majestic, after calling upon the all-seeing God and Savior, . . .
5:1c [and] she stood. . . .

The fact that addition D is interwoven with the translation of the Hebrew text at exactly the same places in both Greek versions indicates that this addition was copied from one Greek version to the other. For otherwise, if addition D came into the LXX and the AT independently from a third source, it is highly improbable that it would have been inserted in identical fashion, splitting sentences apart precisely at the same points. This also indicates either (a) that the Greek texts of chapter 5 in the LXX and the AT were virtually identical, allowing addition D to be positioned in both in exactly the same way, or (b) that the text immediately surrounding addition D was also copied from one Greek text to the other.

Further comparison of the three texts of 5:1 shows other points of interest as well. In line 1, for example, both Greek texts have ἐγενήθη for

47. Because of the imprecision of the siglum LXX, some scholars refer to the LXX translation of Esther, which is found in the vast majority of manuscripts, as the OG, but not everyone agrees that this version is in fact earlier than the Alpha Text. In the Göttingen LXX (Esther was edited by Robert Hanhart), the LXX version is referred to as the *o′*-Text (from the Greek letter *omicron*, which represents the number "seventy") and printed on the top half of the page; the Alpha Text, attested in only four manuscripts, is printed on the lower half of the page and designated by the siglum *L* because at one time it was believed to be the Lucianic revision.

48. Addition A was inserted at the beginning of the book; B between 3:13 and 3:14; C between chap. 4 and chap. 5; E between 8:12 and 8:13; and F at the end of the book. See also illustration 10 on p. 73 above.

וַיְהִי. The Hebrew expression occurs six times in the text of Esther but is translated only here by this aorist passive form. Some LXX manuscripts (including the Hexaplaric recension) attest as a variant reading the more common rendering in the middle voice, ἐγένετο, but all four extant manuscripts of the AT read the passive form. The passive form was in common usage in Egypt during the third century B.C.E.; it seems to have the same semantic sense as the aorist middle form.[49]

19. Esther 5:1–2/D:1–16

	MT			LXX (Göttingen *o′*)	AT (Göttingen *L*)
1	וַיְהִי	**5:1**	**D:1**	Καὶ ἐγενήθη	Καὶ ἐγενήθη
2	בַּיּוֹם הַשְּׁלִישִׁי			ἐν τῇ ἡμέρᾳ τῇ τρίτῃ,	ἐν τῇ ἡμέρᾳ τῇ τρίτῃ,
3				ὡς ἐπαύσατο	ὡς ἐπαύσατο
4					Εσθηρ
5				προσευχομένη,	προσευχομένη,
6				ἐξεδύσατο	ἐξεδύσατο
7				τὰ ἱμάτια τῆς θεραπείας	τὰ ἱμάτια τῆς θεραπείας
8	וַתִּלְבַּשׁ			καὶ περιεβάλετο	καὶ περιεβάλετο
9	אֶסְתֵּר				
10	מַלְכוּת			τὴν δόξαν	τὰ ἱμάτια
11				αὐτῆς	τῆς δόξης
12			**D:2**	καὶ γενηθεῖσα	καὶ γενομένη
13				ἐπιφανὴς	ἐπιφανὴς
14				ἐπικαλεσαμένη	καὶ ἐπικαλεσαμένη
15				τὸν πάντων	τὸν πάντων
16				ἐπόπτην	γνώστην
17				θεὸν καὶ σωτῆρα	καὶ σωτῆρα θεὸν
18				παρέλαβεν	παρέλαβε
19					μεθ᾽ ἑαυτῆς
20				τὰς δύο ἅβρας	δύο ἅβρας
21			**D:3**	καὶ τῇ μὲν μιᾷ ἐπηρείδετο	καὶ τῇ μὲν μιᾷ ἐπηρείδετο
22				ὡς τρυφερευομένη,	ὡς τρυφερευομένη,
23			**D:4**	ἡ δὲ ἑτέρα	ἡ δὲ ἑτέρα
24				ἐπηκολούθει κουφίζουσα	ἐπηκολούθει ἐπικουφίζουσα
25				τὴν ἔνδυσιν αὐτῆς,	τὸ ἔνδυμα αὐτῆς,
26			**D:5**	καὶ αὐτὴ ἐρυθριῶσα	καὶ αὐτὴ ἐρυθριῶσα
27				ἀκμῇ κάλλους αὐτῆς,	ἐν ἀκμῇ κάλλους αὐτῆς,

sources: MT = *Biblia hebraica stuttgartensia*, 1373; LXX and AT = Robert Hanhart, *Esther*, 2d ed. (Septuaginta 8/3; Göttingen: Vandenhoeck & Ruprecht, 1983), 168–71; English translation of LXX and AT = Jobes and Silva. Greek verse numbers follow the o′-text.

49. See John W. Wevers, *Notes on the Greek Text of Exodus* (SBLSCS 30; Atlanta: Scholars Press, 1990), 16.

	MT			LXX (Göttingen *o*′)	AT (Göttingen *L*)
28				καὶ τὸ πρόσωπον αὐτῆς	καὶ τὸ πρόσωπον αὐτῆς
29				ἱλαρὸν	
30				ὡς προσφιλές,	ὡς προσφιλές,
31				ἡ δὲ καρδία αὐτῆς	ἡ δὲ καρδία αὐτῆς
32				ἀπεστενωμένη	ἀπεστενωμένη.
33				ἀπὸ τοῦ φόβου.	
34			**D:6**	καὶ εἰσελθοῦσα	καὶ εἰσελθοῦσα
35				πάσας τὰς θύρας	τὰς θύρας
36	וַתַּעֲמֹד			κατέστη	ἔστη
37	בַּחֲצַר בֵּית־הַמֶּלֶךְ				
38	הַפְּנִימִית נֹכַח בֵּית הַמֶּלֶךְ				
39				ἐνώπιον τοῦ βασιλέως,	ἐνώπιον τοῦ βασιλέως,
40	וְהַמֶּלֶךְ			καὶ αὐτὸς	καὶ ὁ βασιλεὺς
41	יוֹשֵׁב עַל־כִּסֵּא			ἐκάθητο ἐπὶ τοῦ θρόνου	ἐκάθητο ἐπὶ τοῦ θρόνου
42	מַלְכוּתוֹ			τῆς βασιλείας αὐτοῦ	τῆς βασιλείας αὐτοῦ
43	בְּבֵית הַמַּלְכוּת				
44	נֹכַח פֶּתַח הַבָּיִת׃				
45	וַיְהִי כִרְאוֹת הַמֶּלֶךְ	**5:2**			
46	אֶת־אֶסְתֵּר הַמַּלְכָּה				
47	עֹמֶדֶת בֶּחָצֵר				
48	נָשְׂאָה חֵן בְּעֵינָיו				
49				καὶ πᾶσαν στολὴν	καὶ πᾶσαν στολὴν
50				τῆς ἐπιφανείας	ἐπιφανείας
51				αὐτοῦ	
52				ἐνδεδύκει,	ἐνδεδύκει,
53				ὅλος διὰ χρυσοῦ	ὅλος διάχρυσος,
54				καὶ λίθων πολυτελῶν,	καὶ λίθοι πολυτελεῖς
55					ἐπ᾽ αὐτῷ,
56				καὶ ἦν φοβερὸς σφόδρα.	καὶ φοβερὸς σφόδρα.
57			**D:7**	καὶ ἄρας τὸ πρόσωπον αὐτοῦ	καὶ ἄρας τὸ πρόσωπον αὐτοῦ
58				πεπυρωμένον	πεπυρωμένον
59				δόξῃ	ἐν δόξῃ
60					ἐνέβλεψεν αὐτῇ ὡς ταῦρος
61				ἐν ἀκμῇ θυμοῦ	ἐν ἀκμῇ θυμοῦ
62					αὐτοῦ,
63				ἔβλεψεν,	
64				καὶ ἔπεσεν ἡ βασίλισσα	καὶ ἐφοβήθη ἡ βασίλισσα
65				καὶ μετέβαλεν	καὶ μετέβαλε

	MT		LXX (Göttingen *o′*)	AT (Göttingen *L*)
66			τὸ χρῶμα αὐτῆς	τὸ πρόσωπον αὐτῆς
67			ἐν ἐκλύσει	ἐν ἐκλύσει
68			καὶ κατεπέκυψεν	καὶ ἐπέκυψεν
69			ἐπὶ τὴν κεφαλὴν	ἐπὶ τὴν κεφαλὴν
70			τῆς ἅβρας τῆς προπορευομένης.	τῆς ἅβρας τῆς προπορευομένης.
71		**D:8**	καὶ μετέβαλεν ὁ θεὸς	καὶ μετέβαλεν ὁ θεὸς
72			τὸ πνεῦμα τοῦ βασιλέως	τὸ πνεῦμα τοῦ βασιλέως
73				καὶ μετέθηκε τὸν θυμὸν αὐτοῦ
74			εἰς πραΰτητα,	εἰς πραότητα,
75			καὶ ἀγωνιάσας	καὶ ἀγωνιάσας
76				ὁ βασιλεὺς
77			ἀνεπήδησεν	κατεπήδησεν
78			ἀπὸ τοῦ θρόνου αὐτοῦ	ἀπὸ τοῦ θρόνου αὐτοῦ
79			καὶ ἀνέλαβεν αὐτὴν	καὶ ἀνέλαβεν αὐτὴν
80			ἐπὶ τὰς ἀγκάλας αὐτοῦ,	ἐπὶ τὰς ἀγκάλας αὐτοῦ
81			μέχρις οὗ κατέστη,	
82			καὶ παρεκάλει αὐτὴν	καὶ παρεκάλεσεν αὐτὴν
83			λόγοις εἰρηνικοῖς	
84		**D:9**	καὶ εἶπεν	καὶ εἶπεν
85			αὐτῇ	
86			Τί ἐστιν, Εσθηρ;	Τί ἐστιν, Εσθηρ;
87			ἐγὼ ὁ ἀδελφός σου,	ἐγώ εἰμι ἀδελφός σου,
88			θάρσει,	θάρσει,
89		**D:10**	οὐ μὴ ἀποθάνῃς,	οὐ μὴ ἀποθάνῃς,
90			ὅτι κοινὸν	ὅτι κοινόν
91			τὸ πρόσταγμα ἡμῶν ἐστιν·	ἐστι τὸ πρᾶγμα ἡμῶν,
92		**D:11**		καὶ οὐ πρὸς σὲ ἡ ἀπειλή·
93				ἰδοὺ τὸ σκῆπτρον
94				ἐν τῇ χειρί σου.
95			πρόσελθε.	
96	וַיּוֹשֶׁט	**D:12**	καὶ ἄρας	καὶ ἄρας
97	הַמֶּלֶךְ לְאֶסְתֵּר			
98	אֶת־שַׁרְבִיט הַזָּהָב		τὴν χρυσῆν ῥάβδον	τὸ σκῆπτρον
99	אֲשֶׁר בְּיָדוֹ			
100	וַתִּקְרַב אֶסְתֵּר			
101	וַתִּגַּע		ἐπέθηκεν	ἐπέθηκεν
102	בְּרֹאשׁ הַשַּׁרְבִיט׃		ἐπὶ τὸν τράχηλον αὐτῆς	ἐπὶ τὸν τράχηλον αὐτῆς
103			καὶ ἠσπάσατο αὐτὴν	καὶ ἠσπάσατο αὐτὴν

	MT		LXX (Göttingen *o′*)	AT (Göttingen *L*)
104			καὶ εἶπεν	καὶ εἶπεν
105			Λάλησόν μοι.	Λάλησόν μοι.
106		**D:13**	καὶ εἶπεν αὐτῷ	καὶ εἶπεν αὐτῷ
107			Εἶδόν σε,	Εἶδόν σε
108			κύριε,	
109			ὡς ἄγγελον θεοῦ,	ὡς ἄγγελον θεοῦ,
110			καὶ ἐταράχθη	καὶ ἐτάκη
111			ἡ καρδία μου	ἡ καρδία μου
112			ἀπὸ φόβου τῆς δόξης σου·	ἀπὸ τῆς δόξης τοῦ θυμοῦ σου,
113				κύριε.
114		**D:14**	ὅτι θαυμαστὸς εἶ, κύριε,	
115			καὶ τὸ πρόσωπόν σου	καὶ ἐπὶ τὸ πρόσωπον αὐτῆς
116			χαρίτων μεστόν.	μέτρον ἱδρῶτος·
117		**D:15**	ἐν δὲ τῷ διαλέγεσθαι αὐτὴν	
118			ἔπεσεν ἀπὸ ἐκλύσεως·	
119		**D:16**	καὶ ὁ βασιλεὺς ἐταράσσετο,	καὶ ἐταράσσετο ὁ βασιλεὺς
120			καὶ πᾶσα ἡ θεραπεία αὐτοῦ	καὶ πᾶσα ἡ θεραπεία αὐτοῦ,
121			παρεκάλει αὐτήν.	καὶ παρεκάλουν αὐτὴν.

	LXX Esther (Göttingen *o′*)	Alpha Text Esther (Göttingen *L*)
D:1	And it happened on the third day, as she ceased praying, she took off the garments of humility, and put on her glory.	And it happened on the third day, as Esther ceased praying, she took off the garments of humility, and put on the garments of glory.
D:2	Then, when she had become majestic, after calling upon the all-seeing God and Savior, she took two of her attendants;	Then, when she had become majestic, and after calling upon the all-knowing One and Savior God, she took with her two attendants;
D:3	and on one she leaned gently for support,	and on one she leaned gently for support,
D:4	while the other followed, carrying her train.	while the other followed, holding up her train.
D:5	And she was radiant with the full flush of her beauty, and her face looked happy [as if she were] cheerful, but her heart was in anguish from fear.	And she was radiant with the full flush of her beauty, and her face looked [as if she were] cheerful, but her heart was in anguish.
D:6	And when she had gone through all the doors, she stood before the king. And he was seated on the throne of his kingdom, clothed in the full array of his majesty, all covered with gold and precious stones. And he was most terrifying.	And when she had gone through the doors, she stood before the king. And the king was seated on the throne of his kingdom, clothed in the full array of majesty, all covered with gold and precious stones upon him, and most terrifying.

	LXX Esther (Göttingen *o′*)	Alpha Text Esther (Göttingen *L*)
D:7	And he raised his face inflamed with glory and looked at her in the full flush of anger. And the queen staggered, and her color turned pale from faintness, and she collapsed on the head of the attendant who went before her.	And he raised his face inflamed with glory, and he gazed at her like a bull in the full flush of his anger. And the queen was terrified, and her face turned pale from faintness, and she collapsed on the head of the attendant who went before her.
D:8	Then God changed the spirit of the king to gentleness, and alarmed, he sprang from his throne and took her in his arms until she was quieted. And he comforted her with soothing words,	Then God changed the spirit of the king and averted his anger to gentleness. And alarmed, the king jumped up from his throne and took her in his arms. And he comforted her,
D:9	and said to her, "What is it, Esther? I am your brother. Take heart!	and said, "What is it, Esther? I am your brother. Take heart!
D:10	You shall not die, for our law is only for the common person.	You shall not die, for our command is only for the common person.
D:11	Come here."	The threat is not against you. Look, the scepter is in your hand."
D:12	Then he lifted the golden rod and touched her neck with it. And he embraced her, and said, "Speak to me!"	Then he lifted the scepter and touched her neck with it. And he embraced her, and said, "Speak to me!"
D:13	And she said to him, "I saw you, lord, like an angel of God, and my heart was shaken from fear of your glory.	And she said to him, "I saw you like an angel of God, and my heart melted from the glory of your rage, lord."
D:14	For you are fierce, lord, even though your face is full of grace."	And upon her face was a measure of sweat.
D:15	And while she was speaking, she fell from faintness.	
D:16	Then the king was troubled, and all his servants reassured her.	Then the king and all his servants were troubled, and they reassured her.

Εσθηρ is lacking in the additional LXX material in line 4 and in both Greek texts in line 9. One of the characteristics of the Greek texts is that proper nouns are often not translated from the Hebrew. Contrary to what we find in line 4, the LXX typically translates the proper nouns more frequently than does the AT. Esther's name, for example, occurs fifty-five times in the Hebrew, forty-six times in the LXX, and only twenty-six times in the AT.[50] Sometimes a proper noun is not translated from the Hebrew to avoid redundancy because the name was recently mentioned in the additional Greek material.

The Hebrew expression תִּלְבַּשׁ אֶסְתֵּר מַלְכוּת ("Esther put on royal power") in lines 8–11 is translated in the LXX by περιεβάλετο τὴν δό-

50. See Karen H. Jobes, *The Alpha-Text of Esther: Its Character and Relationship to the Masoretic Text* (Society of Biblical Literature Dissertation Series 153; Atlanta: Scholars Press, 1996), 120.

ξαν αὐτῆς ("she put on her glory") and in the AT by περιεβάλετο τὰ ἱμάτια τῆς δόξης ("she put on the garments of glory"). The AT and most English translations specify the reference of the Hebrew phrase to her royal robes, which is literally the case. In the development of the plot, however, when Esther puts on her royal robes, she is also assuming the power that is hers as Queen of Persia and from that point on is the person in charge. The LXX best captures that rhetorical nuance with its metaphorical expression "she put on her glory."

Note the following points in D:2. In line 12, the LXX (except for a couple of manuscripts) uses the aorist passive form where the AT has the aorist middle. As noted above, in line 1 both Greek texts use the aorist passive form, which was in common usage in Egypt during the third century B.C.E. Since both forms seem to have had the same sense, the choice of one form over the other may express only morphological preference. Lines 16–17 exhibit a semantic difference between the LXX, where Esther is said to call upon "the all-seeing God and Savior," and the AT, which reads, "the all-knowing One and Savior God." Finally, in line 19 the AT includes the phrase μεθ' ἑαυτῆς. One of the characteristics of the AT is that it uses reflexive pronouns in prepositional phrases (five times) in comparison to LXX Esther, which never does.

A word-for-word comparison of D:3–6 shows the two Greek versions to be virtually identical in these verses, with no differences whatever in D:3. In D:4, we find two minor variations: the LXX has κουφίζουσα ("bearing, lifting") in line 24 and τὴν ἔνδυσιν ("a putting on, a garment") in line 25, while the AT has forms that convey the same meaning but are arguably better stylistically, namely, the compound verb ἐπικουφίζουσα and the substantive τὸ ἔνδυμα. In D:5 the LXX has two units not found in the AT: the adjective ἱλαρόν ("cheerful") in line 29 and the phrase ἀπὸ τοῦ φόβου in line 33 (which clarifies the previous verb ἀποστενόω in line 32, thus, "her heart was blocked/anguished for fear"). Most of the differences in D:6 are trivial: in line 36 the LXX has the compound form κατέστη and the AT has ἔστη; in line 40 the LXX pronoun αὐτός is specified in the AT with ὁ βασιλεύς; and in lines 50–51 the LXX's phrase τῆς ἐπιφανείας αὐτοῦ corresponds to the single word ἐπιφανείας in AT. The last four elements in D:6 (lines 53–56) contain differences that are somewhat more significant, but even these do not suggest that the two texts arose independently of each other.

D:7 provides another interesting comparison between the LXX and the AT in material that is not found in the Hebrew. In the LXX, the king raises his face inflamed in glory and looks at Esther in fierce anger. The AT includes a distinctive plus: the king "looked at her as a bull in his fierce anger" (lines 60–62). The OL version of Esther also describes the king at this point in the text as an enraged bull, an important clue for shedding light on the history of this text. All four surviving manuscripts of the AT include the reference to the bull. Remembering that the OL text is earlier than the Vulgate, which came into use after the year 400, this clue suggests at least two possibilities: either (a) the AT is closer to the Greek *Vorlage* from which the OL was translated than is the LXX, or (b) one or more manuscripts of the AT were revised to agree with the OL reading at some point early enough in its transmission history that the reading proliferated to all four extant, medieval manuscripts. Further study of the AT looking for other agreements of its text with the OL would certainly be worthwhile.

Students are encouraged to compare D:8–13 on their own, distinguishing variations that are merely stylistic from those that are more substantive. Note also how the Hebrew text of 5:2 has been abbreviated and transformed by the Greek versions in the interests of making the additional material as smooth a narrative as possible.

One final detail merits comment. In D:14–15 the LXX reads, "'For you are fierce, lord, even though your face is full of grace.' And while she was speaking, she fell from faintness." The AT reads simply, "And upon her face was a measure of sweat." Because the text both immediately before and after these verses is the same in the two versions, this wildly variant reading is most peculiar. Moreover, ἱδρώς ("sweat") in line 116 is a rare word in the LXX, occurring only in Genesis 3:19; 2 Maccabees 2:26; and 4 Maccabees 7:8 (the verb ἱδρόω is found in 4 Maccabees 3:8; 6:11).

Charles Cutler Torrey regards this peculiarity as evidence that addition D was translated from an Aramaic source no longer extant. He argues that the translator of the AT, misreading ד (*dāleṯ*) for ר (*rêš*), confused the Aramaic word דֵּעֲתָא ("sweat") with רְעֻתָא ("good will").[51] Once this confusion occurred, scribal attempts to make some sense of the thought resulted in two completely different readings. Perhaps 2 Maccabees 2:26–27 contains a striking allusion to the corrupted reading of the AT: "For us who have undertaken the toil of abbreviating, it is no light matter but calls for *sweat* and loss of sleep, just as it is not easy for one who prepares a banquet [an allusion to Esther?] and seeks the benefit of others" (NRSV). If so, the text of addition D as it stands in the AT must have been known to the author of 2 Maccabees, who is believed to have written to the Diaspora Jews from Jerusalem about 100 B.C.E.

To Continue Your Study

Because of the availability of John W. Wevers's valuable commentaries on the LXX Pentateuch, readers are encouraged to work through

51. Charles Cutler Torrey, "The Older Book of Esther," *Harvard Theological Review* 37 (1944): 1–40, esp. 8.

the running text of several chapters in those books. For example, using his *Notes on the Greek Text of Exodus* (SBLSCS 30; Atlanta: Scholars Press, 1990), the student could profit greatly from translating and analyzing Exodus 1–4 and 12–15.

For further work on LXX Isaiah, the student should consider working through chapters 5–9 and 40–44 with the aid of Richard R. Ottley, *The Book of Isaiah according to the LXX (Codex Alexandrinus)*, 2 vols. (London: Cambridge University Press, 1904–6). Also useful are monographs by Léo Laberge, *La Septante d'Isaïe 28–33: Étude de tradition textuelle* (Ontario: Chez l'auteur, 1978); and especially Arie van der Kooij, *The Oracle of Tyre: The Septuagint of Isaiah xxiii as Version and Vision* (Vetus Testamentum Supplement 71; Leiden: Brill, 1998), chapter 3.

Some scholarly articles are also well suited for the purpose of gaining proficiency in the interpretation of the LXX. Note, for example, Barnabas Lindars, "A Commentary on the Greek Judges?" in *VI Congress of the International Organization for Septuagint and Cognate Studies: Jerusalem 1986*, ed. Claude E. Cox (SBLSCS 23; Atlanta: Scholars Press, 1987), 167–200; and Claude E. Cox, "Job's Concluding Soliloquy: Chh. 29–31," in *VII Congress of the International Organization for Septuagint and Cognate Studies: Leuven 1989*, ed. Claude E. Cox (SBLSCS 31; Atlanta: Scholars Press, 1991), 325–39.

PART 3

The Current State of Septuagint Studies

Throughout the first two parts of this book, we have often had occasion to identify important areas of research in contemporary LXX scholarship and to introduce readers to some of the more significant publications in the field. Part 3 seeks to meet the needs of advanced students and other interested readers who wish to acquire greater familiarization with the *status quaestionis*. It seems appropriate, moreover, to introduce this part of the book with a "human touch": chapter 11 thus provides biographical sketches of earlier scholars whose work established the foundations of current LXX scholarship.

Chapters 12–14 review contributions in three general fields of research. Given the confines of this book, the coverage is selective. We have made a special effort, however, to choose representative works and projects that will facilitate the student's access to the material. Bibliographic suggestions for further study are not included at the end of these chapters. Instead, readers are encouraged to pursue topics of their choice by consulting the relevant works mentioned in the footnotes.

11

Our Predecessors: Septuagint Scholars of a Previous Generation

The Greek versions have enjoyed the attention of many scholars, especially during the last hundred years. In order to appreciate current issues in any field of research, it is helpful to understand the lives, as well as the historical setting, of prominent scholars who have shaped the discipline. Focusing on the period from about the middle of the nineteenth century to the beginning of World War II, this chapter introduces some of the prominent scholars who have set the agenda for LXX studies and on whose work the discipline still stands.

Friedrich Constantin von Tischendorf (1815–1874)

Born January 18, 1815, in Lengenfeld, Germany, Lobegott (Aenotheus) Friedrich Constantin von Tischendorf spent his entire career at the University of Leipzig, first as a student, then as a doctoral candidate, and finally as a professor until his death. His consuming passion was to recover early manuscripts of the Bible, especially the NT, which lay forgotten in monasteries and libraries of the Near East.

No other scholar has discovered and published more biblical manuscripts than Tischendorf. He returned to Leipzig in 1845 from one expedition to Egypt carrying over fifty biblical manuscripts. His first major scholarly achievement was to decipher Codex Ephraemi (C), a fifth-century palimpsest manuscript erased and overwritten with treatises of Syrian church father Ephraem. His most dramatic success came at the Monastery of St. Catherine, where he discovered what turned out to be one of the oldest surviving manuscripts of the Greek Bible, which he named Codex Sinaiticus and designated with the siglum א (normally referred to as S in LXX publications). This event is one of the most frequently told tales of textual history.[1] The forty-three pages he saved from being used as kindling in the monastery's kitchen contained parts of the Greek text of 1 Chronicles, Jeremiah, Nehemiah, and Esther, which he published in Leipzig in 1846 under the title Codex Frederici Augustanus. It was not until 1859 that he acquired the rest of what had survived from the codex.

In 1850 Tischendorf produced his own edition of the LXX.[2] It was little more than a revised Sixtine text, with the variants of uncials A, C, and parts of S (beginning with the third edition, he included variants from the rest of S as well as the variants of B). This work did not mark a significant advance in LXX studies; indeed, it compares unfavorably with his magnificent editions of the Greek NT. Although Count Tischendorf will thus continue to be best known for his work on the text of the NT, we must not forget that he recovered what remains one of the oldest and most important witnesses to the Greek OT.

Edwin Hatch (1835–1889)

Born near Birmingham, England, and educated at the University of Oxford, Edwin Hatch was ordained in 1858 and at the time of his death was the rector of Purleigh in Essex. Shortly after his ordination, he left for Canada to take up an appointment as professor of classics at Trinity College in Toronto. He held this position briefly, until becoming rector of the high school of Quebec. Although capable in scholarship, Hatch was apparently first a churchman. He returned to Oxford in 1867 as vice principal of St. Mary Hall.

In 1880 Hatch delivered the Bampton Lectures on the early organization of the Christian church. This event caused quite a stir among British theologians and brought him to academic prominence. His published Bampton Lectures were translated into German by his dear

1. For the account in Tischendorf's own words, see *When Were Our Gospels Written?* (London: Religious Tract Society, 1866). See also Matthew Black and Robert Davidson, *Constantin von Tischendorf and the Greek New Testament* (Glasgow: University of Glasgow Press, 1981); and Bruce M. Metzger, *The Text of the New Testament: Its Transmission, Corruption, and Restoration*, 3d ed. (New York: Oxford University Press, 1992), 42–45, 126–28.

2. Four revised editions were published during the next twenty-five years. After Tischendorf's death, Eberhard Nestle (1851–1913) supervised the publication of two more editions (1880 and 1887). Although Nestle is best known for his work on NT textual criticism, he also had considerable interest in LXX studies. After the publication of the first edition of his *Novum Testamentum Graece* in 1898, Nestle was commissioned by the Württemberg Bible Society to produce a comparable edition of the LXX, but died before completing it.

friend Adolf Harnack, who later wrote, "Hatch was bound to me by an intimate friendship which to have possessed I count among the highest values of my life."[3] The University of Edinburgh conferred an honorary D.D. upon him in 1883, and he spent his last five years as Reader in Ecclesiastical History at Oxford. At the time of his death his colleagues lamented that "no Englishman of the present generation has given greater promise of becoming a distinguished theologian."[4]

Just a year before his death, Hatch's Grinfield Lectures on the Septuagint, which he had delivered from 1882 to 1884, were published in a volume titled *Essays in Biblical Greek*.[5] Its subtitle—*Studies on the Value and Use of the Septuagint on the Meanings of Words and Psychological Terms in Biblical Greek, on Quotations from the Septuagint, on Origen's Revision of Job, and on the Text of Ecclesiasticus*—indicates the range of his studies. Although some of Hatch's views and methods in this book have not stood the test of time, his studies contain a wealth of detailed and helpful information that shows his mastery of the Greek corpus.

When Hatch died of heart disease suddenly at the age of fifty-five, one of the works he left unfinished was a concordance to the LXX, which his obituary describes as "a work of stupendous labor, to which he devoted the best years of his life."[6] Eventually the project was finished by one of several younger scholars working with him, Henry A. Redpath.[7] The Hatch-Redpath *Concordance to the Septuagint*, published in 1897 (with a supplementary volume issued in 1906), was truly a lasting contribution. Despite some flaws, it remains an indispensable tool for LXX research.[8]

In addition to his pastoral duties and scholarly pursuits, Hatch composed sacred poetry that was collected and published posthu-

3. Quoted in N. F. Josaitis, *Edwin Hatch and Early Church Order* (Gembloux, France: Duculot, 1971), 16. This work, which provides a complete bibliography of Hatch's sermons and scholarly publications, includes a biography as well as his poetry and private letters.

4. *London Times*, 12 November 1889, 10.

5. Oxford: Clarendon, 1889; repr. Amsterdam: Philo, 1970. For a brief discussion of Hatch's linguistic approach, see above, chap. 9, pp. 184–86.

6. *London Times*, 12 November 1889, 10.

7. Redpath (1848–1908) was educated at Oxford and received a D.Litt. in 1901. From that year until 1905 he was Grinfield Lecturer on the Septuagint, following in the footsteps of his mentor.

8. Edwin Hatch and Henry A. Redpath, *A Concordance to the Septuagint and the Other Greek Versions of the Old Testament (Including the Apocryphal Books)*, 3 vols. (Oxford: Clarendon, 1897–1906; repr. Grand Rapids: Baker, 1987). Takamitsu Muraoka's important contribution, *A Hebrew/Aramaic Index to the Septuagint* (Grand Rapids: Baker, 1998), is keyed to the Hatch-Redpath *Concordance*, extending its usefulness to scholars today.

mously. Perhaps Hatch's concordance to the LXX fulfills the wish of his heart expressed in one of the many poems he left:

> . . . to have made one soul
> The better for my birth:
> To have added but one flower
> To the garden of the earth.[9]

Paul A. de Lagarde (1827–1891)

Richard R. Ottley was no doubt speaking for most biblical scholars when he described Paul de Lagarde as the man to whom "students of the LXX must look up to as the leader of modern progress. . . . Lagarde laid down certain rules for the study of the text of the Greek O.T., which still, on the whole, represent the prevailing views and practice."[10] Even today, more than a century after his death, students continue to remember Paul de Lagarde as the father of modern textual criticism of the LXX. German history remembers him for other contributions as well.[11]

Born Paul Bötticher in Berlin in 1827, Lagarde suffered the loss of his eighteen-year-old mother only twelve days after his birth. His grieving father, a teacher of Greek and Latin at a secondary school (*Gymnasium*) in Berlin, never stopped blaming his son for his wife's death. After a harsh childhood, Paul remained embittered toward his father for the rest of his life. When he married Anna Berger in 1854, he initiated proceedings to be adopted legally by his beloved maternal great-aunt, Ernestine de Lagarde. She was more than pleased to have him bear her family name, for she had no sons (Lagarde's marriage, however, produced no children to carry on the family line).

As a young child in Berlin, Lagarde sat on Friedrich Schleiermacher's lap, and in 1844 as a young man entered the university there to study theology under Ernst Wilhelm Hengstenberg, a prominent and conservative professor of OT, and under NT professor David Friedrich Strauss. During Lagarde's years in Berlin, the theological faculty was polarized over Strauss's controversial book, *Das Leben Jesu, kritisch bearbeitet* (The Life of Jesus Critically Examined), published in 1835–36. Hengstenberg publicly accused Strauss of being possessed by Sa-

9. Edwin Hatch, *Towards Fields of Light: Sacred Poems* (London: Hodder & Stoughton, 1890), 38–39.

10. Richard R. Ottley, *A Handbook to the Septuagint* (London: Methuen, 1920), 71, 93.

11. For a biography of Lagarde's life and an analysis of his influence in German history, see Fritz Stern, *The Politics of Cultural Despair: A Study in the Rise of the Germanic Ideology* (Berkeley: University of California Press, 1961), chap. 1. See also Alfred Rahlfs, *Paul de Lagardes wissenschaftliches Lebenswerk im Rahmen einer Geschichte seines Lebens dargestellt* (Mitteilungen des Septuaginta-Unternehmens 4/1; Berlin: Weidmann, 1928).

20. Paul A. de Lagarde (1827–1891)

source: Rudolf Smend

This German scholar is considered by many to be the father of modern Septuagint textual criticism.

tan, and the theological turmoil that ensued deeply disaffected the young Lagarde, who abandoned orthodox Protestant Christianity while at the university. However, it was under Hengstenberg's influence that Lagarde set for himself, even before his twentieth birthday, the goal of reconstructing the text of the Greek OT. Further influenced by Friedrich Rückert, who taught him Arabic and Persian, Lagarde took up philology to further this work.

By the end of his life Lagarde had published critical editions of texts in Latin, Syrian, Babylonian, Arabic, Coptic, and Persian, with occasional papers in Armenian, all in addition to his critical work on the Greek text of the LXX. At his funeral eulogy, the great classicist Ulrich von Wilamowitz-Moellendorff said of Lagarde's scholarly achievements, "There is probably no one among us who can correctly spell the languages in which he published texts."[12]

Lagarde's vision for reconstructing the text of the LXX languished for many years. In 1849 he received his doctorate for a dissertation on the Arabic theory of colors, but failed to find an appointment to a university faculty. He was granted a two-year stipend to work in London

12. Stern, *Politics of Cultural Despair*, 23.

on reconstructing the text of the NT from manuscripts of its ancient daughter versions, and during this stint he found himself welcomed into the circle of the political and literary elite.

Lagarde returned to Germany to marry his fiancée, Anna Berger, and to seek a faculty appointment at a German university. The appointment never materialized, and after his marriage, he taught Latin and calisthenics in a *Gymnasium* in Berlin, growing more embittered year by year. In 1861 the Clarendon Press of the University of Oxford presented him with the five-volume edition of the LXX prepared by Holmes and Parsons almost a century earlier.[13] This gift rekindled his passion for reconstructing the text of the LXX. Two years later he published his first work on the LXX, *Anmerkungen zur griechischen Übersetzung der Proverbien* (Reflections on the Greek Translation of Proverbs), in which he articulated his principles of LXX textual criticism.[14] Lagarde's successors regarded this early publication as perhaps his best work on the textual criticism of the LXX.

In 1869 Lagarde was finally appointed to the faculty at the University of Göttingen, a position he held until his death twenty-two years later. It was during these years that his work on the text of the LXX was to come to its fullest flower. Unfortunately, his research would suffer from his own deeply troubled spirit and a growing involvement in shaping the political ideology of Germany.

In 1883 he published the first volume of *Librorum Veteris Testamenti canonicorum, pars prior graece*, which was intended to be a full critical edition of Lucian's fourth-century text. This first volume turned out to be the only one ever published. Perhaps that was just as well, for it was roundly criticized as an uneven work. In Genesis he included so many variant readings that the critical apparatus was too enormous to afford to print; in other places he published a diplomatic text printed from just one manuscript. The printer received the typescript from him in dribs and drabs, which resulted in numerous typographical errors as well.

Lagarde had seriously underestimated the complexity and size of the task he had undertaken. With reference to this project, Peter Katz later described Lagarde as an impetuous man who "consulted no one but himself" and "rushed prematurely into print."[15] Even Alfred

13. See above, chap. 3, p. 72.

14. See Henry Barclay Swete, *An Introduction to the Old Testament in Greek*, 2d ed. (Cambridge: Cambridge University Press, 1914; repr. Peabody, Mass.: Hendrickson, 1989), 484–86.

15. Peter Katz, "Septuagintal Studies in the Mid-Century: Their Links with the Past and Their Present Tendencies," in *The Background of the New Testament and Its Eschatology: In Honour of Charles Harold Dodd*, ed. W. D. Davies and David Daube (Cambridge: Cambridge University Press, 1956), 187–88; repr. in *Studies in the Septuagint: Origins, Recensions, and Interpretations*, ed. Sidney Jellicoe (New York: Ktav, 1974), 32–33.

Rahlfs, Lagarde's most loyal student, judged the edition to be that scholar's "biggest failure" both in principle and production.[16] Nevertheless, Lagarde imparted to his student his vision and passion for reconstructing the text of the LXX, a task in which Rahlfs was eminently more successful than his predecessor. Although Lagarde announced plans to prepare a critical edition of the Greek Psalter, he soon abandoned his work on the LXX altogether to pursue other interests.

During his university years in Berlin, Lagarde had become disaffected not only by orthodox Protestant Christianity, but by political conservatism as well. Lagarde's loyalty to the Prussian monarchy snapped in 1849 when a compatriot was arrested on trumped-up charges of treason for plotting a German social-democratic republic. His increasing discontent with German politics eventually issued in the publication of *Deutsche Schriften* (1878), which became a classic in cultural criticism for later generations of German readers. Lagarde considered himself foremost a theologian, and his vision was for a new German Reich revitalized and unified by a national religion. Rejecting traditional Christianity, Lagarde became what has been described as a "sentimental theist"[17] who proposed sweeping ideas to reform German politics, theology, and society. Lagarde was regarded as a prophet of the times, and after his death, his vision was embraced by the National Socialists. During World War II, an anthology of his ideological works was distributed to Hitler's army.

In October 1891, Lagarde's health suddenly began to fail. Telling no one but his wife, he entered a hospital in December for surgery for stomach cancer. A few days later he died, but not before bequeathing his LXX work to Alfred Rahlfs and his vision for a new Germany to Julius Langbehn,[18] who moved German political ideology to its next stage. At Lagarde's funeral, a colleague commented, "There exists no task more difficult and therefore more beautiful" than Lagarde's proposed edition of the Greek OT.[19] In the hindsight of history, it was perhaps Lagarde's best thought.

Alfred Rahlfs (1865–1935)

Alfred Rahlfs took up Lagarde's mantle with zeal for the task of reconstructing the original text of the LXX, but with the wisdom gained by Lagarde's failure. Like his mentor, Rahlfs was an impressive philologist who mastered the languages needed to evaluate the textual evidence of the daughter versions of the LXX. He distinguished himself

16. Ibid., 186 (repr. p. 31).

17. Stern, *Politics of Cultural Despair*, 39.

18. For Lagarde's lasting political legacy through Langbehn, see Stern, ibid., chaps. 7–10.

19. Ibid., 23.

21. Alfred Rahlfs (1865–1935)

Rahlfs was the successor to Lagarde's legacy and editor of the only complete critical text of the Septuagint in existence today.

source: Rudolf Smend

in 1889 with an article that came to be foundational in the textual criticism of the Peshitta.[20] Following Lagarde's death, Rahlfs took more than a decade to rethink the work that had been bequeathed to him.

His distinguished series *Septuaginta-Studien* began to appear in 1904, with an issue that he dedicated to the memory of Lagarde. Notably, this first issue dealt with the complexities of using the mixed texts of extant manuscripts that Lagarde had overlooked in his publication of *Librorum Veteris Testamenti*. Three years later the second issue, which addressed the Greek Psalter, appeared. The third and final issue appeared in 1911 as a 298-page tome that exhaustively addressed the manuscript evidence for the books of Kings. All three of these publications were reprinted in one volume in 1965 with a bibliography of Rahlfs's works and a portrait of the author as frontispiece.[21]

The scholarly community began to understand that the task of re-

20. Alfred Rahlfs, "Beiträge zur Textkritik der Peschita," *Zeitschrift für die alttestamentliche Wissenschaft* 9 (1889): 161–210.

21. Alfred Rahlfs, *Septuaginta-Studien*, 3 vols., 2d ed. (Göttingen: Vandenhoeck & Ruprecht, 1965). This edition includes an obituary by Walter Bauer and a previously unpublished paper by Rahlfs on the Ethiopic version.

constructing the text of the LXX would not be accomplished in the lifetime of any one scholar. The importance of Rahlfs's work was recognized by his colleagues Rudolf Smend and Julius Wellhausen, who undertook to establish an institution dedicated to LXX textual criticism. The Septuaginta-Unternehmen was established at the University of Göttingen in 1908 and continues to produce the best available critical texts used in scholarship today.[22] Rahlfs produced a preliminary edition of the Psalms, which first appeared in 1931 and was reissued in 1967 as volume 10 of the Göttingen LXX. Since 1910 the Göttingen institute has also published numerous studies in its distinguished series Mitteilungen des Septuaginta-Unternehmens.

After working many years on Genesis, Rahlfs realized that his original goal of collating all extant manuscript evidence for every book of the LXX, evaluating all the variant readings so identified, and editing a critical text of the entire corpus was a task that would take several lifetimes. Rahlfs redefined his work toward the more realistic goal of producing a critical text of the LXX based primarily on the three major uncials B, S, and A. The Württemberg Bible Society had previously commissioned a similar work from Eberhard Nestle, whose death in 1913 left the task unfinished. Rahlfs took up the project for the Bible Society and spent the last years of his life preparing what has come to be known as "the Rahlfs Septuagint." His edition of the entire LXX was first published in 1935 and has become the most widely used text. It appeared only a few days before Rahlfs died at the age of seventy.

Henry Barclay Swete (1835–1917)

Henry Swete is best known to students of the LXX for his classic work *Introduction to the Old Testament in Greek*.[23] This work was dedicated to the memory of his friend and German colleague, Eberhard Nestle, who had died just a year before its publication. Although Swete's introduction is dated in many ways, the wealth of information it preserves makes it an indispensable tool even today.

Swete also published a three-volume edition of the Greek text entitled *The Old Testament in Greek according to the Septuagint*.[24] The impetus for a new edition of the LXX had come initially from F. H. A. Scrivener (1813–91), who as early as 1875 submitted a proposal to the

22. *Septuaginta: Vetus Testamentum Graecum Academiae Litterarum Gottingensis* (Göttingen: Vandenhoeck & Ruprecht, 1931–). For more information, see above, chap. 3, p. 75, and below, appendix A, p. 313.

23. First published by Cambridge University Press in 1902, then revised by Richard R. Ottley in 1914; the latest reprint is Peabody, Mass.: Hendrickson, 1989.

24. Cambridge: Cambridge University Press, 1887–94. The title is misleading, since apart from a critically reconstructed text there is no such thing as *the* LXX; the text Swete published is actually that of only one manuscript, Codex Vaticanus.

22. Henry Barclay Swete (1835–1917)

British scholar and author of the classic work *Introduction to the Old Testament in Greek*. His three-volume edition of the Septuagint was the forerunner to the Larger Cambridge Septuagint.

source: Henry Barclay Swete, *The Life of the World to Come: Six Addresses* (London: SPCK/New York: Macmillan, 1918), frontispiece.

Syndics of Cambridge University Press.[25] This proposal was later developed by Fenton J. A. Hort (1828–92), having turned to the LXX after many long years reconstructing the critical text of the NT with his University of Cambridge colleague, Brooke Foss Westcott (1825–1901). Two stages were planned. First was a provisional, diplomatic edition of the LXX that would print the text of Vaticanus—judged to be superior to the Sixtine text of previous editions—with a brief apparatus. The second stage was an edition that would present the same text, but with a much larger apparatus (including the variants of all the uncials and of select minuscules, secondary versions, and quotations), thus providing the evidence necessary for reconstructing the original text.

Swete accepted the task of producing the provisional, manual edition, but when he could not commit to supervising the larger work, that project was taken up by Alan E. Brooke and Norman McLean. Swete's edition, although beautifully presented, was widely criticized for its inaccuracies. Peter Katz, for example, describes it as an "uneven compromise between diplomatic reproduction and the exclusion of the most obviously intolerable readings."[26] The larger Cambridge

25. Swete, *Introduction to the Old Testament in Greek*, 189. For what follows, see also Katz, "Septuagintal Studies in the Mid-Century."

26. Katz, "Septuagintal Studies in the Mid-Century," 179 (repr. p. 24).

edition was therefore based on fresh collations, many provided by Rahlfs's Septuaginta-Unternehmen in Göttingen. In spite of these problems, Swete's edition became the most popular text in the first decades of the twentieth century and continued to be widely used, especially in Britain, even after Rahlfs's LXX appeared.

Swete was born in Redland, England, in 1835 and educated at the University of Cambridge. Ordained in 1859, he was a churchman all his life, served a number of parishes, and had been an honorary chaplain to the King of England for six years at the time of his death. In 1890 he succeeded Brooke Foss Westcott in the Regius Professorship of Divinity at the University of Cambridge, a position he held with distinction for twenty-five years.

The 10 May 1917 issue of the *London Times* contained a brief statement that the eminent Professor Swete was lying seriously ill. The next day, it announced his death at the age of eighty-two. Among his many publications and achievements, his obituary notes:

> Students are further indebted to the late Regius Professor for his scholarly commentaries on St. Mark's Gospel and the Apocalypse of St. John. These are works which may be ranked with the great commentaries we owe to Lightfoot, Westcott, and Hort, and form a not unimportant part of the special contribution Cambridge has made to the modern study of the New Testament.[27]

Students of the LXX, including the authors of this book, are also indebted to Swete for the information preserved in his *Introduction to the Old Testament in Greek*, fulfilling his desire as a professor to "supply a want which has been felt by many readers of the Greek Old Testament" and to place "within the student's reach all the information which he requires in the way of general introduction to the Greek versions."[28]

Alan E. Brooke (1863–1939)
Norman McLean (1865–1947)

While Alfred Rahlfs's work was becoming the center of LXX studies in Göttingen, Germany, Alan E. Brooke was one of two British scholars who began to produce what came to be known as the "Larger Cambridge Edition," which was intended to supersede Holmes-Parsons's *Vetus Testamentum Graecum cum variis lectionibus*, published in Oxford by Clarendon Press in the previous century.[29] Brooke was assisted by

27. *London Times*, 11 May 1917, 9. Swete also published significant works on patristic literature and on the history of theology. See the anonymous biography entitled *Henry Barclay Swete: A Remembrance* (London: Macmillan, 1918).

28. Swete, *Introduction to the Old Testament in Greek*, preface.

29. This important work is described above in chap. 3, p. 72.

Norman McLean, a Fellow of Christ's College, University of Cambridge, and a university lecturer there in Aramaic from 1903 to 1931. Well into the project, Brooke was elected to the Ely Professorship of Divinity in 1916 and was not able to devote sufficient time to the LXX project. At this point, Henry St. John Thackeray officially joined the editorial team, but died in 1930 before the final volumes were published.

Brooke, who remained chief editor throughout the project, received his education at King's College, University of Cambridge, where he later served successively as dean, professor of divinity, and provost. In addition to his teaching, administrative work, and LXX scholarship, he served as the Canon of Ely for ten years. In 1918 he was appointed chaplain to the King of England and held that position until his death. Retirement from his illustrious academic career in 1933 allowed him to devote almost full time to the Cambridge LXX, which had suffered since Thackeray's death three years earlier.

Between 1906 and 1940 three volumes of the Cambridge LXX were published in fascicles under the title *The Old Testament in Greek according to the Text of Codex Vaticanus*.[30] When Brooke died after a brief illness in 1939 at the age of seventy-six, the Syndics of Cambridge University Press issued the first fascicle of volume 3 with a notice of his death and the hope to announce their future plans for resuming its publication "as soon as circumstances permit." By this time, however, the Septuaginta-Unternehmen project in Germany was well underway using what many textual critics considered to be a better approach. No other scholar was found to take up the arduous task begun by Brooke, and Cambridge University Press eventually abandoned the project. No further volumes had been published when McLean, the last of the three editors involved, died in 1947. To this day the Cambridge LXX remains incomplete.

Henry St. John Thackeray (1869–1930)

Henry Thackeray was a scholar of King's College, University of Cambridge, who is perhaps best remembered for his work on Josephus.[31] His untimely death at the age of sixty-one in 1930 abruptly ended his work as editor and translator of Josephus's works for the Loeb Classical Library, after producing the first five volumes. At the time he was also at work on an exhaustive lexicon of Josephus, the first volume of which appeared after his death.

In addition to these contributions, Thackeray was deeply involved in LXX studies, and his output in this field was quite extraordinary.

30. For more detailed information, see above, chap. 3, p. 72 n.8.

31. For instance, see the publication of his 1928 Hilda Stich Strook Lectures, *Josephus: The Man and the Historian* (repr. New York: Ktav, 1968).

23. Henry St. John Thackeray (1869–1930)

One of the truly great British Septuagint scholars; his grammar of the Septuagint remains the only such work in English.

source: The Master and Fellows of Selwyn College, Cambridge

His obituary regards as the principal work of his life his collaboration with Brooke and McLean on the Cambridge critical edition of the LXX.[32] To Thackeray we owe an edition of the Greek text of the Letter of Aristeas as well as an important English translation of this document.[33] He also completed the first volume of a full-scale LXX grammar—the only such work in English.[34]

Thackeray's Schweich Lectures, delivered in 1920, became a classic work on the origins of the LXX and on the relationship between Jewish liturgy and the biblical texts.[35] In the first of these lectures Thack-

32. *London Times*, 11 July 1930, 16.

33. His edition of the Greek text is included as an appendix in Swete's *Introduction to the Old Testament in Greek*, 533–606. For the English translation, see Henry St. John Thackeray, *The Letter of Aristeas: Translated with an Appendix of Ancient Evidence on the Origin of the Septuagint* (Translations of Early Documents 2/3; London: SPCK; New York: Macmillan, 1917).

34. Henry St. John Thackeray, *A Grammar of the Old Testament in Greek according to the Septuagint*, vol. 1: *Introduction, Orthography and Accidence* (Cambridge: Cambridge University Press, 1909). Although he was not able to complete the volume on syntax, the introduction to the first volume includes important syntactic discussions. A valuable summary of LXX morphology and syntax may be found in F. C. Conybeare and St. George Stock, *Grammar of Septuagint Greek: With Selected Readings, Vocabularies, and Updated Indexes* (1905; repr. Peabody, Mass.: Hendrickson, 1995).

35. Henry St. John Thackeray, *The Septuagint and Jewish Worship: A Study in Origins* (London: Oxford University Press, 1923). See also above, chap. 7, pp. 158–59.

eray analyzed the Greek text of Samuel–Kings, parts of which, he believed, represented the work of a late translator from Asia Minor. Theodotion, he further suggested, subsequently borrowed this material to produce his famous recension. Thackeray's hypothesis, although no longer held by specialists, has had a long-lasting influence on reconstructions of the history of the Greek text.

When Isaac L. Seeligmann described Richard R. Ottley's work on Isaiah as presenting "a vast amount of material . . . in the unassuming manner of which English writers apparently possess the secret,"[36] he was no doubt also thinking of Swete and Thackeray. Among these British scholars, Thackeray was the most prolific. Moreover, the depth, accuracy, and creativity that characterize his work set him apart as one of the truly great LXX scholars of the past.

Max Leopold Margolis (1866–1932)

The impetus for LXX studies crossed the Atlantic with Max L. Margolis in the late nineteenth century. Born in 1866 in the Russian province that would later become Lithuania, Margolis took his secondary education at the Leibniz *Gymnasium* in Berlin. After his graduation in 1889, he joined his family, who had previously emigrated to New York City. Just two years later, in 1891, Margolis was granted the first Ph.D. degree from the Oriental Department at Columbia University. He wrote entirely in Latin his dissertation on the textual criticism of the Talmud.

Early in his career Margolis was associated with Hebrew Union College in Cincinnati and the University of California at Berkeley. While at Berkeley he met Evelyn Aronson, whom he married in 1906 when he was forty years old. The following year they toured the university towns of Europe, where Margolis gathered research on manuscripts of the Talmud and the LXX that would fuel his writing for years to come.

Margolis's lifelong interest in Bible translation began when in 1908 he accepted the responsibility of editor-in-chief for a new English translation of the Hebrew Bible sponsored by the Jewish Publication Society in Philadelphia.[37] The following year he was appointed profes-

36. Isaac L. Seeligmann, *The Septuagint Version of Isaiah: A Discussion of Its Problems* (Leiden: Brill, 1948), 6.

37. See Max L. Margolis, *The Story of Bible Translations* (Philadelphia: Jewish Publication Society of America, 1917). Two biographies are available, each containing the complete bibliography of his work: *Max Leopold Margolis: Scholar and Teacher* (Philadelphia: Alumni Association of Dropsie College, 1952); and Leonard J. Greenspoon, *Max Leopold Margolis: A Scholar's Scholar* (Society of Biblical Literature Biblical Scholarship in North America 15; Atlanta: Scholars Press, 1987).

24. Max Leopold Margolis (1866–1932)

This Russian immigrant to the United States became the founding scholar of Septuagint studies in North America.

source: Center for Judaic Studies Library at the University of Pennsylvania

sor of biblical philology at Dropsie College for Hebrew and Cognate Learning in Philadelphia, where he served the rest of his life.

During his distinguished career, Margolis made significant contributions to rabbinics, Semitic linguistics, biblical exegesis, and LXX studies. In 1905 Margolis published a constructive critique of the methodological problems in Hatch and Redpath's *Concordance to the Septuagint*. He outlined a plan and method for producing a substantial revision of the concordance that, however, never materialized.[38] More important, he brought his prodigious philological skills to bear on reconstructing the original Greek text of the Book of Joshua, a project to which he devoted his entire scholarly life. His first article on this subject, "The Groupings of the Codices in the Greek Joshua," appeared in 1910.[39]

38. Max L. Margolis, "Entwurf zu einer revidierten Ausgabe der hebräisch-aramäisch Äquivalente in der Oxforder Concordance to the Septuagint," *Zeitschrift für die alttestamentliche Wissenschaft* 25 (1905): 311–19. The article is summarized and translated into English in *Septuagintal Lexicography*, ed. Robert A. Kraft (SBLSCS 1; Atlanta: Scholars Press, 1972), 46–48, 52–64. Other articles by Margolis are reprinted in this volume, including an example based on the Greek verb λαμβάνω (pp. 70–91). On the importance of biblical philology for exegesis, see Margolis's article, "The Scope and Method of Biblical Philology," *Jewish Quarterly Review* n.s. 1 (1910–11): 5–41, in which he takes but one verse, Job 3:3, as his example.

39. *Jewish Quarterly Review* n.s. 1 (1910–11): 259–63. For what follows, see also his "Specimen of a New Edition of the Greek Joshua," in *Jewish Studies in Memory of Israel Abrahams* (New York: Jewish Institute of Religion, 1927), 307–23.

Margolis appreciated the early work of Paul de Lagarde in LXX textual criticism and applied it to reconstructing the Greek text of Joshua with a measure of success never attained by Lagarde in his grandiose attempt to reconstruct the text of the entire LXX corpus. This is one of the ironies of history, that the work of a German scholar whose political ideology was distinctly anti-Semitic should form the foundation of the life work of a man who would become arguably America's greatest Jewish biblical scholar. Instead of Lagarde's identification of three major recensions in the manuscript evidence, Margolis found four for the text of Joshua: P (the Palestinian recension spoken of by Jerome), C (a recension he believed to be produced in Constantinople), S (the Syrian [Antiochian] recension), and E (the Egyptian [Alexandrian] text). His magnum opus on LXX Joshua was published in 1931.[40]

Margolis's dedication to scholarship was matched by his devotion to teaching, and he was well loved by students and colleagues at Dropsie. Noted biblical scholars Cyrus Gordon, Robert Gordis, and Harry M. Orlinsky were among the many who sat under his teaching. Harry Orlinsky recalls, "I entered the Dropsie College in October 1931 in order to specialize in biblical studies under Margolis. He was then already a very sick man. In November he was stricken and I never saw him again. Nevertheless, the influence of Margolis was felt in the College and it led me to become interested in the rather complex field of the Septuagint."[41] Margolis died just months later, in April 1932, of a cerebral hemorrhage at the age of sixty-six.

On the twentieth anniversary of his death, the alumni association of Dropsie College published a memorial volume in which former student Robert Gordis says that Margolis "may fairly be described as the greatest Jewish master of Biblical learning yet arisen in America."[42] But perhaps the full scope of Margolis's contributions was best captured in the words of his wife, Evelyn Aronson Margolis, in that same volume:[43]

> When a teacher dies and his students, in the first flush of grief, establish a memorial to his memory, it does credit to their sincere emotions.

40. Max L. Margolis, *The Book of Joshua in Greek, according to the Critically Restored Text, with an Apparatus Containing the Variants of the Principal Recensions and of the Individual Witnesses*, 4 vols. (Paris: Gabalda, 1931). These volumes contain the text only up to Josh. 19:38. Publication was interrupted by Margolis's untimely death, but the rest of the material was subsequently discovered by Emanuel Tov and published as *Part V: Joshua 19:39–24:33* (Philadelphia: Annenberg Research Institute, 1992).

41. Harry M. Orlinsky, "On the Present State of Proto-Septuagint Studies," *Journal of the American Oriental Society* 61 (1941): 81, introductory note.

42. Robert Gordis, "The Life of Professor Max Leopold Margolis: An Appreciation," in *Max Leopold Margolis: Scholar and Teacher* (Philadelphia: Alumni Association of Dropsie College, 1952), 1.

43. Ibid., vii.

But, when after a lapse of twenty years, mature men holding responsible positions, having obtained stature each in his own field, still feel that they owe a debt of gratitude which must be paid, and prompted by respect or affection, proceed to pay that debt, the memorial they create does great honor, not only to their teacher, but to the men themselves.

My husband was a born teacher and he loved to teach. But more than teaching, he reverenced scholarship. No sacrifice was too great, personal or economic,[44] to uphold the integrity of scholarship. These ideals he passed on to you, his pupils.

And so I wish for you men who have made this book possible, that in your maturity you may live to know that you have stimulated your pupils and disciples as my husband stimulated you. So that the chain of learning may never be broken and the objectivity, tranquillity and honesty of true scholarship may continue to serve a useful purpose in this deeply troubled world.

James A. Montgomery (1867–1949)

James Montgomery was perhaps the first American-born scholar who left an ongoing legacy of LXX studies in North America. Born in the Germantown section of Philadelphia, Montgomery made that city his lifelong home. Educated at the Episcopal Academy, the University of Pennsylvania, and the Philadelphia Divinity School, Montgomery was professor emeritus of Hebrew Languages at the university at the time of his death. He was ordained in 1893, and the same year he married Mary Frank Owen, who died only seven years later. His second marriage, to Edith Thompson in 1902, produced three sons.

Montgomery adopted the methodology of Max L. Margolis in his commentary on Daniel.[45] In turn, he passed this scholarly legacy on to Henry S. Gehman, who became a professor at Princeton Theological Seminary. In the second preface to his International Critical Commentary on Kings, dated 1944, Montgomery notes that its publication had been delayed by "the War" (i.e., World War II) and that the publisher had returned his manuscript for safe keeping until such a time as the publication could proceed. The commentary did not actually go into print until 1951, with a third preface written by Gehman, to whom fell the job of editing and re-

44. This comment is, perhaps, an allusion to the purchase of books for his large personal library, which at the time of his death numbered over 3,900 items (see Greenspoon, *Max Leopold Margolis*, 50). One of the authors of the present book vividly remembers taking courses at Dropsie College in a seminar room that contained part of Margolis's library (as well as countless card files preserving his research). In addition to an impressive collection of works on Semitics and biblical literature, the shelves displayed numerous tools on the classical languages and Indo-European linguistics.

45. James A. Montgomery, *A Critical and Exegetical Commentary on the Book of Daniel* (International Critical Commentary; Edinburgh: Clark, 1927).

vising his mentor's work.[46] In that preface, Gehman thanks his colleague at Princeton Theological Seminary and former student, John W. Wevers, for "valuable assistance in the reading of the proof." Wevers, one of the outstanding LXX scholars of our present day, has on occasion referred to Montgomery as his academic grandfather.

In Summary

The prominent scholars of a previous generation of LXX studies were primarily preoccupied with the textual criticism of the Greek text, in the hopes of reconstructing the original translation of each book and producing ancillary resources, such as concordances and grammars, for future scholars. For this particular task their time in history prepared them well. Most acquired competency in both Greek and Latin in secondary school, later gaining impressive proficiency in Hebrew, Aramaic, Syriac, Ethiopic, Arabic, and other ancient languages. Those who left a lasting legacy of scholarship apparently had an untiring drive for knowledge and a temperament that permitted them decades of long days laboring over minute details, before the aid that computers and photocopying machines could offer. Scholarship of this sustained quality seems to be a thing of the past, even in the European universities that gave it birth. No curriculum today prepares students to master philology to the extent that our predecessors attained.

These scholars are also impressive because, even though making significant and lasting contributions to LXX studies, the LXX was only one part of their academic interests. Many were also outstanding scholars in other closely related fields. Most held active teaching positions for decades at the finest universities. Some were deans and provosts who carried heavy institutional responsibilities. Several were clergy in the church or leaders in the synagogue. Many lived and worked through the tumultuous times of a world war. All had families for whom to provide. Not a few suffered the untimely loss of wife or child. Students today know them simply as names on a page of a book, but these scholars dedicated their lives to us, the future generations of scholars who build on the foundations they laid, so that, as Evelyn Margolis put it, "the chain of learning may never be broken."

Finally, we learn from our predecessors that the attempt to reconstruct the original text of the LXX spans many lifetimes. Although begun more than two centuries ago, the study of the LXX and the reconstruction of its original text continues to be a work that could yet occupy generations of future scholars.

46. James A. Montgomery, *A Critical and Exegetical Commentary on the Book of Kings*, ed. Henry S. Gehman (International Critical Commentary; Edinburgh: Clark, 1951).

> The commemoration of the men of the past is the homage which the present pays to their work and their achievements. The longer the distance is which separates us from them, the more able are we fully to appraise the value of their work, and at the same time to realize the progress which we have made and which was due to the initiative which they have taken. Such a commemoration acts also as a stimulant to take up the thread where they have dropped it, and to continue the work on the lines of our predecessors.[47]

47. Moses Gaster, in the foreword to Henry St. John Thackeray's *Some Aspects of the Greek Old Testament* (London: Allen & Unwin, 1927), the publication of Thackeray's Arthur Davis Memorial Lecture under the auspices of the Jewish Historical Society of England.

12

Current Studies in Linguistic Research

Lexicographic Research. The study of the LXX vocabulary covers various topics. ***Dictionaries and Word Meanings:*** in producing a LXX lexicon, should the meaning of a Hebrew word be our guide in determining the meaning of the corresponding Greek word? ***The Septuagint and Hellenistic Greek:*** is the vocabulary of the LXX distinctive or simply part of the Greek language in general? ***Words and Culture:*** how is the meaning of a word affected by its use in the broader culture? ***Lexicography, Textual Criticism, and Exegesis:*** specialized lexical studies help us determine the original reading of the text as well as its meaning.

Syntactic Research. The study of syntax is important for ***Determining Translation Technique***. Several scholars in Helsinki have been especially prominent in this field of research. ***Quantitative Methods of Syntax Analysis*** have become more feasible because of advances in computer technology. Several methods allow us to identify valid indicators of translation technique.

Much biblical scholarship of the nineteenth and early twentieth centuries focused on philology. Educated people at that time were usually trained in the classical languages early in life. And as was noted in the previous chapter, those who became biblical scholars brought knowledge of several languages to their study of the Bible. It was quite natural that scholars with such training should focus on biblical philology, which emphasized the study of Hebrew words in comparison to other Semitic languages, such as Aramaic, Arabic, and Akkadian. An essential aid in this task is the information furnished by the LXX as well as the other versions, such as the Targumim, the Peshitta, and the Vulgate. Philological studies informed exegesis by shedding light on the sense of ancient words, thus providing a more secure basis for further linguistic and textual study.

The language of the LXX, however, requires special attention, since it contains many features that appear anomalous when compared with other Greek literature. With regard to the vocabulary, an early and important contribution came from Johann Friedrich Schleusner (1759–1831), who in 1820 published his dictionary of the LXX.[1] Another great boon to LXX lexicography was the work of Edwin Hatch and Henry A. Redpath, who compiled and published the standard LXX concordance in 1898.[2]

These tools have not escaped criticism, though, and scholarly concerns have often focused on foundational principles of LXX lexicography that continue to be debated today. Comparable questions arise in the study of LXX grammar. Moreover, influenced by principles of modern linguistics developed in this century, scholars have begun to pay greater attention to the larger structures of language, using syntax criticism and discourse analysis to enlighten our understanding of translation technique, textual lineage, and literary development within the LXX.

Lexicographic Research

Dictionaries and Word Meanings

Scholars study the vocabulary of the LXX with several concerns in mind. Perhaps the most obvious goal of lexical studies is to determine what the words found in the LXX mean. This is not the straightforward task it may at first seem, however. Most of us from an early age learn to look up words in a dictionary to find out what they mean. Seldom do we stop to think about what goes into lexicography, that is, about how the meaning listed in the dictionary is determined or about the complexities involved in producing such a work.

The task becomes even more complicated when the words in question are two thousand years old. And because the words in the LXX translate Hebrew (and Aramaic) words that are themselves even more ancient, the production of a LXX lexicon is burdened with many theoretical and practical problems.[3] Precisely because the LXX is a Greek

1. The full title is *Novus thesaurus philologico-criticus sive lexicon in LXX et reliquos interpretes graecos ac scriptores apocryphos Veteris Testamenti* (Leipzig: Weidmann, 1820). Copies of this work are rare, even though no other comparable lexicon has been produced since that time. See Johan Lust, "J. F. Schleusner and the Lexicon of the Septuagint," *Zeitschrift für die alttestamentliche Wissenschaft* 102 (1990): 256–62.

2. See above, chap. 11, p. 241.

3. See Moisés Silva, "Describing Meaning in the LXX Lexicon," *BIOSCS* 11 (1978): 19–25.

translation of a Hebrew text and a lexicon must give the equivalent word or definition in a modern language, the production of a LXX lexicon is a *tri*lingual task, with semantic issues arising from each of the three languages involved.

Foremost among them is this question: Should the aim of LXX lexicography be to determine the sense of the Greek word as intended by the translator, who had direct knowledge of the Hebrew text, or should the meaning given in a lexicon be whatever was probably understood by a Greek reader ignorant of the Hebrew? For the moment we leave out of consideration those Greek-speaking Jewish readers who may have had some access to the Hebrew text. In any language, the meaning of a given occurrence of a word is determined by its context as intended by the author.[4] In the case of the LXX, the "author" of the text is a translator who had the Hebrew text before him. His immediate mental context for the Greek words he chose would undoubtedly be influenced by the Hebrew words before him. On the other hand, the typical Greek-speaking readers of the LXX had no knowledge of nor recourse to the original Hebrew documents. Their immediate mental context for understanding the Greek words would be formed by how those words functioned in the larger linguistic context of Koine Greek familiar to them.

Consider, for instance, the Greek word δικαίωμα, which in nonbiblical literature has such legal senses as "judgment, penalty" or "justification, legal right" (cf. LSJ 429).[5] Emanuel Tov points out that this word is used in the LXX to translate three Hebrew nouns that usually mean "decree, command": חֹק (46 times), חֻקָּה (26 times), and מִשְׁפָּט (41 times). Accordingly, LSJ gives "ordinance, decree" as a separate meaning of δικαίωμα, listing supporting references only from the LXX and the NT.[6] Does this mean that δικαίωμα was used in a peculiar sense within the LXX, or that it was simply an accident that more occurrences of the word bearing this sense did not survive in the wider Greek world?

Moreover, when a lexicon of the LXX is produced, should the meaning of the Greek word be defined in reference to the Hebrew word it

4. The notion of authorial intent has become a controversial issue in contemporary hermeneutics. See the important work by Kevin J. Vanhoozer, *Is There a Meaning in This Text? The Bible, the Reader, and the Morality of Literary Knowledge* (Grand Rapids: Zondervan, 1998), esp. chap. 2. Our discussion here merely reflects the usual approach in the study of ancient texts.

5. For this and other detailed examples see Emanuel Tov, "Greek Words and Hebrew Meanings," in *Melbourne Symposium on Septuagint Lexicography*, ed. Takamitsu Muraoka (SBLSCS 28; Atlanta: Scholars Press, 1990), 83–126, esp. 85, 89.

6. BAGD 198 gives the similar glosses "regulation, requirement, commandment" for δικαίωμα, and it includes two supporting references from writings that probably were not influenced by the Greek Bible.

presumably translates, or by the use of the Greek word in its larger Hellenistic context? Because surviving evidence of Hellenistic Greek is fragmentary and because we cannot always be certain of the Hebrew *Vorlage* of the extant Greek text, LXX lexicography is a challenging task. One must exercise caution when using BAGD or LSJ to identify the meaning of LXX words, since neither of these lexicons was produced with the purpose of addressing the complicated issues peculiar to the LXX.

Fortunately, two lexicons that do deal with these issues have appeared in recent years. It should be noted, however, that the respective editors take different positions on the problem we have highlighted. Takamitsu Muraoka, on the one hand, argues that a LXX lexicon should give the meaning that would have been understood by a Greek reader with no knowledge of the Hebrew text.[7] On the other hand, Johan Lust takes the position that a LXX lexicon should seek for the meaning intended by the translator, who obviously did have the Hebrew text before him and chose his Greek words under the influence of the Hebrew reading.[8]

What may seem to be a small difference in principle can result in a significant practical divergence, as is shown by comparing the treatment of ἀπορέω in these two lexicons. For the passive form of this verb, Muraoka gives the meaning "to be left wanting food, famished." The citation he gives is Hosea 13:8, ἄκρος ἀπορουμένη ("a hungry bear"), even though the corresponding Hebrew word is שַׁכּוּל ("bereaved"; i.e., robbed of her cubs).[9] In contrast, Lust gives the meaning of this verb as "to be at a loss how to; to be at a loss for, to be in want for." Though he does not cite Hosea 13:8 as an example of this meaning, his definition is closer in sense to the corresponding Hebrew, and quite different from the listing in Muraoka's lexicon. Lust assumes that "the translator appears to have first of all wished to render his *Vorlage* as faithfully as possible."[10]

This example raises the question of how to define "faithfully" as it applies to translation work, because the LXX translators often contextualized their translation for a Greek audience by providing a dynamic equivalent of the Hebrew. In such cases, even though the sense of the expression may be preserved, the underlying Hebrew is not necessarily a good guide to the meaning of individual Greek words. Lust's assump-

7. Takamitsu Muraoka, *A Greek-English Lexicon of the Septuagint: Twelve Prophets* (Louvain: Peeters, 1993), viii.

8. Johan Lust, Katrin Hauspie, and Erik Eynikel, *A Greek-English Lexicon of the Septuagint*, 2 vols. (Stuttgart: Deutsche Bibelgesellschaft, 1992–96), 1.xi.

9. Muraoka discusses this example in the introduction to his *Greek-English Lexicon*, viii.

10. Lust et al., *Greek-English Lexicon*, 1.xii.

tion also raises the question of what Hebrew word the translator actually saw in the text he was translating. Although in the case of Hosea 13:8 we have no reason to believe that the translator's parent text had a word other than שַׁכּוּל, this possibility cannot be excluded in principle.

Muraoka's decision may do justice to what a Greek reader would have expected from common usage, but this meaning does not necessarily reflect what the translator had in mind when choosing the word. Perhaps the word ἀπορέω, while most frequently used in Koine Greek to refer to hunger (want of food), had a less frequently used sense of "wanting for," which in the context of Hosea 13:8 could have been used with reference to bereavement. In that case, the Greek reader may have gathered from the context that the verb was indeed being used in this second, less common sense. This example shows that even though the purpose of a LXX lexicon is to give the meaning of the Greek word as it is used in the LXX, in reality that purpose cannot be served without taking into account both the meaning of the Hebrew word and the use of the Greek word in the Hellenistic world generally.

The Septuagint and Hellenistic Greek

The example discussed above also shows the need to determine the relationship of the LXX vocabulary to the Greek language in general. Is this vocabulary in some way unique, implying perhaps a linguistically differentiated Jewish dialect of Koine Greek? Are there any linguistic traits in the LXX that, while occurring elsewhere, are distinctive to a particular period in the development of the Greek language and thus could help date the translation of individual books of the LXX? Can the occurrence of words in the context of extrabiblical texts, such as the Egyptian papyri, enlighten our understanding of the meaning of those words found in the LXX (or vice versa)?

One important example of the kind of research needed is John Lee's analysis of the Greek Pentateuch.[11] Lee surveys pentateuchal vocabulary by dividing it into two main groups, each with two subdivisions:

1. words in the Pentateuch that are also found in texts outside of biblical and related literature
   a. words known also in older, Classical Greek
   b. words attested only in Koine Greek
2. words in the Pentateuch that are found only in biblical and related literature
   a. words likely to be "normal" Greek
   b. words likely to be peculiar to biblical Greek

11. John A. L. Lee, *A Lexical Study of the Septuagint Version of the Pentateuch* (SBLSCS 14; Chico, Calif.: Scholars Press, 1983).

Most scholars today agree with Lee's conclusion that "the bulk of the Pentateuch vocabulary is the same as that of contemporary Greek."[12] This means that the LXX Pentateuch provides no lexical evidence for a distinctive Jewish-Greek dialect. Any perceived influence of Hebrew on the Greek of the Pentateuch derives from the Hebrew exemplar from which the translation was made, and not from a Hebraized dialect of Greek in use among the Jewish people of the Diaspora.

Lee also uses his study of the vocabulary of the Pentateuch to address the issue of dating the text. He concludes only that the surviving text is "probably older than the middle of the second century B.C."[13] In the case of books for which we have two different Greek texts (e.g., Judges, Daniel, Esther), Lee raises the interesting question of whether comparison of the vocabulary of each to the vocabulary of the Pentateuch may help to determine which Greek text is the earlier of the two.

Lexical studies of the LXX are also useful in determining if the vocabulary is homogeneous throughout a part, or even throughout the whole, of the LXX. This type of information may help to date the production of the translations of various books and to determine if more than one translator worked on a given section or book. As far as the Pentateuch is concerned, Lee concludes that while it is likely that more than one translator worked on the Pentateuch, no lexical evidence supports this case. In other words, if more than one translator produced the Greek Pentateuch, they all apparently drew from the same vocabulary stock so that their individual work cannot be distinguished on the basis of vocabulary.

Words and Culture

In addition to determining the relationship of LXX vocabulary to that of Koine Greek overall and the homogeneity of vocabulary usage within the LXX, lexical studies also seek to determine how a particular word was used in the context of its culture. For instance, to understand the expression *White House* as used in American English, it would not be enough to know that *white* is a color and *house* is a structure where a family lives. Even though those meanings are valid for general English usage, the combination of the terms has a particular referent in American culture that cannot be derived from the meanings of the two individual words. Similarly, some knowledge of Hellenistic Greek society and culture is necessary to understand the meaning of Greek words that have particular referents.

Lexical studies can be focused synchronically (to determine more precisely the meaning of a given Greek word at a particular stage of

12. Ibid., 146.
13. Ibid., 148.

the language) or diachronically (to determine how the meaning of a given Greek word changed through time).[14] The documentary papyri and the inscriptions from the Hellenistic period are of great importance for understanding what a given word meant in Koine Greek and how it was used in contemporary society. Several scholars in Australia, recognizing the need to update Moulton and Milligan's classic reference work *The Vocabulary of the New Testament*, have been gathering the necessary data and publishing some of the material.[15] While this project focuses on early Christianity, much of the work has direct relevance for LXX studies.

On the other hand, the LXX translators sometimes invested common Greek terms with a particular theological or religious sense, and it is that sense that must be understood in the LXX and possibly in the NT as well. Moreover, as we have seen, scholars often debate whether a Greek word in the LXX or NT bears the common sense of the word as it would generally be used in Koine Greek, or a more peculiar sense in the context of theological and religious discourse.

One interesting example of how lexical study can inform our understanding of LXX words (and hence improve our understanding of the message) is found in an article by Gary Alan Chamberlain, "Cultic Vocabulary in the Septuagint."[16] The LXX translators used the word κιβωτός, a common Greek term for "box, chest," with reference to the ark of the covenant (especially in the phrase ἡ κιβωτὸς τῆς διαθήκης κυρίου = אֲרוֹן בְּרִית־יְהוָה). Chamberlain points out that this Greek word may have had a specific sense in Hellenistic culture that made it particularly appropriate for use in this biblical context. An inscription from the island of Paros (not to be confused with Pharos), dating from 175–150 B.C.E., uses this Greek word in a discussion about community archives to refer specifically to the place where authenticated records are to be deposited. The Greek translators of the Hebrew Bible possibly chose κιβωτός not because of its general sense, but because within the Hellenistic setting this word was used in reference to the authoritative, communal documents, which is how the translators understood the ark of the covenant to function in ancient Israel.

14. Diachronic studies are of special interest to NT scholars, who recognize the influence of the LXX vocabulary on the NT. One cannot, however, merely assume that a word used in the NT meant or referred to the same thing as it did centuries earlier when the word was used by the LXX translator. For a discussion of the theoretical issues involved, see Moisés Silva, "Semantic Change and the Role of the Septuagint," in *Biblical Words and Their Meaning: An Introduction to Lexical Semantics*, 2d ed. (Grand Rapids: Zondervan, 1994), chap. 2.

15. See G. H. R. Horsley and John A. L. Lee, "A Lexicon of the New Testament with Documentary Parallels: Some Interim Entries," *Filología neotestamentaria* 10 (1997): 55–84; 11 (1998): 57–84.

16. *BIOSCS* 27 (1994): 21–28, esp. 27.

This example shows the importance of ongoing lexical studies of Greek words occurring in the LXX as new papyri and inscriptions are discovered. It is sometimes not enough to come up with an equivalent word, but it is also necessary to understand the context in which the word was used in Hellenistic culture. In the case of κιβωτός, its more specific meaning may well have influenced the Greek translators' choice, and such information should be included in future editions of LXX lexicons.

Lexicography, Textual Criticism, and Exegesis

Lexical studies of the LXX have additional purposes. One of them is to provide information that can be used by textual critics to determine the original reading of the Greek when variants occur in the manuscripts. For this purpose, each variant reading must be viewed against the larger pattern of LXX vocabulary to determine which is most likely the original reading.

One example of such a lexical study is Claude E. Cox's article on the LXX Psalter.[17] When we examine the verb עָנָה ("to answer") in the Psalms, we find that it is translated thirty-four times by either εἰσακούω ("to hearken") or ἐπακούω ("to listen"). Most of these instances display no textual variation, but in eleven passages the manuscripts are divided between the two verbs. Which was the original Greek verb in these eleven places? To answer that question, Cox considers the use of these verbs within both the wider biblical corpus and the extrabiblical texts. He finds, for example, that the second verb appears with greater frequency. One reason for the variants may have been that scribes replaced the less frequently used verb, εἰσακούω, with its more popular synonym, ἐπακούω; hence εἰσακούω would have likely been the original reading. Furthermore, it appears that εἰσακούω may have been preferred within the Jewish community as an alternative to the more popular verb, which was used widely in the papyri in reference to pagan gods. This preference too suggests that εἰσακούω was the original reading. Many other factors need to be taken into account, however, such as the tendency for ἐπακούω to be used in collocation with κράζω (eight times in uncontested passages, versus one instance of εἰσακούω; four additional passages display textual variation).

Cox's article illustrates another purpose for doing lexical study of the LXX. One would expect עָנָה ("to answer") to be translated by a Greek word with an equivalent meaning, such as ἀποκρίνομαι. Assuming that the Hebrew word in the *Vorlage* of the translator was in fact עָנָה, there was an apparent shift of sense from Hebrew "to answer" to

17. Claude E. Cox, "Εἰσακούω and Ἐπακούω in the Greek Psalter," *Biblica* 62 (1981): 251–58.

Greek "to hear" when the Psalms were translated. As Cox points out, God is depicted in the Hebrew text as an "answering" God. In the Greek, however, God "does not specifically answer prayer (ἀποκρίνω) but is, rather, attentive to man's call (εἰσακούω and ἐπακούω)."[18] Cox concludes that this comparison of the vocabulary of the Greek Psalms to the Hebrew Psalms shows a theological shift in the Hellenistic period concerning how God relates to his people.

In another article, "Vocabulary for Wrongdoing and Forgiveness in the Greek Translations of Job,"[19] Cox focuses on lexical study as a means of contributing "to the understanding of the theology of the book in its Greek form, especially in its LXX form." In this work, Cox identifies a semantic domain of related words ("a circle of words") that the translator uses to refer to wrongdoing. He determines that they are basically synonymous words, not only within the LXX but also outside the biblical corpus. He finds that the vocabulary used in Job in reference to wrongdoing and forgiveness is consistent with that found in other books of the LXX, with one exception. Where the Hebrew word רָע ("wicked") can refer to any class of people, the Greek translator of Job uses the Greek word δυναστής ("ruler"), apparently to specify the Hellenistic rulers as the wicked people in view.

Lexical studies can help interpreters avoid semantic anachronism, especially with terms that later developed a narrower, more technical sense. Ronald Troxel studied the word ἔσχατος to investigate eschatology in LXX Isaiah.[20] It is generally assumed that this word, and particularly the phrase ἐν ταῖς ἐσχάταις ἡμέραις ("in the last days") in Isaiah 2:2, is a technical term for the end-times. Troxel notices, however, that in both geographical and temporal phrases the translator of Isaiah uses this adjective in a general way and that he fails to use the term in passages where he might have been expected to do so to promote an eschatological focus. Troxel concludes that the phrase in 2:2 probably means, more generally, "in days to come." Without denying that there may be eschatology in LXX Isaiah, he argues that "the translation does not use ἔσχατος as a technical term of eschatology, nor does its use of ἔσχατος reflect a translator dominated by expectation of 'die Endzeit.'"[21] Modern readers, therefore, must be cautious not to assume that later theological uses were already present in the Greek versions.

18. Ibid., 258. See chap. 14 below for further discussion of the use of the LXX in theological studies.

19. *Textus* 15 (1990): 119–30.

20. Ronald L. Troxel, "Ἔσχατος and Eschatology in LXX-Isaiah," *BIOSCS* 25 (1992): 18–27.

21. Ibid., 27.

Syntactic Research

In language studies, syntax is the next logical level of linguistic organization after lexical components. The translation process necessarily involves rendering Hebrew words into Greek words not as isolated units, but in syntactic relationships. Because Hebrew and Greek are different languages and do not even belong to the same linguistic family, their syntactic structures are dissimilar. Studies that compare the syntax of LXX Greek with that of the Hebrew text are necessary in order to determine the technique employed by the translator(s) of a given text. Once the translation technique is understood, it can then be used to inform other areas of LXX studies, especially text-critical decisions for establishing the original Greek translation and its Hebrew *Vorlage*.

Determining Translation Technique

The Helsinki school has provided significant leadership in the study of the syntax of the LXX. The impulse comes from Ilmari Soisalon-Soininen's research,[22] which has shaped the work of two successive generations of students at the University of Helsinki. At the Uppsala meeting of the IOSCS in August 1971, Soisalon-Soininen emphasized the reciprocal relationship between syntax study and translation technique with the statement, "No syntax of a translation without serious research on translation-technique; no research purely on translation-technique alone."[23] At that time he proposed a long-term project to study the syntax of the Greek as the proper basis for discussing the translation technique employed by the various LXX translators. He clarified the question of what constitutes the syntax of a translation:

> It is insufficient to point out that a Hebraism or a Greek idiom is found so many times. For a proper evaluation it is necessary to discover the underlying Hebrew expression; how many times it occurs in OT; whether it is uniformly so rendered in Greek, and if not what other renderings are employed elsewhere; and finally whether the expression may also translate another Hebrew term or phrase. Questions of translation-technique rather than syntax may then arise: how far may a particular rendering reflect the subjective influence of the translator?[24]

Soisalon-Soininen began to study the syntax of the Pentateuch as a basis for discussion about its translation technique, since the Penta-

22. See especially his monograph, *Die Infinitive in der Septuaginta* (Annales Academiae Scientarum Fennicae B/132; Helsinki: Suomalainen Tiedeakatemia, 1965).
23. Ilmari Soisalon-Soininen, "Syntax of Translation-Technique," *BIOSCS* 5 (1972): 10.
24. Ibid., 9.

teuch was the first to be translated and presumably set a pattern for the later translators of other books. Recognizing the huge task involved in fulfilling his methodological goal, he ended his paper with the comment, "Time and resources will, of course, determine the extent to which, together with the assistance of my pupils, my hopes in this direction will be realized."[25]

Anneli Aejmelaeus, a pupil of Soisalon-Soininen who now directs the Septuaginta-Unternehmen project in Göttingen, has contributed significantly to the syntactic study of the Greek text. In a book of her collected essays she writes that, in the study of LXX translation technique, it is essential to focus on

> the languages concerned in the process of translating. How do they correspond in the areas of declension, conjugation, language structure, and syntax? It is impossible to describe a translation without paying attention to the linguistic phenomena involved in each detail. The study of translation must always be a study of language.[26]

In her study of Greek participles primarily in the Pentateuch, Aejmelaeus seeks a criterion of translation technique that indicates the translator's ability to master the syntactic relationships of larger units of text.[27] Frequent occurrence of the circumstantial or adverbial participle (*participium coniunctum*) indicates a freedom of translation technique commensurate with such mastery. She identifies six different structures of Hebrew syntax that are translated by the Greek participle:

1. the Hebrew infinitive absolute construction (e.g., Num. 23:25: גַּם־בָּרֵךְ לֹא תְבָרֲכֶנּוּ = οὔτε εὐλογῶν μὴ εὐλογήσῃς αὐτόν)
2. λέγων for לֵאמֹר introducing direct discourse
3. the first verb in an asyndetic pair (e.g., Deut. 1:21: עֲלֵה רֵשׁ = ἀναβάντες κληρονομήσατε)
4. sporadically, a substantive participle in Hebrew (e.g., Jer. 31:15 [= LXX 38:15]: רָחֵל מְבַכָּה . . . מֵאֲנָה לְהִנָּחֵם = Ῥαχὴλ ἀποκλαιομένη οὐκ ἤθελεν παύσασθαι)
5. the Hebrew infinitive construct with the preposition בְּ as a temporal expression (e.g., Deut. 6:7: וּבְלֶכְתְּךָ בַדֶּרֶךְ = καὶ πορευόμενος ἐν ὁδῷ)
6. two clauses connected by וְ in the Hebrew rendered by a finite Greek verb and a subordinating participial phrase[28]

25. Ibid., 11.

26. Anneli Aejmelaeus, *On the Trail of the Septuagint Translators* (Kampen: Kok Pharos, 1993), 2.

27. Ibid., 7–16.

28. Ibid., 8–11. Aejmelaeus finds that the last category covers by far the majority of cases (450 of 740) in the Pentateuch.

Because the adverbial participle is characteristic of Greek style, its frequent use shows the translator's comfort with rendering the Hebrew syntax freely. This information is valuable for making text-critical decisions. For instance, given such evidence, one would be hesitant to adopt a textual variant that reflects a more literal rendering of Hebrew syntax.

Aejmelaeus's comparison of the syntax of coordinate clauses indicates differences in the translation technique employed throughout the Pentateuch. The use of the participle in Leviticus is significantly less frequent than in Genesis, even though there were ample occurrences of the relevant Hebrew constructions that could have been translated with the Greek participle. This suggests that a different translator was at work on Leviticus, or at least that this translation was done with a more literal tendency in mind.

Raija Sollamo, from the University of Helsinki, also a student of Soisalon-Soininen, published work in this same vein, focusing on the resumptive or pleonastic use of the personal pronoun after a relative pronoun (e.g., Num. 13:32: τῆς γῆς, ἣν κατεσκέψατο αὐτήν [lit., "of the land, *which* they had spied *it*"] = הָאָרֶץ אֲשֶׁר תָּרוּ אֹתָהּ). Examining the syntax of Polybius, the Ptolemaic papyri, the inscriptions, Pseudo-Aristeas, and Josephus, she finds that the repetition of the possessive pronoun in contemporary texts composed in Greek is rare and that therefore its frequent occurrence in the LXX reflects the intention of the translator to preserve the syntax of the Hebrew. Comparing the occurrence of the possessive pronouns in each book of the Pentateuch with the other books, Sollamo furthermore finds that pronouns were translated "more slavishly" in the books of Leviticus, Numbers, and Deuteronomy than they were in Genesis and Exodus.[29] This conclusion is consistent with Aejmelaeus's finding that the translation technique that produced Leviticus tends to be more literal than that which produced Genesis.

A third generation of the Helsinki school is using this approach to study other books in the Greek Bible. Seppo Sipilä, for example, applied to the Book of Joshua the same method used by Aejmelaeus in her study of parataxis in the Pentateuch.[30] Noting how the Hebrew introductory formulas וַיְהִי and וְהָיָה are rendered in the Greek text of Joshua, Sipilä finds that the translator did not use just one standard

29. Raija Sollamo, "The Pleonastic Use of the Pronoun in Connection with the Relative Pronoun in the LXX of Leviticus, Numbers and Deuteronomy," in *VIII Congress of the International Organization for Septuagint and Cognate Studies: Paris 1992*, ed. Leonard J. Greenspoon and Olivier Munnich (SBLSCS 41; Atlanta: Scholars Press, 1995), 43–62. See also her monograph, *Repetition of the Possessive Pronouns in the Septuagint* (SBLSCS 40; Atlanta: Scholars Press, 1995).

30. Anneli Aejmelaeus, *Parataxis in the Septuagint* (Annales Academiae Scientarum Fennicae Diss. hum. litt. 31; Helsinki: Suomalainen Tiedeakatemia, 1982).

rendering, but that καί + a form of γί(γ)νομαι is the most frequent way to render the expression וַיְהִי in this book.[31] These results are in contrast to the findings of Aejmelaeus that introductory γί(γ)νομαι is rare in the Pentateuch. The introductory formula וְהָיָה is most often rendered by καὶ ἔσται (seven of eleven times). Sipilä further considers cases where the following clause in the Hebrew functions as an apodosis. Comparing the translation of such cases in Joshua and the Pentateuch, he finds more affinity with Genesis and Exodus than with Numbers and Deuteronomy. This same distinction between the translation technique of Genesis–Exodus and that of Numbers–Deuteronomy was noticed by Aejmelaeus in her study of the conjunction ὅτι.

A characterization of translation technique as reflected in the syntax of the Greek of each book of the LXX emerges from the mutual corroboration of the findings of such studies. The characterization of translation technique is necessary for making informed text-critical decisions about both the original Greek translation and its Hebrew *Vorlage* and for distinguishing textual phenomena from the exegetical and interpretative interests of the translators.

Quantitative Methods of Syntax Analysis

Over the last thirty years, advances in computer technology have made comparative studies of the syntax of the LXX, and hence translation technique, a feasible goal. Using the CATSS database, Emanuel Tov studied the nature and distribution of infinitive absolute constructions throughout the entire LXX.[32] Since Greek has no exact equivalent to the Hebrew infinitive absolute construction, it provides a good test of what translation options might be employed and hence becomes an indicator of translation technique. Tov points out that the Hebrew infinitive absolute is rendered by three distinct Greek constructions: finite verb + participle, finite verb + noun, and finite verb + adverb. Within these three general approaches, he identifies six translation equivalents. For instance, when the Hebrew infinitive absolute is translated into Greek using finite verb + noun, sometimes the noun is cognate with the verb, sometimes not, and the noun will appear in either the dative or accusative case. By presenting such data in chart

31. Seppo Sipilä, "The Renderings of ויהי and והיה as Formulas in the LXX of Joshua," in *VIII Congress of the International Organization for Septuagint and Cognate Studies: Paris 1992*, ed. Leonard J. Greenspoon and Olivier Munnich (SBLSCS 41; Atlanta: Scholars Press, 1995), 273–89.

32. Emanuel Tov, "Renderings of Combinations of the Infinitive Absolute and Finite Verbs in the LXX: Their Nature and Distribution," in *Studien zur Septuaginta: Robert Hanhart zu Ehren*, ed. Detlef Fraenkel et al. (Göttingen: Vandenhoeck & Ruprecht, 1990), 64–73. With regard to CATSS, see below, appendix A, pp. 316–17.

form for the entire LXX, patterns can be discerned that show the translators' preferences.[33]

For instance, the translators of Exodus, Leviticus, Numbers, Deuteronomy, Judges-A, and Ezekiel prefer to render the Hebrew infinitive absolute with finite verb + noun. The translators of Judges-B, 1–2 Samuel, 1 Kings, Jeremiah, and the Minor Prophets prefer finite verb + participle. The translator of Isaiah rendered the Hebrew infinitive absolute with only a finite verb. In Genesis, the two main translation options, finite verb + participle and finite verb + noun, appear with equally large frequency, suggesting that the original translator vacillated between the two in search of the appropriate rendering. However, in the next four books of the Pentateuch, the translator(s) distinctly preferred the finite verb + noun rendering (e.g., in Leviticus, the Hebrew absolute infinitive is rendered twenty-five times with a verb + noun construction and only eight times with a verb + participle construction).

Instead of comparing the syntax of the Greek texts point by point, a methodology developed by Karen Jobes allows the overall syntactic profiles of two or more Greek texts to be directly compared.[34] This means that in the books for which two Greek versions are extant (e.g., Daniel, Esther, Tobit, Susanna, Judges), syntax criticism should be able to determine which, if either, of the two stands closer to the extant Hebrew text, and should therefore possibly shed light on the relationship of the Greek to each other as well as their relationship to the Hebrew text.

For instance, when syntax criticism is used to examine the two Greek versions of Daniel, OG and Theodotion (θ′), a systematic shift in certain elements of syntax is observed that is consistent with a recensional relationship where one text has been produced by modifying the other. On the assumption that OG Daniel is in fact the translation and θ′ the recension, one might intuitively expect the syntax of the OG text to reflect more strongly the Semitic influence of its *Vorlage*. One could imagine the scenario where the first translation made from Hebrew to Greek is influenced by the Hebrew syntax. Subsequent revisions made to the Greek translation without having the Hebrew text as a guide might result in a more idiomatic Greek text as the translation is revised toward the conventions of Koine style.

Current consensus about the recensional history of the Greek versions, however, proposes the opposite effect. The older Greek appears

33. Ibid., 70.

34. Karen H. Jobes, *The Alpha-Text of Esther: Its Character and Relationship to the Masoretic Text* (Society of Biblical Literature Dissertation Series 153; Atlanta: Scholars Press, 1996), 29–47; idem, "A Comparative Syntactical Analysis of the Greek Versions of Daniel: A Test Case for New Methodology," *BIOSCS* 28 (1995): 21–44.

to be a freer translation of the MT than the later revisions, because the later revisions were often made with the specific intent of revising the Greek version to align it more closely to the contemporary Hebrew text. Under this paradigm, it is in fact the younger recension produced from the older Greek version that contains more Semitic elements of syntax, hence θ′ Daniel appears to be a more literal rendering of the Hebrew than OG Daniel.[35]

The existence of two Greek versions of both Daniel and Esther raises the question whether OG Daniel shows affinity with either of the two versions of Esther. If one version of Daniel is a recension of the other, then one might expect the two Greek versions of Esther to have a similar relationship. Moreover, if some affinity between, for instance, OG Daniel and AT (Alpha-Text) Esther could be discovered, it might indicate that both texts were produced during the same period or represent the same recensional activity. With such questions in mind, one might hope to see a similar shift in the syntactic profiles of the two texts of Esther, indicating one is a recension of the other. However, the syntactic profiles of Esther do not support the theory of a recensional relationship between them, suggesting that each may be a separate translation of its Semitic *Vorlage*. AT Esther reflects a slightly more Semitic syntax than does the LXX version, if the six secondary additions are excluded.

Recent work demonstrates that the study of syntax as a basis for the discussion of translation technique can now be facilitated by the judicious use of computer technology. As studies of how other elements of Hebrew syntax are rendered in the Greek throughout the LXX are published, a fuller profile will emerge. Patterns revealed by such a profile may clarify questions about the chronological order in which the books were translated, as well as the place or even the translation "school" in which the Greek was produced.

35. This consensus view has been challenged most recently by Tim McLay, *The OG and Th Versions of Daniel* (SBLSCS 43; Atlanta: Scholars Press, 1996).

13

Reconstructing the History of the Text

The Quest for the Original Greek Text. The recovery of the "Proto-Septuagint" is an unfinished task. ***Theoretical Issues:*** Lagarde's views about the existence of one original Greek version have been generally accepted over against Kahle's position, but some important questions remain unanswered and require further research. ***Recent Contributions:*** Because the LXX can be profitably used for a variety of purposes, scholars have sometimes been distracted from the logically prior goal of reconstructing the original text. Some specialists, however, continue to make significant contributions to this important field of research.

Recensional History of the Greek Translation. Following Lagarde's program, most LXX scholars recognize the need to establish the pre-Hexaplaric form of the text. This goal can be achieved only by reconstructing the later recensions. ***Reconstructing Lucian's Edition:*** in spite of the difficulties involved in distinguishing translation technique from subsequent recensional activity, much progress has been made in recovering the text used in the fourth-century Antiochene church. ***Reconstructing the Kaige Recension:*** Barthélemy's analysis of the Greek Minor Prophets scroll spawned considerable debate regarding the connection between Theodotion and earlier revisions of the OG.

If, as discussed in the previous chapter, the details of Greek syntax are to be used to evaluate translation technique, then we must first determine what the original translation looked like as it came from the pen of the translator. Other uses of the LXX, similarly, depend on knowledge of the original text. The textual criticism of the Greek text itself, however, is hardly a simple enterprise.[1] What are the major issues being debated today?

1. The basic principles are covered above in chap. 6.

The Quest for the Original Greek Text

In a 1956 discussion of the use of the LXX for emending passages in the Hebrew, Peter Katz complained, "Never was the LXX more used and less studied!"[2] Katz pointed out that studies in both the Hebrew Bible and the Greek NT were "branching out widely, without much regard for the LXX, though the LXX is by nature a connecting link between them both."[3] In 1970, Charles T. Fritsch lamented that the LXX was more often used to reconstruct and elucidate the Hebrew text than it was studied in its own right as "the outstanding literary achievement of Alexandrian Judaism and the Scriptures of the Diaspora and the Christian church."[4] A more sharply focused plea was made in 1985 by Albert Pietersma, who called for a return to "the fundamental and methodologically primary aim of LXX research, namely, the recovery of the OG text." Pietersma argued that before the LXX can be used for reconstructing its *Vorlage* or before a history of the various recensions of the Greek text can be written, a "systematic, detailed, verse-by-verse, word-by-word reconstruction" of the OG is necessary.[5]

Theoretical Issues

Pietersma's goal assumes the general validity of Paul de Lagarde's theory about the origin and recensional history of the Greek version(s).[6] On the basis of Jerome's comment that the LXX of his day existed in three forms, Lagarde theorized that all witnesses to the Greek text could be genetically traced back to one of these three recensions. Using these groupings, Lagarde believed the cross-contamination of the texts could be expunged, making it possible to reconstruct the original text of each of the recensions. From those three reconstructed texts, the original OG text (the Proto-Septuagint) could then be recovered. Lagarde therefore argued that there had been one and only one original translation made for each book of the Hebrew Bible.

A quite different theory of the origin of the Greek versions was proposed by Paul E. Kahle (1875–1964).[7] Going against the consensus of

2. Peter Katz, "Septuagintal Studies in the Mid-Century: Their Links with the Past and Their Present Tendencies," in *The Background of the New Testament and Its Eschatology: In Honour of Charles Harold Dodd*, ed. W. D. Davies and David Daube (Cambridge: Cambridge University Press, 1956), 198; repr. in *Studies in the Septuagint: Origins, Recensions, and Interpretations*, ed. Sidney Jellicoe (New York: Ktav, 1974), 43.

3. Ibid., 176 (repr. p. 21).

4. Charles T. Fritsch, "The Future of Septuagint Studies: A Brief Survey," *BIOSCS* 3 (1970): 6.

5. Albert Pietersma, "Septuagint Research: A Plea for a Return to Basic Issues," *Vetus Testamentum* 35 (1985): 296, 297.

6. See above, chap. 1, pp. 35–36.

7. Kahle was director of the Oriental Institute at the University of Bonn and coeditor, with Rudolf Kittel, of the third edition of *Biblia hebraica*. One of Kahle's most nota-

scholarship and the weight of textual evidence, Kahle denied that all extant manuscripts of the Hebrew text go back to a standard single recension, the pre-Masoretic Text of the first century. He extended this hypothesis to the Greek translation, disagreeing that all extant manuscripts go back to three recensions, which in turn go back to one original translation. He alleged that various Greek versions originated in the synagogues in a situation analogous to that of the Aramaic Targumim, so that more than one independent translation of the same Hebrew book would have been produced.[8] Therefore, extant manuscripts do not necessarily have a genetic relationship that can be traced back to some Proto-Septuagint, but rather go back to a number of totally independent, original Greek translations.

Kahle's theories, as well as their application by his student, Alexander Sperber,[9] were roundly criticized. In a landmark paper, Harry M. Orlinsky wrote, "I can see no basis for this sort of hypothetical argument, even apart from the pertinent factual evidence available."[10] Indeed, most scholars rejected Kahle's hypothesis, as pointed out in his obituary:

> Not all his views were everywhere accepted. It is doubtful, for example, whether his suggestions about the Septuagint will be the basis of new editions but even where he was mistaken he had the knack of putting his finger on the important points and his ideas were always stimulating.[11]

How scholars conceive of the origin and history of the Greek text(s) is a fundamental issue in LXX studies. Because the only evidence scholars have are the extant manuscripts themselves, the reconstruction of the origins and recensional history of the Greek text must be based on an interpretation of complex textual evidence that demands some theoretical starting point. Virtually all modern textual criticism of the LXX is based on the Lagardian idea of but one original translation. Caveats are necessary, however. The realization that two distinct

---

ble achievements was his work on the texts discovered in the genizah of an ancient synagogue in Old Cairo. This work was the subject of his Schweich Lectures at the British Academy in 1941, which were published a few years later. After the discoveries at Qumran beginning in 1948, Kahle revised the book, published as *The Cairo Geniza*, 2d ed. (Oxford: Blackwell, 1959).

8. Ibid., 209–64.

9. For instance, see Alexander Sperber, "The Problems of the Septuagint Recensions," *Journal of Biblical Literature* 54 (1935): 73–92.

10. Harry M. Orlinsky, "On the Present State of Proto-Septuagint Studies," *Journal of the American Oriental Society* 61 (1941): 81–91, quotation from 85; repr. in *Studies in the Septuagint: Origins, Recensions, and Interpretations*, ed. Sidney Jellicoe (New York: Ktav, 1974), 86.

11. *London Times*, 24 September 1964, 12.

translations are extant for some books,[12] added to the growing evidence that the earliest Greek translation began to undergo revision at a very early stage, affects the picture. It means, at the very least, that the implementation of Lagarde's program proves much more challenging than is often thought.

In his Grinfield Lectures of 1991 and 1992, Natalio Fernández Marcos spoke of the current ability of scholars to reconstruct the history of the text from available manuscript evidence. While accepting the Lagardian theory, Fernández Marcos nevertheless observes that some LXX books have "several text forms that cannot be reduced stemmatically to a single text, nor stratified chronologically in a sequence of coherent recensions." The complexities involved in reconstructing the history of the Greek texts lead him to conclude that "the alternative between unity/plurality does not appear as final and exclusive as Kahle and Lagarde supposed."[13] After more than a century of work, the task of determining the origin of the Greek text remains incomplete.

Recent Contributions

For the last fifty years, scholarly attention has perhaps been somewhat distracted from the goal of determining the origin of the Greek text because of the discovery of the Judean Desert materials, which stimulated research rather in the direction of the relationship between the Greek and Hebrew texts. Moreover, Dominique Barthélemy's work on the Greek Minor Prophets scroll led to specialized work on the recensional history of the Greek text, which logically is predicated on knowledge of the original translation.[14] As Pietersma observes, the task of writing the history of the LXX text is integrally related to the task of reconstructing its original form, as they are two sides of the same coin. Using this metaphor, he argues that even a coin has an obverse and reverse, with the primary focus on the former, and that for too long, scholars have neglected this primary focus.[15]

A survey of the literature of the last thirty years shows that if one counts only work done directly on reconstructing the OG, then the observations of Katz, Fritsch, and Pietersma are still largely correct. Although much has been written that is certainly relevant to the problem of establishing the original Greek text, most of it is not directly con-

12. See above, chap. 12, pp. 271–72. We shall return to this question later in this chapter.

13. Natalio Fernández Marcos, *Scribes and Translators: Septuagint and Old Latin in the Books of Kings* (Vetus Testamentum Supplement 54; Leiden: Brill, 1994), 23, 24.

14. In other words, we can hardly identify a document as the development of an earlier text unless we know what that earlier text looked like. But a "hermeneutical circle" is involved here. As we have seen, the Lagardian model moves from the later recensions back to the original text.

15. Pietersma, "Septuagint Research," 297.

cerned with the textual criticism of the LXX itself. This is perhaps understandable, given that the science/art of textual criticism is such a specialized skill. Indeed, the availability of quite a few volumes of the Göttingen critical edition of the Greek text may create the impression that not much work is left to do. Fortunately, some scholars continue to make significant contributions to the field.

Pietersma himself, for instance, has substantially advanced work in this area, focusing on the Greek Psalter and paying special attention to the Chester Beatty papyri as an aid in establishing the original text of this book. His article "The Greek Psalter: A Question of Methodology and Syntax" offers a good example of the text-critical issues peculiar to the text of the LXX.[16] He examines variant readings in the Psalter that concern the syntax of neuter plural substantives and asks this question:

> When determining the reading of the Old Greek text and being faced with having to make a choice between a verb in the singular and one in the plural, on what basis is one to decide for the one and against the other? Does one count noses, does one give priority to the most ancient witnesses, does one choose a plural verb because the translator of the book in question seemed to prefer plurals to singulars, or because neuter plural substantives governing plural verbs became a rather common syntactic construction in the hellenistic period—and the Septuagint is after all a product of this period?[17]

These would be the obvious options if one were trying to establish the earliest form of a text originally composed in Greek. But because the LXX is a translation document, another level of complexity must be considered, namely, the need to take into consideration what Hebrew form is being translated. This question, in turn, is itself an intricate problem because we cannot assume that the Hebrew text has remained basically unchanged since the Greek translation was made. Therefore, the textual criticism of the Hebrew becomes inextricably involved.

Pietersma proposes the hypothesis that the number of the Hebrew verb (singular or plural) governed the Greek translator's choice of the form of the verb with neuter subjects in the Psalms. That is, if the Hebrew verb was singular, the original reading of the Greek would be singular; where the Hebrew was plural, the original Greek reading would be plural. For example, plural πεδία takes a plural verb in Psalm 65:11 (LXX 64:12) but a singular verb in Psalm 96:12 (LXX 95:12), both in conformity with the Hebrew. In other words, in this hypothesis, the Hebrew text takes priority over common Greek syntax of neuter substantives and their verbs in the Hellenistic period.

16. *Vetus Testamentum* 26 (1976): 60–69.
17. Ibid., 61.

After examining 162 occurrences of the neuter plural substantive in the Greek Psalter, Pietersma draws the following conclusions:

1. The number of the Hebrew verb was as a rule determinative of the number of the Greek verb, as the same neuter plural substantive was usually found to govern a singular verb in one verse and a plural in another, in exact correspondence with the Hebrew.
2. When a nominal clause in the Hebrew contained a pronoun in the plural number, the translator used a plural of εἰμί, but where there was no explicit pronoun in the Hebrew, he used a singular form of the verb or simply retained the predicate nominative construction.
3. Constructions involving nonpersonal substantives were changed during transmission of the Greek from a plural verb form to the singular.[18]

Even with confidence in his conclusion, Pietersma ends the article by noting the lack of complete agreement between the Greek and Hebrew texts. After all, it is too much to expect a translator to be totally consistent. Furthermore, the Hebrew *Vorlage* of the Greek Psalter may have differed in places from the extant Hebrew text.

Among other contributions, special mention should be made of the editors of the Göttingen LXX. Joseph Ziegler, for example, completed the volumes for all the prophets and several sapiential books and published many important technical studies. Robert Hanhart edited a number of historical and deuterocanonical books. John W. Wevers, Pietersma's former teacher in Toronto and later his colleague, not only edited all five volumes of the Göttingen Pentateuch—itself a colossal undertaking—but also produced individual, accompanying monographs presenting in great detail the basis for his reconstruction of the textual history of each of the books. As if that were not enough, he also wrote substantial commentaries on the Greek text of the Pentateuch that provide a broader context within which to understand his text-critical decisions.[19]

Finally, one must not ignore the technical work being done on the daughter versions of the LXX.[20] In remarks addressed to the IOSCS in

18. Ibid., 68.

19. See appendix B on critical editions and commentaries. Note also John W. Wevers, "Apologia pro Vita Mea: Reflections on a Career in Septuagint Studies," *BIOSCS* 32 (1999): 65–96.

20. These include Arabic, Armenian, Coptic, Ethiopic, Georgian, Gothic, Old Latin, Old Slavic, and Syriac. On this subject, note the papers by John W. Wevers (general issues), Claude E. Cox (Armenian), M. J. Mulder (Peshitta), Melvin K. H. Peters (Coptic), and Eugene C. Ulrich Jr. (Old Latin) in *La Septuaginta en la investigación contemporánea (V Congreso de la IOSCS)*, ed. Natalio Fernández Marcos (Textos y Estudios "Cardenal Cisneros" 34; Madrid: Consejo Superior de Investigaciones Científicas, 1985), 15–80. For an important recent study on the Syriac tradition, see Robert J. V. Hiebert, *The "Syrohexaplaric" Psalter* (SBLSCS 27; Atlanta: Scholars Press, 1989).

1971 at Uppsala, Bo Johnson explained: "The importance of these versions for LXX studies consists primarily in their persistent retention of the characteristics of their Greek *Vorlage* despite the varied course of their subsequent textual history." He concluded that

> all of the daughter versions in their present form, or in an earlier stratum, show affinities with the Lucianic textform. It is an open question how far this affinity should be identified with the Hesychian character of some of the versions, or from another point of view, how purely "Lucianic" the *Vorlage* of the different versions really was.[21]

Before the daughter versions can be reliably used for the textual criticism of the Greek text from which they were translated, textual criticism must be applied to the versions themselves. Melvin Peters, for example, has produced critical editions of the Coptic (Bohairic) Pentateuch, which provide the necessary textual basis for further study of its relationship to the LXX.[22]

In addition to serving scholarship through publishing critical editions of the Coptic texts, Peters has also devoted extensive study to the Coptic translation made from the Greek *Vorlage* in an effort to identify manuscript families and shed light on the history of textual transmission. His study of the Bohairic text of Genesis illustrates how features of the versions are studied in relationship to the LXX.[23] Five hundred variants were selected from the critical apparatus of the first thirty chapters of the Göttingen edition of Genesis from manuscripts known—on the basis of previous study of Deuteronomy—to be related to the Bohairic. The types of variants included pluses (which Peters considers to be the "most accurate indicator of genetic similarity"),[24] unique spellings of proper nouns, unique substitutions, omissions, and transpositions.

These variant readings in the Greek are then compared with the Bohairic text of Genesis to find patterns of agreement. If it agrees primarily with distinctive variants found in certain Greek manuscripts, then those manuscripts probably represent the Greek *Vorlage* of the Coptic version. Peters concludes that this version shows the

21. Bo Johnson, "Some Remarks on the Daughter Versions of the Septuagint," *BIOSCS* 5 (1972): 7–9.

22. Melvin K. H. Peters, *A Critical Edition of the Coptic (Bohairic) Pentateuch* (SBLSCS 15, 19, 22; Atlanta: Scholars Press, 1983–). Already published are volumes on Genesis (1985), Exodus (1986), and Deuteronomy (1983).

23. Melvin K. H. Peters, "The Textual Affinities of the Coptic (Bohairic) Version of Genesis," in *VI Congress of the International Organization for Septuagint and Cognate Studies: Jerusalem 1986*, ed. Claude E. Cox (SBLSCS 23; Atlanta: Scholars Press, 1987), 233–54.

24. Ibid., 236.

greatest affinity with Greek manuscript 509, but that it also shares significant readings with other witnesses, especially certain members of the so-called *y* group. This type of genetic tracing is necessary for reconstructing the history of textual transmission. In Deuteronomy, for example, the Bohairic had been found to represent a pre-Hexaplaric text closer to Alexandrinus than to Vaticanus. Peters's study, however, questions whether in fact this version reflects such a text in the Book of Genesis.[25]

Comparable analyses are being done by scholars on the other versions, especially Armenian, Old Latin, and various Syriac translations. While not many specialists are attracted to this and other narrow fields of study, the results from such work are invaluable pieces in the great puzzle of LXX textual criticism.

Recensional History of the Greek Translation

In an ideal world, discussion of the history of the Greek text and its development after the original translation was produced proceeds from a detailed and sure knowledge of that original Greek text. In the absence of such certainty, but assuming with Lagarde that extant manuscripts contain texts genetically related to the Proto-Septuagint, we need to work backward in time. First, we must seek to identify the recensions known to Jerome. We will then be in a position to establish the pre-Hexaplaric form of the text, that is, the common second-century text that Origen later corrected.

Because Origen's Hexaplaric revisions affected the textual tradition so thoroughly, reconstructing that earlier form becomes an all-important goal, but also one that is most difficult to achieve. As we have seen, the matter is greatly complicated because other translations and revisions, particularly the Three (Aquila, Symmachus, and Theodotion), had been in circulation for some time. Origen himself made use of these, so that their history became intertwined with that of the Hexaplaric recension.[26]

In what follows, we limit our discussion to two areas that have received special attention during the second half of the twentieth century, namely, the Lucianic text and the revision(s) known as *Kaige*-Theodotion.

25. Ibid., 233–34.

26. For a recent volume of essays that treat in detail all major aspects of Hexaplaric studies, see *Origen's Hexapla and Fragments: Papers Presented at the Rich Seminar on the Hexapla, Oxford Centre for Hebrew and Jewish Studies, 25th* [*July*]*–3rd August 1994*, ed. Alison Salvesen (Texte und Studien zum antiken Judentum 58; Tübingen: Mohr Siebeck, 1998).

Reconstructing Lucian's Edition

Within the last thirty years, much effort has been expended in recovering the fourth-century edition of the Greek OT attributed to Lucian, referred to frequently in current literature as the Antiochene (or Antiochian) recension. In particular, the work of Natalio Fernández Marcos and his colleagues in Spain exemplifies both the state of this research and its complexities. In his 1991–92 Grinfield Lectures at the University of Oxford, Fernández Marcos outlined the difficulties facing scholars engaged in reconstructing the recensional history of the LXX.[27] Generally speaking, as we noted above, he agrees with Lagarde that there was only one original Greek translation of each book of the Hebrew Bible, but with the caveat that recensional activity apparently began quite soon after the translation was in existence. Moreover, he points out that it is difficult to isolate recensional activity from original translation technique.

In Fernández Marcos's opinion, for several books the recensional activity was so extensive that any attempt to restore the original Greek from existing manuscripts is precluded. Reconstructing the textual history of the LXX would be complicated enough if there had been but one Hebrew edition (preserved as the MT) from which the original Greek translation was made. The evidence of the Judean Desert material, however, confirms that the Hebrew text itself circulated in more than one form during the very time that the first Greek translation was being made. In other words, at least some of the elements of the LXX previously attributed to translation technique or recensional activity are now known to represent a Hebrew *Vorlage* different from the MT.

Fernández Marcos began his search for the text of the Lucianic recension in the late 1970s by examining the biblical quotations of the Antiochene fathers, which presumably would reflect the version of the Bible in use during the fourth and fifth centuries in Antioch. Special attention was given to the writings of Theodoret (ca. 393–458), a bishop in Syria who quoted extensively from the Octateuch.[28] Because Theodoret's citations show no evidence of a Lucianic recension in the Pentateuch—a conclusion confirmed by Wevers's work on the Göttingen critical edition—and only weak evidence of "Lucian's" distinc-

27. Fernández Marcos, *Scribes and Translators*, chap. 2.

28. Natalio Fernández Marcos, "Theodoret's Biblical Text in the Octateuch," *BIOSCS* 11 (1978): 27–43. Fernández Marcos and A. Sáenz-Badillos subsequently published a critical edition, *Theodoreti Cyrensis Quaestiones in Octateuchum* (Textos y Estudios "Cardenal Cisneros" 17; Madrid: Consejo Superior de Investigaciones Científicas, 1979). Note also Natalio Fernández Marcos and José Ramón Busto Saiz, *Theodoreti Cyrensis Quaestiones in Reges et Paralipomena* (Textos y Estudios "Cardenal Cisneros" 32; Madrid: Consejo Superior de Investigaciones Científicas, 1984).

tive traits in Judges and Ruth, further work has focused largely on the historical books of Samuel–Kings (1–4 Reigns) and Chronicles.

As a result of two decades of research, Fernández Marcos and his collaborators published a reconstruction of these books as they were read in Antioch in the fourth and fifth centuries of our era.[29] The features of the Antiochene recension are the following: (a) stylistic improvements that avoid the Semitisms of translation Greek, (b) frequent varying of synonyms, which produces a high number of lexical variants, and (c) an inconsistent tendency to substitute Attic forms for Hellenistic ones.[30] Fernández Marcos concludes that other corrections are best explained as accommodations of the text for public reading.

The value of this reconstruction, however, lies not only in providing access to the Greek Bible used in an important region of the ancient Christian church. This text is also of great importance for LXX scholars because, as has been shown especially by Dominique Barthélemy, the "Lucianic" manuscripts of Samuel–Kings are the only ones not contaminated by the *Kaige* recension of these books. Furthermore, the importance of the Greek tradition for the textual criticism of the Hebrew text of Samuel–Kings has been dramatically confirmed by Qumran fragments 4QSam$^{a–c}$, which provide a Hebrew form different at significant points from the MT, agreeing sometimes with the OG and at other times with the Antiochene text.

Bernard A. Taylor has employed computer technology to create a critical edition of the Lucianic manuscripts boc$_2$e$_2$ for 1 Reigns (1 Samuel).[31] In contrast to the edition published by Fernández Marcos, Taylor's work prints the majority Lucianic reading as the text, with variant readings among the remaining Lucianic manuscript(s) in the apparatus. He then compares the readings of boc$_2$e$_2$ with those found in Vaticanus, which is widely believed to be the best extant witness to the OG in the non-*Kaige* sections of Samuel–Kings and closest to the textual base used by Origen.

One of Taylor's major conclusions is that the text preserved in manuscripts boc$_2$e$_2$ does not "share the distinctive characteristics of

29. Natalio Fernández Marcos and José Ramón Busto Saiz, *El texto antioqueno de la Biblia Griega*, 3 vols. (Textos y Estudios "Cardenal Cisneros" 50, 53, 60; Madrid: Consejo Superior de Investigaciones Científicas, 1989–96).

30. Fernández Marcos, *Scribes and Translators*, 31–32. Fernández Marcos acknowledges indebtedness to the important 1966 Oxford dissertation by Sebastian P. Brock, now published as *The Recensions of the Septuagint Version of 1 Samuel* (Quaderni di Henoch 9; Turin: Zamorani, 1996).

31. Bernard A. Taylor, *The Lucianic Manuscripts of 1 Reigns*, 2 vols. (Harvard Semitic Monographs 50–51; Atlanta: Scholars Press, 1992–93). See also Taylor's valuable comparison of three editions (Lagarde's, the Spanish team's, and his own) in "The Lucianic Text of 1 Reigns: Three Texts Compared and Contrasted," *BIOSCS* 29 (1996): 53–66.

MS B that set it apart as the exemplar of the Old Greek."[32] Taylor concurs with the claim that B contains the type of text that Origen used as the base of his work, but he disputes the view that the text reflected in the Lucianic manuscripts was essentially the OG. He therefore suggests that the position held by Barthélemy and accepted by Frank M. Cross and many others must be reconsidered and modified.

Biblical quotations in Jewish writings, the NT, and the early Christian fathers provide additional and important data for reconstructing the various recensions. This evidence is problematic for several reasons. With few exceptions, the extant manuscripts of these writings date from after most of the recensional activity had occurred. Furthermore, when these texts were themselves copied, they would often be corrected intentionally or unintentionally toward Origen's (or Lucian's or some other) text at some point in their transmission. Moreover, even if the original quotation within these texts could be recovered with certainty, it is not clear that the text would represent a standard edition of the Bible. It may simply have been an idiosyncratic paraphrase produced by the author.

A useful example is the work of Victoria Spottorno, a collaborator in the publication of the Antiochene text. Spottorno examined the *Antiquities* of Josephus for textual affinities in the 120 readings where the LXX text of 1–2 Kings (3–4 Reigns) disagrees with the critically restored Antiochene text (L). She finds thirty readings where Josephus agrees with LXX against L; seventy readings where Josephus agrees with L against LXX; and twenty readings where Josephus agrees with a text belonging to a mixed group of manuscripts to which L belongs. Spottorno concludes from her comparison of Josephus with the Antiochene text that

> it would not be an accurate conclusion to affirm that the text of Josephus for the books of Kings is of a Lucianic or Antiochene type "in general"; it only can be said that Josephus knew *a* Greek text that probably was at the first step of the development of the Antiochene; this text could be the Old Greek itself or a recension of it called proto-Lucianic. In consequence, it also can be said that the Antiochene text, although culminating in a developed text later in the 5th century, contains very ancient readings. Such readings contribute to give a high evaluation to that text, perhaps too easily considered as second class.[33]

32. Taylor, *Lucianic Manuscripts of 1 Reigns*, 2.127.

33. Victoria Spottorno, "Josephus' Text for 1–2 Kings," in *VIII Congress of the International Organization for Septuagint and Cognate Studies: Paris 1992*, ed. Leonard J. Greenspoon and Olivier Munnich (SBLSCS 41; Atlanta: Scholars Press, 1995), 151–52. Josephus also bears witness to readings distinctive of the *Kaige* recension attributed to Theodotion in the second century of our era (see below). Almost twenty years before Spottorno's work, George Howard observed that Josephus's text often agrees in Samuel–

Reconstructing the Kaige Recension

As we have noted in previous chapters, much attention has been devoted to Theodotion's work and its relationship to the *Kaige* recension. It was Barthélemy's landmark work on the Greek Minor Prophets scroll in 1963 that generated intense scholarly interest in this area of research.[34] Barthélemy argued that the text preserved in the Greek Minor Prophets scroll was produced by a Palestinian school using a method of translation that was driven by first-century rabbinic exegesis.

Prior to Barthélemy, Henry St. John Thackeray proposed that the earliest Greek translation of Samuel–Kings was made in Alexandria, but that it omitted all of the material that was considered derogatory to David, as well as a lengthy section that detailed the decline of the kings of Israel and Judah. The omitted material was later inserted into the Alexandrian text by a translator working in Ephesus, whom Thackeray identified as providing the text later used by Theodotion. (The Ephesian translation of Samuel–Kings possibly made its way to Alexandria when the library at Pergamum was given to Cleopatra as a gift from Mark Antony in the mid-first century B.C.E.) These two large blocks of material originally omitted from the translation of Samuel–Kings but later inserted from the Ephesian translation were labeled βγ and γδ, or together as βδ. Perhaps the most distinctive trait of this material is that Hebrew (וְ)גַם is consistently translated as καίγε (spelled καί γε in Rahlfs's text).

Barthélemy noticed, however, that the Greek Minor Prophets scroll shared some of the characteristics of the *Kaige* sections (βδ) in Samuel–Kings, as did also the B-text of Judges, Ruth, Canticles, the Quinta of Psalms, and the Greek additions to Jeremiah. On that basis, he argued that the *Kaige* sections of Samuel–Kings were not an original translation, as Thackeray proposed, but a recension of the OG.[35] Following Barthélemy, students of the LXX began to produce doctoral

---

Kings with the Lucianic recension against *Kaige*, but that it also often agrees with *Kaige* against the Lucianic; see "*Kaige* Readings in Josephus," *Textus* 8 (1973): 45–54. But should we leave open the possibility that manuscripts of Josephus were corrected to agree with Theodotion's and Lucian's recensions much later?

34. Dominique Barthélemy, *Les devanciers d'Aquila: Première publication intégrale du texte des fragments du Dodécaprophéton* (Vetus Testamentum Supplement 10; Leiden: Brill, 1963). For what follows, see above, chap. 7, pp. 158–61, and chap. 8, pp. 171–73. For a survey of work before Barthélemy, see Sidney Jellicoe, "Some Reflections on the Καίγε Recension," *Vetus Testamentum* 23 (1973): 15–24.

35. Barthélemy also suggested that the OG for those parts of Samuel–Kings is preserved in the Lucianic manuscripts. Other scholars suggest that the OG is simply lost. For a useful article that seeks a compromise between Thackeray's and Barthélemy's views, see Takamitsu Muraoka, "The Greek Texts of Samuel–Kings: Incomplete Translations or Recensional Activity?" *Abr-Nahrain* 21 (1982–83): 28–49.

dissertations identifying more characteristics of this recension and extending the *Kaige* group to still other books.[36]

A confusing situation now exists because the term *Kaige recension*, with its close, though possibly incorrect, association with Theodotion, cannot be precisely defined and has been used to refer to several entities. Sometimes it refers to Theodotion's work, sometimes to Theodotion-like characteristics found in earlier texts, hence to a "Proto-Theodotionic" recension (including the βδ material in Samuel–Kings). In 1988, John W. Wevers strongly urged "that we ban from academic usage the term καίγε recension, reserving the term καίγε either for the καίγε group [of manuscripts] or simply as the common, in fact the excellent, rendering for גַּם and וְגַם."[37] In other words, while it is true that a group of manuscripts represents גַּם as καίγε, the texts of this group do not otherwise share all the characteristics subsequently identified as distinctive of the *Kaige* "recension." This therefore calls into question whether such traits actually derive from the deliberate, unified work of one translation school or from several other possibly unrelated sources.

Peter Gentry's work on Greek Job confirms criticisms of Barthélemy's original theory and further dispels the idea that the *Kaige* group represents a monolithic revision. The asterisked material in Origen's Greek Job (i.e., text marked with an asterisk because it was found in the Hebrew edition Origen used but not in the common LXX of his day) was inserted into the LXX by Origen from Theodotion's version. Gentry's study concludes that Theodotion represents a new translation of Job and not just a revision of the previously existing OG. Moreover, he finds that the asterisked material in Job does not support Barthélemy's explanation of a *Kaige* recension produced by the concerns of first-century, Palestinian rabbinic practice. In fact, "less than a handful of examples in Theod[otion] in Job can be explained this way."[38] Gentry finds rabbinic exegesis as only one of several possible factors that motivated the work that has come to be known as The-

36. For instance, James D. Shenkel, *Chronology and Recension Development in the Greek Text of Kings* (Harvard Semitic Monographs 1; Cambridge: Harvard University Press, 1968); Kevin G. O'Connell, *The Theodotionic Revision of the Book of Exodus: A Contribution to the Study of the Early History of the Transmission of the Old Testament in Greek* (Harvard Semitic Monographs 3; Cambridge: Harvard University Press, 1972); Walter R. Bodine, *The Greek Text of Judges: Recensional Developments* (Harvard Semitic Monographs 23; Chico, Calif.: Scholars Press, 1980); Leonard J. Greenspoon, *Textual Studies in the Book of Joshua* (Harvard Semitic Monographs 28; Chico, Calif.: Scholars Press, 1983). All of these dissertations were produced under the direction of Frank M. Cross, who accepted the basic elements of Barthélemy's work.

37. John W. Wevers, "Barthélemy and Proto-Septuagint Studies," *BIOSCS* 21 (1988): 23–34. (Some scholars believe, against Wevers, that καίγε is a peculiar rendering, especially when used repeatedly.)

38. Peter Gentry, *The Asterisked Materials in the Greek Job* (SBLSCS 38; Atlanta: Scholars Press, 1995), 495–96.

odotionic. The asterisked text in Job bears the influence of the OG, as found in the Pentateuch, Psalms, and Isaiah, and it also shares traits of the *Kaige* "tradition." Gentry concludes that we should not speak of *Kaige* as if it reflected a monolithic revision:

> There is no *Kaige* Recension as such. Instead, there is a continuum from the Greek Pentateuch to Aquila in which approaches and attitudes to translation are on the whole tending toward a closer alignment between the Greek and the Hebrew. Moreover, there is a tradition which developed within this continuum and involved the interplay between various forces in Judaism. To this tradition the καίγε texts belong. We have yet to demarcate clearly between this tradition and the LXX.[39]

These discussions of *Kaige*-Theodotion have also affected scholarly assessment of Aquila. Barthélemy associated Aquila's translation with the exegetical methods of Rabbi Aqiva (often spelled Akiba), following an ancient tradition preserved in both Jerome and the Palestinian Talmud. The assumption is that a literal translation such as Aquila's would have provided a textual basis for the type of exegesis done by Aqiva (or conversely, that Aqiva's style of exegesis could have motivated Aquila's translation technique).

Lester Grabbe compares Aqiva's exegesis of certain biblical passages with Aquila's translations of those passages and finds little reason to associate the two. He concludes that Aquila's translation was not motivated by any particular method of biblical exegesis, but by an "almost mystical notion of being 'faithful to the original'" (a concept that may also have motivated certain types of Jewish biblical exegesis).[40] Other scholars nevertheless think that Aquila's translation technique was influenced in some way by the exegetical method with which he was familiar. Grabbe's call for a "comprehensive study of all the Minor Versions in the light of all the various types of ancient Jewish biblical interpretation" could keep LXX students writing dissertations for years to come.[41]

Before concluding this chapter, some additional comments may be helpful regarding the existence of double versions for some books, such as Judges,[42] Daniel, and Esther. In the case of Daniel, the two ver-

39. Ibid., 497.

40. Lester L. Grabbe, "Aquila's Translation and Rabbinic Exegesis," *Journal of Jewish Studies* 33 (1982): 527–36, esp. 533–34. We have some evidence that Symmachus made use of Jewish interpretation for his translation; see above, chap. 1, p. 40.

41. Ibid., 536. Note also Giuseppe Veltri, "Der griechische Targum Aquilas: Ein Beitrag zum rabbinischen Übersetzungsverständnis," in *Die Septuaginta zwischen Judentum und Christentum*, ed. Martin Hengel and Anna Maria Schwemer (Wissenschaftliche Untersuchungen zum Neuen Testament 72; Tübingen: Mohr Siebeck, 1994), 92–115.

42. On this book, see the previously mentioned work by Bodine, *Greek Text of Judges*.

sions are commonly referred to in such a way as to prejudice their identity, namely, OG Daniel (o′) and Theodotion Daniel (θ′). While work by Sharon Pace Jeansonne and by Dean Wenthe supports the usual view that θ′ was a revision of the OG text and that the reviser had as one of his goals adjusting the translation toward the contemporaneous Hebrew text, that view has been challenged.[43] In any case, the relationship of this second Greek form of Daniel to Theodotion is unclear, hence the name Theodotion Daniel is somewhat of a misnomer.

The two Greek versions of Esther have been studied by Karen Jobes, who finds the relationship between them different from that between the two versions of Daniel.[44] The two texts are referred to as LXX Esther and the Alpha Text, or AT Esther. Until 1965 AT Esther was believed to be the Lucianic recension of Esther, because Lagarde identified it as such on the basis of its being bound with Lucianic manuscripts of other books. In 1965 Carey A. Moore persuasively argued that AT Esther was not the Lucianic recension of this book, leaving the question of its relationship to LXX Esther for further study. Jobes concluded that the two Greek versions were two independently made translations, but that the *Vorlage* of each was similar to the extant MT (contra David Clines and Michael Fox).[45] Once both versions were in existence attempts were made to harmonize the two, which explains the agreements between them, especially the six additional chapters found in both Greek versions but lacking in the Hebrew. LXX Esther has affinities with θ′ Daniel in that it follows the MT more closely; AT Esther has affinities with OG Daniel, such as a more diverse lexical stock. Further study is needed to determine whether this material can shed light on the problems associated with the *Kaige* tradition.

43. Sharon Pace Jeansonne, *The Old Greek Translation of Daniel 7–12* (Catholic Biblical Quarterly Monograph Series 19; Washington, D.C.: Catholic Biblical Association of America, 1988); Dean O. Wenthe, *The Old Greek Translation of Daniel 1–6* (Ph.D. diss., University of Notre Dame, 1991). Contrary views are put forth by A. Schmitt, *Stammt der sogennante θ′-Text bei Daniel wirklich von Theodotion?* (Mitteilungen des Septuaginta-Unternehmens 9; Göttingen: Vandenhoeck & Ruprecht, 1966); idem, "Die griechische Danieltexte («θ′» und o′) und das Theodotionproblem," *Biblische Zeitschrift* 36 (1992): 1–29; and Tim McLay, *The OG and Th Versions of Daniel* (SBLSCS 43; Atlanta: Scholars Press, 1996).

44. Karen H. Jobes, *The Alpha-Text of Esther: Its Character and Relationship to the Masoretic Text* (Society of Biblical Literature Dissertation Series 153; Atlanta: Scholars Press, 1996).

45. David J. A. Clines, *The Esther Scroll: The Story of the Story* (Journal for the Study of the Old Testament Supplement 30; Sheffield: JSOT Press, 1984); Michael V. Fox, *The Redaction of the Books of Esther: On Reading Composite Texts* (Society of Biblical Literature Monograph Series 40; Atlanta: Scholars Press, 1991).

14

Theological Development in the Hellenistic Age

Principles and Methods. The search for interpretative developments within the Greek versions must proceed with careful attention to methodological issues. Questions about textual transmission, the character of theological *Tendenz*, the use of lexical evidence, and the presence of midrashic rewriting need to be taken into account.

Messianism and the Septuagint. Scholars disagree regarding the degree to which messianic expectation can be detected in the Greek translation. We must appreciate the diversity that characterized early Judaism, and distinctions need to be made between texts viewed as messianic prior to the Christian era and texts that were appropriated by the NT writers in reference to Jesus.

Eschatology and the Septuagint. The Jewish concept of a future resurrection developed during the Hellenistic period. Whether this concept is reflected in the LXX cannot be easily determined.

Influence of Hellenistic Philosophy on the Septuagint. Some Jewish writings composed originally in Greek appropriated aspects of Stoic philosophy. It appears, however, that the LXX translators were restrained by their desire to preserve the sense of the Hebrew text.

Theological *Tendenz* of the Three. Because the production of later Greek versions may have been partly motivated by theological concerns, these versions can be a fruitful source for identifying interpretative elements.

More than one hundred years ago attempts were already being made to identify interpretative elements in the LXX and their significance for understanding the theological development of Judaism in the Hellenistic period.[1] A prominent example of this approach in the twentieth century is Isaac L. Seeligmann's analysis of the Greek version of Isaiah "as a document of Jewish-Alexandrian theology."[2] The goal of such research is to trace the development of the theology, practices, and exegetical traditions of Judaism in the Hellenistic period, with attention to the influence that Hellenistic philosophy and culture may have had on the text of the Greek versions. Moreover, the origins of Christianity and its relationship to Second Temple Judaism are also explored through LXX studies, especially because the LXX was the Bible of the earliest Christians.

Principles and Methods

The search for interpretative developments within the Greek versions has been motivated by different interests. For example, because Christianity, with its distinctive claim that Jesus of Nazareth is the long-awaited Messiah, emerged from Second Temple Judaism, the Jewish writings of this period (both the Greek writings of the Diaspora and Semitic documents like those discovered at Qumran) are studied to identify any messianic expectations they may reflect. Other studies of the LXX attempt to understand what, if any, influence Hellenistic philosophy or pagan religious practices had on the translation of Scripture produced for the Greek-speaking audience. More recently, modern sociological concerns have been brought to bear on LXX studies; feminism, for instance, has motivated some scholars to determine whether attitudes toward women reflected in the Greek translation differ from those in the Semitic texts.[3]

The endeavor to find theological development in the LXX logically presupposes that the work of textual criticism has been done and that both the original words that translated the Semitic parent text and any additions to or omissions from that original translation have been identified. This work allows the theological viewpoint (*Tendenz*) of the original translators to be distinguished from that of subsequent revisers. If the theological trait in question is indeed part of the original translation, then one must try to discern if it was introduced by the

1. Z. Frankel, *Über den Einfluss der palästinischen Exegese auf die alexandrinische Hermeneutik* (Leipzig: Barth, 1851; repr. Farnborough: Gregg, 1972).

2. This phrase comes from the title of the fourth chapter of Seeligmann's monograph, *The Septuagint Version of Isaiah: A Discussion of Its Problems* (Leiden: Brill, 1948), 95–121.

3. See, e.g., Susan Ann Brayford, *The Taming and Shaming of Sarah in the Septuagint of Genesis* (Ph.D. diss., Iliff School of Theology and University of Denver, 1998).

Greek translator or if it was already present in the Hebrew *Vorlage*. This distinction is of particular interest, since the majority of extant manuscripts of the LXX were transmitted and preserved within the Christian tradition.

Such a transmission history raises the possibility that Christian scribes harmonized Greek texts of the OT to agree with the use of those texts in the NT, or that they subtly introduced Christian exegesis into the text of the OT books.[4] Any such changes would, of course, be secondary to the original translation and therefore are of no value in determining what, if any, theological interests the original OG version may reflect. Changes introduced by Christian scribes, however, are of value for the history of interpretation, since they help us to understand, for example, how the early church used and interpreted the OT.

Robert A. Kraft groups possible Christian tendencies into three categories: (1) places where the title *Christ* or *Messiah* appears in such a way as to betray Christian interests; (2) the use of specifically Christian terminology in the Greek OT; and (3) passages in the OT that have been rephrased to agree with quotations of them in the NT or in the writings of Christian church fathers.[5] He concludes that while isolated examples of each category may be found in the LXX corpus, overall little evidence is found of distinctively Christian theology being imposed on the Greek text of the OT as it was copied and preserved by Christians. Kraft further points out that what once may have been thought of as distinctively Christian tendencies needs to be reexamined with a new appreciation of "what was possible within the broad framework of what we call ancient Judaism."[6]

When we speak of theological *Tendenz* in the LXX we must clearly remember that we are not speaking of some unified ideology being applied throughout the corpus by one special-interest group, because the OG translation was not a homogeneous work produced at one time by one group of translators. Whatever theological developments one may find in the translation are what Emanuel Tov calls individual *theologoumena*, which may reflect in a particular instance some theological understanding of a singular point.[7] Theological exegesis within the LXX may be evidenced by (1) the consistent choice of a particular translation equivalent for one word, (2) the rewriting of a given verse

4. Robert A. Kraft, "Christian Transmission of Greek Jewish Scriptures: A Methodological Probe," in *Paganisme, Judaïsme, Christianisme: Influences et affrontements dans le monde antique: Mélanges offerts à Marcel Simon* (Paris: de Boccard, 1978), 207–26.

5. Ibid., 211.

6. Ibid., 226.

7. Emanuel Tov, "Theologically Motivated Exegesis Embedded in the Septuagint," in *Translation of Scripture: Proceedings of a Conference at the Annenberg Research Institute, May 15–16, 1989* (Jewish Quarterly Review Supplement; Philadelphia: Annenberg Research Institute, 1990), 215–33, esp. 215.

in translation to reflect a contemporary understanding of it, (3) pluses and minuses of a few words, and (4) the addition of extensive material (e.g., the six additional chapters of Greek Esther).

As many point out, all translation involves interpretation to some extent. One reason is that the use and semantic range of a word in the source language is seldom totally congruent with the use and range of the corresponding word in the target language. Translation equivalents, therefore, most often reflect purely linguistic rather than theological choices and provide at best unreliable indicators of theological *Tendenz*. Lexical choices of this sort must be distinguished from variations that belong on a "higher" level, such as deliberate additions and omissions.[8]

Seeligmann uses the lexical approach to examine the differences between the Hebrew and Greek texts of Isaiah for insight into how Alexandrian Judaism understood God, Torah, and Israel. He admits the difficulties that attend this approach: "The differences between the translation and the original form a fairly narrow basis on which to rest a reconstruction of the independent theological views of the translator."[9]

Seeligmann points out, for example, that at least two Greek words could have been used to render the divine name יְהוָה. Κύριος offered a better lexical choice for rendering the tetragrammaton than does δεσπότης, because the former was used more broadly in the Greek language to refer to someone with a just claim to authority and power.[10] However, once such a lexical equivalent was chosen, presumably by the translators of the Pentateuch, the occurrence of the same equivalence consistently throughout the rest of the LXX corpus may have no particular theological significance for any given book. All we can say is that κύριος became the standard way to render the name of God in Greek.

Theological intent might be discerned, however, when usage deviates from expected equivalents. An example where such intent seems apparent is the translators' handling of מִזְבֵּחַ ("altar"), which is consistently rendered with θυσιαστήριον when it refers to an altar of Israel but with βωμός when referring to a pagan altar. No clear semantic component makes one of these Greek words more appropriate for one

8. For a discussion of the difference between linguistic and conceptual factors, see above, chap. 4, p. 89. The significance of any variations for understanding theological development in the Hellenistic period depends, of course, on whether these differences were already present in the translator's *Vorlage*. If they were, they reflect shifts within the Hebrew tradition over time (many of these would have taken place at a relatively early date). If they were not in the translator's parent text, however, they represent elements introduced during the Hellenistic era and may thus be useful for understanding theological developments during that time.

9. Seeligmann, *Septuagint Version of Isaiah*, 95.

10. Ibid., 97.

type of altar rather than another. We find therefore that theological *Tendenz* is introduced by the way the word consistently distinguishes a heathen altar from one devoted to Yahweh.

Theological reflection may also be found in the rewriting of an individual verse to express the translator's understanding of it. Such rewritings may reflect an attempt to actualize the biblical text for the contemporary reader. That is, this phenomenon is often found in the translation of biblical prophecy if, in the translator's understanding of it, the prophecy had been realized between the time of the original Hebrew text and that of the Greek translation. This is particularly true of biblical predictions that Israel would be sent into exile away from Jerusalem, because it was the very fulfillment of such prophecies that necessitated a translation of the Hebrew Bible into the language of exile!

For instance, Isaiah's prophecies of the destruction of Jerusalem and exile in Isaiah 31 are introduced by the curse, "Woe to those who go down to Egypt for help" (v. 1). Of course, the Alexandrian Jews found themselves living in exile in Egypt precisely because Jerusalem had been destroyed as Isaiah had prophesied. MT Isaiah 31:8–9 continues with a promise that the Assyrians would fail to take Jerusalem because of the burning presence of Yahweh in Jerusalem:

> "Assyria will fall by a sword that is not of man;
> a sword, not of mortals, will devour them.
> They will flee before the sword
> and their young men will be put to forced labor.
> Their stronghold will fall because of terror;
> at sight of the battle standard their commanders will panic,"
> declares the LORD,
> whose fire is in Zion,
> whose furnace is in Jerusalem. [NIV]

Seeligmann notes that the last part of verse 9 (which he regards as a warning to the Jews not to seek the protection of Egypt) is transmuted by the LXX into a blessing not present in the Hebrew: Τάδε λέγει κύριος Μακάριος ὃς ἔχει ἐν Σιων σπέρμα καὶ οἰκείους ἐν Ιερουσαλημ ("thus says the Lord, Blessed is the one who has seed in Zion and relatives in Jerusalem"). The thought seems to express the solidarity of the Diaspora Jews with the remnant in Jerusalem and, according to Seeligmann, reflects the loyalty and yearning of Alexandrian Jews for their Holy City: "This remarkable liberty taken by the translator justifies the assumption that he sought to express an idea very prevalent among Alexandrian Jewry."[11]

11. Ibid., 114.

A similar interpretative element is found in God's provocative statement in Isaiah 19:25, "Blessed be Egypt my people, Assyria my handiwork, and Israel my inheritance," when it is recast in the Greek as εὐλογημένος ὁ λαός μου ὁ ἐν Αἰγύπτῳ καὶ ὁ ἐν Ἀσσυρίοις καὶ ἡ κληρονομία μου Ισραηλ ("blessed be my people *who are in* Egypt, and *who are in* Assyria, and my inheritance Israel"). Apparently the Diaspora Jews thought of themselves (rather than the pagan people of Egypt and Assyria) as the specific referent of this verse, and so the statement was rendered into Greek in such a way as to make that interpretation explicit.

An exacting analysis of Greek Isaiah is found in a recent monograph by Arie van der Kooij. The painstaking labor to distinguish interpretative elements from text-critical concerns is indicated by van der Kooij's decision to focus on but one chapter of the Book of Isaiah, chapter 23, the oracle against Tyre. He finds in the Greek translation of this passage the view that Isaiah's prophecies were fulfilled by contemporary political and military events, such as the destruction of Carthage by the Romans in 146 B.C.E., the Parthian invasion of Babylonia, and the involvement of Tyre in the Hellenization of Jerusalem.[12]

One of van der Kooij's valuable contributions is his discussion (in chap. 6) of the Theodotionic, Hexaplaric, and Antiochene (or Lucianic) revisions of the Greek text of Isaiah 23, along with the interpretation of this passage by church fathers Eusebius of Caesarea, Jerome, Theodoret of Cyrrhus, and Cyril of Alexandria. All four of the church fathers take the same basic approach: they divide the prophecy against Tyre into two parts, the first of which is understood to have historical fulfillment in the sixth century B.C.E. and the second in the Christian era, as Christianity spread all over the world, including Tyre. Van der Kooij finds no specific connection between this exegesis and the recensions.[13] In spite of the existence of a distinctively Christian interpretation of Isaiah 23, it seems significant that none of the three major revisions of the Greek biblical text—not even those by Origen and Lucian—reflects any Christian influence.

The difference in approach between the Jewish translator(s) who produced Greek Isaiah and the Christians who were involved in both transmitting and interpreting that same text is striking. The Jewish Greek translators apparently felt at liberty to change the biblical text

12. Arie van der Kooij, *The Oracle of Tyre: The Septuagint of Isaiah xxiii as Version and Vision* (Vetus Testamentum Supplement 71; Leiden: Brill, 1998), 95–109, in a section entitled "LXX Isaiah 23 as updated prophecy." For a somewhat different perspective on this passage, see Peter W. Flint, "The Septuagint Version of Isaiah 23:1–14 and the Massoretic Text," *BIOSCS* 21 (1988): 35–54.

13. Van der Kooij, *Oracle of Tyre*, 183; he thinks "this is partly due to the fact that not every passage of Isa. 23 is commented upon in the (four) commentaries."

to actualize the prophecies for their contemporary readers, but the Christians apparently transmitted the Greek text as they received it and introduced their interpretative commentary on the relevance of the text in separate writings.

A free approach to handling the biblical text is evidenced not only by Greek Isaiah, but also by those books that include extensive additional material, such as Daniel and Esther. The idea of introducing midrashic commentary within the biblical text seems to have been a distinctively Jewish approach not generally adopted by the early Christian fathers, who were Greco-Roman Gentiles. However, several NT authors were Jewish and one might have expected midrash to be introduced into Greek biblical texts intended for a Greek-speaking Christian reader. For instance, it is interesting that no Christian midrash was introduced into the Greek text of Isaiah itself in light of the apostle Paul's reinterpretation of Isaiah in his christological arguments in Romans and elsewhere. Indeed, one might wonder why Paul himself did not produce a Christian midrash of the Greek text of Isaiah.

That midrashic rewriting of the biblical text is a distinctively Jewish technique suggests that the longer pluses and minuses that exist only in the Greek biblical texts were introduced by Greek-speaking Jewish revisers. For instance, the Greek versions of Esther include six additional chapters not found in any of the Semitic versions. In the Hebrew text of Esther, God is not mentioned, nor is there reference to the central elements of Judaism, such as the covenant, past heroes of the faith, previous events in the history of Israel, the law, the temple, circumcision, prayer, sacrifice, etc. Most of these elements absent in the Hebrew text are introduced in the additions to Esther, especially in the prayers of Esther and Mordecai for the deliverance of their people (addition C). The addition of such extensive material moves the Greek version of the Esther story more into the mainstream of biblical tradition.[14] This and the other additions, as well as smaller insertions containing explicit references to God, clearly show how the Greek reviser was exegeting the story of Esther within the canonical context of the Hebrew Bible. Clearly these additions are intended to reflect how the Esther story was understood and interpreted by the reviser(s). Generally speaking, if the pluses found only in the Greek versions of a given book cohere with an intelligible interpretation or amplification of the

14. See Karen H. Jobes, *The Alpha-Text of Esther: Its Character and Relationship to the Masoretic Text* (Society of Biblical Literature Dissertation Series 153; Atlanta: Scholars Press, 1996), 176–83. For a different approach, see Kristin De Troyer, *Het einde van de alpha-tekst van Ester: vertaal- en verhaaltechniek van MT 8,1–17, LXX 8,1–17 en AT 7,14–41* (Leuven: Peeters, 1997).

surrounding verses, one can conclude that they result from interpretative development.[15]

Once such additional material has been identified, scholars ask if it reflects midrashic exegesis that could have been known to the translator and preserved in later rabbinic writings. Tov defines the term *midrashic exegesis* in the LXX to refer to material introduced into the Greek versions that is also found in the Targumim and rabbinic sources or that interprets the text in a way that resembles the midrashic exegesis found there.[16] The entrance point of such exegesis into the Greek versions is difficult to discern. The midrashic material may already have been present in the Semitic *Vorlage* from which the Greek translation was made, or it may have been introduced at the time the Greek translation was made, or it may have been added by a reviser subsequent to the original translation. Moreover, textual corruption is sometimes mistaken for exegesis. Midrashic exegesis in the LXX was first discussed by Z. Frankel in 1851 and more recently by, among others, David W. Gooding on Kings, Emanuel Tov on Joshua, and Dirk Büchner on Exodus.[17]

Generally speaking, when substantial new material is inserted in the Greek text, that material is not found elsewhere. For instance, the six additional chapters of Esther are not found in any extant Semitic sources, neither in the Targumim nor in rabbinic writings. Midrashic exegesis in the LXX, however, does not normally take the form of inserting large sections into the text. The approach is usually more subtle than that, and so the presence of midrashic influence in the LXX is often quite discreet.

One example is given by Dirk Büchner, who notes that the translator of Exodus 12:16c introduces an extra word that interprets and simplifies a difficult Hebrew reading by bringing it into agreement with halakhic discussion.[18] The MT of this verse, in agreement with the Samaritan Pentateuch and the Peshitta, prohibits work on the Passover "except that which everyone must eat" (אַךְ אֲשֶׁר יֵאָכֵל לְכָל־נֶפֶשׁ). Instead

15. See Arie van der Kooij's discussion of free renderings in "The Old Greek of Isaiah 19:16–25: Translation and Interpretation," in *VI Congress of the International Organization for Septuagint and Cognate Studies: Jerusalem 1986*, ed. Claude E. Cox (SBLSCS 23; Atlanta: Scholars Press, 1987), 127–66, especially his concluding comments on 158–59.

16. Emanuel Tov, "Midrash-Type Exegesis in the LXX of Joshua," *Revue biblique* 85 (1978): 50–61.

17. Frankel, *Über den Einfluss der palästinischen Exegese*; David W. Gooding, "Problems of Text and Midrash in the Third Book of Reigns," *Textus* 7 (1969): 1–29; Tov, "Midrash-Type Exegesis"; Dirk Büchner, "On the Relationship between Mekilta de Rabbi Ishmael and Septuagint Exodus 12–23," in *IX Congress of the International Organization for Septuagint and Cognate Studies: Cambridge 1995*, ed. Bernard A. Taylor (SBLSCS 45; Atlanta: Scholars Press, 1997), 403–20.

18. Büchner, "Mekilta de Rabbi Ishmael and Septuagint Exodus," 408–9.

of representing the verb אֲכָל with ἐσθίω, the LXX introduces the verb ποιέω, resulting in the reading, πλὴν ὅσα ποιηθήσεται πάσῃ ψυχῇ ("except whatever *must be done* for everyone"). The rabbinic commentary *Mekilta* discusses whether what "may be done" on a typical Sabbath is compatible with "what may be done" on the holidays, such as Passover. Büchner approvingly quotes the commentary from La Bible d'Alexandrie on this passage, which concludes that the use of ποιέω is a halakhic variant introduced to conform the text to rabbinic exegesis.[19] This example shows just how subtle midrashic influence may be perceived to be and raises the question whether the LXX translator was intending to reflect known Jewish exegesis or simply drew the same inference from the sense of the Hebrew text.

David W. Gooding provides examples where the sequence of events in LXX 3 Reigns (1 Kings) was reordered to reflect interpretative bias. For instance, chapters 20 and 21 in the MT have been transposed in the LXX in order to reinterpret Ahab's character in a more positive light. Gooding observes:

> On the one hand, the Greek for long stretches agrees with the MT very closely, and many of its differences are readily explainable as having come from Hebrew Biblical manuscripts belonging to text-traditions differing from the MT. On the other hand, the whitewashing re-interpretation of Ahab has so much in common with R. Levi's re-interpretation of Ahab, recorded in the Jerusalem Talmud, that it is difficult not to think that it comes from a similar source. And certainly R. Levi's favourable re-interpretation of Ahab was not based on the discovery of some Biblical manuscript of a non-MT-type, still less on some extra-Biblical historical source. It was totally a matter of exegesis, dictated by theological considerations and achieved by shifting the weight of homiletic emphasis from one phrase of the Biblical text to another, all the while employing the same text.[20]

Gooding argues that the reordering of the material was not in the original translation, but was part of a subsequent revision based on written Semitic traditions that covered the whole book, and possibly beyond.

These examples show that it is often quite difficult to identify unambiguously the presence of midrashic influence in the LXX, and that when it is present, what we find is general agreement with previous exegetical tradition rather than the importation of text from other sources into the Greek.

19. A. le Boulluec and P. Sandevoir, *L'Exode* (La Bible d'Alexandrie 2; Paris: Cerf, 1989), 148.

20. Gooding, "Text and Midrash in the Third Book of Reigns," 26.

Messianism and the Septuagint

Because the NT writers interpret the Hebrew Bible to show that Jesus of Nazareth is the long-awaited Jewish Messiah as well as the Christ of all nations, the development of messianic expectation in Hellenistic Judaism is of interest to both Jews and Christians. It is sometimes claimed that messianic hopes were intensified in the Hellenistic period and that the Greek versions reflect, and possibly even amplify, such expectations.

One must keep in mind that Judaism in the Hellenistic period was politically, sociologically, and religiously diverse. Therefore, it would be unwarranted to assume that there was only one trajectory of development of the messianic expectation. As Marguerite Harl observes, there was apparently a difference between the messianic expectations of the Jews of Palestine and those found in the Diaspora.[21] At least among some Jews of Palestine, as the Qumran writings and the Targumim attest, messianic expectations increased during the tumultuous times of the Seleucid rulers and subsequent Hasmonean independence. Outside of Palestine, these hopes were muted by the political and social climate in which the Greek-speaking Jews found themselves. If the LXX was primarily a text for the Diaspora, it might be expected to reflect a Judaism pressed more by Hellenistic culture and politics than would be the case if it had been produced for Palestinian Jews.

When the LXX is examined for evidence of what, if any, messianic expectation the translators and revisers introduced or amplified, one must keep a further distinction in mind. Some texts of Scripture were understood as messianic by the Jewish people prior to the Christian era, and it is to these that one may rightly look for evidence of development in the LXX. Note, for example, Amos 4:13, where God is described in the MT as making known to humankind "what is his thought" (מַה־שֵּׂחוֹ). Reading the Hebrew as מְשִׁיחוֹ, the Greek translator rendered the clause ἀπαγγέλλων εἰς ἀνθρώπους τὸν χριστὸν αὐτοῦ ("announcing his anointed one to men"). Whether this rendering was the result of a simple mistake or of deliberate interpretation, it certainly reflects a messianic perspective on the part of the translator.

Other texts were later appropriated by the NT writers and early Christian church as prophetic references to Jesus and were henceforth understood as messianic. Johan Lust suggests that such cases should more properly be called "christological applications" rather than mes-

21. Marguerite Harl, Gilles Dorival, and Olivier Munnich, *La Bible Grecque des Septante: Du judaïsme hellénistique au christianisme ancien*, 2d ed. (Initiations au christianisme ancien; [Paris]: Cerf/Centre National de la Recherche Scientifique, 1994), 220.

sianic readings.[22] Any LXX renderings that, in contrast to the Hebrew text, can be understood as messianic must therefore be scrutinized to determine if that understanding was intended by the original translator or was introduced by a pre-Christian reviser or by later Christian scribes.

Lust gives an example from Ezekiel that shows how the Greek text could be "messianized" by later Christian scribes.[23] Ezekiel 17:22b–23a reads: "And I myself will plant [a shoot] on a high and lofty [תָּלוּל] mountain; on the mountain height of Israel I will plant it." Most Greek manuscripts read: "And I myself will plant [it] upon a high mountain; *and I will hang it/him* [κρεμάσω αὐτόν] on the mountain height of Israel." Papyrus 967, however, reads: "And I will plant [it] on a high and *suspended* [κρεμαστόν] mountain."[24] Lust argues that in this case papyrus 967 preserves the original Greek reading (the translator understood the difficult Hebrew *hapax legomenon* to derive from the root תָּלָה, "to hang").

Originally the text had no intentional messianic element. Later Christian scribes associated the idea of the Messiah Jesus hanging on the cross (tree) on the mountain of Golgotha with the planting of a "tree" on a "hanging mountain." By changing the adjective κρεμαστόν to the verb κρεμάσω and adding the explicit direct object αὐτόν, they applied the verse christologically. Lust observes that this Greek verse fits into a series of OT passages that referred to "tree" or "wood" and thus were understood by the church fathers as alluding to the crucifixion of Jesus.

Numbers 24:7 and 24:17 are frequently cited as messianic readings found in the LXX but not in the Hebrew. The former verse reads, according to the MT, "Water will flow from his buckets, and his seed will have abundant water" (יִזַּל־מַיִם מִדָּלְיָו וְזַרְעוֹ בְּמַיִם רַבִּים), but the LXX reads, ἐξελεύσεται ἄνθρωπος ἐκ τοῦ σπέρματος αὐτοῦ καὶ κυριεύσει ἐθνῶν πολλῶν ("*a man* will come out of his seed, and he will rule many nations"). Similarly, in translating 24:17, "A star will come out of Ja-

22. Johan Lust, "Messianism and the Greek Version of Jeremiah," in *VII Congress of the International Organization for Septuagint and Cognate Studies: Leuven 1989*, ed. Claude E. Cox (SBLSCS 31; Atlanta: Scholars Press, 1991), 87–122, esp. 87. In this article, Lust argues that Jer. 23:5–6 and 33:14–26 cannot be used as evidence for a messianic intent on the part of the Greek translator.

23. Johan Lust, "And I Shall Hang Him on a Lofty Mountain: Ezek 17:22–23 and Messianism in the Septuagint," in *IX Congress of the International Organization for Septuagint and Cognate Studies: Cambridge 1995*, ed. Bernard A. Taylor (SBLSCS 45; Atlanta: Scholars Press, 1997), 231–50, esp. 242–43.

24. This portion of the papyrus was not available to Joseph Ziegler in *Ezechiel* (Septuaginta 16/1; Göttingen: Vandenhoeck & Ruprecht, 1952). The revised 1977 edition, however, includes an addendum by Detlef Fraenkel, where the new information is provided (p. 337).

cob, and a scepter [שֵׁבֶט] will rise out of Israel," the LXX uses the word ἄνθρωπος to represent שֵׁבֶט. Tov, who in general finds little messianic interpretation in the LXX, considers the Greek translation in this case to reflect the accepted exegetical tradition, found also in the targum of this passage, that understood "man" to be the Messiah.[25]

Johan Lust, however, argues that ἄνθρωπος ("man") is not used elsewhere in the Greek tradition as a messianic title and that it should be understood in verse 17 as replacing the royal imagery of "scepter" with a much more general reference.[26] He understands the Hebrew, with its conjoined symbols of star and scepter, to be much more messianic than the Greek, despite the apparent individualization present in the latter. Lust points out that when early church fathers Justin and Irenaeus cite this verse in reference to Jesus, they focus their exegesis on the word "star," not on "man." Furthermore, when Philo discusses the verse, he understands "man" to be not the royal Messiah, but an eschatological humankind answering to the primeval human being in the creation and fall. The obscuration of the promise of a royal Messiah in the Greek, achieved by substituting a generic "man" for a reigning king ("scepter"), is perhaps both a politically sensitive and theologically reinterpreted nuancing of the verse for Jews who found themselves living in the Diaspora under Gentile kings.

Joachim Schaper finds more evidence of true messianic development in the Greek Psalms than Lust does in Ezekiel or Numbers. In fact, he argues that two distinct messianic views are present in the Greek Psalter: a political Messiah (e.g., LXX Ps. 59, 107) and a transcendent Messiah (e.g., LXX Ps. 109:3). While discussing a network of messianic Psalms, Schaper takes up the discussion of Numbers 24:7 and 24:17 in relation to LXX Psalm 28:6.[27] Contrary to Lust's claim that ἄνθρωπος does not occur elsewhere in Greek texts as a reference to the Messiah, Schaper cites Testament of Judah 24:1 as evidence that "man" in Numbers 24:17 was indeed understood to be a messianic figure:

25. Tov, "Theologically Motivated Exegesis," 229. On the basis of the LXX and of the targumic tradition, proposals have been made to emend MT Num. 24:7. See, however, John W. Wevers, *Notes on the Greek Text of Numbers* (SBLSCS 46; Atlanta: Scholars Press, 1998), 406; Martin McNamara, *Targum Neofiti I: Numbers* (Aramaic Bible 3; Collegeville, Minn.: Liturgical Press, 1995), 138; Bernard Grossfeld, *The Targum Onqelos to Leviticus and the Targum Onqelos to Numbers* (Aramaic Bible 8; Wilmington, Del.: Glazier, 1988), 137.

26. Johan Lust, "The Greek Version of Balaam's Third and Fourth Oracles: The Ἄνθρωπος in Num 24:7 and 17: Messianism and Lexicography," in *VIII Congress of the International Organization for Septuagint and Cognate Studies: Paris 1992*, ed. Leonard J. Greenspoon and Olivier Munnich (SBLSCS 41; Atlanta: Scholars Press, 1995), 233–57.

27. Joachim Schaper, *Eschatology in the Greek Psalter* (Wissenschaftliche Untersuchungen zum Neuen Testament 76; Tübingen: Mohr Siebeck, 1995), 118.

> And after these things shall a star arise to you from Jacob in peace,
> And a man [ἄνθρωπος] shall arise, like the sun of righteousness,
> Walking with the sons of men in meekness and righteousness,
> And no sin shall be found in him.

Unfortunately, although the pseudepigraphic work known as Testaments of the Twelve Patriarchs probably originated in the Hellenistic Judaism of the second century B.C.E., it may have also experienced Christian interpolations during its history of scribal transmission. The text is extant in only five medieval manuscripts, the earliest dating to the tenth century, making it notoriously difficult to use in LXX studies.

The disagreement of scholars as to whether Numbers 24:7 and 24:17 reflect the development of messianic expectation illustrates several important points. First, the search for such development in the Greek versions rests on subtle differences between the Hebrew and the translation, such as the substitution of a single word or phrase. Although one might expect messianism to be present in the LXX, it is in fact not a prominent element, especially in comparison to the messianic themes in the Semitic Palestinian texts of the same period.

Second, while some subtle differences between the Hebrew and Greek are quite congenial to a messianic reading, especially in hindsight by Christians, other motivations may in fact have been in play. In the study of the history of the messianic idea, one must be able to identify texts that were understood in this way by the Jews before the time of Jesus. This is not always easy or straightforward to do, because most of the extant manuscripts have been preserved by the Christian tradition. Nevertheless, as pointed out at the beginning of this chapter, elements that may have been previously thought of as distinctively Christian tendencies need to be reexamined with a new appreciation of "what was possible within the broad framework of what we call ancient Judaism."[28] In any case, one must appreciate the complexities involved in approaching the LXX as a source for the development of theological ideas.

Eschatology and the Septuagint

Of course, messianism is but one concept of Hellenistic Judaism, and messianic expectation only one part of Jewish eschatology. It is also thought that during the Hellenistic period the Jewish concept of the future resurrection of the righteous developed. The text of 2 Maccabees—a book that was probably composed originally in Greek in the first century B.C.E.—provides evidence that resurrection was the expected reward for those devout Jews martyred under Seleucid perse-

28. Kraft, "Christian Transmission of Greek Jewish Scriptures," 226.

cution (ca. 175 B.C.E.). This book describes the torture and execution of seven sons and their mother and their bold testimony before their tormentors:

> And when he was at his last breath, he said, "You accursed wretch, you dismiss us from this present life, but the King of the universe *will raise us up to an everlasting renewal of life*, because we have died for his laws." . . . When he was near death, he said, "One cannot but choose to die at the hands of mortals and to *cherish the hope God gives of being raised again by him. But for you there will be no resurrection to life!*" . . . "For our brothers after enduring a brief suffering *have drunk of ever-flowing life*, under God's covenant; but you, by the judgment of God, will receive just punishment for your arrogance." [2 Maccabees 7:9, 14, 36 NRSV, emphasis added]

Schaper finds evidence that such hope and interest in the resurrection is also found in the Greek translation of the Psalms, the provenance of which he ascribes to Hasmonean Palestine. Psalm 1:5, for example, reads, "Therefore the wicked will not stand [לֹא־יָקֻמוּ] in the judgment, nor sinners in the assembly of the righteous." The LXX has a straightforward rendering: διὰ τοῦτο οὐκ ἀναστήσονται ἀσεβεῖς ἐν κρίσει οὐδὲ ἁμαρτωλοὶ ἐν βουλῇ δικαίων. Schaper understands the Hebrew of this verse to be a wisdom teaching referring to the "innerworldly" action of God to separate the righteous from sinners. The Greek translator, he argues, reinterpreted a single word, קוּם, by translating it ἀνίστημι, which he takes to be a clear reference to future resurrection. Schaper explains that during the horrors of forced Hellenization that led to the Maccabean Revolt, earlier wisdom literature, with its concept of just retribution in this life, was no longer adequate theology. When the Greek translation was made, the hope of justice for the righteous was deferred to the afterlife.[29]

Schaper's thought is attractive at first, but he apparently overlooks linguistic evidence that complicates the picture. For instance, according to data provided by the Hatch-Redpath *Concordance to the Septuagint*, the Qal of קוּם is very often translated by ἀνίστημι in the LXX, even where the context prohibits the sense of resurrection. Within the Greek Psalter itself, note the intransitive use of the future middle indicative of this verb elsewhere, as in Psalm 93:16, τίς ἀναστήσεταί μοι ἐπὶ πονηρευομένους, ἢ τίς συμπαραστήσεταί μοι ἐπὶ ἐργαζομένους τὴν ἀνομίαν; ("who will rise up for me against the wicked, or who will stand up for me against those who practice lawlessness?"). This evidence renders LXX Psalm 1:5 ambiguous at best for the view that the concept of resurrection was in the translator's mind.

29. Schaper, *Eschatology in the Greek Psalter*, 46.

Schaper examines several psalms, but the eschatological development he finds in each depends on nuancing translation equivalents, a method that is linguistically problematic. If the evidence for theological development in the Greek Psalter is based on subtleties of language, one wonders how extensive such development really is, if it is present at all.

The transmission, preservation, and development of theological concepts such as messianism and resurrection no doubt occurred during the Hellenistic period, but the particular character of the LXX may minimize its usefulness as a window into Jewish thought at that time. Although it may seem natural to expect the LXX to reflect theological perspectives, one must always remember that the people who produced the Greek texts were translators. They had the well-defined task of producing a translation of an existing text, the Hebrew Scripture, not of writing a treatise on the eschatology of their day.

While each translator probably did have a certain messianic concept and view of the afterlife—views undoubtedly shaped by the times in which they lived—it is not obvious that, given the nature of their task, the text they produced would strongly reflect those views. In contrast, books that were composed during the same period might be expected to reflect more directly the perspectives of their authors, who were not constrained by an existing text. Commentaries and midrashim on the Greek Scriptures produced in the Hellenistic period would provide a better window into the development of theological ideas during that time. Unfortunately, such material is rare.

Influence of Hellenistic Philosophy on the Septuagint

An endeavor similar to finding theological exegesis in the LXX is that of identifying what influence, if any, Hellenistic philosophy had on the Greek translation of the Hebrew Scriptures. Greek culture was enamored with wisdom, which was defined as living toward life's highest good. The various philosophical schools, such as Stoics and Epicureans, may have disagreed on the precise articulation of that goal, but the achievement of wisdom was arguably the highest intellectual value of that culture.

When the monotheistic Jews found themselves living in a culture that valued wisdom, they too had a definition of life's highest good: living in accordance with the Torah of God. Moreover, one of their own kings, Solomon, had the legendary reputation of being the wisest man who ever lived. As Jewish monotheism was defended and recommended to the polytheistic Greek culture, Hebrew wisdom literature became a natural point of contact between the Jewish people and their pagan culture.

The pseudonymous Wisdom of Solomon, one of the books usually included in the LXX corpus and originally written in Greek during the Hellenistic period, affirms the Jews as having true wisdom that issues in eternal life and provides an apologetic for monotheistic Judaism in a pluralistic culture. The Greek vocabulary and rhetorical style of this book indicate its Alexandrian origins, and the influence of Hellenistic philosophy on the author is apparent. For instance, Wisdom 8:7 commends the four cardinal virtues previously defined by the Greek philosopher Plato—self-control, prudence, justice, and courage—affirming that "nothing in life is more profitable for mortals than these." Stoic cosmogony is reflected when wisdom is conceived of as an emanation from God that is the soul of the universe (7:24–25). In 13:1–9, the knowledge of God is discussed from a philosophical perspective (as opposed to the perspective of revelation). The Wisdom of Solomon was a composition of Hellenistic Judaism, not a translation of an existing work, therefore it is not surprising that its philosophical tendencies are more apparent.

But what about wisdom books of the Hebrew Bible that were translated into Greek during this same period? Do they also reflect the influence of Hellenistic philosophy in its quest for wisdom? The Book of Proverbs is, of course, the best place to look for such influence. Johann Cook takes up that question in a recent monograph. After examining several chapters of Proverbs, Cook concludes that although the translator used words common to Classical Greek sources, especially Aristotle, he never introduced Greek philosophical or religious ideas in a positive light, but was foremost a conservative Jewish writer, intent on preserving the theological perspective of the Hebrew text.[30]

For instance, Proverbs 6:6–11 extols the ant as a tiny creature whose wisdom is nonetheless exemplified by its industriousness:

> Go to the ant, you sluggard;
>   consider its ways and be wise!
> It has no commander,
>   no overseer or ruler,
> yet it stores its provisions in summer
>   and gathers its food at harvest.
> How long will you lie there, you sluggard?
>   When will you get up from your sleep?
> A little sleep, a little slumber,
>   a little folding of the hands to rest
> and poverty will come on you like a bandit
>   and scarcity like an armed man.

30. Johann Cook, *The Septuagint of Proverbs: Jewish and/or Hellenistic Proverbs? Concerning the Hellenistic Colouring of LXX Proverbs* (Vetus Testamentum Supplement 69; Leiden: Brill, 1997), 318–19.

Between verse 8 and verse 9, the Greek translation includes three extra verses not present in the Hebrew:

> Or go to the bee
> and learn how industrious she is,
> and how seriously she performs her work,
> and whose products kings and commoners use for their health
> and she is respected by all and renowned.
> Although she is physically weak,
> by honouring wisdom she has been honoured.[31]

Cook points out that both the ant and the bee, and in that order, are used by Aristotle in his *Historia animalium* (622B) as examples of industriousness. Moreover, the word translated "industrious" (ἐργάτις) is a *hapax legomenon* in the Greek Proverbs, but is the same word used by Aristotle in his description of the bee. Cook concludes that the Greek translator (and probably the original Greek readers) of Proverbs 6 knew of this description of the ant and the bee and that he makes use of Aristotle's philosophy "in order to explicate a religious issue in the Semitic text he is translating."[32]

This is an example of how a Greek translator may make use of words and motifs that would have been familiar to Greek readers while preserving the original sense of the Hebrew text. Cook concludes that the translator, a conservative thinker, wanted to preserve the sense of the Hebrew, though he was willing to use non-Jewish traditions to explicate that sense. He rejects the idea that the Greek Proverbs embraces explicitly Stoic perspectives. Cook finds the influence of Hellenism to be reflected in the "stylistic and lexical approach" of the translator.[33]

Therefore, the influence of Hellenistic culture on the translation is similar to what we found regarding the development of theological concepts like messianism and resurrection in the Greek text. Philosophical or ideological influence may be found in Jewish texts composed in the Hellenistic period, but the translators of the Hebrew Bible were constrained by their interest in preserving the message of their *Vorlage*.

Theological *Tendenz* of the Three

When looking for theological development or Hellenistic influence, one must distinguish between the original Greek translation (the OG) and its subsequent revisions. Because the books of the Hebrew Bible

31. Cook's translation, ibid., 164.
32. Ibid., 168.
33. Ibid., 320.

were initially translated into Greek by various translators at different times and probably in different places, it may be futile to look for anything but a very general influence of the Greek culture on the Greek text. Examining the work of the revisers of the OG may be a more fruitful task, because a revision is by definition a homogeneous effort by one person (or group of persons), whose motivation would be reflected in his work to the extent he succeeded in his purposes. Moreover, the work of a revision can be compared and contrasted with the OG, provided that all the work of the reviser can in fact be distinguished from the OG. Such a comparison provides a more solid basis of inference concerning theological tendencies, for surely a reviser would let the OG stand except where he was motivated to change it. The comparison of the types of differences between the revision and the OG should indicate whether theological *Tendenz* was one motivating factor.

Considerable debate, however, rages about the relationship of the Three—Aquila, Theodotion, and Symmachus—to the OG text and to each other, which complicates the search for the theological perspective of each. Of fundamental importance is the question whether the Three revised the OG or produced new translations.[34] Additionally, did one or more of the Three know and use the work of the others? And finally a text-critical question: to what extent and with what certainty can the revisions of the Three be untangled from the variant readings presented in the extant manuscripts?[35]

Some proposed rationales for the revisions/retranslations of the Three are the following: (1) to synchronize the contemporaneous Hebrew and Greek texts, which had become sufficiently different (perhaps especially when the pre-MT emerged as the standard text soon after 70 C.E.); (2) to excise Christian interpolations from the Greek text; and (3) to reflect the most recent Jewish scholarship and exegesis.

Aquila's motivation for his revision was explicitly theological, but in the sense that he believed that the linguistic details of the Hebrew Bible were significant. Therefore, his theological conviction led him to decide that every element of the Hebrew text must have a correspondence in its Greek translation. This kind of theological motivation expressed itself in the syntax and style of his revision—which attempted to represent every word, particle, and even morpheme—rather than in

34. See above, chap. 2, pp. 46–47.

35. Evidence from non-Greek sources also needs to be sifted. See, for example, Claude E. Cox, "Travelling with Aquila, Symmachus and Theodotion in Armenia," in *Origen's Hexapla and Fragments: Papers Presented at the Rich Seminar on the Hexapla, Oxford Centre for Hebrew and Jewish Studies, 25th [July]–3rd August 1994*, ed. Alison Salvesen (Texte und Studien zum antiken Judentum 58; Tübingen: Mohr Siebeck, 1998), 302–16.

the development of the sense of the Hebrew text. Aquila's revision is characterized, for instance, by rendering the direct-object marker אֶת with the preposition σύν, and even representing the morphemes of a word one by one (e.g., in 2 Kings 19:25 the words לְמֵרָחוֹק and לְמִימֵי are translated respectively with εἰς ἀπὸ μάκροθεν and εἰς ἀπὸ ἡμερῶν).

Theodotion's revision was not as extreme as Aquila's, but it nevertheless attempted to stereotype translation equivalents by using the same Greek word for a given Hebrew word, even where such a use was unwarranted by the context. For instance, although the Hebrew word אִישׁ bears two senses, "man" or "each," Theodotion translated it with the Greek word for "man" (ἀνήρ) even where it meant "each" and would therefore have been better translated by ἕκαστος. Moreover, Theodotion exhibited some tendency toward Aquila's approach, although not as excessive, by unnecessarily rendering Hebrew גַּם with καίγε and by transliterating Hebrew words rather than translating them.

Of the three, Symmachus most consistently produced a text that translated the sense of the Hebrew without representing every lexical element of the Hebrew or using stereotyped equivalents. Alison Salvesen explores the character of the variant readings attributed to this translator in an attempt to answer the question, Who was Symmachus?[36] Her premise is that enough of the theological *Tendenz* of Symmachus can be seen in his revision of the Greek that his identity as either a Samaritan convert to Judaism or an Ebionite Christian can be determined. Salvesen finds that when the readings distinctive to Symmachus are examined, they show his originality as an exegete and translator, but "they do not seem to point to his participation in any minor sect that is known to us."[37] She finds, among other things, that Symmachus was zealous to uphold the sovereignty of the God of Israel, that he tends to demote and demythologize angels and the heroes of Israel's history, and that he avoids messianic renderings, for instance in Numbers 24:7 and 24:17.[38]

In short, Salvesen finds that Symmachus rendered the text in a way congenial to the monotheism of both Jews and Christians. His work shows no trace of Ebionite belief, but does display a thorough knowledge of rabbinic exegesis. Salvesen views the conflicting historical information given about Symmachus in Eusebius and Epiphanius of Salamis in light of her examination of his extant work, and concludes that he was a Jewish translator working in Caesarea in the third century to produce a Greek version for the Jewish community. She char-

36. Alison Salvesen, *Symmachus in the Pentateuch* (Journal of Semitic Studies Monograph 15; Manchester: University of Manchester, 1991), chap. 9.

37. Ibid., 188.

38. Ibid., 192.

acterizes his revision as combining "the best Biblical style, remarkable clarity, a high degree of accuracy regarding the Hebrew text, and the rabbinic exegesis of his day: it might be described as a Greek Targum, or Tannaitic Septuagint."[39]

Conclusion

The literature surveyed in this chapter represents a very small proportion of the work being done in our day. As we examine the text of the LXX for evidence of theological thought, we must be sensitive both to the ambiguity of much of that evidence and to the significance of the Greek version as a monument of Jewish Hellenistic culture. Only when we have learned to appreciate the LXX on its own terms can we hope to make use of it in a responsible way. And those who are willing to labor in the mines of this rich document will find their work amply rewarded when they discover its treasures.

39. Ibid., 297.

Appendixes

Appendix A

Major Organizations and Research Projects

During the last thirty years, research in LXX studies has become a truly international effort. The work of well-established research projects is focused, generally speaking, toward one or more of the following:

1. establishing the original text of the OG (Göttingen, Germany) or a known recension (Madrid, Spain)
2. translating the LXX into a modern language (*A New English Translation of the Septuagint* and La Bible d'Alexandrie)
3. producing lexical aids for LXX research (Leuven, Belgium)
4. creating computer databases of resources related to the LXX (CATSS in Philadelphia and the Hexapla Working Group in Oxford)
5. publishing editions of the Hebrew Bible that include evidence from the Greek versions (Hebrew University Bible Project and *Biblia hebraica quinta*)

International Organization for Septuagint and Cognate Studies

The most recent issue of the *Bulletin of the International Organization for Septuagint and Cognate Studies* lists current officers and address information (on the Web at http://ccat.sas.upenn.edu/ioscs/).

The founding of the International Organization for Septuagint and Cognate Studies (IOSCS) marked a major milestone in LXX research in this century. The organizational meeting of the IOSCS was held in conjunction with the annual meeting of the Society of Biblical Literature at Berkeley, California, on 19 December 1968. At that meeting each of the three officers, Harry M. Orlinsky (president), Charles T. Fritsch (secretary), and Sidney Jellicoe (editor), addressed timely issues in LXX scholarship.

After noting that the discovery of the Dead Sea Scrolls had given the Greek versions new status for the textual criticism of the Hebrew text, Orlinsky stated that the significance of the LXX for biblical studies is found essentially in its "usefulness for the correct understanding of the Hebrew text, and for the early history of its transmission, and even the reconstruction of original readings."[1] Jellicoe surveyed the then "new problems" of LXX studies, such as "the keenly disputed question of the *Vorlage*, the historical order of 'the Three' (Aquila, Theodotion, Symmachus), and the nature of the *Trifaria Varietas*."[2] Fritsch spoke to the future direction of LXX studies by noting that "sixty years ago Adolf Deissmann lamented that there were few basic tools for LXX research, a situation which has altered little since that time. The three major desiderata in this area are: a lexicon, grammar, and LXX texts."[3] Fritsch identified three other tools that would be useful in LXX studies: (1) a classified, annotated bibliography, (2) commentaries on individual books of the Greek Bible, and (3) a modern, reliable translation of the LXX.

The issues and projects addressed by the founding officers of the IOSCS remain of great importance; happily, over the last thirty years progress has been made toward these goals. Two classified bibliographies have appeared.[4] John W. Wevers, editor of the Göttingen Pentateuch, has produced a set of commentaries on the Greek text of those books.[5] Two LXX lexicons are now in print, one of the complete corpus, another of the Minor Prophets.[6] The IOSCS itself is currently engaged in producing a *New English Translation of the Septuagint* (see below) and has plans for producing a commentary series on the LXX following the completion of the translation.[7]

The IOSCS meets annually in connection with the Society of Biblical Literature, except every third year when it holds an international congress in association with the International Organization for the Study of the Old Testament. Papers presented at the triennial international congresses are published in the IOSCS-sponsored series Society of Biblical Literature Septuagint and Cognate Studies (SBLSCS). Monographs of relevance to the study of the LXX and its daughter versions are also published in this series.

From its inception the IOSCS has published an annual journal: *Bulletin of the International Organization for Septuagint and Cognate Studies (BIOSCS)*.

1. Harry M. Orlinsky, "A Message from the President," *BIOSCS* 2 (1969): 2.

2. Sidney Jellicoe, "Septuagint Studies in the Current Century: A Brief Survey," *BIOSCS* 2 (1969): 5.

3. Charles T. Fritsch, "The Future of Septuagint Studies: A Brief Survey," *BIOSCS* 3 (1970): 4.

4. Sebastian P. Brock, Charles T. Fritsch, and Sidney Jellicoe, *A Classified Bibliography of the Septuagint* (Arbeiten zur Literatur und Geschichte des hellenistischen Judentums 6; Leiden: Brill, 1973); and Cécile Dogniez, *A Bibliography of the Septuagint; Bibliographie de la Septante (1970–1993)* (Vetus Testamentum Supplement 60; Leiden: Brill, 1995).

5. See appendix B on commentaries.

6. See above, chap. 12, pp. 261–62.

7. Not to be confused with a similar commentary series on the text of Vaticanus being planned under the direction of Stanley Porter for Brill.

This publication contains the minutes of the last meeting of the IOSCS, record of works in progress of interest to LXX scholars, announcements of new projects in LXX and cognate scholarship, and a few scholarly articles reflecting current research by members of the organization. Serious students of the LXX should peruse both the congress volumes and back issues of *BIOSCS* to gain an overview of work in the field during the last two or three decades.

Septuaginta-Unternehmen

The Septuaginta-Unternehmen is headquartered at the Lagarde House in Göttingen, Germany. Founded in 1908, this institute has as its primary goal the collection and collation of LXX manuscripts, with a view to publishing a reconstructed text with full critical apparatus, usually referred to as the Göttingen LXX.[8] Alfred Rahlfs was the first director, a position he held until his death in 1935. He was succeeded by Werner Kappler, whose life ended prematurely in World War II. Joseph Ziegler, who had edited the volume on Isaiah (1939), became the sole editor and director of the project. He produced volumes on all the prophetic books, as well as Wisdom of Solomon, Wisdom of Jesus ben Sirach, and Job. During Ziegler's tenure, Robert Hanhart served as the editor of the deuterocanonical books plus Esther and Ezra–Nehemiah and eventually succeeded Ziegler as director. More recently, the Septuaginta-Unternehmen has been under the direction of Anneli Aejmelaeus, who is also editing the books of Samuel.

The collection of materials at the Septuaginta-Unternehmen is the most complete in existence. Under the supervision of Detlef Fraenkel and Udo Quast, student workers collate all available manuscripts of the LXX for a given book with the goal of identifying every extant variant reading. The collation process begins with the production of a notebook in which a full Greek text is carefully written by hand on one line. Every word of every available manuscript must be compared to that text, and every difference is meticulously noted in the collation notebook.[9]

The editor assigned to a particular book receives the collation notebook after all manuscripts have been examined. To this already vast amount of information, the editor adds further collations of papyri, the daughter versions, and patristic quotations. For every variant reading identified by the collation process, the editor must decide which is most likely the original reading and construct the critical apparatus. Understandably, the entire process from the start of collation to the printed edition can take a very long time.

8. See John W. Wevers, "The Göttingen Septuagint," *BIOSCS* 8 (1975): 19–23, for a dated but still useful summary of the work. See also above, chap. 3, pp. 74–75, and chap. 11, pp. 242–47.

9. Because Rahlfs's critical edition of the Psalms was based on only some of the extant manuscripts, that book is currently being collated once again. For the Book of Psalms about 1,200 manuscripts must be collated, and the collation of one manuscript can take as many as 100 hours. Thus, it will take years of collation work before the task of reconstructing the original text of Psalms can begin. For more information on the methods used by the Septuaginta-Unternehmen, see the unpublished paper by Udo Quast, "Einführung in die Editionsarbeit."

In addition to producing the best critical text of the LXX available today, the Septuaginta-Unternehmen publishes a series of volumes, Mitteilungen des Septuaginta-Unternehmens, devoted to a topic of particular relevance for LXX studies. Some of the most important monographs in the field have appeared in this series.

Instituto de Filología del CSIC

The Consejo Superior de Investigaciones Científicas (CSIC) or Higher Council of Scientific Research, based in Madrid, conducts research in both the natural sciences and the humanities (Web page http://www.csic.es/). Under its auspices, the Departamento de Filología Bíblica y de Oriente Antiguo (Department of Biblical Philology and Ancient Near East, which is part of the Institute of Philology) is engaged in an ambitious project, Biblia Políglota Matritense, which consists of editions of biblical texts in five ancient languages (Hebrew, Aramaic, Greek, Latin, and Coptic), Tatian's *Diatessaron* in Syriac, and some biblical books in Armenian. These reconstructed texts, and monographs of related interest, are published in the series Textos y Estudios "Cardenal Cisneros."[10] Many important volumes have been published, including the *editio princeps* of Targum Neophyti 1. The scholars in Madrid collaborate with others at the Complutensian University in Madrid, the Central University of Barcelona, and the City College of Columbia University in New York.

Within this larger project, much attention has been paid to the Greek versions. Natalio Fernández Marcos has published a standard introduction to the field.[11] In particular, he and José Ramón Busto Saiz, along with other collaborators, have devoted their efforts to the reconstruction of the Antiochene (or Lucianic) Text. After much preparatory work over two decades, including a detailed examination of Theodoret's citations, a superb critical edition of this text was published in three volumes in 1989–96.[12] At present, this team of scholars in Madrid is preparing a Greek-Hebrew index of the Antiochene text in the historical books as a complement to the Hatch-Redpath *Concordance to the Septuagint*.

A New English Translation of the Septuagint

The last English translation of the LXX appeared about one hundred and fifty years ago and was based on essentially a single manuscript.[13] Since then,

10. Cardinal Jiménez de Cisneros directed the production of the Complutensian polyglot Bible in 1514–17.

11. *Introducción a las versiones griegas de la Biblia*, 2d ed. (Textos y Estudios "Cardenal Cisneros" 23; Madrid: Consejo Superior de Investigaciones Científicas, 1998) = *The Septuagint in Context: Introduction to the Greek Version of the Bible*, trans. Wilfred G. E. Watson (Leiden: Brill, 2000).

12. See above, chap. 13, pp. 281–82.

13. Lancelot C. L. Brenton's translation was first published in London in 1851 and is currently in print in a Greek-English format as *The Septuagint with Apocrypha: Greek and English* (Grand Rapids: Zondervan, n.d.). See above, chap. 3, p. 76.

significant advances have been made in Greek lexicography, and numerous ancient manuscripts are now available to the textual critic. For instance, the Göttingen critical edition for the Book of Genesis is based on an examination of about one hundred and forty manuscripts (several earlier than the fourth century of our era), ten daughter versions, plus biblical citations in Greek literature. A new translation of the critically reconstructed LXX text into English is therefore needed.

Primarily through the efforts of Albert Pietersma, the IOSCS has undertaken just such a project, known as *A New English Translation of the Septuagint* (NETS), to be published by Oxford University Press. More than thirty LXX scholars are participating in the production of NETS, which seeks to reflect the relationship between the Greek and Hebrew texts. The New Revised Standard Version, an accessible English translation of the Hebrew text, was chosen as the base text. When the NRSV accurately represents the Greek translation as well as the Hebrew text, no changes are necessary. Therefore, a comparison of NETS with the NRSV reflects where and to what extent the Hebrew and Greek differ. For additional information, see the NETS Web page (http://ccat.sas.upenn.edu/nets/).

La Bible d'Alexandrie

In the 1980 issue of *BIOSCS* (vol. 13), Marguerite Harl, professor of postclassical Greek at the University of Sorbonne in Paris, announced a project to translate the Göttingen LXX text into French. The impulse for this project originally came from Dominique Barthélemy. Almost two decades later this project has produced several volumes in the series La Bible d'Alexandrie, published by Cerf and directed by Harl, Gilles Dorival (Aix-Marseille), and Olivier Munnich (Lyon), with the collaboration of Cécile Dogniez (Centre National de la Recherche Scientifique). Each volume contains a French translation of the LXX and a philological and exegetical commentary. The first volume on Genesis appeared in 1986; since then, the remaining books of the Pentateuch, Joshua, Judges, 1 Kings, and some of the Minor Prophets have been published.[14] Other volumes are currently in preparation.

The many collaborators in the project are experts in Hellenistic Judaism, early Christianity, patristics, papyrology, linguistics, Hebrew Bible, and rabbinics, and these scholars are not only producing La Bible d'Alexandrie but other publications resulting from their research as well. In 1988, for example, Harl, Dorival, and Munnich produced an important introduction to the LXX, *La Bible Grecque des Septante* (Cerf/Centre National de la Recherche Scientifique). In 1995 a volume in honor of Harl was published that contains thirty essays on various aspects of LXX scholarship.[15] Also in 1995, as noted above (p. 312 n. 4), Cécile Dogniez published an indispensable 361-page volume, *A Bibliography of the Septuagint: 1970–1993*.

14. See appendix B on commentaries.

15. *Selon les Septante: Hommage à Marguerite Harl*, ed. Gilles Dorival and Olivier Munnich (Paris: Cerf, 1995).

Centre for Septuagint Studies and Textual Criticism

The aim of the Centre for Septuagint Studies and Textual Criticism at Katholieke Universiteit in Leuven, Belgium, is described on their Web page (http://www.theo.kuleuven.ac.be/en/centr_sept.htm): "The study of the Greek translations of the Old Testament . . . in comparison with the Hebrew text. This implies a study of the history of the original text and its Greek translation, including the revisions of Aquila, Symmachus, and Theodotion, an analysis of translation techniques, and an investigation into the exegetical interpretations (*Tendenz*) in the translation."

Under the direction of Johan Lust and in collaboration with Katrin Hauspie and Erik Eynikel, the project has produced *A Greek-English Lexicon of the Septuagint*.[16] This project is associated with the CATSS project (see below) and uses its computer-readable files.

As a second phase of the lexicon project, supplements are being compiled to include the textual variants in Rahlfs's edition and the specific vocabulary of the revisions of Aquila, Symmachus, and Theodotion. A second project underway is a French translation and commentary of LXX Ezekiel, in collaboration with La Bible d'Alexandrie. Preparation of this translation and commentary includes background studies on the vocabulary and style of the Greek version of Ezekiel.

Computer Assisted Tools for Septuagint Study

The vision for using computer technology in biblical studies was discussed in the earliest years of the IOSCS. Kent Smith raised the topic in his 1970 paper in *BIOSCS* by explaining what perhaps seems all too obvious now: if the biblical texts were in an electronic form capable of being searched and sorted by a computer, then various scholarly projects too tedious for manual processing would be facilitated.[17] Smith's immediate interest was to produce a critical apparatus of textual variants and identify their stemma, but he noted that other scholarly resources could be facilitated, such as the production of a descriptive grammar, concordance, and lexicon. Such resources were the desiderata earlier identified by the founding scholars of the IOSCS as they looked toward future goals, and rapidly developing computer technology at that time promised to expedite these projects.

During the 1970s, plans for a computer-assisted project to produce a LXX lexicon developed at the University of Pennsylvania under the direction of Robert A. Kraft, with the assistance of John Abercrombie and a group of graduate students. Emanuel Tov of Hebrew University was designated editor of the lexicon, which was to be produced directly from the computer database. In a 1981 progress report, the aim of the CATSS project was defined as "creating a comprehensive and flexible computer 'data bank' available for efficient scholarly research on virtually all aspects of Septuagintal studies—textcritical, lexical, grammatical, conceptual, translational, bibliographical."[18]

16. See above, chap. 12, p. 261.

17. Kent Smith, "Data Processing the Bible: A Consideration of the Potential Use of the Computer in Biblical Studies," *BIOSCS* 3 (1970): 12–14.

18. Robert A. Kraft and Emanuel Tov, "Computer Assisted Tools for Septuagint Studies," *BIOSCS* 14 (1981): 22–40.

Two monographs describing the database have been produced.[19] The morphologically tagged text of Rahlfs's LXX and the parallel aligned Hebrew text for all books are available on-line at the CATSS Web site (http://ccat.sas.upenn .edu/rs/texts.html).

Hexapla Working Group

In 1994 a conference at the Oxford Centre for Hebrew and Jewish Studies discussed plans for a new edition of Origen's Hexapla.[20] Leonard J. Greenspoon (the president of IOSCS), Gerard Norton of Birmingham University, and Alison Salvesen of the Hebrew Centre organized the conference with funding from the Rich Foundation. The last publication of Origen's work was produced in 1875 by Frederick Field, and the subsequent discovery of new manuscripts warranted a new edition of the Hexapla.[21] At the Ninth Congress of the IOSCS, Norton presented a report on plans resulting from the Rich Seminar.[22] The Hexapla Working Group is currently planning an electronic database for the collection of Hexaplaric data, with eventual access to this information from the Web.

Hebrew University Bible Project

With the initiative and direction of the late Moshe H. Goshen-Gottstein, the Hebrew University of Jerusalem undertook publication of a new edition of the Hebrew Bible. The text itself is a diplomatic edition of the Aleppo Codex, widely regarded as the most authoritative (though incomplete) Masoretic manuscript, accompanied by four apparatuses that seek to give virtually exhaustive textual information.

This edition is of special value for LXX studies because the first apparatus records variant readings retroverted from the ancient versions, and many of these readings are qualified by notations at the bottom of the page. These no-

19. Robert A. Kraft and Emanuel Tov, *Computer Assisted Tools for Septuagint Studies (CATSS)*, vol. 1: *Ruth* (SBLSCS 20; Atlanta: Scholars Press, 1986); and Emanuel Tov, *A Computerized Data Base for Septuagint Studies: The Parallel Aligned Text of the Greek and Hebrew Bible* (CATSS 2/Journal of Northwest Semitic Languages Supplement 1; Stellenbosch, 1986). For detailed information about how the morphology was defined and tagged, see William Adler, "Computer Assisted Morphological Analysis of the Septuagint," *Textus* 11 (1984): 1–16.

20. See *Origen's Hexapla and Fragments: Papers Presented at the Rich Seminar on the Hexapla, Oxford Centre for Hebrew and Jewish Studies, 25th* [*July*]*–3rd August 1994*, ed. Alison Salvesen (Texte und Studien zum antiken Judentum 58; Tübingen: Mohr Siebeck, 1998).

21. See above, chap. 2, p. 51. Even in 1914, Henry Barclay Swete (*An Introduction to the Old Testament in Greek*, 2d ed. [Cambridge: Cambridge University Press, 1914; repr. Peabody, Mass.: Hendrickson, 1989], 76) observed that "materials for an enlarged edition of Field are already beginning to accumulate."

22. See Gerard Norton, "Collecting Data for a New Edition of the Fragments of the Hexapla," in *IX Congress of the International Organization for Septuagint and Cognate Studies: Cambridge 1995*, ed. Bernard A. Taylor (SBLSCS 45; Atlanta: Scholars Press, 1997), 251–61.

tations, characteristically, seek to explain such readings as the result of translation technique and the like, rather than as evidence of a variant parent text. While some scholars object to this method, it has to be recognized that the notes reflect extremely helpful and insightful evaluations of the data. Even if the editor's judgment is rejected, one must be thankful for being alerted to possible alternate ways of understanding the evidence.

Isaiah appeared in three fascicles between 1975 and 1992, with a one-volume edition being published in 1995.[23] It includes the original 1965 introduction, which should be carefully read by all students of the Hebrew Bible. This volume was followed a few years later by publication of *The Book of Jeremiah*.[24] Work on Ezekiel is almost complete.

In connection with this project, the journal *Textus* is published each year. This annual contains important articles on the whole range of biblical textual criticism, including key essays on LXX studies.

Biblia hebraica quinta

Intended as the successor to *Biblia hebraica stuttgartensia* and sponsored by the German Bible Society, *Biblia hebraica quinta* continues to base its work on Codex Leningradensis. The apparatus of the new edition, however, will be heavily influenced by the work of the Hebrew Old Testament Text Project of the United Bible Societies. Distinguishing between text-critical matters based on external evidence and those based on internal evidence, it will take into account the literary development of the text. The apparatus will include evaluative notations and will be accompanied by a textual commentary. In 1998 the Deutsche Bibelgesellschaft published a sample fascicle of Ruth, edited by Jan de Waard. It contains a general introduction that describes in detail the distinctives of this new edition.

23. *The Book of Isaiah*, ed. Moshe H. Goshen-Gottstein (Hebrew University Bible Project; Jerusalem: Magnes, 1995).

24. *The Book of Jeremiah*, ed. Shemaryahu Talmon and Emanuel Tov (Hebrew University Bible Project; Jerusalem: Magnes, 1998).

Appendix B

Reference Works

English Translations

The Septuagint with Apocrypha. By Lancelot C. L. Brenton. Grand Rapids: Zondervan, n.d.

A New English Translation of the Septuagint. Edited by Albert Pietersma and Benjamin G. Wright. New York: Oxford University Press, forthcoming.

Bibliographies

A Classified Bibliography of the Septuagint. Edited by Sebastian P. Brock, Charles T. Fritsch, and Sidney Jellicoe. Arbeiten zur Literatur und Geschichte des hellenistischen Judentums 6. Leiden: Brill, 1973.

A Classified Bibliography of Lexical and Grammatical Studies on the Language of the Septuagint. By Emanuel Tov. Jerusalem: Academon, 1980.

Bibliography of the Septuagint: 1970–1993. Edited by Cécile Dogniez. Vetus Testamentum Supplement 60. Leiden: Brill, 1995.

Critical Editions of the Septuagint Text and Other Primary Sources

Septuaginta: Vetus Testamentum Graecum. Göttingen: Vandenhoeck & Ruprecht, 1939–. Usually referred to as the Göttingen LXX, this is the standard text of the books for which it is available. See chap. 3, p. 75 n. 12, for details.

Septuaginta. Edited by Alfred Rahlfs. 2 vols. Stuttgart: Deutsche Bibelgesellschaft, 1935. One-volume edition, 1979. This is the most commonly used text because it is the only complete critical edition of the LXX in print. Users should carefully read its introductory essay, "History of the Septuagint Text."

The Old Testament in Greek according to the text of Codex Vaticanus, supplemented from other uncial manuscripts, with a critical apparatus containing the variants of the chief ancient authorities for the text of the Septuagint. Edited by Alan E. Brooke, Norman McLean, and Henry St. John Thackeray. Cambridge: Cambridge University Press, 1906–40. Usually referred to as the Larger Cambridge Edition, this work was never completed. For most of the historical books, it is still our primary source of information. See chap. 3, p. 72 n. 8, for further details.

El texto antioqueno de la Biblia griega. Edited by Natalio Fernández Marcos and José Ramón Busto Saiz. 3 vols. Textos y Estudios "Cardenal Cisneros" 50, 53, 60. Madrid: Consejo Superior de Investigaciones Científicas, 1989–96. A critical reconstruction of the Antiochene (Lucianic) text of the historical books of Samuel, Kings, and Chronicles.

Origenis Hexaplorum quae supersunt sive veterum interpretum graecorum in totum Vetus Testamentum fragmenta. Edited by Frederick Field. 2 vols. Oxford: Oxford University Press, 1875. The only printed edition of the extant fragments of Origen's Hexapla. Dated but indispensable.

Linguistic Aids

Conybeare, F. C., and St. George Stock. *Grammar of Septuagint Greek: With Selected Readings, Vocabularies, and Updated Indexes*. Peabody, Mass.: Hendrickson, 1995. A reprint of *Selections from the Septuagint* (Boston: Ginn, 1905).

Hatch, Edwin, and Henry A. Redpath. *Concordance to the Septuagint and the Other Greek Versions of the Old Testament (Including the Apocryphal Books)*. 3 vols. Oxford: Clarendon, 1897–1906. One-volume reprint with a new introduction by Emanuel Tov and Robert A. Kraft and including Takamitsu Muraoka's *Hebrew/Aramaic Index to the Septuagint* (Grand Rapids: Baker, 1998).

Helbing, R. *Grammatik der Septuaginta: Laut- und Wortlehre*. Göttingen: Vandenhoeck & Ruprecht, 1907.

———. *Die Kasussyntax der Verba bei den LXX: Ein Beitrag zur Hebraismenfrage und zur Syntax der Koine*. Göttingen: Vandenhoeck & Ruprecht, 1928.

Lust, Johan, Katrin Hauspie, and Erik Eynikel. *A Greek-English Lexicon of the Septuagint*. 2 vols. Stuttgart: Deutsche Bibelgesellschaft, 1992–96. Includes English equivalents of all Greek words in Rahlfs's edition.

Muraoka, Takamitsu. *A Greek-English Lexicon of the Septuagint: Twelve Prophets*. Louvain: Peeters, 1993. This work provides not only definitions and English equivalents, but much useful additional information.

———. *Hebrew/Aramaic Index to the Septuagint (Keyed to the Hatch-Redpath Concordance)*. Grand Rapids: Baker, 1998. This index is also available in the one-volume reprint edition of Edwin Hatch and Henry A. Redpath's *Concordance to the Septuagint and the Other Greek Versions of the Old Testament (Including the Apocryphal Books)* (Grand Rapids: Baker, 1998).

Taylor, Bernard A. *The Analytical Lexicon to the Septuagint: A Complete Parsing Guide*. Grand Rapids: Zondervan, 1994. Lists in alphabetical order, with grammatical analysis and lexical form, all of the inflected forms of Greek words found in Rahlfs's LXX.

Thackeray, Henry St. John. *A Grammar of the Old Testament in Greek according to the Septuagint*, vol. 1: *Introduction, Orthography and Accidence*. Cambridge: Cambridge University Press, 1909. The only work of this type available in English.

Introductions

Cimosa, M. *Guida allo studio della Bibbia Greca (LXX): Storia–lingua–testi*. Rome: Britannica & Forestiera, 1995. This volume provides minimal information regarding historical and text-critical issues, but includes much linguistic help and extensive readings with valuable annotations.

Fernández Marcos, Natalio. *Introducción a las versiones griegas de la Biblia*. 2d ed. Textos y Estudios "Cardenal Cisneros" 23. Madrid: Consejo Superior de Investigaciones Científicas, 1998. The best available description and evaluation of current research, now available in English translation: *The Septuagint in Context: Introduction to the Greek Version of the Bible*. Translated by Wilfred G. E. Watson. Leiden: Brill, 2000.

Harl, Marguerite, Gilles Dorival, and Oliver Munnich. *La Bible Grecque des Septante: Du judaïsme hellénistique au christianisme ancien*. 2d ed. Initiations au christianisme ancien. [Paris]: Cerf/Centre National de la Recherche Scientifique, 1994. An excellent, comprehensive survey.

Jellicoe, Sidney. *The Septuagint and Modern Study*. Oxford: Clarendon, 1968. Assumes knowledge of Swete's *Introduction to the Old Testament in Greek*.

Swete, Henry Barclay. *An Introduction to the Old Testament in Greek*, 2d ed. Cambridge: Cambridge University Press, 1914. Reprinted Peabody, Mass.: Hendrickson, 1989. The classic work, with a wealth of information.

Commentaries

Genesis

Harl, Marguerite. *La Genèse*. La Bible d'Alexandrie 1. Paris: Cerf, 1986.

Wevers, John W. *Notes on the Greek Text of Genesis*. SBLSCS 35. Atlanta: Scholars Press, 1993.

Exodus

Boulluec, A. le, and P. Sandevoir. *L'Exode*. La Bible d'Alexandrie 2. Paris: Cerf, 1989.

Wevers, John W. *Notes on the Greek Text of Exodus*. SBLSCS 30. Atlanta: Scholars Press, 1990.

Leviticus

Harlé, P., and D. Pralon. *Le Lévitique*. La Bible d'Alexandrie 3. Paris: Cerf, 1988.

Wevers, John W. *Notes on the Greek Text of Leviticus*. SBLSCS 44. Atlanta: Scholars Press, 1997.

Numbers

Dorival, Gilles. *Les Nombres*. La Bible d'Alexandrie 4. Paris: Cerf, 1994.

Wevers, John W. *Notes on the Greek Text of Numbers*. SBLSCS 46. Atlanta: Scholars Press, 1998.

Deuteronomy

Dogniez, Cécile, and Marguerite Harl. *Le Deutéronome*. La Bible d'Alexandrie 5. Paris: Cerf, 1992.

Wevers, John W. *Notes on the Greek Text of Deuteronomy*. SBLSCS 39. Atlanta: Scholars Press, 1995.

Joshua

Moatti-Fine, J. *Jésus (Josué)*. La Bible d'Alexandrie 6. Paris: Cerf, 1996.

Judges

Harlé, P. *Les Juges*. La Bible d'Alexandrie 7. Paris: Cerf, 1998.

1 Samuel

Grillet, B., and M. Lestienne. *Premier livre des Règnes*. La Bible d'Alexandrie 9/1. Paris: Cerf, 1997.

Isaiah

Ottley, Richard R. *The Book of Isaiah according to the LXX (Codex Alexandrinus)*. 2 vols. London: Cambridge University Press, 1904–6.

Minor Prophets

Harl, Marguerite, et al. *Douze prophètes 4–9: Joël, Abdiou, Jonas, Naoum, Ambakoum, Sophonie*. La Bible d'Alexandrie 23/4–9. Paris: Cerf, 1999.

IOSCS Congresses

La Septuaginta en la investigación contemporánea (V Congreso de la IOSCS). Edited by Natalio Fernández Marcos. Textos y Estudios "Cardenal Cisneros" 34. Madrid: Consejo Superior de Investigaciones Científicas, 1985.

VI Congress of the International Organization for Septuagint and Cognate Studies: Jerusalem 1986. Edited by Claude E. Cox. SBLSCS 23. Atlanta: Scholars Press, 1987.

VII Congress of the International Organization for Septuagint and Cognate Studies: Leuven 1989. Edited by Claude E. Cox. SBLSCS 31. Atlanta: Scholars Press, 1991.

VIII Congress of the International Organization for Septuagint and Cognate Studies: Paris 1992. Edited by Leonard J. Greenspoon and Olivier Munnich. SBLSCS 41. Atlanta: Scholars Press, 1995.

IX Congress of the International Organization for Septuagint and Cognate Studies: Cambridge 1995. Edited by Bernard A. Taylor. SBLSCS 45. Atlanta: Scholars Press, 1997.

In addition to the papers presented at the IOSCS international congresses, the SBLSCS series contains monographs generated by the CATSS project, doctoral dissertations on various aspects of the LXX, and collections of essays like the following:

Septuagint, Scrolls and Cognate Writings: Papers Presented to the International Symposium on the Septuagint, Dead Sea Scrolls and Other Writings (Manchester, 1990). Edited by George J. Brooke and Barnabas Lindars. SBLSCS 33. Atlanta: Scholars Press, 1992.

Computer Software

Several Bible programs include the text of Rahlfs's LXX and allow for both lexical and grammatical searches in both Greek or Hebrew.

Accordance for Macintosh is the most powerful computer Bible program available. As of this writing, it is the only program that includes the CATSS parallel Hebrew-Greek aligned texts. It is available from the Gramcord Institute (2218 N.E. Brookview Drive, Vancouver, Washington 98686; on the Web at http://www.gramcord.org), which also produces Gramcord, a sophisticated Bible program for Windows.

BibleWorks is the most versatile Bible program for Windows; it allows for highly complex grammatical searches and includes a large number of reference tools and Bible versions. It is available from Hermeneutika (P.O. Box 2200, Dept. BX-199, Big Fork, Montana 59911-2200; on the Web at http://www.bibleworks.com).

BibleWindows is a capable and user-friendly program. It is available from Silver Mountain Software (1029 Tanglewood Drive, Cedar Hill, Texas 75104; on the Web at http://www.silvermnt.com).

Appendix C

Glossary

anthropomorphism a description of God in terms of human (esp. bodily) characteristics, such as "the arm of the Lord." When human emotions are attributed to God, the term **anthropopathism** is normally used.

anthropopathism see **anthropomorphism**.

Antiochene text (also *Antiochian text*). A revision of the Greek Bible usually attributed to Lucian of Antioch and used widely in Syria and other parts of the Eastern church in the fourth and fifth centuries.

apocryphal see **deuterocanonical**.

Aramaism see **Semitism**.

asterisk a symbol (※) used by Origen to indicate words or phrases that, although found in the Hebrew text, were missing in the LXX of his day (he supplied the Greek of those passages from the later translations). See also **Hexapla** and **metobelus** and **obelus**.

autograph the original manuscript of a work.

catena (pl. catenae) a compilation (from a Latin word meaning "chain") of exegetical comments from ancient Christian writers. Because they include numerous quotations of biblical passages, they are of great value for textual criticism.

codex (pl. codices) a volume of manuscript pages sewn together on one edge rather than rolled in the form of a scroll. The forerunner of the modern book format.

collation the detailed comparison of a manuscript with another manuscript or with a standard text, for the purpose of identifying the differences and drawing text-critical inferences.

collocation a noticeable pattern in the arrangement of words and other linguistic elements.

colophon a note placed at the end of a manuscript often giving the date, the name of its scribe, or other information about its production.

critical apparatus a section (usually at the bottom of the page) of a **critical edition** listing the textual variants found among the extant manuscripts and other witnesses to the text.

critical edition (1) An edition of a text that includes a **critical apparatus.** (2) An edition that provides a critical or **eclectic text**, that is, a text reconstructed by selecting variants from the extant manuscripts, in contrast to a **diplomatic edition**, which simply reproduces the text of one manuscript.

deuterocanonical books writings included in the LXX and the Vulgate OT but not in the Hebrew Bible. These books, almost all of which were originally composed in Greek, are accepted as canonical by the Roman Catholic and Eastern Orthodox churches. The term **apocryphal** ("hidden, inauthentic") has traditionally been used, mainly by Protestants, to refer to the same books. Other noncanonical Jewish writings from the Second Temple period are sometimes also referred to as apocryphal.

diplomatic edition see **critical edition.**

dittography see **haplography.**

eclectic text see **critical edition.**

exemplar a master copy, that is, the manuscript from which one or more copies are made (usually in the same language); contrast ***Vorlage***.

genizah a storage room in a synagogue in which worn-out copies of Scripture and other religious documents were hidden (Aramaic *genaz*, "to hide"), later to be burned. Because the genizah in Cairo was walled over before they were destroyed, valuable manuscripts were preserved there.

hapax legomenon (pl. hapax legomena) a word that occurs only once within a given corpus.

haplography in manuscript production, the mistake of writing only one letter (or word or phrase) where the master copy had two identical forms in close sequence. (In contrast, dittography refers to the mistake of writing two letters or words or phrases where the master copy had only one.) Such an omission—often the result of **homoeoteleuton—**is sometimes referred to as *parablepsis* ("a looking by the side"), a term used of scribal oversights more generally.

Hebraism see **Semitism.**

Hexapla the name of the work containing six parallel biblical texts produced by Origen. The fifth column presented the LXX, probably with his revisions.

homoeoarcton see **homoeoteleuton.**

homoeoteleuton (also *homeoteleuton* and *homoioteleuton*). A similar ending of lines that may cause a scribe to omit the intervening material; the term is often used of the error itself (see **haplography**). Less common omissions are due to **homoeoarcton** (similar beginning of lines).

hypotaxis see **parataxis.**

Indo-European in linguistics, a language family that includes the following groups: *Hellenic* (Greek), *Italic* (Latin and the Romance languages, including French, Italian, Portuguese, Romanian, Spanish), *Celtic* (Irish, Scotch Gaelic, Welsh), *Germanic* (Dutch, German, English, Norwegian, Swedish),

Slavic (Russian, Polish, Serbo-Croatian), *Iranian* (Persian, Kurdish), and *Indic* (Sanskrit, Hindi).

Kaige (also *Kaige recension*). An early revision of some books in the **Old Greek**, characterized by a number of distinctive features, such as the consistent use of *kaige* (καίγε) to render Hebrew *gam* (גַּם, "also"). This work sought to bring the Greek translation into greater conformity with the Hebrew text that was becoming standardized in the first century of our era. The recension may have been a precursor to the work of Aquila and apparently served as the basis for a revision by Theodotion (thus the term *Kaige*-Theodotion).

Koine (Greek *hē koinē dialektos*, "the common dialect"). A form of the Greek language that developed from the classical Attic dialect after Alexander the Great's conquests and that became commonly used throughout the Mediterranean world.

lacuna (pl. lacunae) a gap or missing portion of a text, normally caused by physical damage to a manuscript.

lexical field (also *semantic field/domain*). A defined area of meaning occupied by several words closely related in sense.

lexicography the principles, methods, and task of making a dictionary.

lexicon the vocabulary of a language; also used as equivalent to *dictionary*.

Lucianic recension see **Antiochene text**.

majuscule see **uncial**.

Masoretic Text (also *Massoretic*). The form of the Hebrew biblical text transmitted in the Middle Ages by scribes known as Masoretes ("transmitters"), who also devised a system of markings to represent the vowels and cantillation.

metobelus a symbol (⁄. or ⁒ or ↲) used by Origen to indicate the end of text (if more than one word) that had been marked with an **asterisk** or an **obelus**.

midrash (pl. midrashim) (Hebrew "interpretation"). An explanation of the biblical text. When capitalized, it refers to rabbinic commentaries on biblical books.

minuscule a professional writing style, developed from cursive around the ninth century. The term is used to refer to those manuscripts written in such a style. See also **uncial**.

Mishnah (also *Mishna*). The basic collection of Jewish oral (mainly legal) tradition, compiled around 200 C.E.

obelus a symbol (– or ⸚ or ÷) used by Origen to indicate words or phrases that, although found in the LXX, were missing from the Hebrew text used by the Jews of his day. See also **asterisk** and **Hexapla** and **metobelus**.

Old Greek the presumed initial Greek version of the Hebrew Bible for books other than the Pentateuch.

Old Latin (also *Vetus Latina*). An early translation of the Greek Bible into Latin; this work, produced as early as the second century of our era, may be a collection of independent translations and should be distinguished from the **Vulgate**, a Latin version made directly from the Hebrew.

paleography (also *palaeography*). The study of ancient writings, focusing on their outward form and handwriting, usually with a view to determine their origins and relationships to other texts.

palimpsest a manuscript that has been erased and written over with another text.

parablepsis see **haplography**.

parataxis the joining of independent clauses with a coordinating conjunction, usually "and" (Hebrew *wāw*; Greek *kai*). Hebrew narrative consistently uses this type of syntax. Contrast **hypotaxis**, which refers to the use of subordination (such as participial clauses in Greek).

Peshitta conventional name (Syriac "simple" or "common") for the Syriac translation of the Hebrew Bible. See also **Syro-Hexaplar**.

philology the general study of language and literature. More narrowly, it refers to the comparative, historical branch of linguistics that flourished in the nineteenth century.

polyglot Bible an edition of the Bible that includes the text in more than one language on the same page.

pre-Masoretic a form of the consonantal text of the Hebrew Bible that was standardized around the first century of our era and that became the basis of the **Masoretic Text**. In the present book, this term is distinguished from **proto-Masoretic**, which refers to an earlier ancestor of the MT, prior to the time of standardization (e.g., the great Isaiah Scroll from Qumran).

proto-Masoretic see **pre-Masoretic**.

recension a deliberate, systematic revision of an entire text.

retroversion a "back-translation"; the hypothetical reconstruction of an original text (see ***Vorlage***) inferred from an existing translation.

semantic field/domain see **lexical field**.

Semitic in linguistics, a language family that encompasses the following groups: *Canaanite* (Ugaritic, Hebrew, Phoenician, Moabite), *Aramaic* (Palestinian Aramaic, Syriac, Mandean), *Akkadian* (Babylonian, Assyrian), and *"South" Semitic* (Arabic, Ethiopic, South Arabian).

Semitism a (Greek) word or expression borrowed from a Semitic language or used in a way that reflects the influence of such a language, especially Hebrew (**Hebraism**) or Aramaic (**Aramaism**).

Septuagint the first translation of the Hebrew Pentateuch into Greek (from the Latin term for "seventy"). By extension, the term also refers to the Greek translation of the other biblical books (including the **deuterocanonical** books composed originally in Greek) as found in most manuscripts or in modern editions. See also **Old Greek**.

Septuagintalism (also *Septuagintism*). A Greek word or expression used in a way that reflects the influence of the LXX.

siglum (pl. sigla) an abbreviation used to identify and catalog manuscripts.

stereotyping the unconscious tendency or deliberate technique of translating a word or phrase consistently ("literally"), even when the context calls for a different rendering.

Syro-Hexaplar (also *Syro-Hexapla*). The Syriac translation of Origen's revised (Hexaplaric) text of the LXX; it often includes the **asterisk** and other symbols Origen used to identify differences between the LXX and the Hebrew. This version is a translation from the Greek into the Syriac and thus should be distinguished from the **Peshitta**, which is a Syriac translation directly from the Hebrew.

Talmud the authoritative written body of Jewish tradition, consisting of the **Mishnah** and later commentary (*Gemara*).

Tanak (also *Tanakh*). An acronym for the Jewish Bible formed from the first syllable of the Hebrew words for the Pentateuch (*Torah*), Prophets (*Neviʾim*), and Writings (*Ketuvim*).

targum (pl. targumim) (Hebrew "translation"). Often capitalized and normally used specifically with reference to the Aramaic versions of the Hebrew Bible.

Tendenz a German term used of discernible tendency or bias in the work of a writer, translator, or redactor.

tetragrammaton (Greek "four letters"). God's name in Hebrew, *yhwh* (probably pronounced *Yahweh*), traditionally translated in English as "LORD."

textus receptus the "received text" of the Bible that by historical precedent is given a privileged standing; usually refers to the Greek NT produced by Erasmus in the sixteenth century.

Three, The a collective term that refers to the later Greek translations of Aquila, Symmachus, and Theodotion.

Torah (Hebrew "instruction, law"). This term may refer specifically to the Sinaitic Covenant, but is most commonly used with reference to the Pentateuch (see **Tanak**), and sometimes by extension to the Hebrew Bible as a whole.

uncial a professional writing style, developed from **majuscule** (capital letter) writing and used until about the eighth century. The term is used to refer to manuscripts written in such a style. See also **minuscule**.

Ur-Theodotion (also *Proto-Theodotion*). A hypothetical revision of the **Old Greek** thought to have served as the basis for Theodotion's work. Most scholars now identify that earlier revision with the first-century ***Kaige*** recension.

variant (also *variant reading*). A portion of text that varies from a given standard. Differences among manuscripts are referred to as *variants*, *variant readings*, or *textual variants*.

Vetus Latina see **Old Latin**.

***Vorlage* (pl. *Vorlagen*)** a German word used of the parent text from which a translation was made.

Vulgate Jerome's translation of the Hebrew Bible (and of the Greek NT) into Latin. It includes the **deuterocanonical** books. See also **Old Latin**.

Appendix D

Differences in Versification between English Versions and the Septuagint

The vast majority of verse numbers in the LXX and English Bible correspond, and readers approaching the LXX from the English should have no trouble finding the corresponding verse in the Greek. On the other hand, some verses in the English Bible do not appear in the LXX, an absence that becomes obvious only when one looks for them in a standard edition of the LXX. Falling between these two groups are verses in the English Bible that appear in the LXX under a different chapter and/or verse number (the MT versification variously agrees with the LXX or English in these situations). The table below deals with this third group by correlating verses found in both versions but with divergent numbering. (Since versification differs even among editions of the LXX, the numbering of the Rahlfs edition of the LXX has been followed.) In many of the verses listed here, the correspondence between the English and Greek texts is not exact; the LXX may omit some of the material or otherwise introduce variations.

A baseline letter following a verse number indicates that only part of the verse is intended (e.g., Gen. 31:48a is the first part of the verse). A superscript letter following a verse number indicates Rahlfs's enumeration of additional LXX material not found in the Hebrew or English (e.g., Exod. 28:29[a] marks additional material coming after Exod. 28:29).

The descriptive titles of most of the Psalms are assigned verse 1 in the Greek (and Hebrew) text. Since these titles are not included in the English numbering, verse numbers in English translations of the Book of Psalms are usually one number lower than those in the LXX (and MT). As it would greatly expand the size of this index without appreciably increasing its usefulness, we have chosen not to indicate this deviation for each individual psalm.

If a verse number is not included in the following table, readers may infer either (a) that the verse numbers in the English and LXX correspond exactly or (b) that the verse is missing from the LXX. Which inference is true of a particular verse can be determined only by opening the English and LXX texts and comparing them.

	English	Rahlfs
Genesis	31:48a	31:46b
	31:50b	31:44b
	31:51–52a	31:48
	31:55–32:32	32:1–33
	35:21	35:16a
Exodus	8:1–32	7:26–8:28
	20:13, 14, 15	20:15, 13, 14
	21:16, 17	21:17, 16
	22:1–31	21:37–22:30
	28:23–28	28:29[a]
	35:15, 17	35:12[a]
	36:8b–9	37:1–2
	36:34	38:18
	36:35–38	37:3–6
	37:1–24	38:1–17
	37:29	38:25
	38:1–7	38:22–24
	38:8	38:26
	38:9–23	37:7–21
	38:24–31	39:1–8
	39:2–31	36:9–38
	39:32	39:10
	39:33–43	39:13–23
	40:30–32	38:27
Leviticus	6:1–30	5:20–6:23
Numbers	1:24–25	1:36–37
	1:26–37	1:24–35
	6:27	6:23b
	10:34, 35, 36	10:36, 34, 35
	16:36–17:13	17:1–28
	26:15–18	26:24–27
	26:19–27	26:15–23
	26:28–43	26:32–47
	26:44–47	26:28–31
	29:40–30:16	30:1–17
Deuteronomy	12:32–13:18	13:1–19
	22:30–23:25	23:1–26
	29:1–29	28:69–29:28
Joshua	8:30–35	9:2[a–f]
	19:47, 48	19:48, 47
	24:29, 30, 31	24:30, 31, 29
1 Samuel = 1 Reigns	20:42b–21:15	21:1–16
	23:29–24:22	24:1–23

	English	Rahlfs
2 Samuel = 2 Reigns	18:33–19:43	19:1–44
1 Kings = 3 Reigns	3:1	2:35[c]
	4:17, 18, 19	4:19, 17, 18
	4:20	2:46[a]
	4:21	2:46[k]
	4:22–23	5:2–3
	4:24, 25, 26	2:46[f,g,i]
	4:27–28	5:1
	4:29–34	5:9–14
	5:1–16	5:15–30
	5:17–18	6:1[a,b]
	5:18b	5:32
	6:14	6:3b
	6:37–38	6:1[c,d]; 2:35[c]
	7:1a	7:38
	7:1b	7:50
	7:2–12	7:39–49
	7:13–18	7:1–6
	7:19, 20, 21	7:8, 9, 7
	7:23–24	7:10–11
	7:25, 26	7:13, 12
	7:27–45	7:14–31
	7:46, 47	7:33, 32
	7:48–51	7:34–37
	8:12–13	8:53[a]
	9:15–22	10:22[a–c]; 5:14[b]
	9:23–25	2:35[h,f,g]
	11:3	11:1
	11:5, 6, 7, 8	11:6, 8, 5, 7
	12:2	11:43b
	14:1–18	12:24[g–n]
	20	21
	21	20
2 Kings = 4 Reigns	11:21–12:21	12:1–22
1 Chronicles	6:1–81	5:27–6:66
	12:4b–40	12:5–41
2 Chronicles	2:1–18	1:18–2:17
	14:1–15	13:23–14:14
Nehemiah	1–13	2 Esdras 11–23
	4:1–5a	2 Esdras 13:33–37a
	4:7–23	2 Esdras 14:1–17
	9:38–10:39	2 Esdras 20:1–40

	English	Rahlfs
Esther	1:1	1:1[s]
Job	41:1–34	40:25–41:26
Psalms	10:1–18	9:22–39
	11–113	10–112
	114:1–8	113:1–8
	115:1–18	113:9–26
	116:1–9	114:1–9
	116:10–19	115:1–10
	117–146	116–145
	147:1–11	146:1–11
	147:12–20	147:1–9
Proverbs	16:4	16:9
	16:6, 7, 8, 9	15:27[a], 28[a], 29[a,b]
	20:20–22	20:9[a–c]
Ecclesiastes	5:1–20	4:17–5:19
Song of Songs	6:13–7:13	7:1–14
Isaiah	9:1–21	8:23–9:20
	64:1–12	63:19b–64:11
Jeremiah	9:1–26	8:23–9:25
	25:15–38	32:15–38
	26–43	33–50
	31:35, 36, 37	38:36, 37, 35
	44:1–30	51:1–30
	45:1–5	51:31–35
	46	26
	47	29
	48	31
	49:1–5	30:17–21
	49:7–22	30:1–16
	49:23–27	30:29–33
	49:28–33	30:23–28
	49:34	25:20
	49:35–39	25:15–19
	50	27
	51	28
Ezekiel	7:3–9	7:7–9, 3–6
	20:45–21:32	21:1–37
	32:19	32:21b
	42:18, 19	42:19, 18
Daniel	3:24–30	3:91–97
	5:31–6:28	6:1–29
Hosea	1:10–2:23	2:1–25
	11:12–12:14	12:1–15
	13:16–14:9	14:1–10
Joel	2:28–32	3:1–5
	3	4
Jonah	1:17–2:10	2:1–11
Micah	5:1–15	4:14–5:14
Nahum	1:15–2:13	2:1–14
Zechariah	1:18–2:13	2:1–17
Malachi	4:1–3	3:19–21
	4:4, 5, 6	3:24, 22, 23

Indexes

Subject Index

Author Index

Scripture Index

Chapter and verse numbers follow Septuagint versification; for Masoretic/English equivalents, see appendix D.